SEAFARING
AND SEAFARERS

IN THE BRONZE AGE EASTERN
MEDITERRANEAN

Sidestone Press

SEAFARING AND SEAFARERS

IN THE BRONZE AGE EASTERN MEDITERRANEAN

A. Bernard Knapp

Once again, for Stella

© 2018 A. Bernard Knapp

Published by Sidestone Press, Leiden
www.sidestone.com

Imprint: Sidestone Press, Leiden

Lay-out & cover design: Sidestone Press
Photograph cover: The Mediterranean sea and Es Malgrat rocks, Morro d'en
    Pere Joan Bay, Mallorca, Balearic islands, Spain.
      Photo: bortnikau (stock.adobe.com)

ISBN 978-90-8890-554-4 (softcover)
ISBN 978-90-8890-555-1 (hardcover)
ISBN 978-90-8890-556-8 (PDF e-book)

Contents

Preface and Acknowledgements

There are several scholars better trained and equipped than I am to write a book such as this. Amongst those who have dedicated much of their research output to examining the multiple aspects of seafaring and seafarers in certain periods of the Bronze Age eastern Mediterranean — each in their own distinctive way — are Ezra Marcus, Shelly Wachsmann, Caroline Sauvage, Cyprian Broodbank and Christopher Monroe. I have been fortunate to be able to call upon one of them, Christopher Monroe, to read a draft of the final manuscript, and I thank him sincerely for his comments and corrections.

Of course, my whole involvement with the subject matter — always on the periphery of my interests — is due to my wife, Dr Stella Demesticha, a maritime archaeologist whose main period of focus is Late Antiquity, but whose interests have no temporal bounds. She has encouraged and supported my fledging attempts to write about maritime matters, and her always very critical reading of what I write has enhanced not only the present volume, but also the two previous books that we wrote or co-edited together (Demesticha and Knapp 2016; Knapp and Demesticha 2017).

Beyond that, I am indebted to the following scholars for comments on various sections or chapters of the book, and/or for providing me with unpublished or recently published work that helped to ensure this volume is reasonably well up-to-date:

Kathryn Bard: for comments on drafts of a section on Wadi Gawasis and for providing a recent publication on the site.

Michele Massa: for comments on drafts of sections related to Early and Middle Bronze Age Anatolia.

Vasif Şahoğlu: for comments on drafts of sections related to Early–Late Bronze Age Anatolia.

Jennifer Webb: for reading and commenting in detail on drafts of sections related to Early and Middle Bronze Age Cyprus.

Yuval Yekutieli: for providing key details concerning Early Bronze Age Egypt and Levant, and for reading a draft of that section.

Yuval Goren: for providing recent analytical information on pottery and the stone anchor from the Cape Gelidonya shipwreck.

I thank Luke Sollars for preparing the maps, and Irini Katsouri for producing several of the drawings that illustrate this volume. In addition, I am grateful to the following people or institutions for providing me with several images used in this volume:

Department of Antiquities, Cyprus: Figures 18, 19, Bellapais Vounous 'boat' model; Kamares Ware cup from Karmi *Palealona*

Lennart Åström: Figure 7, bronze trident from Hala Sultan Tekke

Michal Artzy: Figures 25, 28, Aerial photo of Haifa Bay; Tel Akko 'altar'

Kathryn Bard: Figure 12, wooden cargo box from Wadi Gawasis, Egypt

Peter M. Fischer: Figures 42, 44, Hala Sultan Tekke stone anchors and murex shells

Raphael Greenberg: Figures 9a-b, EB II-III 'metallic ware' jars from Tel Dan

Duncan Howitt-Marshall: Figure 41, satellite image of stone anchors from Achni

Ann Killebrew: Figure 17, drawing of Late Bronze Age Canaanite jars

Sturt W. Manning: Figure 43, Maroni stone anchor

Michele Massa: Figure 10, Anatolian Trade Network and 'super-network'

Penelope Mountjoy: Figure 49, drawing of Bademgediği Tepesi LH IIIC sherd with warriors

Cemal Pulak: Figures 47, 48, 51, glass ingots, boxwood lid and stone anchor from Uluburun

Vasif Şahoğlu and Hayat Erkanal: Figure 11, overview of excavations at Liman Tepe

Elias Spondylis: Figure 16b, drawing of oval-mouthed amphora from Koulenti, Laconia

Shelly Wachsmann: Figures 30, 32, relief drawing from tomb of Iniwia at Saqqara; Gurob wooden boat model

Jennifer Webb: Figure 35, drawing of ships' graffiti at Kition

Jennifer Webb and David Frankel: Figure 20, location of Early-Middle Cypriot sites on north coast, Cyprus

Yuval Yekutieli: Figure 8, reconstructed 'D-ware' sherd from Taur Ikhbeiheh

Finally, I would like to thank Karsten Wentink and Sasja van der Vaart-Verschoof of Sidestone Press, the former for facilitating every aspect of the submission and publication process (including the cover image), the latter for her careful work on the layout and design of this book. Thanks also to Ayla Çevik, who produced the index.

LIST OF ILLUSTRATIONS

MAPS

FIGURES

TABLES

Map 1: *The Aegean and western Anatolia.* Prepared by Luke Sollars.

SEAFARING AND SEAFARERS IN THE BRONZE AGE EASTERN MEDITERRANEAN

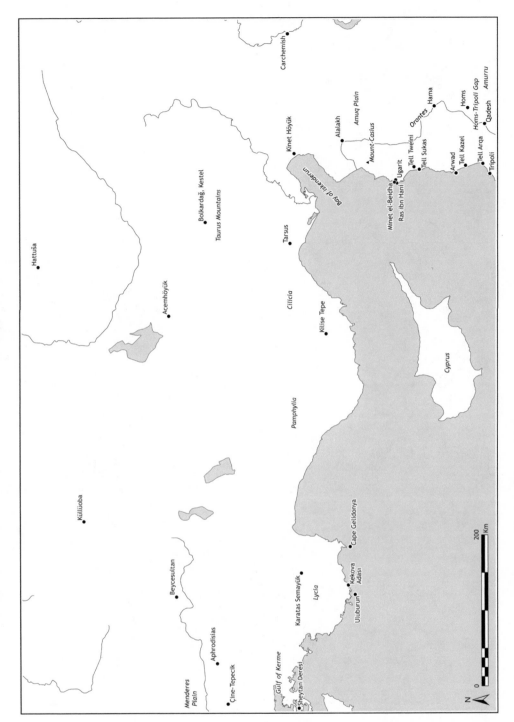

Map 2: *Anatolia and northern Levant.* Prepared by Luke Sollars.

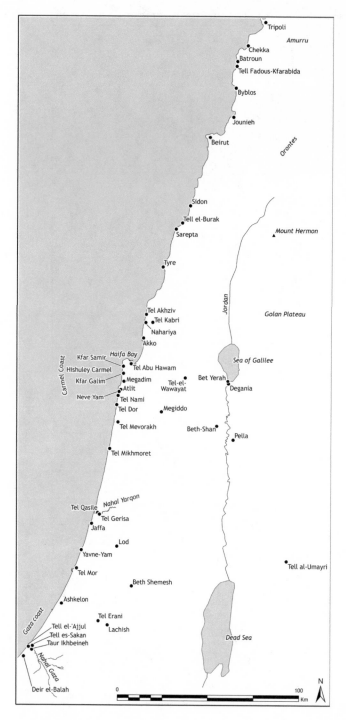

Map 3: *Levant.* Prepared by Luke Sollars.

SEAFARING AND SEAFARERS IN THE BRONZE AGE EASTERN MEDITERRANEAN

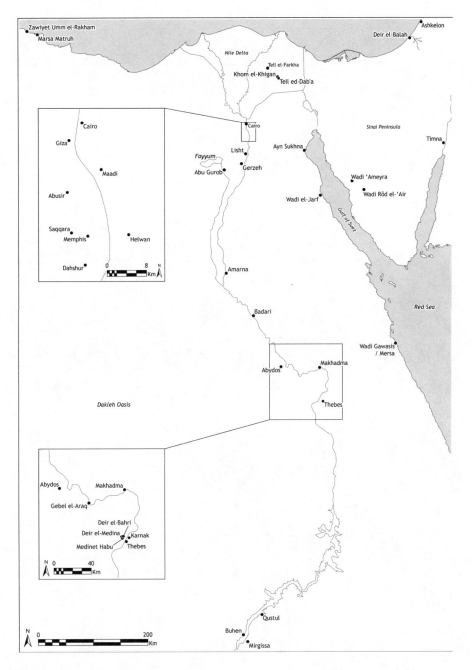

Map 4: *Egypt.* Prepared by Luke Sollars.

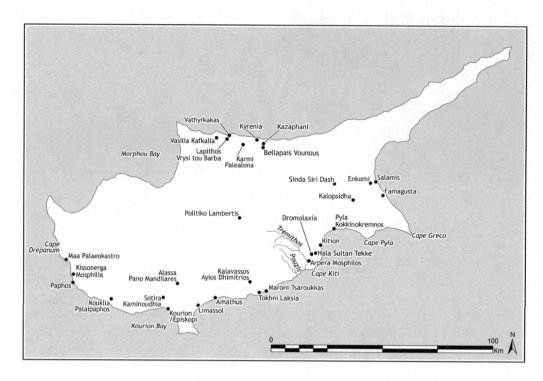

Map 5: *Cyprus.* Prepared by Luke Sollars.

SEAFARING AND SEAFARERS IN THE BRONZE AGE EASTERN MEDITERRANEAN

CHAPTER 1

INTRODUCTION

In his study of seafaring in the Mediterranean from the Late Neolithic through the early Iron Age, Broodbank (2010: 249) asked a stimulating question: how has the Mediterranean, '… occupying less than one percent of the planet's blue expanses, made such a disproportionate impact on the archaeology of seafaring and the maritime history of humanity'? In an exhaustive study devoted to Bronze Age ships, their representations and their construction, Wachsmann (1998: 3) noted that by the Late Bronze Age (LB), the Mediterranean had become transformed into a 'super-highway' for inter-cultural communication, and asked: 'what insights into a culture can be gleaned from studying its ships and the manner in which it interacted with the sea'? In this study, I attempt to address these questions once again and to evaluate the wealth of available evidence — shipwrecks, harbours, ships' representations and boat models, stone anchors and fishing equipment, ancient documentary evidence, and more — to consider how seafaring and seaborne trade in the eastern Mediterranean (the Levant, Cyprus, Anatolia, Egypt) emerged during the Early Bronze Age (EB) (from ca. 3000 BC onward), and made the region an economic epicentre by the LB (after ca. 1700/1600 BC).

Wachsmann (1998: 9-204) reviewed in detail the available material, textual and iconographic evidence of seagoing ships from Bronze Age Egypt, the Levant, Cyprus and Aegean, and I repeatedly refer to his perceptive comments in the present study. It should be noted that Basch (1987) had already provided a nautical analysis of the relevant Bronze Age iconographic evidence in a single chapter of his wide-ranging work on 'la marine antique' —from predynastic Egypt to the Roman empire. Taking a broader view, Broodbank (2010) presents some of the evidence for seagoing, sailing ships, their representations and ship-building technology in the Late Chalcolithic through Iron Age Mediterranean, discussing their sociocultural impact. In a more recent work, Broodbank (2013) explores the nature of Mediterranean prehistory and early history, and the obstacles and affordances presented to the people and polities who lived and functioned within and around the Middle Sea. His three chapters on the Bronze and early Iron Ages cover in remarkable detail the art, archaeology, history, economics and mentality of the peoples of the entire Mediterranean — from the 'long third millennium to the 'collapse' of eastern Mediterranean high cultures (1200-1000 BC) and the narrowing of horizons that followed. Invariably, given his interests, he touches upon ships, seafaring, merchants and mariners to some degree, but always within the context of his broader cultural, historical, environmental, climatic and chronological concerns. Finally, Sauvage (2012) surveys and synthesizes evidence from multiple disciplines in order to counterbalance prevailing views on maritime routes and systems of exchange in the LB Aegean and eastern Mediterranean (see also Yon 2016, which attempts to relate this evidence to trade with LB Cyprus). Sauvage treats much of the same Late Bronze Age data (published up to 2010) that is presented here, but does not attempt to engage with the mechanisms that moved people, materials and objects around the eastern Mediterranean. Because her main focus falls on the LB period, there is little consideration of diachronic developments in maritime commerce vis-à-vis social, political and economic change, or of why and how long-distance maritime exchange emerged in the first place.

The present study thus differs significantly from all these works. Unlike Wachsmann or Basch, my emphasis, not to mention my expertise, does not fall upon the style, design, construction and function of ships, but rather considers who might have built the ships with which Bronze Age maritime trade was conducted, and who captained or sailed them? Which ports and harbours were the most propitious for ships, merchants, mariners and maritime trade? My concern with seafaring is how it serves as a mode of travel, transport and connectivity, a way of traversing maritime space that facilitates the transport of goods and materials but at the same time affords the movement of people and ideas — communicating and sharing knowledge across the sea and between different lands.

Seagoing ships under sail were operating between the Levant, Egypt, Cyprus and Anatolia by the mid-third millennium BC and within the Aegean by the end of that millennium (Broodbank 2010: 255-256). By the mid-second millennium BC, seaborne trade in the eastern Mediterranean seems to have become so well and widely developed that there was no place for Aegean, Canaanite or Egyptian trading monopolies, i.e. 'thalassocracies' (Wedde 1991; Knapp 1993; Lambrou-Phillipson 1993). The world of eastern Mediterranean seafaring and seafarers had become much more complex by this time, and involved several different peoples in multiple networks of economic and social exchange. This much is known, or in many cases widely presumed. But is it possible to trace the origins and emergence of these early trade networks? Can we discuss at any reasonable level who was involved in these maritime ventures?

What other evidence exists for seafaring, fishing, the exploitation of marine resources and related maritime matters? This study seeks to address all these questions by examining a wide range of archaeological, documentary and iconographic evidence, and by re-examining a multiplicity of varying interpretations on Bronze Age seafaring and seafarers in the eastern Mediterranean — from Anatolia in the north to Egypt in the south and west to Cyprus. The Aegean world operated on the western boundaries of this region, but is referred to in this study more in passing than in engagement. My approach in citing and treating (much of) the relevant data cannot be exhaustive, something that is increasingly difficult in the twenty-first century, after 200 years of archaeological research in the region. Instead, my aim is to be consistent and systematic in detailing these data and to be coherent in attempting to interpret them.

Because the social aspects of seafaring, the relationship different peoples had with the sea and the whole notion of 'seascapes' are seldom discussed in the literature of the eastern Mediterranean Bronze Age, this volume devotes significant attention to such factors. These include but are not limited to mobility, connectivity, the length and purpose as well as the risk of the journey, the knowledge and experience of navigation and travel, 'working' the sea, the impact of distance and access to the exotic upon peoples' identities and ideologies, and much more.

All sites, regions and geographic features mentioned are indicated on the five maps (the Aegean and western Anatolia, Anatolia and northern Levant, Levant, Egypt, Cyprus) provided at the beginning of this volume.

A BRIEF (PRE)HISTORY OF THE MEDITERRANEAN BRONZE AGE

Broodbank (2010: 250, fig. 20.1) identifies the eastern Mediterranean as one of the 'major maritime interaction zones' during the third millennium BC (Early Bronze Age), when early states had formed in Egypt and Mesopotamia, eventually transforming social, economic and technological links between and amongst various Levantine regions and the Nile Delta in Egypt (see, *e.g.*, Marfoe 1987; Gophna 2002; Marcus 2002: 406-407; Hartung *et al.* 2015). Comparable polities, albeit with considerable variation in their socioeconomic makeup, emerged across northern Syria and Anatolia and, eventually, in conjunction with 'bottom-up developments', in the Aegean, on Minoan Crete (Broodbank 2014: 53). By the mid-third millennium BC, Egypt most likely had secured access to certain resources it lacked, or desired (*e.g.* oils, wine, timber, resins, lapis lazuli, possibly metals), via seaborne trade with the central-southern Levant (Marfoe 1987: 26-27; Wengrow 2006: 149-150; Marcus 2007: 137; Sowada 2009: 128-141).

During the second millennium BC (Middle and Late Bronze Ages), as economic productivity grew, various coastal or island polities became involved in moving both prestige items and bulk goods over long distances, or at least in controlling their movement (Sherratt and Sherratt 1991: 372-373). Material and documentary sources alike indicate the emergence of standardised commodities such as ingots, weight systems, units of precious liquids, maritime transport containers ('branded' or not), and regimes of value based on metal-based equivalencies (Bevan 2010; Broodbank 2014: 53; Monroe 2015: 10-11; Knapp and Demesticha 2017). The demand for prestige goods, coupled with an increase in maritime mobility, proved to be key factors in emerging systems of long-distance trade during the Middle and especially the Late Bronze Age, if not the early Iron Age (Sherratt and Sherratt 1993). Those polities that had the economic capacity and people with sufficient seafaring knowledge to mount trading expeditions increasingly seem to have gained a pre-eminent position amongst their neighbours (Broodbank 1993: 323).

Nonetheless, because seafaring had by now become a more common activity, wherein various social groups and individuals engaged with the sea (at least on the local level), it was difficult to establish any level of sociopolitical or even economic control (Purcell 2014: 67). Over the long term, and despite some convincing arguments for later periods (*e.g.* Abulafia 2014), the evidence for maritime 'thalassocracies' — whether Egyptian, Aegean, Levantine or Cypriot — in the LB Mediterranean is fleeting at best (Wedde 1991; Knapp 1993; Lambrou-Phillipson 1993; Wachsmann 1998: 332). Instead, maritime connectivity within the Late Bronze and early Iron Age Mediterranean should be associated with coastal polities that were independent of land-based powers like New Kingdom Egypt, the Hittites in Anatolia or even the reputedly seagoing Minoans (Wachsmann 1998: 10). Eastern Mediterranean interconnections were most intensive between Egypt, the Levant and Cyprus, less so with Anatolia, and more episodic with the Aegean. Prestigious goods from near and far flowed through these networks of interaction, best exemplified by the cargo of the late fourteenth century BC Uluburun shipwreck: Cypriot copper, Levantine anchors and pottery, Egyptian resin and glass ingots, African ebony and ivory, Baltic amber, central Asian tin, possibly Levantine wine and Italian weapons (Pulak 1998, 2008, 2009; Jung and Mehofer 2005-2006; Broodbank 2014: 53; McGovern and Hall 2016).

The (natural) 'proto-harbours' of the Middle-Late Bronze Ages (and the purpose-built harbours of the Iron Age) became key centres of long-distance exchange, ports of entry for goods or people and ideas coming into the Mediterranean from afar. Because their basic purpose was to serve transport and mercantile needs, the ports themselves were not necessarily urban centres. For example, the coastal site of Minet al-Beidha (Figure 1) in northern Syria served as one port of entry for the palatial centre at Ugarit, which was located about one km inland. The same applies to the sites of Poros-Katsambas and/or Amnisos on Crete, which served as gateways for the palatial centre at Knossos, some 5-7 kms inland (Schäfer 1991; Dimopoulou-Rethemiotaki et al. 2007). Along with their surrounding farms, estates and even villages, such ports and their urban centres formed the socioeconomic basis of the 'palatial' polities of the LB. Based on the amount of Aegean painted pottery found at LB sites throughout the Aegean and eastern Mediterranean, Broodbank (2013: 358, 413) estimates a network of some 40-50 key trading centres, extending from the Nile Delta to the Aegean. No doubt countless further communities — including smaller seaports, shelters and natural havens — filled in the wider system of connectivity and mobility that typified the LB eastern Mediterranean.

Within a century around 1200 BC, several politico-economic regimes that had been dynamically integrated in maritime transport and exchange over the previous

Figure 1: *Minet el-Beidha, port of Ugarit.* Photo by Machteld Johanna Mellink, Bryn Mawr College (MJM-00911).

300-400 years fell into disarray. Whilst multiple causes — migrations, the 'sea peoples', political inequalities, climate change, etc. —have been argued for this collapse, there is no convincing explanation to account for all the economic, social and political disruption that seem evident in both archaeological and documentary sources (Cline 2014; Knapp and Manning 2016). Both at sea and on land, 'piracy' (see further below, Chapter 2—*Merchants, Mariners and Pirates*) and brigandage accelerated the demise of international trade. An Egyptian account by Ramesses III (Kitchen 1983: 39-40) has long been argued to portray Egypt's defeat of the 'sea peoples'. Amongst others, however, Roberts (2009: 60; 2014: 359-360) has questioned the historicity of Ramesses III's year 8 reliefs and inscriptions, arguing that their main purpose was to magnify the accomplishments of the pharaoh in accordance with the Egyptian worldview. Middleton (2015) regards the 'sea peoples' narratives as 'colourful stories', essentially historical myth. The reliefs on the outer walls of Ramesses III's temple at Medinet Habu portray one segment of these villians as a group of mariners, but their accompanying ships, depicted only once in any detail (Wachsmann 2000: 105-106, fig. 6.1), look very similar to the independent, small-capacity vessels that came to characterise much of Iron Age shipping (see further below, Chapter 5—*Ships' Representations (Egypt)*).

The lack of stability in exchange networks, leading to problems in supply and demand, tends to impact negatively on the maintenance of long-term trading patterns (Arnaud 2011a: 72-73). As many key Bronze Age ports and harbours in the eastern Mediterranean were destabilised or even destroyed, the business of merchants, mariners or even 'pirates' suffered, or failed. As Monroe (2015: 7-8) states so clearly, the interdependencies that resulted from the risk-taking behaviour of merchants outpaced any state-level oversight of an 'immature' international network of exchange. Nonetheless, some coastal towns and island ports survived the chaos (*e.g.* Beirut and Byblos in the Levant, Kition (Figure 2) and Palaipaphos on Cyprus), whilst new, purpose-built harbours emerged elsewhere as commercial centres (*e.g.* Sidon, Tyre and Dor in the Levant, Salamis and Amathus on Cyprus), engaging in a new type of economy that became integral to Mediterranean connectivity. Although it remains uncertain if Iron Age ports like Tyre, Sidon or Dor were organised at any level on a 'palatial' model like those of the LB, it is assumed that these new mercantile towns and ports replaced earlier, palace-centred diplomatic and trading networks, and that more independent, merchant enterprise became the dominant mode of trading activity.

Broodbank (2014: 53) has encapsulated all these events crisply and concisely:

> ... *the ability of strongly centralized, dynastically embedded palace structures to control an ever more powerful and volatile network in the east must have become strained beyond endurance, and ever more at odds with the overtly mercantile values with which they had once cohabited. From this perspective, it is extremely suggestive that those parts of the east that were least invested in palatial institutions, in particular Cyprus and by now parts of the Levant, enjoyed effectively seamless records of ebullient town-based economic activity straight across the 1200-BCE "crisis" (regardless of short-term destructions), while the clearest victims were those most committed to centralized, hierarchical economic management.*

Figure 2: *Main excavated area at LB site of Kition, Cyprus.* © User: Jerrye and Roy Klotz md /wikimedia commons / CC-BY-SA-3.0.

Singer (2011: x), in one of his last papers, presented a similar view:

> *I have designated this period [13th century BC] as 'The Age of Complacency' because underneath the façade of splendor and stability lurked strong destabilizing forces that were either ignored or unsuitably fended off by the self-confident emperors and their advisers. Each great power had its own set of inner problems, but, upon closer examination, they all shared similar difficulties: internecine rifts within the royal houses, schisms within the ruling elites, regional attempts to secede from central rule, overextended supply lines, and restless ethnic groups operating on the fringes of the states, increasingly undermining the authority of the central powers: Arameans on the fringes of Assyria and Babylonia, nomadic Shasu groups in Egyptian Canaan, and "Sea Peoples" subverting both Hittite and Ahhiyawan control in western Anatolia. These unconventional forces proved to be the hardest to deal with. The great powers knew how to recruit enormous armies and resources in order to fight each other, but when it came to dealing with these elusive rebels on the fringes of the kingdom they were at a loss. Repeated campaigns to quell the insurrections turned increasingly ineffective.*

In the chapters that follow, I present first a general discussion of two different aspects of the maritime world of the Bronze Age eastern Mediterranean: (1) social— seascapes and seafaring; merchants, mariners and pirates; and (2) material— shipwrecks; ports and harbours; ships' representations and boat models or wall paintings; stone anchors and fishing equipment. I then present a broad selection of the actual evidence — material, iconographic and documentary — for each period

SEAFARING AND SEAFARERS IN THE BRONZE AGE EASTERN MEDITERRANEAN

under discussion: the Early, Middle and Late Bronze Ages. This is followed by a chapter that summarises all this evidence, and engages it in discussions of seafaring, seafarers and seaborne trade, the various routes and networks of exchange that characterised the Bronze Age eastern Mediterranean, and the impact of seafaring and seafarers on Bronze Age polities. In the conclusion, I outline developments in the Bronze Age eastern Mediterranean in light of the materials and ideas presented in this volume, revisiting some of the social and material aspects of Bronze Age maritime matters, and considering just what we have learned from them. I return to the questions raised in this chapter, and gauge the extent to which the present work has been able to answer them. In closing, I offer a few final thoughts about seafaring and seafarers in the Bronze Age eastern Mediterranean.

CHAPTER 2

Maritime Matters
and Materials

SOCIAL ASPECTS

SEASCAPES AND SEAFARING

Seascapes are both mental and material, many-layered but without chronological strata; knowledge of such aspects is essential if we wish to understand past maritime cultures (Westerdahl 1994: 266; Pungetti 2012: 52-54). Whereas the surface of the sea therefore cannot be 'mapped' like a landscape, certain coastal features (*e.g.* harbours, anchorages, shelters or havens, fishing installations) and submerged cultural remains can (Parker 2001: 23). Westerdahl (1994: 267-268) defines such features, or nodes, as *transport zones* (parallel but lying at right angles to the coast) and *longitudinal zones* (lying in belts directly parallel to the coast). The contact between these zones comprise what Westerdahl terms transition points, or maritime enclaves. Such enclaves would be marked in the seascape by, for example, uplift zones, rapids or dangerous seas, but in the cultural landscape by ports, harbours, offshore islands or beaches that served for offloading or transhipping goods, people, even ideas.

In Parker's (2001: 23) view: '… a full understanding of the landscape [sc. seascape] involves a functional interpretation — the web of interactions which constitute the maritime cultural landscape, … or the system, the total of all activities which have taken place in a given sea area'. Westerdahl (2010: 283) sees it differently: the liminal zone along any transition point between the sea and land is dangerous, at times even supernatural, loaded with magical or spiritual meaning (see also Cunliffe 2001: 9; McNiven 2003). Similarly, Monroe (2011: 90-96) views maritime trade through the lens of 'liminality', pointing out its ambiguity but at the same time its potential for fostering autonomy, power and transformation. Perhaps we might say that a 'full understanding' of seascapes involves engaging the functional, social, symbolic and liminal aspects of maritime space, considering not just the landscape but its marine counterpart, and where possible or plausible using the eyes and ears of mariners, fishermen or seafaring merchants in attempting to portray and understand shorelines, coastal structures and natural features, ports, harbour installations, fishing fleets, and the people and things within and amongst them.

It is impossible, of course, to reconstruct the specific physical or mental conditions that seafarers may have experienced in the past. Any number of changes may and probably have affected the marine environment, including relative sea-level, the range and force of tides, the silting of harbour entrances, the enlargement of estuaries, the effects of storms and, not least, human impact (Parker 2001: 25). Some prehistoric seamen followed shoals of fish whilst others followed up rumours of distant or exotic lands: such factors propelled open-sea ventures on ships. Even in deep water, a ship's position and direction could be gauged from the sun or the stars, the swells of the sea, sea-birds and clouds (around islands) (Figure 3). Hazards for a seafarer include violent storms, traversing low-lying coasts with hidden rocks or sand bars, navigating through shoals, shallows and deeps, making a forced landfall, or other dangers. Coastal sailing in shallow waters with reefs was always a hazardous exercise, and a working knowledge of coastal topography, of the prevailing seasonal and local winds, was essential to navigate from place to place (Morton 2001: 46-56; Beresford 2013: 99-100, 184-185; see also Karyda 2016: 79). Parker (2001: 32-33) thus maintains that the 'underwater landscape' was well known to seafarers and fishermen, one that helped them to determine their position and direct their voyages.

Guided by such features of the sea as well as by knowledge of currents and tides (the last insignificant in the Mediterranean), the stars, landmarks etc., seafarers approaching land would look for hills, mountains or cliffs (especially with a crown of cloud) (Figure 4) and other topographic features (Morton 2001: 185-201), as well as prominent promontories, ridges, built structures or shrines known by their ships' graffiti and/or seafarers' offerings (Parker 2001: 35) — *e.g.* the castle of

Figure 3: *Salina (Aeolian islands) with clouds. View northwest from Lipari island.* Photo: A. Bernard Knapp.

SEAFARING AND SEAFARERS IN THE BRONZE AGE EASTERN MEDITERRANEAN

Figure 4: *View of Gozo cliffs (Maltese islands), from sea.* Photo: A. Bernard Knapp.

Saint Hilarion or the abbey of Bellapais, situated in the mountains above and behind (south of) Kyrenia on the north coast of Cyprus, both clearly visible from the sea (Michail 2015: 50, 59). There are references in Homeric literature (*Iliad* and *Odyssey*) mentioning mortuary structures ('barrows') on headlands, which may well have been designed to serve as navigational 'signs' for seafarers (Morton 2001: 194; Beresford 2013: 199 and n.102, with refs.). Maori communities, to take another example, used prominent landmarks to identify — from the sea — the location of their fishing grounds (Barber 2003: 444). Phillips (2003: 375-380), in turn, maintains that Neolithic megaliths on Scotland's Orkney islands were placed so that they could be seen from the sea.

In a prehistoric context, the term *mare* ('sea') was just as significant symbolically as *domus* ('home, house') and *agrios* ('wild') (Hodder 1990: 44-46, 85-87; Westerdahl 2010: 284); in other words, people could construct their worlds into home, or away from home, or at sea (for the Greeks of later periods, see Arnaud 2011b). Early seafarers and seafaring communities must have had an 'attitude' to the sea (Parker 2001: 37-39), and seagoing would have been a normal activity in such communities. This attitude might be expressed in terms such as 'maritime consciousness' or even invoked to describe, for example, the intensification of mobility and connectivity in the Middle-Late Bronze Age eastern Mediterranean. Although some people who took to the sea may have done so in order to showcase their ability to travel to distant places and return with 'exotic' goods or knowledge, not to mention renown for their own ventures (Helms 1998; Kristiansen 2004: 116; Knapp 2006: 56-59), others were propelled by economic motives — *e.g.* the search for basic materials, finished goods or even new lands — to instigate seafaring ventures.

Archaeologists can gain some access to such ideas and attitudes by considering material features like the development of port facilities or coastal settlements, by identifying landmarks and zones of transport or interaction, by tracking the movement of maritime transport containers or other products in demand (Demesticha and Knapp 2016), and by being ever aware of the ideology of the sea in the conceptual worlds of earlier peoples (*e.g.* Westerdahl 2005, 2010). As Parker (2001: 39) put it:

> *An appreciation of the maritime aspects of the historic landscape [sc. seascape] requires archaeologists to adopt a mariner's perspective, in which the sky, the sea, the seabed, seamarks and landmarks articulate navigation, pilotage and safe arrival in port.*

Turning to seafaring, we may define this as a mode of travel, a way to traverse maritime space that enables the transport of all kinds of goods, materials, peoples and ideas — communicating and sharing knowledge across the sea and between different lands. The 'business of seafaring' (Anderson 2010) involves travelling upon and making a living from the sea — i.e. 'working' the sea. In prehistoric or protohistoric cases, seafaring would have extended peoples' habitats and given them access to resources that lie near and beyond the shore: it increased the range and links of fisher-foragers, migrants and, ultimately, merchants and colonists; it facilitated the bulk transport of goods and the expansion of trade; and it enabled the establishment of sea-based states and kingdoms.

Anderson (2010: 3) suggests that archaeologists should focus upon '… the active or dynamic side of the broad field of maritime archaeology, i.e. upon the history, modes and results of seaborne mobility and their implications for prehistory'. Seafaring involved particular types of skills — *e.g.* the ability to 'read' seascapes, sea-lanes and coastlines — and knowledge: of navigation, fishing, foraging or trading; of boats, jetties and harbours (where to locate and how to construct them); of social patterns and seasonal mobility; of traditions or rituals related to the sea.

The coastline represents the interface between two different worlds, sea and land, virtual 'environments on the edge', where change in any biotic, climatic or ecological parameter or process can test the resilience of coastal dwellers or seafarers who exploit that land- or seascape (Walsh 2014: 31) The core activities of seafaring revolved around the exploitation of marine resources, the transport and exchange of goods and the mobility of people. In the Mediterranean, the 'agency' of winds, currents, erosion or progradation must have influenced not just the economies but even the social structures of those who dwelt on the coast and exploited the sea (Walsh 2014: 67).

Ancient seafaring, however, can be difficult to demonstrate archaeologically (Anderson 2010: 4). Travelling on the sea itself leaves few and often disputed material traces, while rising sea levels since the Late Glacial Maximum (i.e. after about 26,000 years ago) have left ancient coastlines, settlements and other terrestrially-related evidence of seafaring submerged under some 120 m of water (Peltier and Fairbanks 2006). In the Mediterranean, the most significant rise in sea level occurred between about 17,000–11,000 BP (Shackleton *et al.* 1984; Lambeck and Purcell 2005: 1985-1987, fig. 14). A dramatic rise in sea level around 14,500 years ago — estimated to be around 20 m in less than 500 years (Clark *et al.* 2002; Weaver *et al.* 2003) — would have transformed seascape and landscape alike (Stewart and Morhange 2009: 402). By the eighth millennium BC, sea level had risen to some 7 m lower than present levels (van Andel 1989: 736; Lambeck and Chappell 2001: 683; Pirazzoli 2005: 1996–1999): any shorelines that existed before that time are now submerged, tens if not hundreds of metres beyond present-day coasts (Bailey and Milner 2002: 132–133).

These submerged prehistoric coastal shelves included some of the most favourable environmental settings of the Late Pleistocene–Early Holocene Mediterranean, but they have been largely inaccessible to archaeologists. Moreover, the most striking thing about such material markers of fisher-foragers as we have (*e.g.* boats, fishhooks, shells, harpoons, even representations in cave art) is their paucity in the pre-Holocene archaeological record (in general, see Broodbank 2013: 126-127 on the westernmost Mediterranean). As a result, seldom can we portray adequately the activities of those who plied the seas or exploited the coastal landscapes and seascapes of that era (Flemming 1983; Westley and Dix 2006: 11).

The origins of seafaring, from early hominims to the coastal dwellers or riverine settlers of the terminal Pleistocene, are widely hypothesized and just as widely debated (Anderson 2010: 4-7). For example, although there is little secure evidence for maritime ventures to the Mediterranean islands during the Pleistocene (Cherry and Leppard 2015; cf. Simmons 2014; Howitt-Marshall and Runnels 2016), recent survey work on the south coast of Crete has identified chipped stone assemblages of Mesolithic type. The survey team also assigned (controversially) a Lower Palaeolithic date to various tools, flakes, cores and debitage made of massive quartz and found in the region around the Preveli gorge (Strasser *et al.* 2010; 2011; Runnels *et al.* 2014; Runnels 2014; cf. Leppard 2014a; Cherry and Leppard 2015: 3, 12). Whatever the case may prove to be on Crete, by the eleventh millennium Cal BC, the limited and tentative forays into the sea (*seagoing*) that typified the Late Pleistocene rapidly morphed into a more adept, practiced form of *seafaring*, i.e. the sea now became a 'vector for travel', not just a 'provider of resources' (Broodbank 2006: 200). There is solid and still-accumulating evidence from the Late Pleistocene-Early Holocene transition indicating that for at least two millennia before the advent of farming, seafaring fishers and foragers plied the coasts and islands of the Mediterranean. The maritime capabilities developed by these early seafarers enabled them to explore new landscapes and seascapes, tap new marine resources and make use of accessible coastal sites — whether on islands or mainlands.

Gamble (2003: 232-233) maintained that such seafaring began deep in human prehistory, not just as a response to environmental or climatic stress but because it offered attractive options for exploration and subsistence. By contrast, Broodbank (2006: 208) felt that an era of more intensified seafaring emerged during the climatic downturn of the Late Pleistocene, giving rise to seaborne networks that brought to the fore 'trans-Mediterranean societies'. Since the present volume is devoted to Bronze Age seafaring, here it must suffice to state that short-range seafaring, which probably followed upon earlier coastal or freshwater developments, emerged under certain environmental and social conditions, favourable or otherwise, and that travelling by sea in the Mediterranean cannot be demonstrated unequivocally before the Middle if not the Upper Palaeolithic (Broodbank 2006: 205-208; 2013: 126-128, 154-156).

Broodbank (2010: 258-260) highlights the advantages of seafaring under sail as opposed to oared ships: (1) optimising travel time, thus expanding the margins of the Mediterranean to embrace the unknown; (2) lowering transport costs and thus enabling some key centres to produce specialised goods; (3) bringing distant and different peoples and cultures, and their material and social practices, into contact in the main ports; and (4) facilitating the bulk transport of diverse goods — maritime transport containers and their contents, grain and other staples, and metals (with no evidence yet for metric tonnage exceeding roughly 20-25 tons in the Bronze Age—Monroe 2007).

With reference primarily to the Aegean world, Georgiou (1997) discussed generally the emergence, development and location of ('urban') harbours, and how seafarers used their knowledge and navigational skills — *e.g.* the position and orientation of bays and inlets, winds and currents, proximity to natural resources — to sail the open sea whenever it was advantageous (i.e. during any season) and to make a profit. Indeed, seamanship and an intimate knowledge of the local land- and seascape may compensate for certain navigational difficulties, *e.g.* sailing at night or during the off-season (Arnaud 2011a: 62, 70-71). Although ancient mariners may have avoided night-time or wintertime ventures on the sea, certain regional conditions or specific sea routes may have remained an option: travelling between Greece and Egypt, for example, would have been safe for winter sailing (Morton 2001: 255-265).

In Arnaud's (2011a: 75) view, winter sailing was riskier than summer sailing, and so involved different (coastal) routes and sailing times, and probably the use of smaller ships (more quickly and cheaply built, and easier to navigate in estuaries and shallow anchorages), which in turn meant different trading patterns on different scales. Beresford (2013: 181-183) too suggests that winter navigation would have required mariners to modify their sailing strategies. The relation between a ship's size and seaworthiness during winter, however, remains unresolved, not least because of such factors as the manoeuvrability of bigger vs smaller craft, their ability to shelter or the weight of a ship's cargo (Morton 2001: 153; Beresford 2013: 125-134). Even if we accept that there was no closed season as far as merchant shipping was concerned, throughout classical antiquity most recorded open sea trips during summer were related to prevailing winds and seldom lasted longer than three days (Arnaud 2005: 121).

The situation in the prehistoric eastern Mediterranean is less clear. According to Monroe (2007: 15): '... little is securely known about the details of Bronze Age ships — their size, construction details, costs, sailing properties, and ownership issues. Some of these questions may never be answered satisfactorily until more evidence is uncovered'. One aspect of ancient seafaring we can discuss in some detail, however, concerns the people involved in maritime practices: merchants, mariners and — perhaps — pirates.

MERCHANTS, MARINERS AND PIRATES

> *...maritime traders operated spatially and socially in between worlds, with greater autonomy, economic potential, and risks than their inland neighbors. In addition to common terrestrial terrors, coastal dwellers and seafarers faced the inherently chaotic sea* (Monroe 2009: 280 n.3).

Merchants, traders and seamen, together with their contacts onshore, 'connected' people and things from different, often distant lands. As Horden and Purcell (2000: 224-230) observed regarding historic times on the Aegean islands, production resulted from 'all around connectivity'. Maritime trade, and the connectivity that flowed in its wake, were instrumental in determining the degree of mobility that coastal and island communities enjoyed. Such communities and their ports were oriented toward the sea and relied on its connecting role to meet the demands and exploit the opportunities afforded by engagement in wider, maritime networks.

The real as well as the cognitive worlds of ancient mariners were fluid, with ever-shifting boundaries and the ever-present threat of natural and human disasters: high winds, storms, rogue waves, rocky shores, sinking and drowning (Monroe 2015: 44, 46). This transformative capacity of maritime space not only shaped cultural practices but also impacted on commercial exchange in all its manifestations: reciprocity, redistribution, markets, trade diasporas, world systems and more (Monroe 2011: 95; Nakassis *et al.* 2016).

Even the most enterprising merchant or most experienced mariner had much to cope with in their everyday life. Moreover, the risks involved in their work were not just economic in nature: documents from Ugarit (Syria) and Amarna (Egypt) allude to the theft of goods, ships wrecked, hostage-taking and murder on land and at sea (Holmes 1978; Monroe 2009: 174-178; see further below, and in Chapter 5: *Late Bronze Age—The Documentary Record*). The upside for the merchants, of course, is that there was also much to gain from living on and working the sea. Maritime trade traditionally was heterarchical in nature, enticing not just rulers and royal fleets but also independent and entrepreneurial merchants and traders of all sort — 'experts inhabiting the liminal world of shorelines' (Monore 2015: 46).

In much later periods, European maritime traders often invested their earnings in banking or finance, because they aspired to join the landed aristocracy (Braudel 1982: 478-481), and thus to earn a less precarious living. Bronze Age merchants who took to the sea also must have known that commerce always involves risks — natural and human — and they may have accepted that some form of 'piracy' was the price of doing business. After all, many of them were probably engaged in similar activities themselves. To be sure, piracy, as well as the social and legal customs that regulated it, is likely as old as the emergence of sailing ships on the high seas; some have even suggested that the Mediterranean was the birthplace of piracy (Backman 2014: 170; see also Bono 2013):

> *The Mediterranean is a headstrong and willful beauty. Since the first peoples settled her shores, societies have had to adapt to her dictates. The characteristics that make the sea so naturally a commercial bazaar are the very qualities that made it a natural zone for piracy. Ease of movement and navigation, and a superabundance of islands and of coastal crags and inlets made it as easy for pirates to find sanctuary as it did navigation for the merchants they targeted* (Backman 2014: 181).

In general, the sea is a lawless space, and the Mediterranean was '… an anarchic, free-for-all zone for anyone with the skill, daring and funds to set out upon it' (Broodbank 2013: 394). For example, according to Appian (*Mithridatic Wars* 92), a Roman historian of Greek origin writing in the second century AD, sailors from throughout the eastern Mediterranean, suffering from the severe and drawn-out Mithridatic war, '… preferred to do wrong rather than suffer it, and for this purpose chose the sea instead of the land'.

The practice of piracy required at least some people who had essential maritime skills, the watercraft in which to engage them and ideally access to a network of commercial contacts (Rauh 1997: 270). As is known better from post-Roman times (and no less today, *e.g.* renewed episodes in the waters off the coast of Somalia—http://www.aljazeera.com/news/2017/03/somalia-pirates-anger-fuels-return-ship-attacks-170315191915900.html), pirates often used small, swift boats and attacked merchant vessels as they were approaching a port or anchored at port. Attacking a ship as it approached land was probably preferable, as the vessel would not yet have been under any jurisdiction or protection from the target port. Geospatial and political factors in any specific region must also be taken into account. For example, Venetian traders operating in the relatively narrow Adriatic Sea were highly vulnerable: pirates from Dalmatia or any of the hundreds of small islands along the eastern shore of the Adriatic struck and vanished quickly. Intense local loyalties and political rivalries in the region meant that pirates could always find a shelter or port with a harbour master amenable to granting refuge — for a small share of the profits (Backman 2014: 179).

But how should we define 'piracy', in particular as it may be related to prehistoric periods? De Souza (1999: 1) described pirates in the Graeco-Roman world as 'armed robbers whose activities normally involve the use of ships'; they are people who have been designated 'pirates' by their enemies and their victims, not by themselves. To keep to a straightforward definition, and to sidestep the debate over whether piracy was just another form of warfare at sea (see below), I define piracy as an irregular, typically hostile, ongoing economic activity carried out for personal benefit and involving the use of ships, maritime mobility and plundering, at sea and along coastal areas (following Leeson 2009: 195; Samaras 2015: 191). Moreover, there is a positive correlation between trade and piracy, as both are dependent on a flourishing system of maritime exchange (Braudel 1972/2: 883-884).

The case has been made — based on eighth century BC Neo-Assyrian documents — that Ionians (*Iaunaya/Iamnaya*—Greeks?) were involved, perhaps as mercenaries, in piratic activities (Parker 2000: 74-75; Luraghi 2006; Deszö and Vér: 2013: 334, 342, 359; *cf.* Kuhrt 2002: 18-20, 24). Yet it is only with classical authors that we gain literary insights into piracy and into people who are actually termed 'pirates' (see below on possible Bronze Age cases). Both the Homeric and classical word *lêistes*, and the later (third century BC onward) word *peiratis*, meant 'pirate' or 'bandit' but could also be translated as 'plunderer'. Strabo (*Geography* 11.2.12) stated that people from Colchis in the Bosphorus area 'live by plundering [*lêisteriôn*] at sea'. Another, less common term — *katapontistes* (from a verb meaning 'to throw into or drown in the sea') — refers exclusively to 'pirate', not 'bandit': the third century AD author Cassius Dio (36.20.1) wrote: 'The pirates [*katapontistai*] had always attacked shipping, just as the bandits [*lêisteias*] did those who live on land'. In de Souza's (1999: 8-9) view, therefore, 'pirates operate mainly at sea and use ships', unlike bandits whose activities typically are restricted to land. The pirates' use of ships also meant that they needed anchorages or harbours, and thus their bases become crucial for their activities (de Souza 1999: 11). These are important distinctions to which I return below.

Surviving ancient Greek records often refer to pirate attacks at sea and on land (usually coastal areas): pillaging, kidnapping and murder by seaborne raiders must have been familiar phenomena for many Mediterranean people during the classical era (de Souza 1999: 1). Homer, to begin with, was clearly negative about merchants but rather ambivalent about pirates. Although generally disapproving, Homer twice has Odysseus boasting about his escapades at sea, whilst Menelaus stated that it took him seven years and great hardships to amass his fortune 'and bring it home in my ships' (*Odyssey* 4:75-85). Most Greeks of the classical era tended to view pirates as brigands who threatened not only trade but civilised life as well. Although Thucydides regarded piracy (*lêisteia*) as an impediment to progress, in reminiscing about Aegean seafaring before the 'Minoan thalassocracy', he commented that there was 'no disgrace', 'even some glory' attached to attacking and plundering small towns (*History* I:5:1-3). Piracy flourished in the eastern Mediterranean during the Hellenistic era: the waters off southern coastal Cilicia and the western coastal Balkans were infested with pirates (Rauh *et al.* 2013; Álvarez-Ossorio Rivas 2013; Backman 2014: 176-177).

Plutarch's *Life of Pompey*, fanciful as it may be, describes how Roman commerce was harassed by a vast fleet based in coastal hideaways in Cilicia and Crete, involving some 20,000 pirates aboard 1000 ships. These pirates reputedly held for ransom the people of 400 port cities, ransacking their temples and looting their treasuries. Plutarch states that these pirates were so successful that many wealthy men in these ports — good citizens all —not only hastened to invest in these thieving ventures but also to take part in them. Plutarch's tale relates many other aspects of piracy, but it rings false throughout; it seems that some ancient sources romanticised pirates as much as modern media do (Backman 2014: 170-171, 174). Moreover, whereas Cicero (writing in the first century BC) castigated pirates as 'the common enemy of all mankind', St Augustine (writing in the fourth century AD) expressed the view that piracy was relative, as beauty is in the eye of the beholder — what we would term today a social construct (Gabrielsen 2013: 133, with refs.).

The lesson we may take from all these examples is that 'piracy' was very much an individual initiative, not restricted to any class, upper or lower: it may have offered to certain elements amongst seafaring peoples a way to enter the lucrative commerce of the eastern Mediterranean world.

The literature on 'piracy' during the Bronze Age is relatively recent and, in most cases, limited in scope, controversial and often contradictory (*e.g.* Wachsmann 1998: 320-321; Cesarano 2008; Jung 2009; de Miroschedji 2012: 283-284; Gilan 2013; Hitchcock and Maeir 2014, 2016, 2018; Samaras 2015; Emanuel 2015, 2016; Molloy 2016). Some of it refers to the work of de Souza (1999: 241), who implied that the piracy — as we think of this practice today — did not exist during the Bronze Age, and that any form of seaborne raiding or plunder could not be distinguished from warfare in general before the fifth-fourth centuries BC. Liverani (2014: 383), a more realistic source for the Bronze Age, suggests that 'the boundary between piracy and organised military endeavours, and between the indifference of the palaces and their participation in these activities, was not always clear'. Elsewhere, Liverani (2001: 109) refers to various hostile, tribal groups in the Bronze Age ancient Near East as 'small people, of small moral texture' who engage in 'guerrilla activity'; although he did not refer specifically to piracy, their activities might be so categorised. Most scholars who have previously written about piracy in the Bronze Age simply made very generic references. For example, in discussing the troubled times between about 1250-1150 BC, I once wrote that '… communications were disrupted severely, while brigandage on land and piracy at sea complicated international trade' (Knapp 1992: 126).

De Souza (1999: 2), in any case, argued that '… *all* evidence of piracy in the Graeco-Roman world is textual' and that '… pirates did not leave any distinct trace in the archaeological record'. Such a perspective, if taken seriously, presents an unreasonable obstacle to archaeologists working mainly with the material record, seeking to find material insignia of piracy or pirates. Whereas I don't ascribe to de Souza's restriction, like him I take a sceptical approach in considering possible instances of piracy in the Bronze Age.

One of the earliest cases made for 'piracy' stems from textual evidence, and involves a recent re-reading of the 'autobiography' of the Sixth Dynasty Egyptian court official Uni (Weni) (de Miroschedji 2012). Uni repeatedly fought with the *Ḥeryu-sha*, who may have interfered with the maritime connections between Old Kingdom Egypt and Early Bronze Age Byblos, and against whom Uni undertook a campaign by sea. In de Miroschedji's (2012: 283-284) view, the actions of the *Ḥeryu-sha* could be considered one of the earliest documented instances of 'piracy' in the eastern Mediterranean, occurring just when Egypt's maritime trade with Byblos had become most significant economically.

When we turn to (mainly) archaeological treatments of the Late Bronze Age (LB), it may be noted that Morgan (1988: 159, 164) long ago suggested that the 'miniature fresco' from Thera, with its drowning men and Mycenaean-attired warriors, might represent an attempt to portray a coastal community plagued by pirates (see also Höckman 2001: 224). More recently, Cesarano (2008) maintains there was no such thing as 'Mycenaean piracy', yet Gilan (2013: 53-54) unhesitatingly discusses Mycenaean 'sea raiders'. Jung (2009: 78-79) too proposed that the Mycenaeans engaged both in (legitimate) trade as well as piracy, and that '… the immigration of persons from Italy to Mycenaean Greece may have been part of the piracy of the so-called Sea Peoples starting in the time of Ramesses II'. More by assertion than demonstration, Jung sought to reconcile a thick description of bronze metallurgy, especially weapons (Naue II swords, socketed spearheads) and pottery (multiple Mycenaean types, Handmade Burnished Ware of Italian origin) with historical interpretation. In turn, Araque-Gonzalez (2014: 153-154) rather too easily views these same 'sea peoples', i.e. coming from the LB eastern Mediterranean, as pirate-like immigrants to nuragic Sardinia.

In a long series of publications, Wachsmann (1981; 1998: 172-196; 2000a; 2013: 33-40) has maintained that the 'sea peoples' ships from Medinet Habu have their closest parallels in Aegean (Mycenaean) galleys depicted in representations of Late Helladic and Iron Age warships. He suggests, for example: 'Either the ships in use by the Sea Peoples were Mycenaean, or such ships were patterned closely on Mycenaean prototypes' (Wachsmann 2000a: 121). More recently, he has argued that the Abu Gurob ship-cart model found in Egypt, and radiocarbon dated (2σ) to 1256-1054 BC (XIXth Dynasty), represents a (Late) Helladic type of galley used by the 'sea peoples' (Wachsmann 2013: 26, 28, 33, 59, 201-203) (discussed further below, Chapter 5: *Late Bronze Age—Ships' Representations (Egypt)*).

Emanuel (2016: 267-268) suggests that piracy posed a 'significant threat' during the LB and that polities (like Ugarit) and merchants alike may have addressed such a threat by maintaining small fleets of 'combat-capable' vessels to defend their coastal waters. He mentions in passing that the anchorage at Marsa Matruh, along Egypt's westernmost frontier, might have served as a base for pirates, just as the coastal waters off Crete and Cilicia may have done at times. Turning to his comfort zone, Emanuel (2016: 271) points out that the end of the LB was a time of 'accelerated innovation' in maritime technology and tactics, and asks whether it was pirates and raiders who developed more efficient hull designs and sailing rigs for plundering opportunities, or whether such innovations emerged in response to piracy and in order to protect coastal waters as well as ships at sea. In fact, the documentary evidence (discussed in detail below) suggests neither: coastal polities likely developed such maritime technology as they did in the attempt to promote maritime trade, and such 'pirates' as can be identified in these documents were primarily coastal raiders. One could also counter that the ships of the presumed LB pirates would have been smaller, more manoeuvrable vessels (as pointed out by Hitchcock and Maeir 2016: 256); in any case, there is neither documentary nor material evidence of any 'pirate' ships *per se* during this period.

Hitchcock and Maeir (2014, 2016, 2018) seek to link piracy more generally to the 'sea peoples' phenomenon at the end of the LBA. They associate multiple aspects of the Mycenaean world — Linear B texts, disadvantaged workers, feasting and drinking, representations on pottery, ships (the 'Mycenaean galley'), site locations, 'slavery', pottery (Handmade Burnished Ware), even 'grooming and depilatory habits' — to a 'culture of piracy' (Hitchcock and Maeir 2016: 247 and *passim*). Their arguments, however, are based more on assertion than demonstration. For example, even if it is clear that 'Cilician' pirates operating in the second and first centuries BC placed importance on their dress and manner (Rauh 1997: 276-277), it is pure speculation to argue on that basis that 'the display of Sea Peoples' regalia … contributed to maintaining tribal identity within pirate cultures' (Hitchcock and Maeir 2014: 626), or that piratic tribes like the 'sea peoples' developed '… a unified culture aboard their ships that coalesced around dress, weaponry and warrior culture, Mycenaean styles of drinking, and Mycenaean and Italian grooming habits' (Hitchcock and Maeir 2016: 260). More thoughtful is Molloy's (2016: 367, 371) take on piracy and the 'sea peoples': he posits a 'maritime movement of warriors' following the collapse of Mycenaean polities and reflecting the devolution of trading into raiding and involving 'multi-ethnic confederations that were soluble, transient, archaeologically ephemeral but potentially sizeable in both numbers and socio-political impact'.

All these scholars, each in their own way, view events at the end of the Bronze Age as involving mixed tribal groups comprised of non-elites, the disenfranchised from all classes, and peasants and immigrants such as Mycenaeans or 'sea peoples'. However, the whole question of large scale migrations leading to 'deep change' in the material record (Yasur-Landau 2010: 234-238, 267-268) can be challenged (*e.g.* Voskos and Knapp 2008), whilst the 'crisis' at the end of the LB was much more complex than allowed by most of those writing on the issue of Bronze Age piracy (Knapp and Manning 2016). Moreover, Ben-Dor Evian (2016, 2017) has now made compelling arguments — based on a wide range of material evidence from Late Bronze and early Iron Age Levantine sites — that the 'sea peoples' (or at least the Philistines) mentioned in the texts from Medinet Habu were of north Levantine and Anatolian origin and that, consequently, Aegean 'pirates' had nothing tō do with the infamous naval battle(s) recorded in the Nile Delta.

Two further strains of archaeological evidence are commonly cited to infer the existence of Bronze Age pirates: defensible site locations and ships' representations on pottery. Taking the latter first, a few Late Helladic (LH) III kraters show what have been interpreted as weapon-wielding warriors aboard ships, *e.g.* from Enkomi (LH IIIB), Bademgediği Tepesi in western Turkey (LH IIIB-C; see below Figure 49) and Kynos in east Lokris (LH IIIC) (Mountjoy 2011: 484-486, figs. 2-3; see also Mountjoy 2005). As Mountjoy (2011: 487) notes, the scenes on the Bademgediği Tepesi and Kynos kraters could well portray a sea battle, with warriors on deck prepared to board another ship. A small body sherd from another LH IIIC vessel (most likely a krater) from Liman Tepe depicts what is interpreted as an 'oarsman', like the one depicted on the Bademgediği Tepesi krater, perhaps standing below deck with the legs of another figure/warrior above (Aykurt and Erkanal 2017: 62-66, figs. 4-5). From Çine-Tepecik, inland from Miletos, the rim of yet another krater preserves the figure of what appears to be a warrior standing on the deck of a ship (Günel and Herbordt 2014: 4-5, figs. 3-5). Along with the representation of a naval battle seen in the wall reliefs of Ramesses III's temple at Medinet Habu (Wachsmann 2000: 106, fig. 6.1), these are the closest we come in any medium to what is commonly viewed as 'piracy', i.e. ship-borne raiders attacking another ship at sea in the attempt to plunder, loot cargo or seize captives (for further discussion of both the Anatolian representations and Medinet Habu reliefs, see below, Chapter 5: *Late Bronze Age—Anatolia, Ships' Representations*).

Regarding site location, Rediker (1987: 257-258) has noted that, in general, pirates ('sea robbers') typically sought bases located near major maritime trading routes, 'as distant as possible from the powers of the state'. Samaras (2015: 195-196) also notes several locational features of sites that might have been attractive as pirate bases during the postpalatial period in the Aegean (after ca. 1150-1100 BC), and again during the Geometric period (after 900 BC). These include naturally defensible sites; sites with defensive features such as fortifications or towers; and sites situated on or near the coast but invisible from the sea. Nowicki (2000: 264-265) has suggested that several defensible coastal sites on postpalatial Crete might have been established as bases by mobile 'sea-warriors' (but *cf.* Dickinson 2006: 47-48).

Hitchcock and Maeir (2014: 629-630) suggest that the Cypriot sites of Maa *Palaeokastro* and Pyla *Kokkinokremnos* — both easily defensible with excellent surveillance qualities — might be associated with piracy, the former as a refuge for pirates, the latter to protect against them. Long ago, Sherratt (1998: 300-301 n.15; 2016: 292) made a similar argument, maintaining that Maa and Pyla may have been 'bypass and outflanking centres' serving mercantile elites who had broken away, respectively, from longer established ports at *Palaipaphos* and Kition, to set up their own seaside bases, perhaps a reflection of piratic activities. Of course, most earlier studies had argued that these sites served defensive functions (Karageorghis 1998: 127-130; Steel 2004: 188-190; Keswani 2009: 123), specifically as local 'strongholds' that served as outposts of neighbouring sites. Alternatively, it must be pointed out that Caraher *et al.* (2005: 246-248; 2014: 5 fig. 1.5, 43-47) have now identified what they term 'the definitive characteristics of a prehistoric to historic harbour' and a palaeocoastline some 150 m inland from the present-day beach near Pyla (see also Zomeni 2014). In a more recent study that attempts to place Pyla *Kokkinokremnos* in its broader landscape context, Brown (2017: 291) notes: 'The now defunct natural harbour at Pyla would have rivalled the nearby Larnaca Salt Lakes as a sheltered anchorage for Bronze Age shipping on the south-east coast'. The existence of this Bronze Age harbour at Pyla supports earlier suggestions that the site likely served as an intermediary in moving traded goods from coastal ports to inland settlements (*e.g.* Stanley Price 1979: 80-81; see also Knapp 2013a: 357-358).

Whether indicative of the presence of pirates or the potential victims of piracy, the two Cypriot sites, along with many other sites in the Aegean or eastern Mediterranean might be construed that way (*e.g.*, postpalatial Koukounaries on Paros, or the islet of Modi just east of Poros in the Saronic Gulf—Samaras 2015: 195-196). Korfmann (1986a: 13) even described Troy as a 'pirate fortress'. One point that might support such a notion is that Troy, like the strait between Rhodes and the Marmaris region in southwestern Turkey, could well be seen as a 'choke point', where maritime routes are constricted by capes, straits or islands (Galvin 1999: 12; cited by Hitchcock and Maeir 2016: 255).

Beyond any generalisations one might make about piracy or pirates on the basis of all this material and locational evidence — their social status and organisation, their ethnicities or gender, the 'culture' of piracy, it remains problematic to apply the notion of piracy or to demonstrate the existence of pirates during the Bronze Age. Indeed, we know little if anything about any group of people or community involved in prehistoric or early historic pirate-like practices: their leaders and crews, their insignia and memorabilia, their dress or the tools of their trade (*contra* assertions by Hitchcock and Maeir 2016). Can we think of them as a 'buccaneer' 'society against the state' (Araque Gonzalez 2014: 155)? Or, perhaps more appropriately, as a socially ephemeral group of varying origins that brought together diverse material and cultural practices, objects and 'know-how', and whose influences, once these groups fragmented, were spread far and wide in the Mediterranean (Molloy 2016: 371)? Broodbank (2013: 466) argues that characterising the 'sea peoples' as pirates only validates the viewpoint of a land-based authority as to what constituted legality on the high seas, a legality over which such authorities had no control.

All this archaeological manoeuvring and more does little to instil confidence in our ability to detect piratical activity or to establish the existence of pirates in the material record of the Late Bronze Age (Rauh *et al.* 2013: 59). Moreover, there is no mention in any LB cuneiform or Linear B document of 'piracy' or 'pirates' *per se* — or of any words translated as such. Indeed, the Greek word that best reflects English 'pirates' — πειρατής, *peiratis* — is not attested until the late fourth or third centuries BC (Ormerod 1924: 59; de Souza 1999: 3-7). To be sure, there are several references to groups of people or the raiding and sacking of coastal towns that may point to the existence of Bronze Age pirates or, better, coastal raiders. Depending on the definition one uses, these groups include the *Šikila, Lukki, miši*, the 'enemy' noted in certain cuneiform letters from Ugarit and *Alašiya*, and more (discussed further below).

To gain some insight into what is clearly a rather intractable problem, I turn now to consider some contemporary documentary evidence from the eastern Mediterranean. It may be added here that in an otherwise compelling discussion of regulations regarding Late Bronze Age maritime travel, Sauvage (2011: 432) maintains that 'Late Bronze Age texts show that piracy was common', citing five documents in support of her statement. Moreover, on the basis of two letters exchanged between Ugarit and Cyprus (RS 20.18, RS 20.238–see below), Kopanias (2017: 127-128, and n.78) suggests that 'Piracy was apparently a serious problem' in the fourteenth-thirteenth centuries BC in the eastern Mediterranean. As we shall see, however, there are at least 25 such documents that bear upon this issue, but they are far from clear about the extent of piracy at this time.

Amongst the LB textual references to various individuals, groups of people or acts and events that mention ships, sea battles, enemy raiders sacking ports or abducting captives, and the like, and that thus may point to the existence of pirates or piracy, are the following:

1. RS 34.129: an Akkadian text from Ugarit in Syria referring to the *Šikila*-people. In it, an unnamed Hittite king writes to the governor of Ugarit, demanding an interview with someone named 'Ibnadušu, who had been captured by the '… *Šikila*-people, who live on ships' (Bordreuil 1991: 38-39, no. 12).

2. KUB XIV 1+KBo XIX 38: Hittite document from Hattuša (Boğazköy) in Anatolia, in which Madduwatta, a vassal of the Hittite king (most likely Arnuwanda I), responds to a royal complaint that he had been involved in raiding *Alašiya* (Cyprus—at that time claimed by the Hittite king) and taking captives (Otten 1969; Beckman *et al.* 2011: 69-100).

3. KUB XIX 5+KBo XIX 79: Hittite document from Hattuša, in which Manapa-Tarhunta, of the Seha River Land (a Hittite vassal) writes to the Hittite king (Muwatalli II?), stating that a person named Piyamaradu had organised a raid against *Lazpa* (Lesbos in the eastern Aegean) and abducted two groups of skilled craftsmen, perhaps dyers of purple (murex-shell) wool (Singer 2008; Beckman *et al.* 2011: 140-144).

4. CTH 105: Hittite document from Hattuša, in which the Hittite king (Tudhaliya IV) forbids Šaušgamuwa, the last king of Amurru, to let any 'ships of *Ahhiyawa*' travel via his country to Assyria (Beckman *et al.* 2011: 50-68, esp. 63). This text evidently refers to a Hittite ban on trade between *Ahhiyawa* and Assyria, i.e. involving merchandise brought by *Ahhiyawa* ships to the Levant before being conveyed overland to Assyria (*e.g.* Devecchi 2010: 254; Beckman *et al.* 2011: 68, 279-280). Bryce (2016: 70), however, suggests it is a ban on *Ahhiyawa* ships as transport carriers of mercenaries to Amurru, and thence to Assyria (see also Cline 1991). Steiner (1989) argued, largely in vain, that the term *Ahhiyawa* was not fully preserved in the text and suggested the vessels in question were 'warships' belonging to Amurru (*cf.* Wachsmann 1998: 129). Monroe (2009: 181) rightly observes that any restrictions on *Ahhiyawa* trade with Amurru was only one aspect of Tudhaliya's military embargo against Assyria, with whom he was at war.

5. KBo XII 38: Hittite document from Hattuša, in which the Hittite king Šuppiluliuma II states that he set out to sea and '…the ships of *Alašiya* met me in battle three times' (Güterbock 1967), indicating that this Hittite ruler, and the state of *Alašiya* (i.e. Cyprus), both had warships ('long boats') in their fleets. Here it may be noted that EA 39 and EA 40 (two Akkadian letters from Amarna in Egypt—Moran 1992: 112-113) demonstrate that the king of *Alašiya* also owned merchant ships ('round boats').

6. Südburg inscription: Hieroglyphic Hittite inscription from Hattuša, stating that the Hittite king Šuppiluliuma II conducted three military campaigns along Anatolia's Mediterranean coast, including in the *Luk(k) a*-land (Hawkins 1995: 59; Singer 2000: 27-28). If any of these campaigns were against *Alašiya*, perhaps it was the same event mentioned in the previous document, KBo XII 38 (see also Bryce 2016: 73).

7. RS 18.113A: a letter written in Ugaritic from an unnamed official to an unknown king (most likely of Ugarit), indicating that royal approval was needed to sell ships to the king of *Alašiya* (Virolleaud 1965: 1-15, no. 8; Dietrich *et al.* 1976: 2.42; Knapp 1983).

8. RS 20.238: an Akkadian letter from Ugarit, in which an (unnamed) king writes to an unnamed king of *Alašiya*, stating that while his own army was engaged in Hatti and his navy in the *Lukka*-land, seven 'enemy' ships arrived, set fire to his towns and ravaged the countryside (Nougayrol *et al.* 1968: 87-89). This document may refer to the same event as in the following two letters (Singer 2006: 250).

9. RS 94.2523, RS 94.2530: two Akkadian letters from Ugarit, in which the Hittite king (Šuppiluliuma II?) and an official (Penti-Šarruma) reprimand king 'Ammurapi of Ugarit for failing to send his ships to the *Hiyawa*-men (*Ahhijawa*?) who awaited them in the *Lukka*-land (Lackenbacher and Malbran-Labat 2005: 237-238; 2016: 25-31; Singer 2006: 251-258; Bryce 2016: 70-73). Gander (2012: 284-286) disputes the *Hiyawa-Ahhijawa* equation.

10. RS 20.18: an Akkadian letter from Ugarit, written by a high-ranking official in *Alašiya* to the king of Ugarit, referring to certain actions conducted against the people of Ugarit and its ships. The official denies any responsibility, warns that 20 further ships of 'the enemy' have been launched (to/from a 'mountainous region'?) and that the king of Ugarit should take defensive measures (Nougayrol *et al.* 1968: 83-85 no. 22; Singer 1999: 721).

11. RSL 1: an Akkadian letter from Ugarit, in which an unnamed king from an unknown country states that if indeed enemy ships had been sighted at sea (as in the previous letter?), the king of Ugarit should gather his infantry and chariots within the city walls and fortify them (Nougayrol *et al.* 1968: 85-86 n.1, no. 23).

12. RS 20.212: an Akkadian letter from Ugarit, in which the Hittite king reprimands the king of Ugarit for reneging on his obligations, notably for failing to provide a large ship and crew to transport 2000 measures of grain from Mukish (north Syria) to Ura (Cilicia) under the supervision of two Hittite officials (Nougayrol *et al.* 1968: 105-107, no. 33).

13. RS 34.147 lists 14 unseaworthy ships of the king of Carchemish harboured in the port at Ugarit, while RS 34.138 is a letter sent from the king of Carchemish to the queen of Ugarit, which indicates she is permitted to send some ships as far as Byblos and Sidon but no farther (Bordreuil 1991: 23-25, no.5; 31-32, no.8). Both texts, written in Akkadian, suggest that the Hittites, whose vassal occupied the throne at Carchemish, were concerned to maintain a fleet of ships at Ugarit (Singer 2000: 22), and to keep close track of their movements (Singer 1999: 659). Emanuel (2016: 268) speculates that Ugarit may have maintained a small military fleet charged with defending coastal waters against pirates and/or escorting valuable shipments to foreign ports (but *cf.* Singer 1999: 659).

14. EA 38: Akkadian letter from Amarna in Egypt indicating the *Lukki* had raided Egyptian-controlled territory in the Levant, and coastal villages on Cyprus (see further below).

15. EA 101, 105: two Akkadian letters from Amarna, referring to the *miši*, in which Rib-Addi of Byblos asks pharaoh to send ships for support or rescue (see further below).

16. EA 113: Akkadian letter from Amarna, in which Rib-Addi of Byblos accuses Yapah-Adda of Beirut of plundering two Byblian ships.

17. EA 114: Akkadian letter from Amarna, in which Rib-Addi of Byblos informs pharaoh that the ships of Tyre, Beirut and Sidon are in *Wahliya* (unknown place) and that Yapah-Hadda (of Beirut?) has seized one or more of his ships on the 'high sea'.

18. EA 98, 101, 105, 149: Akkadian letters from Amarna that mention the 'men' and 'ships of *Arwada*', used to intercept other vessels at sea, to cut off maritime communications and to seize or blockade ports.

Various Egyptian documents of the thirteenth through eleventh centuries BC, in particular those of the pharaohs Ramesses II, Merneptah and Ramesses III, describe seaborne raiders or battles often associated with the 'sea peoples'. For example, on the Aswan stele of his second year, Ramesses II claims to have 'captured' or 'destroyed' the warriors of the 'Great Green' (the Mediterranean?) (Kitchen 1996: 182). On the so-called Tanis II rhetorical stele, this same pharaoh boasts of defeating seaborne warriors known as the *Sherden*, 'who came bold-[hearted], in warships from the midst of the Sea' (Kitchen 1996: 120). Ramesses III's Medinet Habu inscription claims that certain elements of the 'sea peoples' (*Peleset, Tjeker, Shekelesh, Denyen*, perhaps also *Sherden* and *Weshesh*) 'devastated' Hatti and Arzawa (Anatolia), Qodi and Carchemish (Syria), and *Alašiya* (Cyprus) (Breasted 1906.4: §64).

Despite long-standing consensus in the general literature that these 'sea peoples' swept victoriously through the Aegean, Anatolia, the eastern Mediterranean and Egypt at various times between the fourteenth and eleventh centuries BC (see further in Middleton 2015: 45-46), Egyptologists and Assyriologists alike remain sceptical about the historicity or purpose behind the Medinet Habu inscription (*e.g.* Lesko 1980; Liverani 1990: 121; Cifola 1994; Redford 2000: 7). Roberts (2009: 60), an Egyptologist, has argued that the main purpose of the Medinet Habu inscriptions '… was not to record an invasion by hostile northerners, but rather to record the actions of Ramesses III'; more recently, he has questioned the validity of virtually all past scholarship on the 'sea peoples', in particular the historicity of an invasion as recorded at Medinet Habu (Roberts 2014: 359-60; see also Middleton 2015). More generally, Wilkinson (2010: 56) suggests: '… the Egyptians were adept at recording things as they wished them to be seen, not as they actually were'. Weeden (2013: 5-6), an Assyriologist, questions the value of assigning to specific and known ethnic or geographic names any of the ethnonym lists used in the texts of Ramesses III, as such lists simply provided the means to construct a stereotype of Egyptian enemies. In his view, they more likely referred to 'peripheral groups destined by geography or status to commerce and its sister piracy, who would profit from a collapse of an international system based on centralized palace economies' (Weeden 2013: 6).

In an 'iconic analysis' of the Medinet Habu reliefs, Ben-Dor Evian (2016) maintains that most historical reconstructions of the battles between the Egyptians and 'sea peoples' have ignored the basic iconic and narrative principles of ancient Egyptian art, and consequently produced scenarios full of misconceptions about the sequence and geographic settings of the land and naval battles as well as the nature of the 'sea peoples' themselves. She argues elsewhere (Ben-Dor Evian 2017) that the land battles mentioned in the Medinet Habu inscription occurred in the northern Levant, whereas the naval battle, a completely separate enterprise, took place in the Nile Delta. In her view, the 'sea peoples' were 'displaced' groups from the northern Levant, Anatolia, Cilicia and Cyprus, some of whom established the kingdom of *Palistin* locally, in the Amuq Plain (Singer 2012; Weeden 2013); others, notably the Philistines, eventually settled in the southern Levant, once Egyptian control over that region ceased (Ben-Dor Evian 2017: 278-279).

Sauvage (2011: 432-433) mentions two further Egyptian texts of possible relevance to piracy. The first is from the fifth campaign in year 29 of Tuthmosis III (late fifteenth century BC) against the territory of Ullaza, after which pharaoh seized two ships laden with 'servants', metals, wood, etc. (Sethe 1907: 686-687). The second is the Papyrus Harris I (Grandet 1994: 230), from the reign of Ramesses III (early twelfth century BC), which mentions the construction of ships 'made for the sea', manned by troops with weapons (archers). Wiener (2013: 164-165), in a brief and ill-informed discussion of piracy vis-à-vis what he regards as a 'Minoan empire' and the 'Minoan thalassocracy', cites the Egyptian text of Tuthmosis III and another from the reign of Amenhotep III, as well as two Hittite texts (Madduwatta, Piyamaradu—nos. 2-3 above), the last three dealing with coastal raiders.

Finally, the eleventh century BC Egyptian Tale of Wenamun includes certain events that may suggest pirate-like activity (Lichtheim 1976: 224-229). On his venture to Byblos, some of Wenamun's goods were stolen by one of his own crew at the site of Dor on the Carmel coast, probably the main early Iron Age port between Egypt and Lebanon (Gilboa 2015: 248-250). Wenamun made a legal appeal for these goods to the prince of Dor, but it fell on deaf ears (Brinker 2011). Having grown impatient for retribution, he departed for Byblos; on the way, he confronted a ship of the *Tjeker* and seized some goods to replace what he had lost. Later, having concluded his business (obtaining local timbers) at Byblos, Wenamun prepared to leave the port just as eleven ships of the *Tjeker* appeared along the shore. The *Tjeker* appealed to the prince of

Byblos to arrest Wenamun, but the prince demurred, and Wenamun then set sail, ostensibly to return to Egypt but his ship was blown off course to *Alašiya*. Throughout all this, only the confrontation between Wenamun and the *Tjeker* on the high seas should be construed as related to piracy; even then, however, we might have expected the *Tjeker* — not Wenamun — to be doing the pillaging.

Wachsmann (1998: 123-130) presented a more limited range of cuneiform texts and Linear B documents than that treated here, but elsewhere has referred to '… the ever present danger of shore-based pirates/privateers/enemy ships' recorded in the Amarna letters (Wachsmann 2000b: 809). Whether any of these documents are actually concerned with piracy or pirates, however, remains a matter of opinion. Even so, there are three main groups of people whose activities might be regarded as piratic in nature: the *Lukki* (men of the *Lukka*-lands), the *miši* and the men of *Arwada* (Linder 1981: 38-39 classes as pirates the *Lukki, miši* and the *Ahhiyawa*). The *Šikila*, moreover, 'live on ships' and, assuming they are to be equated with the Šekelesh (*Tjeker*) known from the Egyptian documents of Merneptah, Ramesses III and Wenamun (Singer 1999: 722), certainly conducted seaborne raids on coastal ports. I consider each of these groups in turn.

Regarding the *Lukki*, in Akkadian letter EA 38 from Amarna, the king of *Alašiya* wrote in response to pharaoh's complaint that some men from Cyprus had accompanied the *Lukki* in raiding Egyptian-controlled territory; in his own defence, the Cypriot king protested that the *Lukki* repeatedly had also attacked various (presumably coastal) villages on Cyprus (Moran 1992: 111). Wachsmann (1998: 130) suggested that these raids by the *Lukki* '… presumably refer(s) to piratical attacks on Alashia for the express purpose of taking captives'. At one time, as indicated by Akkadian letter RS 20.238, the navy (and army) of the king of Ugarit had been engaged somehow in the *Lukka*-lands (and Hatti), whereas at another time (RS 94.2523, RS 94.2530) king 'Ammurapi of Ugarit was reprimanded by the Hittite king for failing to send his ships to the *Hijawa*-men who awaited them in the *Lukka*-land. Here, Bryce (2016: 73) sees the Hittites engaging the services of the *Hiyawa*-men to provide support (by land and sea) in some of the increasingly vulnerable frontier zones of their kingdom in the south and southwest, an area the Hittites always found difficult to control (Liverani 2014: 383). Moreover, if these actions are to be related to claims that the Hittites had 'conquered' *Alašiya* (KBo XII 38, Sudburg Inscription), it may be that Cyprus was included in this area. If the *Lukka*-lands formed part of the region extending from western Pamphylia through Lycia, on the south-central to southwestern coast of Anatolia (Bryce 2005: 56), this rocky, semi-mountainous area with its numerous bays and harbours certainly could have served as a haven for pirates (see also Singer 2006: 251-252, 258; Gilan 2013: 54-56), as it did in the centuries following, just like the region of Cilicia immediately to its east (Ormerod 1924: 190-241; Rauh 1997: 269-270; Rauh *et al.* 2013; Liverani 2014: 383).

The *miši* are mentioned in the Amarna letters concerning Byblos and the land of Amurru. Lambdin (1953), followed by Moran (1992: 174, 178), equates this term with Egyptian *mš'*, and thus regards this group simply as the 'army, troops' of the Egyptians. Linder (1970: 94; 1981: 39 n.38), however, sought to extend the meaning of *mš'* to 'warship' (based on its Old Kingdom meaning) and thus defined the *miši* as 'men of the warships', or 'marines'. Although the cuneiform documents in question are not fully transparent, Rib-Addi of Byblos often refers to the *miši*, who are typically linked with hostile, sea-based activities (Wachsmann 1998: 130; see also Linder 1981: 38-39). In EA 101, Rib-Addi tells pharaoh that '… the ships of the *miši* are not to enter the land of Amurru'. Recall here that a Hittite letter (CTH 105) instructed the king of Amurru not to allow entry to any 'ships of *Ahhiyawa*', which seems to indicate a Hittite boycott of trade with Assyria. In EA 105, the men of Amurru themselves (under their king Abdi-Aširta) have seized the ships of the *miši* (or, the 'army ships') and their cargo (Lambdin 1953: 76; Moran 1992: 178). EA 110 is a brief, very fragmentary text that simply mentions the ships of the *miši* (or 'army ships'—Moran 1992: 185). Wachsmann (1998: 130) cited a British Museum painted papyrus showing boar's-tusk-helmeted warriors fighting alongside Egyptians (Schofield and Parkinson 1994), and suggested that '… the *miši* ships mentioned in the Amarna tablets may refer to Aegean (Mycenaean?) ship-based mercenaries in the employ of the Egyptian court at Amarna'. Such an association is in no way implied by the cuneiform documents themselves.

The men and ships of *Arwada* are mentioned in five Amarna letters; from them, it would seem they were closely involved in naval warfare during the fourteenth century BC (Vidal 2008: 8). Arwad is a small, approximately 40-ha island lying some 2.5 km off the Levantine coast near modern-day Tartus in Syria. With two large bays suitable for anchorages, *Arwada* became a key port — along with Byblos, Beirut and Tyre — in the trade linking Ugarit and the northern Levant with Egypt and the southern Levant (Liverani 1979b: 1330). The main activities of the ships and men of *Arwada* were: (1) an attack against and a naval blockade of the Amurru port town of Ṣumur (EA 104, 105); (2) intercepting three Byblian ships at sea, bound for Ṣumur (EA 105); (3) the sacking of Ullaza (northern Lebanon), another, nearby port (EA 105); (4) blockading, or at least controlling the ports of Šigata and Ambi to prevent the delivery of grain to Ṣumur (EA 98); and (5) an attack against Tyre's port (?) of Ušu in support of Sidon, thus threatening the seaborne activities of Tyre itself (EA 149). In EA 101, a difficult letter to interpret (Liverani 1998), the author (probably Rib-Adda, ruler of Byblos) asks pharaoh (Amenhotep III or IV) to seize the ships of the men of *Arwada* to prevent them from attacking Byblos.

Vidal (2008: 10-12) has interpreted all these activities to mean that Ṣumur (the main town of the Amurru), with Egyptian support, had replaced Arwad as a key trading centre, leading the 'men and ships of *Arwada*' to act as a 'mercenary force' — using 'marauding practices and piracy' — for their very subsistence; he thus compares them with Artzy's (1997) 'economic mercenaries' (see also Sasson 1966: 130). Although none of the Amarna letters explicitly indicates that the men of Arwad were 'pirates', Vidal (2008: 11) stresses that the island of Arwad would have provided some essential features as a base for piratic practices (isolation, inaccessibility, refuge). Indeed, the size and possible lack of arable land on an island like Arwad, presumably a wealthy port with a sizeable population, might indicate that some of its people were involved not just in fishing and farming, but also in raiding coastal towns. Broodbank (2000: 191-197, 253-258) makes a similar case for some islands of the Early Bronze Age Cyclades. As cautionary points, however, it is worth noting (1) that the Bronze Age archaeological record of Arwad is a virtual blank (Badre 1997: 218), and (2) that

Liverani (2004) questions the historical veracity of the Byblos letters found at Amarna, attributing them to the 'siege mentality' of the city's ruler, Rib-Adda.

Whereas Altman (2014) refers in passing to pirates and piratic activities as documented in the Amarna letters, his main concern is to examine the alliances and hostilities that developed amongst various central-northern Levantine ports (Byblos, Beirut, Tyre, Sidon, Arwad, Amurru region, Ugarit) over the control of seaborne trade during the mid-fourteenth century BC. In his view, there were two major confrontations between these ports and/or coalitions they formed: (1) between the rulers of Tyre and Sidon in the south; and (2) between Rib-Addi of Byblos and the rulers of the Amurru region (Abdi-Aširta, Aziru), in the north (Altman 2014: 13-17; see further below on relations between Amurru and the men/ships of *Arwada*, and the *miši*). We need not linger over the details of the ever-shifting alliances that Altman documents: *e.g.* Tyre and Byblos, Sidon and Amurru, Beirut and Arwad allied with Amurru, Sidon and Beirut allied with Byblos, and so on, changing with some frequency. Rather we should note that these alliances were motivated and nourished by commercial factors, not least (1) the access that Amurru had to expansive and fertile inland regions, as well as to the overland route through the Homs-Tripoli gap and thus to trade with Mesopotamia and the east, and (2) the ability to attract and maintain exchange relations with various polities within but especially beyond the Levantine littoral: Egypt, Cyprus and the Aegean (Altman 2014: 20-24). Altman thus argues that the impetus behind the conflicts amongst the various Levantine ports during the mid-fourteenth century BC was the desire to gain access to maritime as well as overland commercial traffic, markets and trade.

One crucial lesson to take from all these maritime encounters, 'sea peoples' activities and ships' actions is that LB polities had little success in curbing the commando-like raids evident in the relevant written documents. Although Levantine coastal ports were often engaged in hostilities against one another, it is also clear that foreign seaborne raiders took port/coastal towns by surprise, sacking and destroying them, and often taking hostages. Although most scholars who write on LB 'piracy' necessarily base their arguments on the plundering of coastal towns, it must be reiterated that the activities of pirates, as we understand them today, are predicated upon sea-based encounters.

There are but few instances of such maritime activity in the documentary evidence discussed here:

1. KBo XII 38 (sea battle between ships of *Alašiya* and the Hittites)
2. RS 20.238 (the ships of the ruler of Ugarit somehow engaged in or against the *Lukka*-lands)
3. EA 105 (ships of *Arwada* intercept three Byblian ships at sea, preventing them from reaching Ṣumur)
4. EA 113-114 (Byblian ships seized at sea by Amurru and/or Beirut)
5. RS 20.18 and RSL 1 (actions taken against the people of Ugarit and its ships, involving 'enemy' ships); and, for the sake of completion
6. the Tale of Wenamun (who seized some goods from a *Tjeker* ship at sea and later confronted them in the harbour of Byblos).

Most other texts deal with raids carried out on coastal sites, or blockades of them, or taking their inhabitants as hostages: this included ports like Ugarit, Byblos and Ṣumur, as well as unknown coastal sites on Cyprus (*Alašiya*) and Lesbos (*Lazpa*).

Perhaps such acts of plunder and the seizing of captives point to the economic lure of piracy, as well as the positive correlation between piracy and trade. Any level of piracy depended on reliable information about trade networks. Artzy (1997, 1998) long ago argued that fringe groups were employed as 'hirelings' or 'economic mercenaries' to facilitate exchange within and amongst various LB polities and trading networks. Their expertise in navigation, trade or simply possession of a boat made them an essential part of these trade networks, 'intermediaries' who impacted on coastal settlements throughout the Levant. This very expertise, however, would have enabled them to shift from cabotage or tramping, to directed commercial ventures, to 'piracy', as conditions warranted (Monroe 2011: 94). Their involvement in what Artzy calls 'sailors trade', entrepreneurial in nature, eventually meant they came into competition or conflict with land-based powers or port centres, and as economic conditions declined at the end of the LB, they effectively became 'sea peoples'.

If, as I have suggested, piratic activity is to be defined as an irregular, ongoing and economic activity that involves maritime mobility, the use of ships, and plundering for personal benefit, then the activities outlined in all these documents may be construed that way. Moreover, we should keep in mind that pirates are not easily 'found' in Bronze or early Iron Age material or textual evidence because such people were, perhaps, first and foremost not 'pirates' *per se* but rather merchants, mariners (like Artzy's 'hirelings', 'intermediaries' or 'economic mercenaries') or even rulers (like Odysseus and Menelaus, kings who plundered on occasion). The boundary between pirates, corsairs (ex-pirates authorised by states to conduct raids at sea), privateers, buccaneers or even organised naval endeavours is difficult enough to disentangle in Medieval and later documents, when the indifference of any given state or its rulers, and their participation in such activities, is far from clear.

This situation is only compounded when it comes to the material record and archaeological interpretation where, as far as the Bronze and early Iron Ages are concerned, most arguments are based on vague representations of warriors on ships, or the interpretation of 'defensible' coastal sites, or other, even less tangible associations, all of which rely more on subjective assertion than convincing demonstration. Unlike later, especially post-Roman times, we cannot show that Bronze Age 'piracy' was ubiquitous with, for example, grain merchants turning an occasional hand to seaborne marauding during the growing season, or spice merchants finalising a successful trading mission with a raid on shipments of wine or silks, or naval commanders replenishing their personal coffers by moonlighting as pirates (Backman 2014: 180). In other words, unlike the situation that we may reconstruct for the LB eastern Mediterranean, post-Roman Mediterranean piracy…

... showed all the fluidity, pragmatism, and at times contradiction of other forms of Mediterranean life.... it thrived on many of the same elements of cross-cultural adaptation as did Mediterranean trade and intellectual exchange.... it was widely regarded as a risk of doing business, a problem to be regulated and managed rather than solved (Backman 2014: 182).

Virtually all the recent literature that treats the phenomenon of piracy or the activity of pirates during the Late Bronze Age assumes and asserts their existence, perhaps rightfully so. If anything, adding a detailed analysis of the relevant, contemporary documentary evidence — as I have attempted to do here — may seem to corroborate these arguments. Nonetheless, I would emphasize three points:

1. there is no word or term in the rich textual record at our disposal that can be equated with either 'pirates' or 'piracy';
2. there is no unequivocal association between the wide sweep of material culture that has been linked to LB piracy and what has been termed a 'culture of piracy' (Hitchcock and Maeir 2016: 247, 259; but *cf.* Molloy 2016);
3. there is little correlation between the type of sea-based encounters known from any later period and the actions or representations called into evidence for the Late Bronze Age.

If we use the terms 'pirates' and 'piracy' at all, then we should do so with more caution and less hyperbole, setting aside the type of intellectual inflation that art theorists label 'post-critical' (*e.g.* Foster 2015).

MATERIAL ASPECTS

SHIPWRECKS

Ships were the largest and most complex 'machine' of antiquity (Oleson 2014: 510; see also Steffy 1994: 23; Pomey 2011). Small ships could be launched from land and beached upon arriving at their (unexposed) destination: river mouths, estuaries and protected coves facilitated these practices, which were simplified in the Mediterranean by the absence of large tidal changes. With respect to a ship's size, Monroe (2007) maintains that seagoing, sailing vessels in the Mediterranean during the Bronze Age were probably not much larger than the ship wrecked at Uluburun off the southern coast of Turkey, i.e. about 20 metric tons capacity and up to 16 m in length. The seafaring ships sent by the Egyptian pharaoh (Queen) Hatshepsut to the land of Punt (anywhere from the Red Sea coast of Sudan south to Somalia) most likely were also about 20 m in length (ca. 16 m at the waterline, and thus hull capacity) (Wachsmann 1998: 19-29; Monroe 2007: 6; see also Ward *et al.* 2012 on Hatshepsut's replica ship). The two well preserved early Iron Age (eighth century BC) wrecks found off the coast of Gaza and surveyed by Ballard *et al.* (2002) are each estimated to have carried approximately 25 tons of cargo (wine, in amphorae). All the available textual and material evidence suggests that we should assume smaller as opposed to larger ship capacities in any reconstruction of Bronze Age trade networks.

Depending on their state of preservation, shipwrecks offer the basic material evidence for the study of seafaring and seafarers, and often shed light on the type of goods traded, the routes sailed and, more problematically, the possible ports of origin and destination. Although recent theoretical work in maritime archaeology (*e.g.* Adams 2001; Flatman 2003; Farr 2006; Westerdahl 2010) has refined the ways we approach issues related to seafaring and exchange, shipwrecks still have the potential to contribute crucial chronological information as well as details on nautical aspects and maritime activities more generally.

There are, of course, some limiting factors involved in studying shipwrecks or wreck deposits. Some underwater sites, situated close to the coast but devoid of any wooden ship remains, may not actually involve shipwrecks (Frost 1976; Parker 1981). For example, about one km south of Haifa on the southern Levantine coast, Galili *et al.* (2013) identify a 'wreck deposit' they date to the LB (thirteenth century BC), mainly on the basis of copper and tin ingots found on the seabed. The authors also postulate four more LB shipwrecks along a three-km stretch of beach south of Haifa; these are much more likely to be the result of dumping, taphonomic or other factors, at least until some evidence of an actual ship can be demonstrated (also noted by Wachsmann 1998: 208-209). Wachsmann (1998: 205; 2011: 17, n.14) also questions certain Aegean cases, namely an Early Helladic wreck from Dokos (Argo-Saronic Gulf) and another, Minoan wreck from Pseira (east Crete), although he stands on less firm ground here.

Be that as it may, as of this writing, there are eight known, at least partially published shipwrecks of Bronze Age date in the eastern Mediterranean and Aegean: in Turkey, Sheytan Deresi (Bass 1976), Uluburun (Pulak 2008) and Cape Gelidonya (Bass 1967, 1973); in Israel, Hishuley Carmel (Galili *et al.* 2013); and in the Aegean, Cape Iria (Phelps *et al.* 1999), Modi island, near Poros (Agouridis 2011), Koulenti, Laconia (Spondylis 2012) and Pseira island (Hadjidaki and Betancourt 2005-2006). Another shipwreck found near Bodrum, Turkey (at Hisarönü), has been dated to the early second millennium BC but thus far is only reported in the Turkish press. Of all these, only the deposits at Cape Gelidonya and Uluburun preserve some of the actual wooden ship remains. Even in the four centuries of the early Iron Age (through the Late Geometric-Early Archaic period), only three further shipwrecks are known: the deepwater Tanit and Elissa wrecks off the Gaza coast (Ballard *et al.* 2002), and another at Kekova Adası off southwestern Turkey (Greene *et al.* 2011). Despite their fragmentary (Kekova Adası) or inaccessible (*Tanit* and *Elissa*) conditions, these wreck deposits still present a great deal of specific information on the composition and nature of their cargo (Knapp and Demesticha 2017: 118-121).

The Uluburun shipwreck, of course, offers by far the most striking evidence for the material aspects of Bronze Age trade, including amongst many other materials copper from Cyprus, anchors and pottery from the Levant, resin and glass from Egypt, ebony and ivory from Africa, amber from the Baltic Sea area, tin likely from central Asia, weapons possibly from Italy, and perhaps wine from the Levant (Pulak 1988, 1998 2008, 2009; McGovern and Hall 2016) (discussed further below in Chapter 5: *Late Bronze Age—Anatolia, Shipwrecks*). Given the numbers of copper and tin ingots as well as some 150 Canaanite jars from the Uluburun wreck, not to mention all the other manufactured goods, the cargo can only be defined as 'compound' (mixed) as opposed to 'bulk' (homogeneous, i.e. made up mainly of a single component). By contrast, the *Tanit* and *Elissa* shipwrecks (off the coast of Gaza) each carried classic 'bulk' cargoes — nearly 400 torpedo-shaped Phoenician 'transport amphorae' (Ballard *et al.* 2002); the Kekova Adası wreck held some 130 amphorae in its cargo (90-100 Cypriot amphorae; 20 southeast Aegean amphorae and 7-10 Corinthian Type A amphorae—Greene *et al.* 2011; 2013: 23-28). Moreover, of the much greater number of shipwrecks known from the Hellenistic and Roman Mediterranean, few could be regarded as 'compound' cargo carriers (Parker 1990; 1992: 20-21). In sum, it seems clear that all eight of the Bronze Age shipwrecks currently known and published held compound cargoes; from the mid-late first millennium BC onward, however, the majority of ships' cargoes were characterised by a single, bulk component (*e.g.* wine, olive oil, fish sauce) carried in maritime transport containers (Knapp and Demesticha 2017).

PORTS AND HARBOURS

> *By studying harbours, one can feel the heartbeat of the people, their virtues and potential, even their courage and determination. A harbour should be a place of protection and lull, the hospitable entrance or the exit from or to the unknown, the sea — rough or calm, the foreign place, the other cultures and other unknown goods. It should be a place where the facilities for the loading and unloading of merchandise, for the embarkation and the disembarkation of passengers, [are] accessible for any ship* (Marangou 2002: 23).

By the mid-third millennium BC, the development of larger craft involved in long-distance trade would have motivated the development of specially defined places to accommodate ships and to facilitate the loading or off-loading of cargo. Such a development in harbour design and capacity would surely have been driven by the changing characteristics of the ships that used them, the economic needs of those who constructed and made use of them, and changes in the tools and technology available (Oleson 2014: 510). Because coastal settlements often were established at a safe anchorage, or at a critical juncture along sea-lanes, they must have been founded intentionally to serve as harbours (Papageorgiou 2009: 216). Even so, a coastal location does not necessarily demonstrate a site's status or function; some places might serve for accomodating pilgrims or refugees rather than for receiving goods; others might be involved more in fishing than in maritime trade. The material assemblages of such sites may reveal few if any indicators of foreign contacts (Parker 2001: 27).

In general, beyond Blackman's (1982) well established and essential studies on the subject, Leidwanger (2013: 221 n.1) recently defined a 'harbour' as a protected, often enclosed space used to shelter vessels, whereas a 'port' is a location where goods or people pass between sea and land. Both terms might equally be used, as they are in this study, in the broader sense of an 'emporion', i.e. a place oriented around the needs of maritime trade (*emporia*) and the activity of maritime traders (*emporoi*) (Hansen 1997; Arnaud 2011a: 65). Whatever services they may

Figure 5: *Scene from Tomb of Kenamun, Thebes.* After Amiran 1970: fig. 43.1.

have provided for ships (*e.g.* shelter, repair, provisioning), most harbours were fundamentally economic entities; they prospered or failed along with the volume and level of successful commercial exchange.

The material evidence recovered from harbour sites offers a key source for investigating the mechanisms of Mediterranean trade. Gates (2011: 381) suggests that harbours were established and endured largely because of the people, goods and ships involved in maritime exchange. Purcell (2014: 67) points out that harbours of the classical era were subjected to surveillance and taxation, because the polities that received revenues from duties on travellers and traded goods relied on them not just for support but also for their own access to the sea.

What we know about prehistoric and protohistoric harbours is based on a few pictorial representations, scattered and very limited documentary evidence, plentiful stone anchors, some underwater explorations, and excavations carried out in those sectors of ports or anchorages situated on land. One informative pictorial representation from the eastern Mediterranean is that from the Late Bronze Age tomb of Kenamun at Thebes (Egypt) (Figure 5), which shows people unloading goods on ramps from merchant ships moored to a dockside platform (Davies and Faulkner 1947: pl. 8). Hatshepsut's mortuary temple at Deir el-Bahri has reliefs showing Egyptian cargo ships at Punt, anchored near a beach, with goods being carried through shallow water and up the gangplanks (Wachsmann 1998: 17, fig. 2.11). The well known 'miniature fresco' from the West House at Akrotiri on Thera (late Middle Bronze Age in date) depicts a representation of a double harbour, situated on a peninsula or headland, with shore-side structures like ship-sheds nearby (M. Shaw 1985: 22-25; Shaw 1990: 429-433; Morgan 2007: 120-121; Blackman 2011, 2013).

Early harbour sites in the Mediterranean were typically situated in open or partly enclosed bays, deltas, protected anchorages (*e.g.* in the lee of a promontory; behind offshore reefs or small islands) and at the mouth of river valleys (see also Oleson 2014: 511). The earliest Bronze Age harbours were concentrated around natural anchorages — small coves, pocket beaches, estuaries and wadis — that required little modification to serve their purpose (Marriner and Morhange

2007: 175). Other Bronze Age harbours were situated on the open shore, often in combination with a small offshore islet (Frost 1995; Shaw and Shaw 2006: 854).

Several general studies have been published on maritime (cultural, social, economic) landscapes, including harbours and port facilities (*e.g.* Blackman 1982; Blackman *et al.* 2013; Westerdahl 1992; 2010; Blue 1997; Knapp 1997; Gates 2011; Rogers 2013). Taking examples from Cilicia and Cyprus to construct a 'topographical typology' of second millennium BC harbours and anchorages, Blue (1997) long ago suggested that many Bronze Age coastal landscapes have largely disappeared; thus before we can even begin to understand these coastal configurations, it is necessary to engage interdisciplinary, palaeogeographic and topographic work along with landscape reconstructions. Increasingly maritime archaeologists have engaged with the geomorphological, hydrological or sedimentary processes that affect the building and maintenance of harbours (*e.g.* Marriner and Morhange 2007; Marriner 2009; Carayon *et al.* 2011). Regional or local tectonic activity, including erosion or aggradation, seriously affects our ability even to recognise ancient harbours. Some are now silted in, and stranded some distance inland — *e.g.* Troy, Ephesos or Miletos along the western coast of

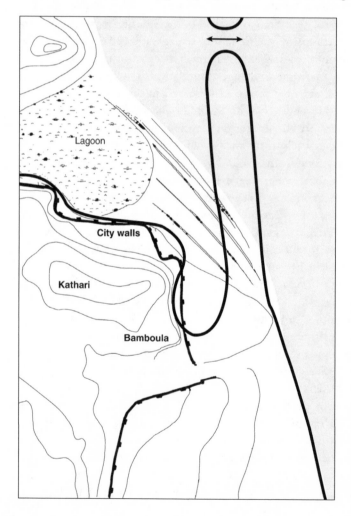

Figure 6: *Coastal reconstruction at Kition, Cyprus, show-ing Bamboula basin as a small cove within a larger lagoon. A more recent reconstruction indicates the harbour/ lagoon extended to the northern edge of the Late Cypriot site at Kathari (Bony et al. 2016: fig. 3). After Marriner and Morhange 2007: 163, fig. 22. Drawing by Irini Katsouri.*

SEAFARING AND SEAFARERS IN THE BRONZE AGE EASTERN MEDITERRANEAN

Anatolia (Marriner and Morhange 2007: 154), Kinet Höyük in Cilicia (Beach and Luzadder-Beach 2008) and Kition on Cyprus (Morhange *et al.* 2002; Marriner and Morhange 2007: 162-164; Bony *et al.* 2016) (Figure 6); others are embedded in a peninsula, *e.g.* the Bronze Age harbour site of Liman Tepe on the southern shore of the Bay of İzmir (Erkanal 2008; Erkanal and Şahoğlu 2016).

The study of Bronze Age ports or harbours — mainly on land, not underwater — in the eastern Mediterranean has received a fair amount of attention, at least with respect to individual sites. These are discussed in more detail in the respective chapters below but include, in Israel, Tel Nami (Artzy 1995, 2005), Ashkelon (Stager 2001), Dor (Raban 1987, 1995), Akko (Raban 1991; Artzy 2005), Tell Abu Hawam (Artzy 2005, 2016), Atlit (Haggi 2006; Haggi and Artzy 2007); in Egypt, Tell ed-Dab'a (Marcus 2006; Bietak 2008), Marsa Matruh (White 2002a, 2003); on Cyprus, Kition (Morhange *et al.* 2000; Bony *et al.* 2016) and Hala Sultan Tekke (Devillers *et al.* 2015). Frost's work (*e.g.* 1971, 1972, 1973, 1995) led her to suggest that, during the Bronze Age, offshore islands and reefs along the Levantine coast (*e.g.* at Tyre, Sidon, Arwad) were quarried and/or shaped to provide facilities for large trading ships. Wenamun visited the harbours of Dor and Byblos (Gilboa 2015; see also Helck 1986; Frost 2004), the latter with a small natural bay, not that typical along the eastern Mediterranean littoral. In the Aegean, the Akrotiri 'miniature fresco' shows a few buildings (towns?) along a coast but no constructed harbour facilities. Whilst there certainly seem to have been ship-sheds at Kommos on Crete (Shaw 1999; Blackman 2011), and perhaps a basin constructed for ships at Pylos (Zangger 2008), Oleson (2014: 512) suggests that Bronze Age harbours were 'passive in character', and consisted largely of naturally sheltered beaches and bays, or of basins excavated in riverbanks or shorelines. Although the same designs, as well as some of the same (Levantine) harbours continued in use into the Iron Age, new sites were also constructed for shipping from at least the ninth-eighth centuries BC, using walls built into the sea as breakwaters (fuller discussion in Knapp and Demesticha 2017: 20-25).

MARITIME TRANSPORT CONTAINERS (MTCS)

Bronze Age maritime transport containers (MTCs) are known under several different rubrics (*e.g.* Oval-mouthed amphora, Canaanite jar, Egyptian amphora), and have long formed the focus of specific and detailed pottery studies (*e.g.* Grace 1956; Parr 1973; Sagona 1982; Killebrew 2007; Pedrazzi 2007; Pratt 2016). The maritime transport of bulk goods in such containers offers insights into many facets of trade: *e.g.* exchange networks, merchants, economic transactions, distribution and consumption patterns. The production and shipment of MTCs also had other, socioeconomic impacts (Bevan 2014: 413): they were easily manufactured to a standardised shape; their design facilitated easy movement over long distances and the preservation of their contents; they were easily counted for economic transactions; and their widely recognisable shapes would have enhanced the reputation and credibility of those responsible for their movement.

Given such factors, it is important to define an MTC and to present briefly its design and function (for detailed discussion and relevant references, see Knapp and Demesticha 2017: 36-42). The basic criteria for identifying an MTC are the following: the vessel should be of closed type and found in quantities, either on shipwrecks or at sites distant from their place of origin. The most significant attribute of MTCs is that they were *designed* for maritime transport, not just used for it. Storage is another key, constituent attribute of MTCs, but a vessel's morphology or function alone is insufficient to characterise it as an MTC.

Whereas their archaeological context (*e.g.* on a shipwreck, in a harbour site) may be more informative, context cannot always be linked to primary usage, as transport containers were extensively recycled and re-used throughout their history (*e.g.* Peña 2007: 61-118; Lawall 2011; Abdelhamid 2013). Because the very existence of MTCs presupposes the need for low-cost packaging containers, the amount of exported or traded MTCs found at some distance — near or far — from their place of production also provides an indicator of their function. The manufacture of MTCs mediated between local production and overseas demand (Greenberg, in Bevan 2014: 406). The very design of MTCs, which became increasingly elaborate and sophisticated through time, suggests that they were made and used within local communities of practice—something often confirmed by chemical or petrographic analyses. For example, Sugerman's (2000; 2009: 445-446) petrographic analyses of Canaanite jars in the Late Bronze Age southern Levant suggests some directionality in the distribution of locally produced wares, and a dendritic network through which they were transported to larger export centres.

In brief, then, the term 'Maritime Transport Container' can be applied to any pottery vessel that was designed or used repeatedly to move bulk organic cargoes over long distances by sea. These containers had to be airtight, sealable either on the interior (with pitch, pine sap, etc.) or exterior (by an applied slip or burnish), and made from materials that would not react with their contents or lead to spoilage when exposed to bilge water or sea spray (Marcus 1995: 601). Their basic morphological features are as follows: (1) a narrow or restricted orifice (mouth, neck), (2) durable walls, (3) at least two handles and (4) a narrow base (although flat bases are attested). Their minimum capacity is 4-5 litres, but there was a great deal of variability involved when such vessels were used for bulk transport (Demesticha 2017). Finally, as already emphasized, in order to distinguish an MTC from other vessels used for storage or transport, it should be possible to demonstrate its primary use in maritime transport by its presence (a) on shipwrecks and/or in storage installations, and (b) beyond its production centres, in considerable numbers.

The archaeological record of the third millennium BC eastern Mediterranean offers substantial evidence for intensified maritime connectivity, through which local trading networks gradually linked into wider regional systems (Broodbank 2010: 250-254; 2013: 300-314). To summarise briefly what is presented in the following chapters, it may be noted here that significant numbers of Early Bronze Age (EB) Levantine ledge- and loop-handled jars found in Egypt (Hartung 2002: 437-443; 2014; Watrin 2002: 453-455) already point to an industry of standardised transport containers at the outset of the third millennium BC. By the EB II–III periods (ca. 3050-2400/2200 BC), mass-produced 'metallic' or 'combed' ware jars were being exported from the Levant to Egypt (Greenberg and Porat 1996; Thalmann and Sowada 2014).

During the Middle Bronze (MB) IIA-IIB periods (ca. 2000-1650 BC), thousands of Canaanite jars (CJs) were exported to Tell ed-Dab'a in the Egyptian Delta (Bietak 1996: 20; Kopetzky 2008) and farther south, in Middle to New Kingdom deposits at several other sites, leaving no doubt that Levantine products were shipped to Egypt packaged in MTCs. A few CJs of MB date have also been found beyond the Levanto-Egyptian regional sphere of interaction, *e.g.* on Crete at Knossos (Macgillivray 1998: 90), on Cyprus at Bellapais *Vounous* and Arpera (Merrillees 1974: 75-76), and at Kinet Höyük in southern coastal Anatolia (Akar 2006: 17). During the same period, Cretan Oval-mouthed amphorae were distributed around the island, and exported both to Tell ed-Dab'a ('Ezbet Rushdi) in Egypt (Czerny 1998; Bietak and Marinatos 2001: 40) and to the Greek mainland (Laconia—Spondylis 2012).

During the Late Bronze Age, Levantine CJs were exported widely throughout the eastern Mediterranean; their presence in the cargoes of the Uluburun and Cape Iria shipwrecks (Pulak 2001, 2008; Lolos 1999) (see Figure 33, below) demonstrates their function as MTCs (see also Cateloy 2016; Pedrazzi 2016). The Levantine tradition of CJ production continued into the Iron Age, pointing to continuity in seaborne trade practices but perhaps not by the same agents; this, however, takes us beyond the scope of the present study (but see Pedrazzi 2010, 2016; Martin 2016). The detailed study of MTCs enables us to understand better the earliest phases of systematic seaborne trade in the eastern Mediterranean, including the increasingly large-scale transport of goods, and demonstrates how these containers served as markers of trade mechanisms of different scale, or indicators of economies that more or less depended on seafaring and seaborne trade.

SHIPS' REPRESENTATIONS

Wachsmann (1998) presented a comprehensive study of the representational evidence for Bronze Age Levantine and Aegean ships, whilst Broodbank's (2010) study of seagoing Bronze Age ships includes some representations as well as a discussion of ship-building technology. Ward (2010a: 149) includes representations of ships and boats as one aspect of the 'primary' evidence available on ancient seafaring and trade in the Bronze Age Aegean. Amongst indicators of a maritime culture, Westerdahl (1994: 265) includes toy boats, ship models, symbolic representations of ships and the sea in votive offerings or mortuary rituals, and 'maritime iconography' — *e.g.* representations of ships engraved on the walls of buildings and churches (i.e. ships' graffiti or ships' carvings—Westerdahl 2013). He also suggested (Westerdahl 1994: 266) that some maritime societies — like that of Minoan Crete — have a 'conspicuous absence' of maritime symbols, especially depictions of boats or ships. More recent works, however, refute Westerdahl's suggestion: see, for example, Wedde (1991, 2000), who discusses Minoan 'oared sailing ships' in the context of the wider Aegean world, or Wachsmann (1998: 83-122; 2000b: 804-807), who discusses, respectively, Minoan ship representations and Aegean ship construction techniques.

In general, ship iconography and ships' graffiti are difficult to interpret (Le Bon 1995), as those who created them were not necessarily concerned with nautical reality (Basch 1987: 230; Sawicky 2007: 39; Wedde 2000). It is difficult to determine whether such representations followed specific artistic traditions or, even if they did, the extent to which such traditions reflect how ships were actually built (Kristiansen 2004: 111). Producing a representation typically involves its maker in calling upon a range of conventions, skills and constraints with which s/he is familiar, and then addressing the purpose for which the image was intended.

Renfrew (2003: 205) suggests that all representations, or representational art, may be deemed 'symbolic' inasmuch as the work (*e.g.* the depiction of a ship in this case) symbolises an actual ship (or at least one in the artist's mind) in a real or ideal context through which that ship is to be understood. Whilst visual representations are intended to portray or symbolise the likeness of something, at the same time the resulting image may lead viewers to re-imagine, redefine or reconstruct the perceived world as it relates to that image (Skeates 2007: 199): it has the potential to represent reality but equally to lead one astray. Images, in other words, are not only symbolic, but also 'a system of action, intended to change the world' (Gell 1998: 6); they may play a significant role in creating and maintaining society and social identities, or in representing society in a predetermined manner. For example, a set of 21 water-colour drawings of Spanish colonial presidios (fortified bases) in Mexico produced between 1766-1768 tend to misrepresent indigenous vernacular traditions in order to convey the message that the defensive and administrative facilities of these bases were more important than the residential communities surrounding them (Voss 2007: 147-148).

Thus we cannot always and equally identify images with the realities they are presumed to represent. On the one hand, the truer or more realistic the representation, the more likely it is deemed to have captured the essence, agency or power of the original. On the other hand, the more abstract the representation, the more likely its meaning will be ambiguous, unstable or malleable, and open to different interpretations. In the game of representation, the meaning(s) of even the most realistic images may be contested by their makers as well as their consumers.

Wachsmann (1998: 5) strikes a similar note, and cautions that ancient ships' representations were 'refracted' through the eyes, skills and traditions of those who created them and as a result diverged considerably from the original. Typically, they tend to be schematic and illusive, conceptual rather than realistic. Quite who made or drew most of the ships' representations considered in this study — their producers (artists, sailors, ship owners, merchants) — is unknown, whilst who might have made up their audience(s) — their consumers — is an equally challenging question (on 'producers' and 'consumers', see López-Bertran *et al.* 2008: 345). Any answer(s) must rely heavily on examining the item's broader cultural or historical context and its links to other material or documentary evidence (Voss 2007: 147). For example, given their context, the representations of the ships, harbours and events depicted on the 'miniature fresco' from Thera (recently, Strasser 2010), or the representations of the naval battle carved in relief on the walls of Ramesses III's temple at Medinet Habu (Wachsmann 2000: 106, fig. 6.1; Ben-Dor Evian 2016), must have involved specialist artisans as well as elite consumers. With the exception of ships painted on pottery, most Bronze Age images that concern us here were crafted or drafted by unskilled hands (perhaps those of fishermen or seafarers attempting to depict themselves or their vessels), or else were represented in a medium that challenged the artist in depicting the prototype.

Representations of ships in the Bronze Age Mediterranean help to illustrate the key role that seafaring and seafarers played in everyday maritime practices. Images of ships or other nautical representations may have served as performative elements in various social, ritual or mortuary practices (López-Bertran *et al.* 2008: 348-352). Some performances are public and spectacular, others may be private and involve mundane or everyday events (Soar 2014: 226). The former may be geared to display social power or enhance social prestige and connections, the latter simply to emphasize presence or social action in context. Drawing or carving ships on the walls of a building (*e.g.* the 'temples' at Kition—Basch and Artzy 1985) might indicate the performance of 'ceremonial' activities within the building, or it might signal some level of 'patronage' on the part of building's users or inhabitants for seafarers. Equally, of course, it may simply point to the importance of landmarks associated with seafaring and trade routes (Artzy 1999). Or, to take another example, namely the Late Helladic (LH) IIIB krater from Enkomi that depicts two boats with larger than life-sized 'warriors' above deck and beside the ships, and smaller figures below deck (Sjöqvist 1940: fig. 20.3) (see Figure 38, below): is the size of the warriors meant to be important, a performative act of 'display'? Again, and equally, it may simply point to a generic act of naval warfare, or to the challenge the artisan faced in working on this medium.

In the chapters that follow, a diverse range of Bronze Age boat and ship representations are presented: clay models, graffiti, wall paintings, carved reliefs, depictions on pottery and seals. They were made of, or painted, carved, incised, drawn or outlined with and on a variety of materials: clay, stone (often precious stones), metal, pottery and ivory, and were found in a variety of contexts: in houses, on the walls of buildings and in tomb deposits. They may have served individual, royal, ritual, performative, symbolic or everyday, practical purposes.

STONE ANCHORS, FISHING AND FISHING EQUIPMENT

Fish and other marine resources are a key component of the mixed economies that form the basis of most Mediterranean societies, ancient and modern. Amongst the fisherman's toolkit are such objects as hooks (metal, bone), weights (lead, stone), floaters and sinkers (usually of stone), and tridents or harpoons (metal). Such resources are evident to some degree in the material, iconographic and ichthyofaunal evidence of the Bronze Age cultures under consideration here. Representational art depicts not only fish and shells but the ships and people who manned and sailed them. The close links between fishing and seafaring as well as maritime exchange may seem obvious, but are seldom studied in a comprehensive manner (*cf.* Brewer and Friedman 1989; Powell 1996; van Neer *et al.* 2004; Bekker-Nielsen 2005).

Frost (1991: 364-366), concerned about the loss of archaeological evidence related to fishing tackle, whether practical or votive, laid out some criteria for recognising, identifying and classifying such materials. In the process, she discussed the feeding patterns and routines of various types of fish and shellfish, and noted that each variety had to be caught with specific 'tools': hooks, lines, metal-forks and tridents, harpoons, baskets, nets, traps, etc. Some, like baskets and nets, have to be kept in place by floats and two kinds of weights, one for anchoring or immobilising, the other for sinking buoyant cordage or basketry ('sinkers').

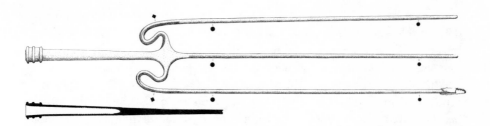

Figure 7: *Bronze trident from Tomb 23, Hala Sultan Tekke.* Length: 87.5 cm; width 14.8 cm. After Niklasson 1983: 174, 206 fig. 493. Courtesy of Lennart Åström. Drawing by Irini Katsouri.

Excepting the occasional finds of hooks (often made of metal), net weights (stone, lead, terracotta) are typically what survives in the archaeological record. Set, long-line fishing involves suspending a rope (or similar) at an appropriate distance from the sea bottom, and stringing along it stone weights as well as underwater floats, from which hang baited hooks; for certain fish, such as conger eel or fork-beards (a type of cod), the lines can rest on the bottom (Frost 1991: 365). Stone weights can be found in most maritime archaeological settings (see Frost 1969: 432 and pl. VI for an example from Hellenistic levels at Byblos), but their value for drawing wider conclusions is limited unless one is able to draw upon a wider range of evidence for 'the husbandry of the sea' (Frost 1991: 365).

Other material evidence of fishing, if not seafaring, includes fish bones, marine invertebrates (shells) and various objects that may have served for fishing, like the bronze trident from Hala Sultan Tekke on Cyprus (Åström 1986: 14-16, figs. 17, 24) (Figure 7). Powell (1996: 1) suggests that the study of fishing *per se* can provide 'insights into the beginning of seafaring itself'. Fish can be preserved by smoking or sun-drying, and at least one 'Late Palaeolithic' site in (Middle) Egypt, Makhadma, seems to have been used mainly for fish-smoking (van Neer *et al.* 2000). The salting or preparation of fish products in brine, or of fish sauces like the famed, fermented Roman sauce *garum* (Smith 1998), represent another, presumably not uncommon way to store and utilise fish. When it comes to marine shells, their recovery is more common in archaeological practice, not just because they are so obvious but also because they were often used for other purposes, not least personal display (Bar-Yosef Mayer *et al.* 2017). There is much less consistency of field practice regarding ichthyofaunal data, although van Neer *et al.* (2004: 110-120) presented a summary of the Bronze Age evidence known at that time for 'traded' fish in Egypt and the Levant.

Accordingly, iconographic evidence pertaining to the marine world has an important role to play. One of the best iconic representations of fishing comes from the reliefs in the Old Kingdom mastaba of Akhtep, which shows grooved or waisted stones holding down a net (Ziegler 1993). Abundant iconographic representations of nautical and marine subjects are equally evident in the Aegean world, especially the 'marine style' pottery of Late Minoan Crete, Late Helladic pictorial pottery, seals, painted shells, plaques (gold-leaf), and decorated frescoes, floors and walls (Powell 1996: 62-76). Such representations are less common in the material records of Cyprus, the Levant and Anatolia.

Turning to stone anchors, in a series of papers Frost (1963, 1970a, 1970b, 1985: 282) has emphasized their significance in the wider Mediterranean and on Cyprus in particular. Based on detailed studies of anchors from Kition on Cyprus and Ugarit in the northern Levant, she suggested that some of the largest Late Bronze Age ships traversing the sea-lanes in the eastern Mediterranean were of Cypriot and Levantine origin (Frost 1985; 1991: 370-371). Wachsmann (1998: 211-212), in turn, discussed several problems associated with identifying a wrecked ship's port of origin or 'ethnic' affiliation, but suggested that the ship's anchors might, in certain cases, provide more secure evidence. Even so, in most instances it continues to be problematic if not erroneous to attribute a specific type of anchor to a single region or culture (Toth 2002; Howitt-Marshall 2012: 109; Harpster 2013).

Pierced anchors from the Mediterranean have been divided into three types: (1) sand anchors (with multiple holes for wooden pieces); (2) weight anchors (with a single hole for the mooring cable); and (3) composite anchors (with three holes, for the mooring cable and wooden arms) (Frost 1985: 283-284, fig. 1). Most sailing vessels probably had more than one type on board, for anchoring on different types of sea-beds (*e.g.* sandy or rocky bottoms). Some of the smaller, single-holed anchors might also have served as line weights, spaced at intervals along a mooring cable, and with a larger, composite anchor at the end. Alternatively, as noted above, they could be used for 'set-long-line' fishing, in which baited hooks were held on the sea bottom by rough stone weights (Frost 1985: 319). One of the crucial differences between stone weights used on land and at sea is that the latter usually have holes or extra piercings for holding wooden 'arms' (Frost 1991: 366).

Having now considered both the social (seascapes and seafaring; merchants, mariners and pirates) and material (shipwrecks, ports, MTCs, ships' representations, stone anchors and fishing gear) aspects of the maritime matters with which this study is concerned, in the following three chapters I consider all these aspects, or at least those that are evident in the archaeological and documentary records of the Early, Middle and Late Bronze Ages in the eastern Mediterranean.

CHAPTER 3

EARLY BRONZE AGE

EGYPT AND THE LEVANT

Documentary evidence from the Early Bronze Age (EB) related to maritime matters is limited but not without interest. Sauvage (2012: 234-235) recently suggested that the 'Byblos ships' recorded in Old Kingdom texts may refer to the technological origins of this type of seagoing vessel. Ward (2010b: 43), however, maintains that *kbnt* refers specifically to the Levantine source of cedar wood used to build Egyptian seagoing ships.

Beyond 'Byblos ships' (*kbnt*), two brief passages of the Fourth Dynasty pharaoh Sneferu (ruled ca. 2600 BC) on the Palermo Stone refer to ships 'of 100 cubits' (50 m) made of *meru* wood (Strudwick 2005: 66); these passages are often taken as indicators of a major trade in cedar between Egypt and the central Levant (*e.g.*, Prag 1986: 59; Wengrow 2006: 149). Esse (1991: 116, based on Wilson's translation in Pritchard 1969: 257 and n.2) argued that, on the open sea, ships of such a size would have been fully seaworthy, and particularly suitable for transporting heavy cedar timbers from the central Levant. Monroe (2007: 5), however, basing his argument on the hieroglyphic of the Palermo Stone and Strudwick's reading of it, felt that ships 'of 100 cubits' must refer to royal craft used on the Nile, which were to be built from the wood imported in other, seafaring ships, whose size is never stated.

Another interesting text of possible relevance is the 'autobiography' of the Sixth Dynasty court official Uni (Weni), whose combined land and sea battle against the *Heryu-sha* ('sand dwellers', from southern coastal Palestine?) must have relied on seagoing ships capable of transporting troops (Marcus 2002: 408; for the text, see Lichtheim 1973: 18-23; see above, Chapter 2: *Social Aspects—Merchants, Mariners and Pirates*). In de Miroschedji's (2012) elaborate reconstruction of events, Uni's campaigns against the *Heryu-sha* represent recurrent conflicts between Egypt and some EB III coastal settlements (*wenet*) in the southern Levant (between the mouths of the Yarqon and Gaza rivers), punitive operations geared to safeguard maritime links between Egypt and Byblos. In his view, the actions of the *Heryu-sha* could be considered one of the earliest documented instances of piracy in the eastern Mediterranean, occurring at the point when Egypt's maritime trade with Byblos, during the reign of pharaoh Pepi I, had reached its greatest extent (de Miroschedji 2012: 283-284).

Beyond this limited array of documentary evidence, how can the archaeological record related to harbours, ships' representations, maritime transport containers and stone anchors extend our understanding of Early Bronze Age seafaring and seafarers in Egypt and the Levant?

PORTS AND HARBOURS

Although not on the Mediterranean, ports along the Red Sea coast are recorded at Wadi el-Jarf and Ayn Sukhna already in the EB Age, during Egypt's Old Kingdom (ca. 2680-2180 BC); they may have been used by Egyptian vessels for short trips (*e.g.* across the Suez Gulf to the Sinai peninsula) or for longer-distance ventures (Tallet 2012). The first site, Wadi el-Jarf, is situated some 200 km southeast of Cairo on the Red Sea (Gulf of Suez), and has been dated tentatively to the beginning of the Fourth Dynasty, ca. 2600 BC. Along the shoreline here were various facilities, including an L-shaped pier and at least 21 limestone anchors; some large storage jars — tentatively dated to the Fourth Dynasty — turned up in underwater explorations. A further 99 'boat anchors' were uncovered some 200m inland from the pier area, between two possible storage structures (Tallet *et al.* 2012; Tallet and Marouard 2014: 11-12, figs. 17-18). Excavations carried out in at least 25 storage galleries, located some five km inland, produced the wooden parts of ships (long hull pieces, fragments of oars), tenons, ropes and pieces of sail (Tallet and Marouard 2014: 7-8, fig. 10).

The second port site, Ayn Sukhna, located about 100 km north of Wadi el-Jarf and 120 km southeast of Cairo, was also used during the Old Kingdom and into the Middle Kingdom. Fieldwork here has identified ten galleries — used as both living and storage areas, and containing two large limestone anchors, as well as the charred cedar planks of at least two Middle Kingdom ships, whose estimated lengths are 14-15 m (Tallet 2012: 149-150, figs. 9-10). An inscription dated to the reign of the penultimate pharaoh of the Fifth Dynasty (Djedkare-Isesi, ca. 2400 BC) commemorated a short trip across the Suez Gulf to the 'terraces of turquoise', *i.e.* the Sinai peninsula (Tallet 2012: 151); this would seem to confirm the close relationship between these early ports and pharaonic mining activities (Moreno García 2017: 98). Another inscription found in one of the galleries (G1) may indicate that the same pharaoh initiated an expedition to Byblos, since it mentions *kbnt*-ships, long understood as a class of large, seagoing ships used on the journey from Egypt to Byblos (Faulkner 1940: 3; Wachsmann 1998: 19).

Early Predynastic (fourth millennium BC) Egyptian links with Byblos or its environs have long been argued, based on a presumed Egyptian demand for timber, resin, ivory and other exotics (Ward 1963: 5-7, 53; de Miroschedji 2002; Braun and van den Brink 2008; Hartung 2014). Both Prag (1986: 59-63) and Marfoe (1987: 32) suggested that the roots of urban formation at Byblos may go back to the Late Chalcolithic, when there are signs of 'social ranking', a traffic in silver and other resources, and an emphasis on orchard crops such as the olive (on olive cultivation in the southern Levant from EB Ia onward, see Gophna and Liphschitz 1996: 146-147; Langgut *et al.* 2016). Material and analytical examples of these early contacts between Egypt and the central Levant, and especially Byblos, include wood from Lebanese cedar (*Cedrus libani*) found at Maadi at the apex of the Nile Delta (von Kroll 1989: 134-135; Rizkana and Seeher 1989:76), coniferous wood (cedar, pine, cypress, probably juniper) found at Badari far up the Nile (near Asyut) in fourth millennium BC contexts (Brunton and Caton-Thompson 1928: 38, 62-64, 95), and pollen evidence (Sea of Galilee) of large scale olive production from EB I onward (Langgut *et al.* 2016). From Byblos Tomb 1823, a bone or ivory bracelet with Badarian parallels must represent an Egyptian import (Brunton and Caton-Thompson 1928: pl. XXIII.14; Prag 1986: 70). This find and others like it, together with the wood (noted above), as well as resins, if not silver (Prag 1986: 71-73), surely signal the likelihood of Egyptian maritime trade with the EB Levant (see also Moorey 1990: *67-*68; Ward 1963: 53-57).

Marfoe (1987: 26-27) noted that the keel-less Egyptian vessels of Naqada II times (mid-late fourth millennium BC), mainly used for Nile riverine travel, could also have been used for north-bound trips along the Mediterranean coast, but only with the aid of favourable westerly winds and the northerly current (see also Prag 1986: 59-60). In such cases, he posits that a trip to Byblos would have taken six days. The return trip, by contrast, with countervailing winds and currents, would have taken at least 8-10 days from the Carmel Ridge, the area closest to Egypt. Even if such limiting factors might have made overland travel seem more reasonable, the amount of pottery exchanged between the Levant and Egypt from the late fourth millennium BC onward suggests otherwise (see further below).

In any case, it is likely that by the time of Egypt's First Dynasty (ca. 3000 BC), frequent, state-sponsored expeditions, perhaps supported by smaller anchorages or trading ports along the Levantine coast, were established in the wake of more intensive exchange activity. The level of exchange between Egypt and the Levant probably waxed and waned over the centuries, but by the end of the Second Dynasty (ca. 2680 BC), the abundance of Egyptian pottery and other, Egyptian-influenced material found at Byblos (Saghieh 1983: 99, 103-106) indicates a significant amount of maritime-based exchange. Levantine pottery found in Egyptian tombs (nobles, court officials), as well as Egyptian inscriptions, also point to heightened trade activity from the end of the Second through the Sixth Dynasties (ca. 2680-2180 BC) (Chehab 1969). By the time of the Fifth and Sixth Dynasties, there is little doubt that maritime connections between Egypt and Byblos had become well established and economically significant (*e.g.* Sowada 2009: 128-141; de Miroschedji 2012: 281-282; Ahrens 2015: 141-142, 151). Of course, this is also the time when others have posited the emergence of newer and larger, seagoing ships under sail (Broodbank 2010: 254-255), which would unquestionably have made maritime transport quicker and cheaper (carrying larger cargoes) compared to overland traffic.

Broodbank (2013: 301-303) discusses the early third millennium BC emergence of Byblos as a 'local entrepôt', a maritime community that promoted sea traffic north and south along the Levantine coast and enjoyed a special relationship with Egypt, perhaps even between their royal households (see also Bevan 2007: 77-78). In Marfoe's (1987: 27) still compelling view, the scale of this seaborne traffic may have resulted from the 'spiralling interdependence between timber procurement, ship construction and carrying capacity', not least for the shipment of maritime transport containers carrying olive oil or resins (see below—*Maritime Transport Containers*). The intensification of Egyptian-Levantine interconnections at nodal harbours such as Byblos — where certain people would have the capacity to control

imports and exports as well as the transhipment and/or redistribution of goods —
also would have facilitated inland trade throughout Lebanon and inner Syria, and
likely in the southern Levant as well (Langgut *et al.* 2016: 124-125). Marfoe's (1987:
34-35) discussion of major reorientations in Levantine and Syro-Anatolian trading
relationships, not least in metals, must now be reassessed through the lens of Şahoğlu's
(2005) 'Anatolian Trade Network' and the contemporaneous 'super-network' that
extended from Egypt and the Levant as far east as the Indus Valley (Massa and
Şahoğlu 2015: 69, 71 fig. 10) (see further below—*Anatolia*, and Figure 10).

Stager's (2001) 'port power' model for the southern Levant envisages a standard,
three-stage settlement system: local villages ('communities of exchange'), regional or
'intermediate' markets, and the seaport, which in turn links into international trade.
Essentially, Stager (2001: 629) suggests that the 'Phoenician model of trade' as we know
it from the first millennium BC may also be applied to the eastern Mediterranean of
the third and second millennia BC. However, the more substantial parts of Stager's
study focus on the inland villages or 'markets', and the major maritime entrepot he
postulates at Ashkelon still has no material basis. Stager (2001: 630) claimed that
'vestiges of the EB seaport have been discovered by the Leon Levy Expedition to
Ashkelon'. And yet, beyond the site's seaside location and finds of 'metallic combed
ware' sherds (see the following section), neither the land nor underwater surveys
conducted by the long-term archaeological project at Ashkelon have provided any
material evidence; there is nothing beyond the likelihood that it was '… an important
seaport for thousands of years, from the Middle Bronze Age (if not earlier) until
the medieval period' (Raban and Tur-Caspa 2008: 67). Despite hopes raised by the
detection underwater of a rock formation whose shape suggested human intervention,
the divers eventually determined it was a natural formation, and '… thus Ashkelon's
harbour remains undiscovered' (Wachsmann 2008: 97). On the positive side, wood
from two native Lebanese trees (which never grew in the southernmost Levant) —
Cedrus libani (Cedar of Lebanon) and *Quercus cerris* (Turkish Oak) — found in EB Ia
strata at sites along the 'Ashkelon trough' (Afridar) would seem to indicate direct
maritime trade between the central Levantine coast and the Ashkelon region (Gophna
and Liphschitz 1996: 146-148). Although it thus remains very likely that seaborne
shipping became the primary means to conduct long-distance trade during the EB
period, and however appealing the 'port power' model may be, to this day that model
remains largely theoretical rather than demonstrable.

In sum, we may postulate that small-sized communities like Byblos, and perhaps
others like Ugarit, Tell Tweini, Tyre and Ashkelon had the capacity to invest in
sailing technology, and thus *could* have established ports no later than the mid-third
millennium BC. Some 'natural' harbours in the southern Levant had important (EB III)
sites nearby, *e.g.* Tell es-Sakan at the mouth of the Gaza River, and Tel Gerisa near the
mouth of the Yarqon (de Miroschedji 2012: 282-283). Ports or anchorages such as
these all along the Levantine coast are said to have been in 'full development' by the
Middle Bronze Age (MBA), and continued to play a key role in eastern Mediterranean
exchange systems thereafter (Al-Maqdassi 2013: 78-79; see also Morhange *et al.* 2005).
I return to consider such developments in Chapter 4: *Middle Bronze Age*.

There are no shipwrecks in the eastern or southern Mediterranean that can be
dated to the Early Bronze Age, only the documentary mention of 'Byblos ships',

and the few ships' representations presented in the following section (some of which appear to depict cargoes of pottery jars).

SHIPS' REPRESENTATIONS

Within the Mediterranean, the (independent) emergence of seagoing, sailing ships appears to have occurred earliest in Egypt and the southern Levant (Broodbank 2010: 254-255) — by the mid-third millennium BC if not earlier. Ships under sail could cover twice the daily distance that a longboat could, and at the same time transport much more cargo. It is argued that such ships sailed between the mouth of the Nile and into the Levant, as far north as Byblos if not beyond it (Marcus 2002; Broodbank 2013: 301-303). Broodbank (2010: 255) also suggests that this sailing technology spread as far north as Tarsus in Cilicia, perhaps even to Cyprus, during the course of the third millennium BC. Such a scenario, however, also needs to be assessed in light of the 'Anatolian Trade Network' (Şahoğlu 2005), which tends to firm up and expand the parameters of overland and seaborne trade (discussed in detail below—*Anatolia*). However, as there are no known shipwrecks dated to the third millennium BC in the eastern or southeastern Mediterranean, what can we actually say about these early sailing ships?

Pictorial evidence during this time period is limited. From the late fourth millennium BC, a square sail may be seen on one of three ships depicted on an incense burner from an 'elite tomb' at Qustul, close to the modern Sudanese border (Williams 1986: 138-145, pl. 34). One 'D-ware' jar of unspecified Naqada III date also depicts a vessel with a forward-set sail (Bowen 1960: 117-118, figs. 1-2), but its provenance is unknown and its authenticity has been questioned (see, *e.g.*, Lacovara 1982). A small pottery sherd of 'D-ware' from Taur Ikhbeiheh in Gaza depicts a part of a (boat's?) canopy, whilst the reconstruction (Figure 8) shows a restored boat, based on an example seen on a complete, red-painted (Naqada IIC-D) parallel from Gerzeh in Egypt (Oren and Yekutieli 1992: 369-370, pl. 8, 372 fig. 8:12; for the parallel, see Stevenson 2016: 439 fig. 2). Perhaps the best-known ships' representations of this time are the two different types of vessel — both with elaborate vertical prows and sterns but no sails — depicted on the ivory knife handle from Gebel el-Araq (Sievertsen 1992); Basch (1987: 57) regards the scene as the earliest known representation of a naval battle.

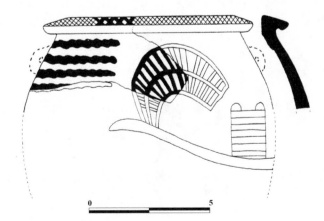

Figure 8: *Reconstruction of 'D-ware' sherd from Taur Ikhbeiheh.* Courtesy of Yuval Yekutieli and Eliezer Oren.

From the site of Wadi 'Ameyra in the southwestern Sinai come six ships' graffiti, dated by the excavators according to the *serekhs* engraved with them over a long period of time — from Naqada IIIA-D (ca. 33/3200-2800 BC), *i.e.* during Egyptian Dynasty 0 and the early First Dynasty (Tallet and Laisney 2012). Unlike these well-dated examples, I pass over here without further mention the boats seen on an array of rock carvings in Egypt's eastern desert, Nubia and elsewhere in the region, as their chronology remains contentious (see Wengrow 2006: 111-114 for general discussion and further refs.) Whilst all these representations tell us something about the early use of the sail within Egypt or, in the case of the Sinai engravings, about an early and unexpected Egyptian presence in this region, none of them really speak to the likelihood of Egyptian shipping in the southeastern Mediterranean at this time.

The same could be said about the obviously seaworthy ships — from the Egyptian Fifth Dynasty (ca. 2500–2350 BC) — depicted in the temple of Sahure at Abusir (12 ships) and in the causeway of Unas at Saqqara (Marcus 2002: 408; see also Kantor 1992: 20-21). Relief fragments from the former, however, depict what may be a shipment of (Levantine?) jugs, whilst the latter shows a more generic cargo of pottery vessels (Wachsmann 1998: 13 figs. 2.2-2.3 [Sahure], and 16 fig. 2.9 [Unas]). I also omit here discussion of the plank-built boats from First Dynasty Abydos and the Fourth Dynasty funerary barge of Khufu; these and others like them were riverine vessels used on the Nile in Egypt (Lipke 1984; Ward 2006), and so do not really shed light on the role of seagoing vessels in the Mediterranean. From the southern Levant, there are only a few incised representations of (riverine?) boats on pottery sherds from Megiddo, and a miniature clay boat model from Tel Erani (Marcus 2002: 406-407, fig. 24.1).

STONE ANCHORS

Marcus (2002a: 408-409) makes the point that hewn stone anchors are key indicators of maritime activity, although they appear in this period largely as pictorial representations or in terrestrial contexts. They may be seen in both the Sahure and Unas reliefs noted above (Wachsmann 1998: 14, fig. 2.5, 256-259; fig. 12.2). Various types of stone anchor were found in Fifth Dynasty tombs at Abusir and Saqqara. In the Levant, six stone anchors ('replicas') formed the lowest course of a flight of steps leading up to an imposing structure (termed the 'Tower Temple', perhaps a lighthouse?) on the shorefront at Byblos, dated to the late third millennium BC (Frost 1969: 429-430, figs. 23-28, pl. 3; 1970b: 384-385, pl. 2A; 2004: 320-321, fig. 5). In Frost's view, these stone-anchor 'replicas' may never have been used at sea but instead represent the complement of anchors carried by a single ship. Wachsmann (1998: 271-272, fig. 12.28: 17-18, 22) suggests that three further stone anchors of the same date were found within the 'Tower Temple' structure.

Both Wachsmann (1998: 262-265) and Marcus (2002a: 408-409) discuss the *shfifonim*, a heavy, anchor-shaped object, typically with a single hole. These objects have been found on land sites around the Sea of Galilee, notably at EB II Bet Yerah, but primarily in fields and thus not in any archaeological or stratigraphic context; none have been found underwater. Wachsmann (1998: 262) concludes that they may be understood as 'dummy' anchors, perhaps intended as symbolic representations of real anchors. Marcus (2002a: 409) seems more inclined to regard them as anchors — because of the occasional powerful winds that arise on the Sea of Galilee — or else in use as mooring stones that would have been buried in the muddy shores of the sea. In either case, they tell us little about Mediterranean seafaring, and are not considered further here.

Dating stone anchors found in the sea is a hazardous exercise, and even the most reliable dates, from stratigraphic contexts at land sites, are seldom more than *termini anti quem*. Although 'Bronze Age' anchors — some incised with enigmatic signs — have been recorded at or near coastal sites such as (in Israel) Megadim, Dor, Kfar Samir (south of Haifa), Tell Abu Hawam and Tel Akko (Wachsmann 1998: 265-270, with refs. and illustrations), none can be associated directly with Early Bronze Age contexts. Beyond the nine anchors already described (above) from Byblos, the only other Levantine examples presented by Wachsmann (1998: 271-273, from Byblos, Ugarit) can only be dated very generally to the Middle or Late Bronze Age.

Meanwhile, more secure evidence for the emergence of seaborne trade in the third millennium BC is provided by the maritime transport containers exchanged between the Levant and Egypt (for a more detailed account, see Knapp and Demesticha 2017: 42-46).

MARITIME TRANSPORT CONTAINERS (MTCS)

Links between the Levant and Predynastic–Early Dynastic Egypt, as seen from the perspective of pottery wares imported into Egypt via seaborne trade, present a complex picture. Marcus (2002: 410) argued that during the EB of the southern Levant (mid-late fourth millennium BC), potters began to adapt various attributes of the common storage jar to make it more suitable for transport. For example, EB IA ledge- and loop-handled jars were likely exported to Maadi near the apex of the Nile Delta (Rizkana and Seeher 1987: 31-32, 52-54, 108-111, pls.72-77) and to Tell el-Farkha in the northeastern Delta (Czarnowicz 2011: 122-123, fig. 3, 126; 2012). From the nearly contemporary royal cemetery at Abydos, over 200 wine jars were found in chambers of Tomb U-j (Hartung 2002: 437-443, figs. 27.2-27.6; Watrin 2002: 453-455, figs. 28.3-28.4). There is some question, however, whether the loop- and ledge-handled jars found in Tomb U-j were actually Levantine imports (Braun 2011: 112). The plot thickens with the existence of an ivory handle found at Abydos, showing people in Levantine-style dress carrying what seem to be ledge- or loop-handled jars (Shaw 2000: 314). Broodbank (2013: 278, 287 fig. 7.16) has suggested that local production of these jars may represent an attempt to suggest more exotic origins for local vintages than was actually the case (see also Porat and Goren 2002: 266; Wengrow 2006: 204), whilst Watrin (2002: 459) maintained that local, Egyptian potters may have adapted these shapes to store or transport 'Delta wine'. Murray (2000: 577, fig. 23.1, 596), however, maintains that wine-making in Egypt cannot be demonstrated before the First Dynasty, when wine presses appear in seal impressions; the word for wine appears in Dynasty 2 (see also McGovern 2001; 2009: 168-170, on the Levantine origin of the wine in the Abydos jars).

Hartung *et al.* (2015: 324-326) recently conducted further work on 20 EB IB II 'shale-derived' ceramic imports found in Cemeteries U and B at Abydos, which indicate a likely origin in northern Lebanon. The date of all these vessels extends over about 400 years, and indicates that some 500 years before the start of the Old Kingdom, *i.e.* from the earliest stages of the EB period, trading links — almost certainly seaborne — thrived between Lower Egypt and much of the Levant, north and south (see also Mączyńska 2013; Stevenson 2016: 441-444, 448-449).

Another possible indicator of late fourth millennium BC maritime links between the southern Levant and Egypt is the identification of freshwater, Nile River valley molluscs (*Aspatharia rubens*) in a large (storage?) jar recovered on the seabed some 700 m offshore at north Atlit bay in Israel (Sharvit *et al.* 2002: 159-161, fig. 3a-b). Eighteen of these shells were found in or around the jar, petrographic analysis of which indicates that it was produced from alluvial Nile clay. Because such shells have also been found at several Chalcolithic–EB I sites in Israel (Bar Yosef Mayer 2002; van Neer *et al.* 2004: 110, 117), they may have been common imports from Egypt. Finally, amongst several Egyptian vessels imported into the southern Levant during late EB I, one 'wine jar fragment' from Lod (Israel) has a potter's mark that may indicate the determinative for wine (*irp*) (Braun 2011: 114-115, fig. 12.17).

By the EB II–III periods (ca. 3050-2400/2200 BC), other pottery vessels from the central and southern Levant were being imported into Egypt, and again to Abydos (Knoblauch 2010). Scholars have long posited a close petrographic relationship between the (misleadingly labelled) EB II 'Abydos Ware' jars and juglets and Levantine 'metallic ware' vessels produced in the southern Levant (*e.g.* on the Golan plateau, Mount Hermon, upper Jordan valley) (Greenberg and Porat 1996; Porat and Goren 2002; Greenberg and Eisenberg 2002: 219-221; de Miroschedji 2014: 320) (Figure 9a,b) and along the central Levantine coast (Thalmann and Sowada 2014: 369-372). Recent petrographic analyses of five EB II-III Red Polished and 'metallic ware' vessels found in tombs at Helwan (near Memphis) indicate an origin in the Akkar Plain near Byblos and Tell Arqa; further analyses on 18 (EB III) 'combed ware' sherds from Giza also point to a Lebanese origin (Ownby 2012: 24; see also Köhler and Ownby 2011: 43; Wodzińska and Ownby 2011: 287-293). Recent petrographic analyses of a few samples of EB II-III 'metallic ware' from Tell Fadous-Kfarabida indicate that such 'shale-derived' ceramics may have been produced throughout central and northern Lebanon (Badreshany and Genz 2009: 78; Hartung *et al.* 2015: 325).

Many of these imported jars, like later MTCs, increasingly were produced with thickened walls and bases, an elongated body, a shaped rim, etc. Such features may have emerged to meet the growing demands of seaborne trade (Marcus 2002: 410; see also Stager 1985: 179-180). Given the size, capacity and possible standardisation of combed ('metallic') ware jars, they may well have been used to transport commodities such as olive oil, wine and resins (Sowada 2009: 248-255). Indeed, organic residues analysis indicates the presence of resin in imported Levantine jars from the tomb of First Dynasty pharaoh Djer at Abydos (Serpico and White 1996). Thalmann and Sowada (2014: 369-372) suggest that such jars became iconic vessels in Levantine trade with Old Kingdom Egypt, displacing the more globular 'metallic ware' containers whose production then quickly declined.

Thus on the basis of certain technological and typological characteristics of EB II-III Levantine vessels, as well as the numbers involved, we may assume they

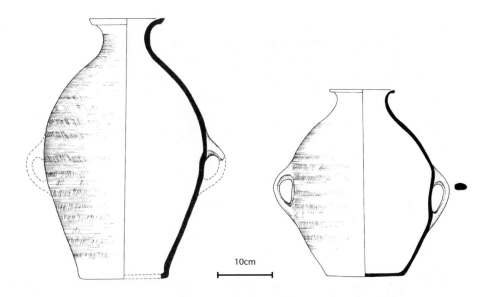

10cm

Figure 9a, b: *EB II-III 'metallic ware' jars from Tel Dan, Israel: (left) tall; (right) short.* After Greenberg and Porat 1996: 8, figs. 2:3, 2:5. Courtesy of Raphael Greenberg.

were produced to transport liquid or other organic goods to Egypt in newer and perhaps larger sailing vessels. The emergence of such pottery containers (MTCs) designed for commercial purposes suggests that potters and merchants, perhaps even winemakers, in the Levant had become involved in long-distance seaborne trade in the eastern Mediterranean (Marcus 2002: 410).

CYPRUS

Unlike the comparatively rich material evidence for maritime commerce and connectivity within and between the Levant and Egypt during the Early Bronze Age, relevant archaeological data from Cyprus are different in nature and limited to metallurgical and ceramic evidence (beyond MTCs) related to long-distance trade. Because such material could only have been exchanged by sea, however, it speaks directly to the phenomenon of seafaring and seafarers in the Aegean and eastern Mediterranean during the Early Bronze Age.

Although the Australian archaeologist James Stewart (1962: 290) once quipped: 'The Cypriote has never been a great sea-farer ... nor has he been a keen fisherman', evidence for the Late Bronze Age, at least, suggests otherwise (Knapp 2014). But what about the earlier periods of the Bronze Age that concern us here? To be sure, there are limiting factors for seafaring on certain parts of the island: anchoring a ship along the island's north and northwest coasts, and parts of the south coast, for example, may have been a precarious exercise in bad weather. Given the prevailing northwest winds, even the old harbour at Kyrenia was unsafe when strong northerlies or gales arose (Georgiou 1997: 121). Georgiou (1997: 121) also maintains that (modern?) wreck sites are not uncommon on the western coastal shelf between Paphos and Cape Drepanum (no refs. are provided).

Over the course of time, Cyprus's most prominent harbours or anchorages were established in bays and inlets along the south and southeast coasts, from the region around modern-day Famagusta on the central eastern coast, down to Larnaca in the southeast and around to Limassol on the central southern coast. This is where the island's best known Bronze Age harbours or anchorages are to be found — *e.g.* at Enkomi, Kition, Hala Sultan Tekke and, possibly, Kourion/Episkopi (discussed below, Chapter 5: *Late Bronze Age—Cyprus, Harbours*).

Other natural constraints also may have limited the foreign contacts of Cyprus during the Early (and parts of the Middle) Bronze Age, but constraints should also be seen as potentials. For example, distance and perhaps even location (*i.e.* coastal vs. inland) may have had little impact on Cyprus's external contacts at this time, a pattern that holds true even for the Late Bronze Age, when the island was intensively involved in interregional trade (Portugali and Knapp 1985). Even so, both the key (mortuary) sites of Vasilia (Early Cypriot, EC) and Lapithos (Middle Cypriot, MC) were situated on/very near the coast (see further below). Moreover, in the increasingly interconnected world of the third millennium BC eastern Mediterranean (Peltenburg 2007; Broodbank 2009: 692-701; Bolger 2013; Webb 2013), the entanglement of socioeconomic forces with landscape and resource diversity served to stimulate emerging mechanisms of shipping and commerce.

As already argued with respect to the numbers and types of materials exchanged (MTCs, timber, resin), as well as certain indicators in representational art, sea-going ships under sail were operating between Egypt and the Levant by the mid-third millennium BC (Marcus 2002: 407-409). To that picture, we must now add the likelihood of seaborne contacts between coastal Anatolia, the Cyclades, Cyprus and the southern Levant (Philip *et al.* 2003; Şahoğlu 2005; Webb *et al.* 2006; Kouka 2009a, 2016).

Lead isotope analysis of some metal objects, dated to the early third millennium BC and found in Jordan and Crete, indicates they were made of copper consistent with production from a Cypriot ore source: an axe from an EB II hoard found at Pella in Jordan (Philip *et al.* 2003); a fishhook and an awl from the EB I cemetery at Hagia Photia on Crete (Stos-Gale and Gale 2003: 91-92, table 5). Both the Pella hoard and the Hagia Photia cemetery are dated ca. 3000 BC, or shortly thereafter (Philip *et al.* 2003: 87; Davaras and Betancourt 2004: 4). Moreover, according to Kayafa *et al.* (2000: 43-44), a few EB metal objects from Lerna and Tsoungiza on the Greek mainland are consistent with production from Cypriot ores.

Chemical and lead isotope analyses carried out on sixteen Early-Middle Bronze Age metal artefacts found in Cypriot tomb or hoard deposits (notably at the key EC site of Vasilia near the north coast) suggest that metallurgical developments on mid-third millennium BC Cyprus emerged within a complex regional interaction sphere — the 'Anatolian Trade Network' (discussed further in the next section, *Anatolia*) — involving the seaborne movement of metals and metal artefacts between coastal Anatolia, the Cyclades and eastern Aegean, and Cyprus (Şahoğlu 2005; Webb *et al.* 2006). Links with Anatolia are evident in some metal objects dated to the Philia phase (ca. 2400/2350-2200 BC—but *cf.* Manning 2014a; on the sites, see Webb 2013: 63 fig. 4). Two spearheads, most likely from tombs near

Vasilia, have no Cypriot parallels but are similar in form to examples from Cilicia and north Syria; they may be 'the first objects of direct Anatolian origin to be identified in Cyprus' (Webb *et al.* 2006: 265). One of the spearheads and a rat-tang sword are tin bronze objects, otherwise known from Philia-phase metalwork only in the case of four small spiral earrings from Tomb 6 at Sotira *Kaminoudhia* (Giardino *et al.* 2003: 388–90) and reportedly from Vasilia *Kafkallia* Tomb 1 (Hennessy *et al.* 1988: 26). The tin used in these objects had to be imported by sea, in some form or other. Lead isotope analysis indicates that the tin-bronze spearhead, rat-tang sword and a knife are consistent with production from copper ores stemming from Bolkardağ in the Taurus mountain range (Webb *et al.* 2006: 265, 271). Two further metal artefacts (a ring-ingot and a perforated axe) are reported to be consistent with production from Cycladic copper ores.

Finally, even if we adopt a minimalist view on the origins of the Philia culture and the contacts that brought new ideas and technologies to Cyprus early in the EC period (Knapp 2013a: 263-277), there is little question that new species of animals (cattle, donkeys, screw-horned goats) also reached the island during this time and can only have arrived via seaborne transport. And, to reiterate, both lead isotope and compositional analyses suggest that copper and tin, whether as raw materials or imported artefacts, reached Cyprus via the sea during the both the Philia phase and EC period.

The raw materials and/or finished artefacts analysed may have come to Cyprus through various trade mechanisms (*e.g.* through Cycladic, Anatolian or Cypriote merchants, or Anatolian migrants or metalsmiths, or Cypriote elites who travelled to Anatolia), but the relevant point is that they had to come via the sea. Moreover, several of the metal weapons or tools arguably stem from tombs around Vasilia, which was located near '… a sheltered inlet suitable for early shipping' (Webb 2013: 59) and enjoyed access to the ore bodies of the northern Troodos mountains (Webb *et al.* 2006: 279). Stewart (1962: 288-289) long ago suggested (a) that Vasilia must have been a key terminal of an inland copper route and perhaps the main export terminal for Cypriot copper, and (b) that its later (MC) counterpart, Lapithos, had 'better harbour facilities' and enjoyed access to copper sources in both the northwest and northeast Troodos (Stewart 1962: 289). Webb (2013: 68) succinctly summarised the situation: '… some communities in Cyprus in the mid-third millennium BC were connected to external markets and engaged in establishing and promoting levels of integration between coastal outlets and hinterland and mining areas'.

Concerning contacts with the Aegean, Stos-Gale (2001: 200-201, fig. 10.2) has argued that 25 copper-based metal artefacts from mortuary contexts in Prepalatial Crete (ca. 2600-1900 BC) were consistent with production from Cypriot ores. Thus not long after bronze weapons and rod- or ring-shaped ingots were being exchanged amongst coastal Anatolia, Cyprus, the eastern Aegean and the Cyclades, other metal artefacts from Crete — consistent with production from Cypriot copper ores — may also have been involved in this interaction sphere. Whilst it is unknown how ores of likely Cypriot origin might have made their way to Crete during the Prepalatial period, like all the other ores and objects under consideration here they had to travel by sea.

With respect to ceramic evidence for seaborne trade during Cyprus's Early Bronze Age, examples of Black Slip and Combed ware, long associated with Red and Black Streak-Burnished ware from EB II levels at Tarsus in Cilicia (Goldman 1956: 112-113, 130; Mellink 1991: 170-172; *cf.* Bachhuber 2014: 143), have been found in at least six Philia-phase sites (Webb and Frankel 1999: 25-28 and fig. 18). Stewart (1962: 231) regarded the larger Cypriot shapes of these wares as variants of (Cypriot) Red Polished Philia wares, whilst Peltenburg's (1991: 31, 33 n.5) re-examination of the Black Slip and Combed ware led him to conclude that the Tarsus examples were imported from Cyprus. Swiny *et al.* (2003: 68) also mention a (Cypriot) Red Polished ware bottle and jug from an earlier EB II level at Tarsus.

Some 'discoid' faience beads found at several EC III-MC I sites on Cyprus may have been imported (Frankel and Webb 1996: 215-216, with further refs; *cf.* South 1995: 190). Peltenburg (1995) reports on 21 even earlier (Late Chalcolithic) faience disc beads from Kissonerga *Mosphilia*; he cautiously suggests they may have been imported from the Levantine mainland or Egypt. Three gypsum vessels — two bowls and a jug — from Vasilia *Kilistra* Tomb 103 were most likely imports from Egypt (Merrillees 2009). Beyond these examples, up to 20 further objects stemming from Crete, the Levant, Anatolia and Egypt were imported to Cyprus during the Early Bronze Age (for a list of EC and some MC imports and exports, see Knapp 1994: 281, fig. 9.4). Although it is has been argued (*e.g.* Webb *et al.* 2006: 282; Webb 2013: 65; Webb 2014: 364) that there was a lack of tin and absence of imported copper during the EC I-III periods, and that during the last centuries of the third millennium BC Cyprus was largely isolated from the surrounding world (receiving only a single Syrian jar), Manning (2014a: 210-211) points out on the basis of the available radiocarbon evidence that EC I-III may represent a very short period of time (ca. 2200-2100/2050 BC). If this was indeed the case, then it may be premature to argue that Cyprus was so isolated throughout the late third millennium BC: any chance finds of new materials or re-dating of old, and/or further radiocarbon analyses, may render such an argument void.

The number and quality of copper and bronze weapons and implements found in some EC IIIB-MC I tombs at Lapithos (Keswani 2004: 208-213, tables 4.11b-c) may represent not just internal production and consumption but also a growing external demand for Cypriot copper (Knapp and Cherry 1994: 161-162). Ongoing research by Jennifer Webb on materials from the tombs at Lapithos, however, indicates that the real take-off in metal deposition at the site occurs during the MC period (and increases markedly from MC I to MC III) (J. Webb, pers. comm., 23 November 2016; see also Webb 2016; 2017: 132-133). Thus the Lapithos 'phenomenon' —with respect to internal metal production and consumption as well as external demand — more properly belongs in a discussion of the MC period (see below, Chapter 4: *Middle Bronze Age—Cyprus*). Nonetheless, it is worth mentioning that, toward the end of the Early Bronze Age (ca. 2000 BC), the number of bronze objects alloyed with tin begins to increase on the island (Balthazar 1990: 161-162), suggesting that Cyprus was already involved in the regional exchange system(s) that brought tin to the island (Yener 2000: 75).

ANATOLIA

Current understandings of Anatolia's role(s) in seafaring, connectivity and trade during the Early Bronze Age (EB) revolve largely around Şahoğlu's (2005) model of the Anatolian Trade Network (ATN), as well as certain finds from the monumental EB site at Liman Tepe on the southern shore of the Gulf of İzmir. Drawing upon archaeological data from the İzmir region (including inland Bakla Tepe), Troy, the site of Küllüoba in central northwestern Anatolia and others, as well as various islands within the north and east Aegean, Şahoğlu (2005) presents a distinctive set of material features — new pottery shapes and wheelmade wares, tin bronzes, large settlements with monumental fortifications — that emerged at the end of EB II-beginning EB III (after ca. 2500 BC) and extended from western and southern Anatolia, through the eastern Aegean islands, to the Cyclades and mainland Greece (see also Şahoğlu 2008a, 2008b, 2011; Erkanal and Şahoğlu 2016). Efe (2002: 55-61; 2007: 60-61, and fig. 17a) questions the maritime component of materials exchanged between Cilicia and the northeast Aegean/Troy during EB III, arguing that materials, innovations (*e.g.* wheelmade pottery, tin bronzes) and ideas reached the latter area via overland trade — what he terms the 'Great Caravan Route' — and only thence filtered into the Aegean.

Both Şahoğlu and Efe maintain that the relatively sudden appearance of these features over such a wide geographic area can only be explained by an increased demand for various raw materials, in particular metals, and the associated technologies. The extraction and 'controlled distribution' of gold, silver and tin from the Taurus mountain range and the Cilician region in south central Anatolia would have accelerated hierarchical social change and eventually led to the emergence of an 'international' maritime and terrestrial trading network (Şahoğlu 2005: 340-344, figs. 1-2; 2008a: 162-163; on the Aegean and Anatolia, see also Kouka 2002: 296-302). Related to this and contemporaneously, Kouka (2002: 238-247, 297-299; 2016: 205-211) argues for the rise of an elite group of metalworkers and traders on the Aegean islands of Lemnos, Lesbos, Chios and Samos. Rahmstorf (2016: 234-235, 254-256) maintains that the emerging use of seals and sealings in the Aegean world during the EB II period resulted via transmission from central and western Anatolia, whilst the use of weights emerged in both areas about this same time. Massa and Şahoğlu (2015: 69, 71 fig. 10), finally, postulate a contemporaneous 'super-network' or 'ensemble of interlocking networks' extending from the Indus Valley to the Aegean, of which the ATN is the westernmost component (Figure 10).

At Troy, the relevant levels (Troy II-III) demonstrate rich architectural, ceramic and metallurgical finds (see, *e.g.*, Jung and Weninger 2015: 208-211; Bachhuber 2015: 114-115, 122-128, 143-145, 160-167, 171-172). Whilst numerous attempts over the years have yet to identify a harbour near the site (*e.g.* Cook 1984; Korfmann 1986a; Kayan 1990; Kraft *et al.* 1982, 2003), Troy's maritime impact during the mid-late third millennium BC is readily demonstrated by its numerous Aegean pottery imports, and by a material culture shared with Poliochni on Lemnos and Thermi on Lesbos (Kouka 2002). Moreover, its strategic location on the Dardanelles, between the Aegean and the Black Sea, makes it an obvious point of connectivity, where land and sea routes intersect. Troy is also one of only two sites in Anatolia (the other is Kilise Tepe, some 50 km inland from the southern, Cilician coast) that

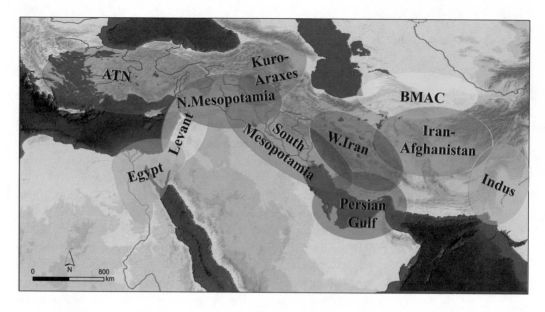

Figure 10: *The proposed Anatolian Trade Network, and the 'super-network' (BMAC stands for Bactria-Margiania Archaeological Complex).* From Massa and Şahoğlu 2015: 69, 71 fig. 10. Courtesy of Michele Massa.

have actually recorded fish remains (Uerpmann and Van Neer 2000; Van Neer and Waelkens 2007), even though fish bones and mollusc shells are common at sites such as Çeşme-Bağlararası and Liman Tepe (Michele Massa, pers. comm. 6 December 2017). Şahoğlu (2005: 344-347) suggests that Troy was linked inland and northward, to Kanlıgeçit in Thrace (a 'small scale copy of Troy II'), and eastward to Küllüoba (with its 'palatial' complex), and thence southeast to sites such as Acemhöyük, and the sources of silver (and tin?) at Kestel and Tarsus/Gözlükale, the last a gateway to the Mediterranean in the south. Another branch of this network extended inward from a proposed port at Liman Tepe to key sites such as Aphrodisias, Beycesultan (north) and Karataş-Semayük (south). Closer to the coast and just southeast of Liman Tepe lay the site of Bakla Tepe, whose cemeteries contained rich metal finds (gold and silver jewellery, earliest tin bronzes from the İzmir region), as well as (ceramic) mortuary goods indicating links that extend from central and western Anatolia to the Aegean (Şahoğlu 2005: 347-349; 2016). Whilst it is not a coastal site, Bakla Tepe is located strategically at the head of the Menderes plain and is linked directly to the Aegean sea through a narrow valley.

On the Gulf of İzmir, Liman Tepe itself is one of the key coastal sites in Sahoğlu's ATN; it was inhabited throughout the EB II-III periods and is discussed in more detail in the following section (*Ports and Harbours*). Şahoğlu (2005: 352, with refs.; 2008a: 162-163) suggests that the İzmir region functioned as a bridge between Anatolia and the Aegean, its traders playing a key role in both maritime and overland trade. The seafaring branch of these traders may also have been instrumental in establishing outposts of the ATN that extended throughout the Cyclades — *e.g.* on Syros, Naxos, Keos, Delos, Amorgos and Keros — and ultimately to the Greek mainland, especially Euboea, or Kolonna on Aegina. Ünlü

(2016) discusses the increasingly close relations between western Anatolia and the Aegean toward the end of the third millennium BC in terms of a 'communal' consumption of wine and fermented beverages in a 'west Anatolian drinking set' (cups with oversized handles and beak-spouted pitchers). At Kastri on Syros, a suite of pottery types that may be construed as drinking vessels (*depata* and bell-shaped cups, incised *pyxides*) are, like the fortification system and metallurgical remains, said to be 'entirely Anatolian in character' (Şahoğlu 2005: 352). Like Kanlıgeçit in Thrace, Kastri is regarded as a small 'colony' established to facilitate the movement of goods through the ATN.

In contrast, Aegean prehistorians regard communities like Kastri to be Cycladic trading centres, pure and simple (*e.g.* Broodbank 2013: 322, 335; Knappett and Nikolakopoulou 2014) (see further below). In turn, the entire assemblage of ceramic finds from Ayia Irini on Keos — *depata*, tankards, cutaway-spouted jugs, two-handled cups, wheelmade plates (Wilson 1999: 94-101) — finds counterparts elsewhere in the ATN. Such finds, which suggest some level of association with Anatolia during the EB period, indicate that Keos might have served as a stepping stone for the extension of the ATN to mainland Greece (*e.g.*, at sites such as Lerna, Tiryns, Manika, Lefkandi, Raphina, Thorikos and Pevkakia — for refs., see Şahoğlu 2005: 352-353, nn. 15-18).

From a more western and self-consciously insular perspective, Knappett and Nikolakopoulou (2014: 28-30) see only a short-term 'reverberation of Anatolian trends' in the Cycladic islands, a side effect of 'intangible' features like the transmission of metallurgical technology or the circulation of rare metals (gold, silver, tin). In their view, the Cyclades did not necessarily serve either as insular colonies of the ATN or as stepping stones for the transmission of ATN traits and technologies to the wider Aegean world (see also Angelopoulou 2008; Sotirakopoulou 2008). Given the strategic position and involvement of the Cycladic islands in maritime trade, Knappett and Nikolakopoulou (2014: 29) regard them instead as 'active participants' in the spread of metals as well as metallurgical technology along two routes, one from Lavrion on the Greek mainland, Kythnos and Siphnos, the other from Troy and the northeast Aegean (see also Broodbank 2000: 211-246). Thus the multiple sites in the Cyclades that are seen as 'expatriate trading centres' of the ATN might instead be regarded as (1) parts of a 'buffer zone' for the spread of Anatolian traits westward, and (2) a home to communities that made a conscious choice to expand their already thriving networks of interaction to the east and northeast.

Nonetheless, the Anatolian Trade Network, as already indicated in the previous section (*Cyprus*), formed a significant part of what seems to have been more widespread systems of trade and material practices involving Cyprus, the broader Aegean world (Cyclades, mainland Greece, and likely Crete) and the southern Levant (and beyond that linking to northern Syria and eventually to Mesopotamia and the east—see Figure 10, above). The basis of all these interaction systems lay mainly in the production and maritime exchange of metals such as copper (or copper alloys), silver and tin, as well as metal goods (ring ingots, weapons, jewellery) (Mellink 1986, 1993; Kayafa *et al.* 2000; Efe 2002, 2007; Philip *et al.* 2003; Stos-Gale and Gale 2003; Şahoğlu 2005; 2011; Webb *et al.* 2006; Knappett and Nikolakopoulou 2014). Many of the pottery forms said to characterise the

ATN (or any other mechanism of maritime trade between western Anatolia and the Aegean) are pouring or drinking vessels (*depata*, cups, *pyxides*), which suggests that wine or other alcoholic ('elite') drinks, as well as perfumes or scented oils, may also have played some role in this trade network (Şahoğlu 2005: 354; see also Zimmerman 2005; Rutter 2008). By the second half of the EB III period (sometime after ca. 2300 BC), these exchange networks collapsed, for reasons unknown, even if 'climatic events' and the socioeconomic pressures associated with them increasingly are cited as a primary cause (*e.g.*, most recently, various papers in Meller *et al.* 2015; see also Dalfes *et al.* 1997; Staubwasser and Weiss 2006; Roberts *et al.* 2011). Henceforth, the 'western' branch of the ATN increasingly looked towards the Aegean whilst the central Anatolian branch was gradually integrated into the wider Near Eastern world (Massa and Şahoğlu 2015: 69).

PORTS AND HARBOURS

Sahoğlu (2015: 593) maintains that Çeşme–Bağlararası, situated at the westernmost tip of the Urla Peninsula, in the centre of Çeşme (İzmir province) near its modern harbour, was … 'an important harbour settlement from at least the EBA onwards'. The excavated part of the EBA settlement, however, indicates only a domestic quarter (chipped stone tools, weights, loomweights), whilst the pottery assemblage points to local development with no visible imports (very different from contemporary Liman Tepe, just 50 kms distant, at least in terms of imported pottery).

Liman Tepe ('harbour hill') was a major Bronze Age settlement, inhabited continuously from the Chalcolithic period onwards; it is situated in the Bay of İzmir on the northern side of the Urla peninsula (Figure 11). The site is ideally situated for an anchorage and lay at a crucial crossroads between the northern and southern Aegean Sea, just east of the large island of Chios (Erkanal 2008; Erkanal and Şahoğlu 2016: 165). Physical and material evidence for an EB harbour at Liman Tepe, however, remains limited. The northern part of the 'citadel' area now lies underwater, but the topography and to some extent the architectural remains have been documented. At least some of these underwater remains formed part of the Archaic-period settlement at Klazomenai, submerged as the result of severe tectonic changes (Ersoy 2004: 53). Current thinking is that the harbour area of the Bronze Age must lie in the eastern part of the settlement, which became filled with alluvial deposits through time and eventually led to the construction of a breakwater during the Archaic period (Vasif Şahoğlu, pers. comm., 8 November 2016).

The implication is that at least some of the underwater remains at Liman Tepe represent an anchorage or harbour of one or more of the ancient settlements: two rubble-strewn features, a tongue-shaped mole and a secondary mole projecting from it, well-preserved organic materials (olive pits, *poseidonia*, etc.), all tend to corroborate this notion. Underwater excavations within the area of the larger mole indicates that it was constructed during the Archaic period and remained in use until the fourth century BC (Artzy 2009: 14). Recent work has also identified the arm of a wooden anchor, dated to the sixth century BC on the basis of associated pottery (Votruba *et al.* 2016), and stone (stock) and metal ('teeth') parts of other anchors dated to the fourth century BC (Votruba and Erkanal 2016). Beyond these much later remains, however, there is still no published evidence of Liman Tepe's harbour.

Figure 11: *Overview of excavations at Liman Tepe.* Photo by Hakan Çetinkaya. Courtesy of Hayat Erkanal and Vasif Şahoğlu, İzmir Region Excavations and Research Project (IRERP) Archives.

Nonetheless, the interregional maritime links of Liman Tepe are evident from the earliest period of occupation on the site, with its imported Melian obsidian and various other finds indicating contacts with the Cyclades and various Aegean islands during the Chalcolithic period (Liman Tepe VII) (Kouka 2009b: 143-145, figs. 4-6; Şahoğlu 2010: 1572). The site was transformed during the following Liman Tepe VI period (EB I, ca. 2950-2650 BC) into a 'proto-urban' centre with a lower town, a fortified citadel boasting a monumental gateway complex, and blocks or 'insulae' of long rooms (typical of the period) attached to the fortification wall (Kouka 2009b: 144-146; Erkanal and Şahoğlu 2016: 157-158, fig. 1, 160 fig. 3). Imported Melian obsidian, Naxian emery and Cycladic pottery found in the long-room houses demonstrate the continuation of Liman Tepe's maritime contacts with the central and southern Aegean during the EB I period (Erkanal and Şahoğlu 2016: 161; Şahoğlu 2008b: 487-488, 499 figs. 7-9; Kouka 2009b: 145-146, figs. 7, 9). By the mid-third millennium BC (EB II, Liman Tepe V), the settlement expanded into a major regional centre, and exchange with the Aegean world intensified. The monumental fortifications were rebuilt and enforced with a horseshoe-shaped bastion, whilst a second round of fortifications was built 300 m southwest of the first one (Erkanal and Şahoğlu 2016: 162-163, figs. 9-10; Massa and Şahoğlu 2015: 68, 71 fig. 9; Şahoğlu 2008b: 488; Erkanal 2008: 181-184, 189 figs. 7-8: Kouka 2016: 210-211, figs. 9.4-96). Liman Tepe continued to be an important regional centre during the Middle Bronze Age, and by the Late Bronze Age its role as a key maritime centre in the eastern Aegean is signalled by rich finds of Mycenaean pottery.

CHAPTER 4

MIDDLE BRONZE AGE

THE LEVANT AND EGYPT

There are no shipwrecks yet documented for the Middle Bronze Age (MB) in the southeastern Mediterranean. During this period, however, it is likely that Levantine port towns such as Ugarit, Tell Tweini and Byblos were in 'full development', and played a prominent role in eastern Mediterranean exchange (Al-Maqdassi 2013: 78-79); the port established at Ugarit became a key centre of connectivity in regional as well as interregional trade (Bordreuil *et al.* 1984; Yon 2006: 16). Marcus (2007) has admirably summarised much of the material, representational and documentary evidence for Egyptian seafaring and transport during the Middle Kingdom in his detailed evaluation of the Mit Rahina inscription of the Twelfth Dynasty pharaoh Amenemhet II (ca. 1928-1878 BC); the following account of maritime related material frequently calls upon that study for reference as well as guidance.

Most Egyptian Middle Kingdom documentary or epigraphic references to seagoing ships pertain to the Red Sea and/or the Land of Punt, not to the Mediterranean. These include especially several inscriptions (ostraca, stele) from the Red Sea port of Wadi Gawasis referring to the Twelfth Dynasty rulers Amenemhet II, III and IV (Sayed 1977: 159-163, 170; Bard and Fattovich 2010: 5-6, 8, 10-11, and fig. 7). The story of *The Shipwrecked Sailor* mentions a large ship with a crew of 120 mariners who raised sail in the Red Sea (Lichtheim 1973: 212–213; Simpson 2003: 48; *cf.* Der Manuelian 1992: 224-225, who argues against any specific location for this tale). By contrast, the Papyrus Lythgoe, a partially preserved late Twelfth Dynasty text from El-Lisht, refers to a *kbnt* (usually understood as a 'Byblos ship', but *cf.* Ward 2010b: 43) and may be part of a literary tale about an Egyptian travelling to the Levant (Marcus 2007: 155; Simpson 1960).

The most relevant textual evidence concerning Egyptian seafaring and seafarers stems from some inscribed granite blocks found at Mit Rahina (Memphis) — court records of the Twelfth Dynasty pharaoh Amenemhet II (Altenmüller and Moussa 1991: 14-16). These documents discuss building activities, endowments and Egyptian foreign relations. One record that treats a commercial expedition has been described by Marcus (2007: 154, with further refs.) as the Mediterranean's earliest known 'cargo manifest'. Two 'transport ships' returning home from *Hnty-s* (central-northern Levant) carried a large variety of goods: raw materials (timber, precious metals, minerals, stones), organic products (aromatics, oils and resins, wine, medicinal plants, spices) and finished pieces (*e.g.* seals, bronze daggers decorated with gold, silver and ivory). Such a cornucopia of diverse materials and goods is unlikely to have originated in a single place (unless all goods were collected there prior to loading), probably not even in a single region, but rather from several (likely Levantine) ports of call.

Beyond these textual references, the archaeological record boasts a significant corpus of MB material and representational evidence related to ships, seafaring, maritime transport containers and harbours, all of which suggest an expanding interest and involvement in seaborne trade, and the movement of goods and people throughout the eastern Mediterranean.

SHIPWRECKS

No MB shipwrecks are known from the Levant or Egypt. Nonetheless, strontium isotope analysis on wood from the Egyptian Pharaoh Senwosret III's (Twelfth Dynasty, ca. 1889-1836 BC) 'Carnegie Boat' (Patch and Haldane 1990; Peters *et al.* 2017) — found in his funerary complex at Dahshur — indicates that the timbers originated in the cedar forest of Horsh-Ehden in northern Lebanon (Rich *et al.* 2016). Whilst it has long been assumed that Egypt imported cedar from Lebanon, notably from Byblos, as early as the Old Kingdom (see above, Chapter 3: *Early Bronze Age—The Levant and Egypt)*, these analyses provide the first direct evidence for Middle Kingdom imports of Lebanese cedar, and by extension of seafaring craft — Levantine or Egyptian — that carried them from the (central) Levant to Egypt.

From Senwosret III's mortuary complex at south Abydos, the remains of a royal boat burial have been identified and recently excavated (Wegner 2017). Like the group of Early Dynastic (ca. 3000-2800 BC) royal boat burials found earlier at Abydos (O'Connor 1995), these vessels provide a great deal of information on the technology of early boats that may have travelled upon the Nile, if not the open sea (Ward 2006), but they do not speak directly to seafaring or maritime ventures in the Mediterranean. From the walls of the same subterranean building that housed Senwosret III's large (ca. 18-20 m) funerary boat, however, come 120 surviving, incised drawings of watercraft that are nothing short of remarkable; they are discussed in more detail below (*Ships' Representations*).

PORTS AND HARBOURS (EGYPT)

In Egypt's Nile Delta, just west of the MB complex at Tell ed-Dab'a (ancient Avaris), geophysical survey has revealed a large, 450 x 400 m harbour basin linked by canals to the main (Pelusiac) branch of the Nile, as well as two other likely harbours to the north and northeast (Forstner-Müller 2009; see also Bietak 2008: 111 fig. 35, 112 n. 2; 2010: 18; 2013: 188-189, figs. 1-2). According to the excavator, (unpublished) radiocarbon dates from the associated inlet canal belong 'to the time of the Middle Kingdom' (Bietak 2010: 18, n.65). Marcus (2006: 188) glowingly described the port complex at Tell ed-Dab'a as 'Venice on the Nile'. Excavations at the location 'Ezbet Rushdi have produced some of the earliest MB Levantine and Middle Minoan pottery known from Egypt (Marcus 2007: 160), including maritime transport containers such as the 'Canaanite jar' and the Minoan oval-mouthed amphora (see below, *Maritime Transport Containers*). It seems reasonable to assume that this harbour complex surrounding the site of Tell ed-Dabʿa served not only as a key nexus in eastern Mediterranean trade but also as a gateway for trade extending farther up the Nile (Bietak 2010: 20-21).

Some 400 km to the southeast of Tell ed-Dabʿa, on the coast of the Red Sea, lay another Middle Kingdom harbour facility, Mersa/Wadi Gawasis (Sayed 1977; Frost 1996; Bard and Fattovich 2010; 2011; 2015). Situated in an optimal harbour position, the mouth of the Wadi Gawasis was — in the late third–early second millennium BC — a deep lagoon within a large embayment. Above this ancient lagoon and cut about 20m deep into the western wall of the fossil coral terrace at Wadi Gawasis were two isolated rock-cut chambers and six long galleries containing a treasure-trove of seagoing paraphernalia: up to 30 coils of rope from ships; 43 wooden cargo boxes (Figure 12); about 90 timbers from the hull, deck and rudders of ships, along with tenons, dovetails and copper strips used as fastenings (Ward and Zazzaro 2010). Seventeen ostraca recorded quantities of food and ships; one included the name of the pharaoh Amenemhet III. A poorly preserved stela lists offerings to ʿOsiris of the Great Green/Seaʾ, suggesting that Osiris here took the form of a maritime deity at this harbour (Bard and Fattovich 2011: 125).

Nine radiocarbon dates compliment the pottery typology at Wadi Gawasis, indicating that this harbour was used primarily during the Middle Kingdom (ca. 2060-1740 BC) (Bard and Fattovich 2011: 109, table 1; 2015: 5). The excavators emphasize that seafaring expeditions launched from this port were most likely directed southward, along the east African coast, toward the ancient lands of Punt and Bia-Punt — modern southern Sudan and Eritrea — or perhaps to Yemen on the opposite, eastern coast of the Red Sea (Fattovich 2012; Bard and Fattovich 2015: 9-10). In fact, the existence of an exchange network centred on the Red Sea itself seems quite likely, given the ʿexoticʾ pottery (Nubian, Eritrean, Yemeni) found at the site (Manzo 2012; Moreno García 2017: 99-101). Unlike the large harbour basin at Tell ed-Dabʿa, therefore, these impressive remains from Wadi Gawasis only provide indirect evidence for any attempt to understand Egypt's role in eastern Mediterranean — as opposed to Red Sea — seafaring and trade during the Middle Bronze Age.

Figure 12: *One of 43 wooden cargo boxes from the ships' para- phernalia excavated at Wadi Gawasis, Egypt.* Courtesy of Kathryn Bard.

PORTS AND HARBOURS (LEVANT)

The establishment of early ports and harbours necessitated the development of schemes to mitigate environmental impact: *e.g.* changes in sea level or in coastal configuration resulting from sedimentary deposition and progradation. Moreover, selecting a suitable location for a port or harbour meant that sea currents and the dominant winds had to be taken into account (Walsh 2014: 64-65). Even if sea conditions in the Mediterranean have not changed since antiquity (Morton 2001: 6), climate changes and shifting weather systems would have led to variations in wind and current patterns, potentially altering the timing and seasonality of the winds (Walsh 2014: 66 and fig. 3.16).

The earliest Bronze Age harbours in the eastern Mediterranean were most likely concentrated around small coves, estuaries and the mouths of wadis — 'natural' anchorages or 'proto-harbours' that required little modification by the mariners or fishermen who used them (Marriner and Morhange 2007: 175). Such proto-harbours probably existed at Levantine Bronze Age sites such as Byblos, Arwad, Beirut, Tyre and Sidon (Carayon *et al.* 2011; Carayon *et al.* 2011-12: 442-447; Doumet-Serhal 2013). Of these, Byblos may well have been the most important but remains the least well known: its spatial layout is regarded as typical for the Bronze Age, namely one or more sheltered coves or natural, juxtaposed anchorages (Carayon 2012-13: 19 fig. 25). Underwater prospection (Frost 1988-1989) and geomorphological exploration (Morhange 1988-1989) at Byblos have indicated that if any Bronze Age anchorage or harbour existed, it would most likely have been situated in the southern part of the town's headland (Skhineh Bay).

At Middle-Late Bronze Age Beirut, the spatial configuration looks similar: a promontory (Ras Beirut) overlooking two natural harbours (Carayon *et al.* 2011: 51-53; Carayon 2012-13: 25-34). Geomorphological reconstruction of the promontory suggests that an anchorage was situated between the Nahr ('River') Beirut to the east, two rocky promontories and a tiny offshore islet (Carayon *et al.* 2011: 53, fig. 11).

Using 'high resolution geoscience techniques' and a series of calibrated radiocarbon dates, Marriner *et al.* (2006a: 1-2) identified pre-Phoenician harbours at both Tyre and Sidon, lying beneath and around their present-day urban centres (Marriner *et al.* 2006a: 3 fig. 4, 4 fig. 5; Marriner *et al.* 2008: 1282). They identify at least four harbour phases (six are noted at Sidon in Marriner *et al.* 2006b); during the MB, they suggest that semi-open marine coves at Tyre and Sidon served as proto-harbours. At the same time, natural downwind embayments and coves north of the promontories at Tyre and Sidon could have served as attractive sites for anchorages.

Tyre was once an island, and may have been connected to the mainland by a tombolo (sand isthmus) as early as the ninth century BC (Carmona and Ruiz 2008; *cf.* Marriner *et al.* 2008). Once eustatic sea level reached broad stability, no later than 4000 BC, the northern coast would have become at least partially protected by a small Quaternary ridge complex, and it is assumed the 'northern harbour' had Bronze Age origins (Marriner *et al.* 2008). Shallow draft boats could have been hauled onto the beach at Tyre's semi-open marine cove, but larger merchant vessels would have had to anchor in the bay, using smaller vessels to transfer their cargos to and from the shore (Marriner *et al.* 2005: 1319). Based on geomorphological analyses of 25 cores taken to elucidate the coastal stratigraphy, it is suggested that the maximum extent of Tyre's harbour basin was 40-50% larger than it is today (Marriner *et al.* 2006a: 3 fig. 4; Carayon *et al.* 2011: 46-49, figs. 2-4).

Sidon was ideally situated for a harbour site: it has two natural embayments on the northern and southern sides of a promontory, and another potential anchorage on the small offshore island of Zire, just north of the northern embayment (Marriner *et al.* 2006: 1516-17, figs. 2-3) (Figure 13). A proto-harbour in the northern embayment may be dated to the late MB and early Late Bronze Age (ca. 1700–1450 BC). Protected by a 600m-long offshore Quaternary ridge (Marriner *et al.* 2006a: 2), Sidon's northern basin afforded better shelter than the coast at Tyre; larger ships also would have been better accommodated in this northern harbour, or on the leeward side of the 'outer harbour' on Zire. From the large, semi-circular embayment to the south, the so-called 'Egyptian harbour', studies of bio- and litho-stratigraphic cores point to a natural, fair-weather open harbour with wide sandy beaches that could have served the landing purposes of smaller vessels (Marriner *et al.* 2006b: 1519-1520, 1525).

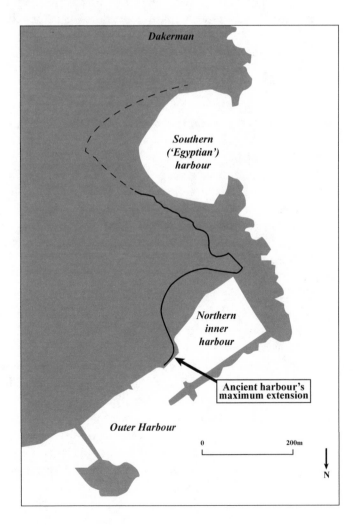

Figure 13: *Sidon MB harbour plan.* After Marriner and Morhange 2005: 188 fig. 6. Drawing by Irini Katsouri.

In both Tyre and Sidon, the MB was a time of increasing international contacts (Egypt, Crete, Cyprus) and related socioeconomic development (Doumet-Serhal 2003: 9-14; 2013: 132-137; see also Ward 1961). The semi-protected proto-harbour(s) proposed for this period would thus be contemporary with the growth of an early port infrastructure. Having retraced the maximum limit of Tyre and Sidon's Middle Bronze Age basins, Morhange et al. (2006a: 4; 2006b: 1532) have also shown that coastal progradation (advance of land from sediment deposition on river deltas) has not only silted up large portions of these sites but also buried them beneath the present-day town centres: their historical coastlines are now situated some 100-150m inland. The fact that both Tyre and Sidon are located at the distal margins of small deltas helps to explain why their two harbours are still in use, unlike the coastal progradation that has made sites like Troy and the Maeander delta in Anatolia landlocked today (Kraft et al. 2003; Brückner et al. 2002).

In Artzy's (2006: 45-46) view, the Bay of Haifa — especially the site of Akko —provides an obvious point for a key harbour along the coast of modern Israel. The importance of the area's anchorages or harbours depended on the nearby rivers and their estuaries, which led inland. During parts of both the Middle and Late Bronze Ages, coastal installations in this region — such as Tel Nami, first inhabited during MB IIA (Artzy 1995: 19-22; Lev-Yadun et al. 1996) — would have served as a focus for maritime as well as terrestrial trading networks. At Tel Dor on Israel's Carmel coast, it can only be speculated whether an early, MB harbour (Gilboa and Sharon 2008: 148) had the same configuration as its Iron Age counterpart, namely two natural anchorages — a bay on the north and a large lagoon protected by offshore islets on the south. Underwater surveys at Dor produced MB IIA pottery, anchors and a Middle Cypriot import (Wachsmann and Raveh 1984: 239). The excavators maintain — on the basis of intrusive MB pottery in later contexts — that the site was inhabited from at least MB IIA onward (Gilboa and Sharon 2008: 148), but there is no physical evidence of an actual harbour. In principle, then, Dor represents a good example of a natural anchorage that could have served as a stopping point for local, regional or international (e.g. Egyptian) maritime commerce. Farther south, submerged boulder piles at the MB site of Yavne-Yam may indicate an attempt to improve upon a natural anchorage there (Marriner and Morhange 2007: 175).

Raban (1985: 14-23), Marcus (2007: 165-170) and Burke (2011: 65-67) have all considered the possible existence of MB ports or source areas along the Levantine littoral (Raban in present-day Israel only). Such studies also need to take into account the work of Sivan et al. (2001), which used archaeological data as 'constraints' on isostatic models for sea level change along the southernmost Levantine coast (Israel). This study determined that, overall, sea level was lower than −3 m at the outset of the Bronze Age and remained below its present level until the end of the Bronze Age, with notable impacts at both Tel Nami and Tel Dor (Sivan et al. 2001: 114-115; see also Walsh 2014: 42, 44, 51). How this phenomenon might have impacted on other likely harbour or anchorage sites is uncertain. Nonetheless, what follows is a summary of the evidence for such sites (amongst others already noted), moving from south to north (see Map 3, p.18):

Southern Coastal Plain

- Tell el-'Ajjul (Šaruhen?), today situated about 2 km inland on the Wadi Gaza (Tufnell 1962: 1; Fischer 2000: 212-213)
- Ashkelon (Stager 2001)
- Tel Mor, near the outlet of Nahal Lachish
- Yavne-Yam, just south of the estuary at Nahal Soreq, a possible natural anchorage (Marriner and Morhange 2007: 175)
- Jaffa, a possible anchorage or port just south of the ancient outlet of Nahal Ayalon (Raban 1985: 17, 27, nn. 87-88; de Miroschedji 2012: 273-274); beyond imports such as some Middle Cypriot wares and 'Hyksos' scarabs, however, MB evidence at the site is very limited (Burke 2011: 66-67; Burke *et al.* 2017: 90)
- Nahal Yarqon, but with no coastal site at the mouth of the estuary, only some MB IIA material remnants; the MB IIA site of Tel Gerisa today lies 4 km upstream
- Tel Mikhmoret on a promontory bordering the northern side of the estuary at Nahal Alexander, with possible anchorage in a lagoon just southeast of the tell (Raban 1985: 17, 19, fig. 5).

Carmel Coast

- Tel Dor and Tel Nami (as already noted, neither has yet revealed physical evidence of a MB harbour)
- Atlit, on a peninsula on the southern side of the outlet of Nahal Oren, inhabited during both EB and MB periods (Sharvit *et al.* 2002: 164), and perhaps nearby Megadim
- Tell Abu Hawam, at the outlet of Nahal Qishon; the earliest remains excavated here are Late Bronze in date (Artzy 2006: 46-49; 2016).

Northern Israel and Southern Lebanon

- Tel Akko (Raban 1991: *31-*32; Artzy 2006: 49-50)
- Nahariya, next to the outlet of Nahal Ga'aton, with its MB II 'sanctuary' (Ben-Dor 1950; see now D'Andrea 2014: 45, 49, fig. 3, with other, earlier refs.)
- Tel Akhziv on a peninsular promontory north of the estuary at Nahal Keziv, with at least a few MB II remains and possible signs of harbour construction (Raban 1985: 18-19, fig. 4)
- Tyre and Sidon (already treated above)
- Tell el-Burak (Lebanon), but the site lacks any evidence even for a good anchorage, and may instead have served as a defensive element within the territory of Sidon, which lies nine km to the north (Sader and Kamiah 2010: 139; Pederson 2011: 287).

Northern Lebanon and Southern Syria

- Beirut and Byblos (already treated above)
- Tell Arqa, with MB remains including likely MTCs (Thalmann 2007: 435-436, fig. 5:3; Ownby 2010: 62-64, fig. 3.11) (see further below, under *Maritime Transport Containers*)

- Tell Kazel, with remains primarily of Late Bronze–early Iron Age date (Badre 2011); the built 'Phoenician' harbour at Tabbat el-Hammam may have served as the port for Tell Kazel.

North Syrian Coast
- Tell Sukas, located on a promontory between two natural bays, but its southern harbour dates mainly to the Late Bronze–early Iron Ages (Riis *et al.* 1995)
- Tell Tweini (ancient Gibala?), at the confluence of two rivers (Rumailah, al-Fawar), inhabited from the EB onward (Bretschneider *et al.* 2014: 349-351); often cited as the southernmost harbour of the LB Ugaritic kingdom, today it lies 1.7 km inland but geophysical survey and geomorphological analyses indicate that the site lay on the sea during the Bronze Age (Al-Maqdissi *et al.* 2007)
- Ugarit, with obvious anchorages at Minet el-Beidha and Ras Ibn Hani, but mainly lacking physical remains of a harbour (Schaeffer 1933; Bordreuil *et al.* 1984; Bounni *et al.* 1998). The town itself witnessed substantial 'urban' development during the MB, especially during its later phases (Yon 2006: 16-18).

Burke (2011: 66, table 6.1) points out that the average distance between the major, MB ports along the Levantine coast is about 38 km (20.5 nautical miles), which might reflect an average minimum distance sailing during daylight hours in a single day. His calculations led him to conclude that the nearly 380-nautical-mile trip from the Lebanese coast to the Egyptian delta would have taken an average of 11 days; he notes, however, the unpredictability of winds and other weather conditions that would impact on such calculations.

Approaching the problem from just that angle, Safadi (2016: 350-351, table 1, fig. 1), in a strikingly original study of 20 Bronze and Iron Age harbour sites located in modern-day Lebanon, evaluates their maritime accessibility and sheltering potential through the modelling of wind speed and direction, and of the wave heights for harbour sites. Some of these sites have already been noted: Tyre, Sidon, Tell el-Burak, Beirut, Byblos and Tell Arqa. Seven sites afforded what was determined to be a significant level of protection and accessibility (from south to north): Sidon, Beirut, Jounieh, Byblos, Batroun, Chekka and Tripoli. In Safadi's (2016: 358) view, these sites had a 'natural maritime predisposition' — providing both shelter and enhanced accessibility — and may have operated on local and regional scales of interaction. The site of Tyre turns out to be unique as a harbour or place of anchorage, especially in terms of wind directions, as sailing to and from the site in either a northerly or a southerly direction is possible during all seasons of the year. Safadi cautions that her study constitutes a point of departure, not an end result. Beyond the wind and waves, it is necessary to take into account other factors, such as human agency or regional, local socio-economic contexts, the needs and skills not only of the mariners but of those who settled in, and enhanced or failed to develop the use of any given place as a harbour or anchorage. Not every site that afforded good shelter was necessarily used as a Bronze Age harbour or anchorage and, conversely, those sites with limited affordances did not necessarily play a limited role.

For differing reasons, then, many of the sites listed above may never have served as MB ports. Even so, ships sailing to or from Egypt's Nile Delta could have anchored at one or another of these Levantine destinations for various commercial purposes, including the acquisition of raw materials (*e.g.* cedar timber, silver), organic goods (*e.g.* aromatics, oils, resins, wine) and finished products (*e.g.* MTCs and other pottery, metal tools and weapons) — as the Mit Rahina inscription suggests. Nilotic fish remains are attested at MB coastal or near coastal sites such as Tel Dor and Tel Kabri, and at inland sites such as Lachish, Megiddo and Tel el-Wawayat, where they often represent the only evidence for Egyptian imports (van Neer *et al.* 2004: 117, 119). Tel Kabri and Lachish also have various fish taxa imported from the Mediterranean (van Neer *et al.* 2004: 134).

In general, the Middle Bronze Age was a time of intense maritime exchange between Egypt and the Levant, including Syria and Anatolia (Moreno García 2017: 115, with further refs.). Clearly some people — producers (miners, farmers, loggers), merchants and shippers, seamen — recognised the commercial if not military importance of exploiting and exchanging various commodities in demand via seaborne transport by developing maritime networks in the eastern Mediterranean and the ports and anchorages that supported them (Marcus 2007: 175-176). Moreover, given the significant amount of 'urban' expansion at sites along the eastern Mediterranean coast during this period, it seems reasonable to suggest that maritime trade all along the Levantine littoral, and its likely extension along the Cilician coast of Anatolia, impacted positively on urban development, the inland production associated with it, as well as 'port power' (Stager 2001).

SHIPS' REPRESENTATIONS

Both Basch (1987: 62) and Wachsmann (1998: 18) noted that there were few if any known depictions of Egyptian Middle Kingdom (roughly MB in date) or Levantine seagoing vessels or seafarers. Several possible exceptions, however, must be noted. The first is the ship carved on a Syrian-style hematite cylinder seal found at Tell ed-Dab'a in the Nile Delta and dated to the eighteenth century BC (Porada 1984: 485-486, fig. 1, pl. 65:1; Wachsmann 1998: 42, fig. 3.1) (Figure 14). With a mast positioned amidships, two highly stylised figures on either side of it and oars depicted beneath the figures, such a vessel could have been both wind-driven and oar-powered. Both Porada (1984: 487) and Marcus (2006: 188) suggest that other motifs on the seal — a 'smiting weather god', a charging bull, a lion and a serpent — may represent a patron gods of seafarers, in particular Ba'al Ṣapon. Brody (1998: 18-19, 29-30, 97) adds that the Canaanite goddess Asherah had 'marine attributes' and that two of her symbols — the snake and lion represented on the Tell ed-Dab'a seal — indicate that she was the 'guardian' of the ship depicted.

Another other possible exception is a wall painting from the Middle Kingdom tomb of Amenemhet at Beni Hassan in Egypt that depicts two Nile ships towing a funerary barge (Wachsmann 1998: 248-249, fig. 11.3; 2000: 808-809, fig. 4; Newberry 1893: pl. XIV). Strictly speaking, these may not be regarded as 'seafaring', but each ship sports a sail, of different size.

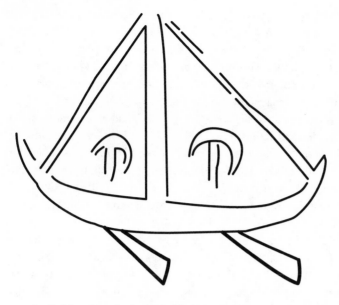

Figure 14: *Boat with sail engraved on Syrian-style cylinder seal from Tell ed-Dab'a.* After Porada 1984: 486, fig. 1. Drawing by Irini Katsouri.

At Byblos, Brody (1998: 44-45, 143 figs. 37-39) refers to the presence of at least 20 bronze ship models in MB deposits at the 'Temple of Obelisks' and the 'Champ des offrandes' (Dunand 1954: nos. 15068-15077, 17265, 10086-10087, 10089-10092, 10642-10643, 8816). Wachsmann (1998: 54-55, fig. 3.21) interprets at least some of these as Egyptian ship models or local Byblian copies of Egyptian models. Brody (1998: 45-46, n. 31) disputes Wachsmann's overly specific comparisons, and maintains that these are some of the very few representations of MB Canaanite ships. Whether Egyptian or Levantine, they are ships representations, and given what seem to be long-standing, intimate connections between Byblos and Egypt conducted by sea, need occasion no surprise.

Beyond these, Wachsmann (1998: 32-38, figs. 245-260) presented a unique group of 13 ships' graffiti incised on the smooth rock faces within the Sinai's Wadi Rôd el-'Air, dated to both the Middle and New Kingdom. As Marcus (2007: 154 n.49) pointed out, however, the only example depicting even a furled sail (no. 13—Wachsmann 1998: 38 fig. 2.60) lacks a secure date. These petroglyphs most likely represent riverine vessels, or perhaps vessels used to cross the Red Sea, from Egypt's Suez coast to the Sinai. Finally, two terracotta and several metal ship models excavated at Byblos were originally regarded as Levantine in origin and design (Dunand 1937: pl. 140, nos. 3306, 6681; 1954: 337-338, nos. 10089-92). Wachsmann, however, argues that one of the terracotta models is of a known New Kingdom Egyptian type (Wachsmann 1998: 52, figs. 3.16-3.17), whereas the second model is similar to Egyptian boats of the Middle Kingdom or the preceding First Intermediate period (Wachsmann 1998: 53-54, fig. 3.19). The best preserved of the metal boats finds its closest parallels in Middle Kingdom Egyptian 'traveling ships' (Wachsmann 1998: 54, 55 fig. 3.21, with further refs.).

Recent excavations at Abydos (2014–2016) have uncovered the remains of a large funerary boat, buried intact within a subterranean vaulted structure and dated to the reign of the Twelfth Dynasty pharaoh Senwosret III (ca. 1889-1836 BC). Incised on the interior walls of this structure is an extensive 'tableau' with up to 120 diverse drawings

Figure 15: *Ship's 'tableau' from MB Abydos.* After Wegner 2017: 19 fig. 11, top. Drawing by Irini Katsouri.

of pharaonic watercraft (Wegner 2017: 18-22, figs. 11-14) (Figure 15). In addition, an extensive deposit of 'necked liquid storage or transport jars' ('beer jars') was found within a trough leading to the boat-building's entrance (Wegner 2017: 23, fig. 15). The morphology of these jars' neck and rims suggests that they are contemporary with the boat building and the incised ships' drawings (Arnold 1988: 140-143).

The cluster of ship drawings on the side and end walls of this building extends over 25 m in length (Wegner 2017: 18-19, figs. 11a-b). In the excavator's view, these images were created over a brief time period by people intent on commemorating a specific event—a royal funerary procession of Senwosret III, whose subterranean tomb lies in an adjacent funerary enclosure (Wegner 2017: 26-28). Some of the vessels depicted have masts, sails, rigging, rudders, oars (in some cases with rowers) and deckhouses or cabins amidships; other boats are depicted more schematically. One distinctive feature of many images is the portrayal of a sailing vessel with mast, as well as the deckhouse amidship.

The main question that arises in the context of the present study is whether these drawings represent exclusively Nile watercraft, or if they might also illustrate seagoing vessels that could have operated in the Mediterranean or on the Red Sea. In earlier studies, a distinction was typically made between the hull remains of seagoing ships vs those used for travel or transport on the Nile (*e.g.* Ward 1963: 44 n. 1; Wachsmann 1998: 215-222). Cheryl Ward (2006; 2010b: 45-46), however, maintains that riverine ships used on the Nile were designed to be disassembled and portaged overland to the Red Sea, where they could be used for seagoing ventures. Specifically, she emphasizes the similarity between (1) the planking of the Middle Kingdom boats from El-Lisht and Dashur and those from First Dynasty Abydos, and (2) the planking of seagoing cedar ships from the Middle Kingdom port at Wadi Gawasis on the Red Sea (Ward 2010b: 43-45; Ward and Zazzaro 2010; Bard and Fattovich 2011: 117-118). Citing also the charred remains of Middle Kingdom ship timbers, planks, fastenings and lashing channels from Ayn Sukhna (Tallet 2012, discussed above, Chapter 3: *Early Bronze Age—The Levant and Egypt, Ports and Harbours*), Ward also contends that the Egyptians of the MB had developed the technology to build and use seagoing ships, *i.e.* for sailing not just on the Nile but also on the open sea, not least in connection with the trade networks of the Red Sea (Moreno García 2017: 98-99). Taking Ward's arguments into account, it seems that at least some of the masted, sailing vessels with deckhouse amidship might represent seagoing vessels that were also used to transport various goods and products to Abydos.

The pottery jars (at least 145 in number) found just outside the entrance to the structure containing the ship representations are bulbous in shape and roughly 45 cm in height; they are clearly intended for storage and/or transport. Found in context with them are some 'decayed' mud jar stoppers. At this point, it may be recalled that over 200 wine jars and 150 wine jar impressions were recovered from Tomb U-j in the Proto-Dynastic cemetery at Abydos (Hartung 2002: 437-443; Watrin 2002: 453-455). Although analytical work (chemical and petrographic) on these vessels proved to be controversial with respect to their origins (*e.g.* McGovern 1998: 31; Porat and Goren 2002), more recent petrographic studies of 20 examples from Cemeteries U and B at Abydos (with a broader database for comparison) indicate that these jars are not of Egyptian origin but more likely come from the region of present-day northern Lebanon (Hartung *et al.* 2015, already noted above, Chapter 3: *Early Bronze Age—The Levant and Egypt, Maritime Transport Containers*).

Despite the distance of Abydos from the sea, then, there is a precedent for a large deposit of (imported) transport containers containing wine or other alcoholic beverages (McGovern *et al.* 2009), arriving in Egypt from the Levantine coast and being deposited in a mortuary context at the same site under discussion here. Even so, beyond their likely storage or transport function, the morphological differences between the earlier 'Abydos Ware' vessels and the 'beer jars' found in the Middle Kingdom contexts under discussion are significant. Moreover, the 'beer jars' do not conform to the criteria established for MTCs (Knapp and Demesticha 2017: 42), particularly given their rounded bases and lack of handles.

In terms of possible function, closed domestic ceramic containers like jars, jugs and amphorae typically have multiple uses: storage, processing and transfer or transport (Orton *et al.* 1993: 217-218; Rice 2015: 412-415, fig. 25.1, table 25.1). As far as the 'necked liquid storage or transport jars' from MB Abydos are concerned, we must await further analyses and research on their origin(s), contents and other, relevant morphological features before deciding upon their possible origin and function. Nonetheless, given the proximity of their findspot, just outside a structure whose walls contained some 120 incised drawings of sailing, masted, pharaonic ships, it may at least be suggested that these jars served transport as well as storage purposes, and that they may have arrived at Abydos on vessels like those depicted in the boat building. Elsewhere, in the Nile Delta, there is no question that maritime transport containers were arriving from the Aegean and the Levant during the Middle Kingdom.

MARITIME TRANSPORT CONTAINERS (MTCS)

As Marcus (2007: 162) states: '… the Middle Minoan imports to 'Ezbet Rushdi [Tell ed-Dabʿa] offer unequivocal evidence for maritime contact', this time in the form of fragmentary oval-mouthed amphorae (OMA). This amphora — a product of Minoan Crete — is one of the earliest Aegean vessel types that may be defined as an MTC: the most common examples have an ovoid or piriform body, a short tapering neck and two thick, wide, strap handles (Knapp and Demesticha 2017: 75-79). OMAs have been found at several sites on the Greek mainland, on the island of Thera and on two Minoan shipwrecks, one off the islet of Pseira in Mirabello Bay (Hadjidaki and Betancourt 2005-06; Bonn-Muller 2010), the other off the Laconian coast in the Peloponnese (Spondylis 2012) (Figure 16). They turn up most prominently on Crete, notably in Quartier Mu at the north coast site of Malia (Poursat and Knappett 2006: 153).

During the early-mid second millennium BC, it is likely that 'Ezbet Rushdi — situated about one km north of the main excavations at Tell ed-Dab'a — served as a Deltaic port for receiving and transhipping foreign goods. At least ten fragments of OMAs —body sherds, handles and a rim — have been recovered from excavations at the site (Czerny 1998: 46, fig. 21). Based on his understanding of the Mit Rahina inscription, part of the court records of the Twelfth Dynasty pharaoh Amenemhet II (ca. 1911-1877 BC), Marcus (2007: 162-164) suggests that containers like the OMA were used for transporting organic goods, liquids, resins and the like — from the Aegean to Egypt. The inscription in question (already discussed in more detail above) records a seaborne, commercial expedition involving two 'transport ships' returning from the central-northern Levant with all manner of goods for redistribution. The OMA is one material indicator of a new and broader economic reorientation to longer distance seaborne trade within the eastern Mediterranean.

Even more representative of such a reorientation are the earliest examples of the Canaanite jar (CJ). These vessels have found by the thousands in Middle Bronze (MB) IIA-IIB levels (ca. 2000-1650 BC) at Tell ed-Dab'a and represent the largest group of imported pottery at the site, between 15-20% of the estimated vessels in the total assemblage (Bietak 1996: 20; Kopetzky 2008; Bader 2011: 139, fig. 1). Provenance studies (Neutron Activation Analysis [NAA] and petrographic analyses) have produced differing results, but all agree that these vessels are Levantine in origin, most likely from the coastal plain of Lebanon (Griffiths 2011-12: 160; see also McGovern and Harbottle 1997; Cohen-Weinberger and Goren 2004).

Figure 16: *Oval-mouthed Amphorae (a) from Pseira (Crete) wreck deposit. (b) from Koulenti wreck deposit in Laconia (Inv. no BE 2009/3-3).* a) After Hadjidaki 2004: 46, fig. 2. Drawing by Irini Katsouri; b) Courtesy of Elias Spondylis. Drawing by Y. Nakas.

0   10 cm

a

BE 2009/3-3

b

Many more examples (mainly sherds) of CJs, dated to the MB IIB/C periods (ca. 1750-1550 BC), derive from other sites in Egypt: Kom Rabia (Memphis) (Bourriau 2010; Ownby 2010: 99, 178; Ownby and Bourriau 2009: 177-181); Khom el-Khigan, a northeastern Delta site near Tell ed-Dabʿa (Ownby 2012: 26); Dashur (Bourriau 1990: 19*, n.7); and Lisht, the capital of Middle Kingdom Egypt (Arnold *et al.* 1995: 14, 27). Ownby (2010: 88-90, fig. 3.39) lists eight sites, from Tell ed-Dabʿa in the north to Buhen in Nubia, that have produced MB Canaanite jar fragments. A range of petrographic studies indicates that most of the CJs found in Egypt and dated to the MB II period stemmed from a network of sites stretching all along the Levantine coast, but perhaps primarily from the north-central Levant (Ownby and Bourriau 2009: 183-184). Finally, we may note that some fragmentary remains of CJs have been identified at Middle Minoan (MM) IIB or early MM IIIA (ca. 1800 BC) Knossos on Crete (MacGillivray 1998: 90), in MB levels at Bellapais *Vounos* and Arpera on Cyprus (Merrillees 1974: 75-76), and at MB Kinet Höyük along the southern Anatolian coast (Akar 2006: 17).

The Canaanite jar is arguably the best known and most widely represented example of an MTC in the Bronze Age Mediterranean. In terms of quantities, even if one reduces Bietak's (1996: 20) inflated estimate of two million examples from Tell ed-Dabʿa by a factor of ten, we are still dealing with thousands of examples from a single site. Despite the ongoing work of scholars such as Pedrazzi (2007, 2016), Killebrew (2007), Ownby (2010), Cateloy (2016) and others, as well as the

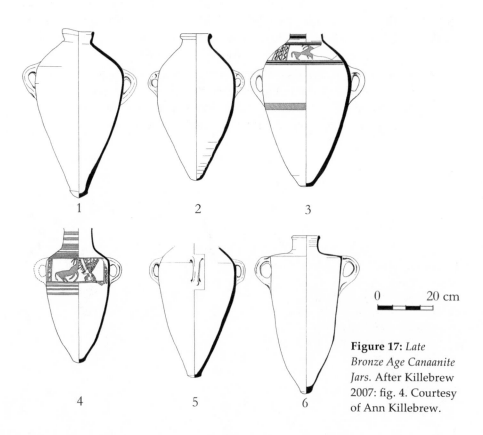

0   20 cm

Figure 17: *Late Bronze Age Canaanite Jars.* After Killebrew 2007: fig. 4. Courtesy of Ann Killebrew.

SEAFARING AND SEAFARERS IN THE BRONZE AGE EASTERN MEDITERRANEAN

work of the Canaanite Amphora Project (http://www.amarnaproject.com/pages/recent_projects/material_culture/canaanite.shtml), it is impossible to quantify the number of CJs found within the Levant, not least because older publications often list only complete examples, while more recent excavations tend to publish only the rims from 'storage jars' (Ownby 2010: 85). A conservative estimate of currently known and reasonably well-published CJs found beyond the Levant and Egypt would be at least 500 vessels, although that number also includes Late Bronze Age examples (Knapp and Demesticha 2017: 65-66) (Figure 17).

Foremost amongst the products that were shipped in these widely circulated jars — with a capacity ranging between about 7-30 litres — are wine, resins and olive (as well as other) oil. Beginning in the Middle Bronze Age with their transport to Egypt, Cyprus, Anatolia and the Aegean, and continuing during subsequent centuries with an even broader pattern of distribution (see further below Chapter 5: *Late Bronze Age, The Levant and Egypt, Maritime Transport Containers*), they became the signature vessel of maritime transport in Mediterranean seaborne trade.

STONE ANCHORS

In Egypt, stone anchors have been recorded in Middle Kingdom contexts in an Upper Egyptian fort at Mirgissa (Nibbi 1992; Basch 1994a) and at Wadi Gawasis on the Red Sea coast (Sayed 1977; Wachsman 1998: 259-262; Zazzaro 2007; Bard and Fattovich 2011: 188 and *passim*). In the Levant, four stone anchors (one-hole, 'weight' anchors) of likely MB date are recorded from the 'Temple of Obelisks' at Byblos (Frost 1969: 428-429; Wachsmann 1998: 271 reports seven anchors from 'in and around' this structure). Brody (1998: 44), in a re-interpretation of Dunand's site plans, suggests that an offering deposit — including ten bronze ship models — was placed very near one of the anchors built into the courtyard surrounding the 'Temple of Obelisks'; he thus views this structure as a 'repository' for maritime offerings. Four additional stone ('weight') anchors come from the 'Sacred Enclosure' at Byblos (Frost 1969: 430-431; Brody 1998: 45, 142 fig. 36). Frost (1991: 366-367) also mentions three 'miniature anchors' (wt: 6-7 kg) of triangular shape from the 'temple area' at Byblos, which may date to the nineteenth century BC.

The stone anchors excavated at Ugarit (Brody 1998: 46-49; Wachsmann 1998: 273) present dating problems, as the excavator assigned the structure in which they were found very generally to the Middle and/or Late Bronze Age (Schaeffer 1978; Courtois 1979: 1195-1197). Even so, he suggested a MB date for all the anchors found within this structure, the 'Temple of Ba'al' (Schaeffer 1978: 375). Frost (1991: 375-380) published a catalogue of anchors from Ugarit; those from in and around the 'Temple of Ba'al' supposedly included five 'wall anchors' (i.e., built into the wall) and eleven others. However, she only catalogued 13 of them, with little further information that might help to refine or secure the dating; she cited Schaeffer's suggestions and noted some parallels from Kition on Cyprus, all of which are Late Bronze Age in date (only one example, no. 9 in her catalogue, was suggested to be possibly of MB date). Brody (1998: 47-48, and n.39, 146 fig. 43) cites twelve 'votive' stone anchors from the 'Temple of Ba'al' but argues that all of them probably came from LB levels; he suggests they may be considered as 'thank-offerings' to the Canaanite storm god (Ba'al Ṣapon).

Two *shfifonim* form part of a tomb construction at the site of Degania 'A' in Israel (Wachsman 1998: 265). Marcus (2006: 188; 2007: 155) also mentions 'at least 26' anchors of 'Byblian' or 'Syrian' type found mainly along the Carmel coast of northern Israel (at Neve Yam, Kfar Samir, Kfar Galim, Megadim, Atlit), which have been assigned a MB IIA date mainly on the grounds of their typology or material (*i.e.* limestone) (Galili 1985; Galili *et al.* 1994). Wachsman (1998: 265-270) also mentions many of these same 'sea anchors' but notes that it is difficult to date or identify them securely.

CYPRUS

SHIPS' REPRESENTATIONS

Basch (1987: 70, 72, fig. 137) suggests that an enigmatic vase from the north coast site of Bellapais *Vounous* (Tomb 64.138) may be the earliest representation of a Cypriot ship (Schaeffer 1936: pl. 22.2) (Figure 18). He dates it to the very end of the Early Cypriot (EC) period, around 2000 BC (see also Frankel 1974: 47). Any Cypriot contact with the surrounding world obviously necessitated watercraft, but it may well be questioned whether the *Vounous* vessel or any of three further ceramic models — dated to the Middle Bronze Age — actually represent ships.

1. Red Polished III ware bowl of unknown provenance (now in the Louvre, no. AO 17521); although badly damaged and largely reconstructed, this could represent a boat (Westerberg 1983: 11, no. 4, fig. 4; Caubet *et al.* 1981: 10, 74 suggest *Vounous* as the possible site of origin). Date: likely Middle Cypriot (MC) or possibly Early Cypriot (EC), in either case early second millennium BC.

VOUNOUS V.T.64-138

Figure 18: *'Boat' model of Early Cypriot date, from Bellapais Vounous (Tomb 64.138).* Courtesy of and with permission of the Department of Antiquities, Cyprus.

SEAFARING AND SEAFARERS IN THE BRONZE AGE EASTERN MEDITERRANEAN

2. White Painted II ware model of unknown provenance (now in the Louvre, no. AM 972), thought to show a boat with rounded hull and projecting stem- and stern-posts, and depicting eight people and two birds atop what might be a ship's railing (Westerberg 1983: 9-10, no.1, fig. 1; Basch 1987: 70-71, figs. 132-135). Date: MC I, ca. 1900/1800 BC (see also Frankel 1974: 46).

3. White Painted IV ware deep bowl — six sherd fragments that join to form three separate pieces — from Politiko *Lambertis* (now in the Cyprus Museum, nos. 1941/III–6/1, 1941/I–18/1), with five people sitting on the edge of what Westerberg (1983: 10, no. 2, fig. 2) suggested might be a ship's hull; atypically these people face outward, and Frankel (1974: 43-47, figs. 1-2, pl. VIII) does not regard this object as a boat model. Date: MC II or MC III (ca. 1800/1700 BC).

4. White Painted IV ware, probable boat model of unknown provenance (now in the British Museum, no. C 261), with rounded hull, depicting one person sitting at the stern (?) and leaning backward (Westerberg 1983: 10, no. 3, fig. 3). Date: MC III, ca. 1700 BC (see also Frankel 1974: 46-47).

MARITIME TRANSPORT CONTAINERS AND OVERSEAS TRADE

In earlier publications that mention MB Canaanite jars (CJs) found on Cyprus, authors typically referred to them as, for example, Syrian (or Levantine) jars, store jars or amphorae (*e.g.* Åström 1965: 120; Merrillees 1974: 47). The most prominent, complete vessel that is clearly a CJ stems from a MC III burial (Tomb 1A) at Arpera *Mosphilos* (Merrillees 1974: 44 fig. 29.5, 47, 54 fig. 35). Crewe (2012: 230-232, fig. 2) identifies six examples of what she terms CJs (or, alternatively, 'Levantine jars') in MC III-Late Cypriot (LC) I tombs across the island; of the six, however, only the jar from Arpera is a true CJ, by any definition (*e.g.* Pedrazzi 2007: *passim*; Knapp and Demesticha 2017: 47-48). Crewe (2012: 232) also claims to have identified at least 26 examples of CJs in MC III or MC III-LC I settlement contexts at Kalopsidha, from the excavations of Gjerstad (1926: 269) and Åström (1966: 9, 76); no examples are illustrated, however, so this identification cannot be confirmed. In any case, most of the examples cited date to the LC I period, and so are not treated here (but see below, Chapter 5: *Late Bronze Age—Cyprus, Maritime Transport Containers*).

Crewe (2012: 237-239; 2015a: 122-124) argues that the Plain White Hand-made *pithoi* of the MC III-LC I period were nearly contemporaneous with the first appearance of the few identifiable CJs found on Cyprus. She asserts that these *pithoi* were intended to emulate the CJ and thus might have represented an 'international shorthand' for transport containers. Thus these *pithoi* may represent a Cypriot attempt to become engaged in the bulk exchange of organic goods and would have 'slotted seamlessly' into the networks of CJs circulating in the eastern Mediterranean. Although Crewe sees these vessels as the local Cypriot counterpart of the Canaanite jar, it must be reiterated that the Plain White Handmade *pithos*, with a wide mouth and broad flat or ring-base, and lacking handles, cannot be classified as a MTC (Knapp and Demsticha 2017: 42; various papers in Demesticha and Knapp 2016).

Even so, there is no question, as Crewe (2012) and others (*e.g.* Knapp 2013b) have demonstrated, that Cyprus increasingly became involved during the MC period in overseas trade, which of necessity involved ships and maritime mobility. Perhaps the best known examples of Cypriot involvement in such trade are the Cretan spouted jar from Tomb 806A at Lapithos (Grace 1940: 24-27, pl. IA) and the Kamares Ware cup from Karmi *Palealona* (Webb *et al.* 2009: 252) (Figure 19); both vessels are of Middle Minoan date. The return trade, such as it was, may be seen in a fragmentary Red Polished III 'amphora' from Knossos (Catling and MacGillivray 1983) and some copper products at Malia argued to be consistent with production from Cypriot ores (Poursat and Loubet 2005: 120). Bassiakos and Tselios (2012) have speculated that the lack of evidence for Aegean copper extraction after about 2000 BC may have stimulated the production of copper for export on Cyprus, and made the island a valuable resource for the Aegean world. To the east, this is also the time (post-1900 BC) that documentary evidence from Mari and Babylon refers to copper imported from *Alašiya* (Knapp 1996: 17-19; 2008: 307-308). If these documents are taken to indicate an increase in foreign demand for Cypriot copper, it is worth noting that this is approximately the same time, around or just after 2000 BC, that tin bronzes reappear on Cyprus (Weinstein Balthazar 1990: 161-162); tin, of course, had to be imported to the island. In turn, this suggests that Cyprus increasingly became involved in whatever system(s) of exchange that brought tin to the island (Yener 2000: 75). Finally, to the south, multiple types and notable amounts of (late) Middle Cypriot pottery have been documented at Tell ed-Dab'a in the Egyptian delta (Maguire 2009).

Turning to other likely imports, Keswani (2005: 388-389, table 13) lists a series of imported or 'foreign-influenced' goods — pottery, gold jewellery, metal objects, weapons and jewellery, faience beads and pendants, horse teeth and bones, alabaster items — from Crete, the Levant, Anatolia and Egypt, all dated to the MC period. Webb (2015: 249; 2016: 62-63, both with further refs.) has observed an increased range of 'exotic' goods in MC tombs at Lapithos, which she believes may well be imports: new pin types (with 'umbrella' or forked heads, splayed centres

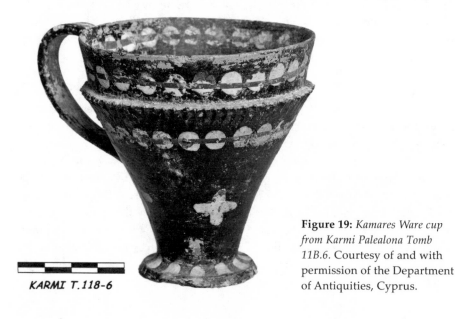

KARMI T.118-6

Figure 19: *Kamares Ware cup from Karmi Palealona Tomb 11B.6.* Courtesy of and with permission of the Department of Antiquities, Cyprus.

and faience inlays); silver or silver-lead rings, earrings, bracelets, diadems and pins; gold spirals and other ornaments; faience necklaces; frog-shaped and bushy-headed globular paste beads (Webb, pers. comm., November 2016; Webb 2017: 133). Moreover, the take-off in metal deposition that can be seen in the Lapithos tombs — reflecting both increased (internal) metal production/consumption and external demand (Keswani 2005: 391; Knapp 2008: 81, 84-87) — is a MC phenomenon, and increases markedly from MC I to MC III. Lapithos, with its coastal location in a protected bay, was well situated to take part in an expanding system of seaborne trade (Webb *et al.* 2009: 251-252; 2013: 65-66; 2017: 132).

Webb and Frankel (2013: 219-221) further suggest that the copper ore used in the intensified metal production at Lapithos most likely arrived at the site via coastal transshipment from various production communities in the northwest Troodos. Crewe (2015b: 145), discussing possible earlier (EC) links between the island's southwest (the region around Kissonerga) and the north coast, also suggests that '… it is possible that coastal traversion [sic] in small boats was extensive'. And Manning (from 1993: 47 through 2014b: 24-25) has long argued that there must have been some key, Philia-phase centre or port, either along the north coast or in the Morphou Bay area. Of course, as long as archaeologists are unable to work in the occupied, northern part of Cyprus, there is little chance of demonstrating the likelihood of such suggestions. Moreover, it remains strictly an assumption that that those who were producing and moving copper and/or other goods during the MC period had ships capable of such transport ventures; the only material evidence that might support such suggestions are the (possible) ship models noted above, none of which seem suitable as vessels for transporting large amounts of ore.

Nearly all the imported objects mentioned above stem from cemeteries along the north coast of Cyprus—Vasilia *Kafkalla*, Bellapais *Vounous*, Lapithos *Vrysi tou Barba* and Karmi *Palealona* (Figure 20). In Keswani's (2005: 387-391) view, the limited number of imports currently identifiable in the material record of the MC I-II periods suggests that the scale of long-distance trade was 'more sporadic than systematic'.

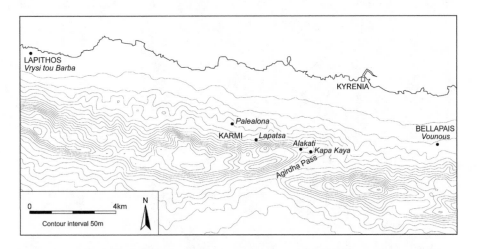

Figure 20: *Early-Middle Bronze Age sites, central north coast, Cyprus.* From Webb et al. 2009: 3 fig. 1.4. Courtesy of Jennifer Webb and David Frankel.

Similarly, Peltenburg (2008: 153) felt that the same evidence for imports, including those from Crete, indicated only a 'passive' involvement of Cypriot communities in long-distance exchange, whilst Kouka (2009a: 40) suggested that the Cretan pottery arrived indirectly, via Minoan outposts in the southeast Aegean. None of these views, of course, were able to take into account Webb's (2015, 2016, 2017) more recent work at Lapithos, which may well change our views on MB Cypriot trade.

Despite all the signs that Cyprus's overseas trade, perhaps especially in the export of copper, was intensifying during the MB, we have no secure evidence to indicate the means by which such materials may have been shipped by sea. Although the evidence increases dramatically in the subsequent, Late Bronze Age (see already Knapp 2014, and below, Chapter 5: *Late Bronze Age—Cyprus*), there are no shipwrecks associated with the island until the late Classical and early Hellenistic periods (Steffy 1985; Demesticha *et al.* 2014).

ANATOLIA

SHIPWRECKS AND STONE ANCHORS

At Sheytan Deresi, some 25 km east of Bodrum, on Turkey's southwest coast, the cargo of a late Middle or early Late Bronze Age (ca. 1600 BC) wreck has been excavated (Bass 1976; Margariti 1998; Catsambis 2008). The cargo, found some 100 m offshore, included some possible maritime transport containers, which are discussed further below. Based on his detailed study of the pottery from Sheytan Deresi, Catsambis (2008: 85) concluded that the ship itself was '... a fairly small Middle Bronze Age coastal trading vessel that capsized rounding a dangerous cape, not far from its point of origin'. There is little else that can be said about this particular wreck deposit. Another, new shipwreck dated to the early second millennium BC has been reported from Hisarönü, near Bodrum, but thus far has only been mentioned in the Turkish news (e.g. http://www.hurriyetdailynews.com/archaeologists-find-bronze-age-shipwreck-off-turkeys-southwest-94665/ ; Michele Massa, pers. comm., 7 December 2017). No

Figure 21: *Stone anchors of uncertain date, Museum of Underwater Archaeology, Bodrum, Turkey.* From http://gardendaily. blogspot.com. cy/2013_10_01_ar-chive.html.

other Middle Bronze shipwrecks or ship representations are known from the eastern Mediterranean. Wachsmann (1998: 274) notes that there are some (unpublished) stone composite- and weight-anchors of uncertain date exhibited in the Museum of Underwater Archaeology at Bodrum, Turkey (Figure 21).

PORTS AND HARBOURS

The Bronze Age settlement at Liman Tepe (Bay of İzmir, west central Anatolia) continued to be an important regional centre during the Middle Bronze Age. Although Liman Tepe is well situated to serve as a harbour or anchorage, there is no physical evidence for a Bronze Age harbour at the site. The MB site at Çeşme-Bağlararası (already noted above: *Early Bronze Age: Anatolia, Ports and Harbours*) became an important hub of interaction with the Aegean world, as evidenced by finds of Minoan or Minoanizing pottery and some Minoan loomweights (Şahoğlu 2007; 2015: 599-605, figs. 12-13, 17). Another likely harbour site — Maydos Kilisetepe, on the European side of the Dardenelles, with cultural levels reportedly dating from the Chalcolithic period onward, has been excavated in recent years, but the extent of its Bronze Age remains is not yet clear (for now, see Sazcı 2013). Finally, a 'Hittite port' at Kinet Höyük, in a well-protected corner of the Bay of Iskenderun, may have been operational by the end of the MB (Gates 2013). Excavations there uncovered two types of Canaanite jars, one dated to Middle Bronze III, as well as an array of Cypriot imports dating from the very end of the Middle Cypriot or early in the Late Cypriot period, *i.e.* MC III-LC I (Gates 2013: 227, figs. 7-8, 229-232 figs. 15-16, 234 n.2). Thus far, however, no physical remains of a harbour have been identified. Inland from the Cilician coast, at Kilise Tepe, bones of two types of fish (shark, and *capoeta*, the latter a freshwater fish) have been identified in MB levels (Van Neer and Waelkens 2007: 608 table 41).

MARITIME TRANSPORT CONTAINERS

It is possible that three 'piriform amphorae' from the Sheytan Deresi ship's cargo may have served as MTCs (Catsambis 2008: 21-25, figs. 9-11). Some possible parallels from Anatolia, the Aegean, mainland Greece and, especially, Crete have been noted, but the lack of strong similarities in shape and fabric may indicate the local (*i.e.* southwest Anatolia) nature of the cargo (Catsambis 2008: 51-42, 77). Petrographic analyses (conducted by Yuval Goren) on examples of all vessel types from the wreck deposit indicate a generally homogenous group (of uncertain origin), suggesting they belong to a single shipwreck event (Catsambis 2008: 61). Neutron Activation Analysis (NAA) on a subset of the Sheytan Deresi vessels, including one of the 'piriform amphorae', were inconclusive but did not contradict the petrographic analyses. Although Catsambis (2008: 77-78) is cautious, he points out that the narrow bases and restricted mouths of the 'piriform amphorae', as well as the bases and 'strap-handles' of some *pithoi* from the wreck deposit, would have made them suitable for transport, and may well link them to maritime trade. His summary statement thus seems most appropriate (Catsambis 2008: 11): 'Being coarse, utilitarian vessels, the main assemblage of pottery may have served as merchandise containers and/or constituted local trade items themselves, while some may have held the crew's food and drink supply'.

Two further vessels, termed 'small jugs' (Catsambis 2008: 19-20, figs. 7-8), resemble — in fabric, profile and size — the larger-sized examples of 'southwest Anatolian reddish-brown burnished jugs' from Late Bronze Age Kommos (Crete) but do not have the lug or handle on the lower body. Rutter (2006: 139-144, 148-149) has argued convincingly that these 'reddish-brown burnished' jugs could be of Anatolian origin, specifically from the southwestern coastal area between the Gulfs of İzmir and Kerme, *i.e.* the very area of the Sheytan Deresi wreck deposit. Less convincing are his arguments that this type of vessel functioned as a MTC and could have served to transport organic goods, perhaps wine, from Anatolia to Minoan Crete (Rutter 2006: 142-143, 149; see also Catsambis 2008: 76; *cf.* Knapp and Demesticha 2017: 96-98). In any case, the two 'small jugs' from the Sheytan Deresi cargo have been dated provisionally to the end of the Middle Bronze Age and thus are much earlier than the Kommos examples (Rutter 2006: 149; Bass 1976: 298-299).

CHAPTER 5

LATE BRONZE AGE

THE DOCUMENTARY RECORD

In the chapters on the Early and Middle Bronze Ages, I prefaced presentation of the material record with brief summaries of the most relevant, contemporary textual evidence on seafaring and seafarers. For the Late Bronze Age (LB), however, the documentary record demands a separate section of its own: the evidence is much more extensive, complex and controversial, especially the large corpus of cuneiform texts from Ugarit, in particular with respect to the reading(s) of those written in the alphabetic cuneiform of Ugarit.

In a series of studies, Linder (1970, 1973, 1981) discussed his — at times, somewhat inflated — interpretation of all the then-available texts from Ugarit that treated maritime matters: ships and shipping, merchants (royal, private) and trade. Wachsmann (1998: 39-41) presented a brief, general treatment of a range of Egyptian, Ugaritic and Akkadian texts that deal with 'Syro-Canaanite' ships; in the same volume Hoftijzer and van Soldt (1998: 333-344) provided translations and extensive philological commentary on both Ugaritic and Akkadian texts from Ugarit that pertain to seafaring, ships and merchants. Singer's (1999) 'political history of Ugarit' includes several sections in which he offered his own, invaluable views on various maritime matters mentioned in that site's documentary record: international trade, economic relations with Egypt, Cyprus, the Aegean and other Canaanite ports and polities, grain shipments, seaborne raids, and more.

Sauvage's (2012) volume on maritime routes and international trade in the LBA considers several matters also treated in the present study: ships and sea routes, commercial goods and ship's cargoes, coastal ports and (natural) harbours, economic systems and international relations, piracy, and more (see also Yon 2016). Like Sauvage's work, Monroe's (2009) epic study of 'trade and transformation' in the Late Bronze Age eastern Mediterranean is a revised PhD thesis, essentially what it takes to tackle these topics meaningfully. Monroe engaged a wide range of Ugaritic, Akkadian, Hittite, Egyptian and biblical texts to discuss maritime matters as diverse as trade models and economic motivations, shipwrecks, ship cargoes and traded goods, ships' capacities and equipment, terms for ships, ownership and control of ships (*e.g.* owners vs merchants vs rulers), trader-state relations, maritime finance and maritime law, the enthnicity of trade, and above all the role of merchants in seaborne trade in the Late Bronze Age eastern Mediterranean.

All this only scratches the surface of a much greater range of secondary literature that treats in a more limited or circumscribed manner the documentary evidence related to ships, seafaring and seafarers. This body of material includes further works by Monroe himself (2007, 2010, 2015, 2016) as well as others by Artzy (1985, 1987, 1988, 1997, 2003), Singer (2006, 2013), Gestoso Singer (2010), Sauvage (2005, 2011; Sauvage and Pardee 2015), Yon (2016; Yon and Sauvage 2015), and the extensive documentary evidence related to 'piracy' and 'pirates' already presented above (Chapter 2: *Maritime Matters and Materials—Social Aspects*).

There is no straightforward way to present a concise and coherent interpretation of all this material. For one thing, translations of certain Ugaritic and even some Akkadian texts differ significantly amongst scholars; even philological interpretations can be difficult. The types of formulaic, abbreviated and often broken or missing texts or entire passages that characterise these tablets (in which *hapax legomena* are not infrequent, especially in the Ugaritic documents) force philologists, translators or would-be interpreters to infer or restore missing content or context, which often results in cases of special pleading or of historical scenarios that are controversial if not contradictory.

Taking such factors into account, what follows is an attempt to list and discuss a range of the more relevant texts that treat the issues with which this study is concerned: ships and their cargoes; merchants and mariners, ports and harbours, and seafaring more generally. The intention is not to be exhaustive but rather representative, *i.e.* to indicate the variety and diversity of the relevant documentary evidence (see Tables 1-4, below). I repeatedly call upon many of the works listed above (especially Monroe 2009), without which this summary of maritime matters in the LB texts simply could never have been written.

SHIPS AND CARGOES

> *I built ships. I loaded soldiers onto the ships, I approached the land of Mukiš by sea, and I reached dry land in front of Mount Hazzi. I moved inland, and when my land heard about me, they brought oxen and sheep to me. In one day, as one man, the lands of Niya, Ama'e, (and) Mukiš and the city of Alalah, my city, turned to me* (Electronic Idrimi — http://oracc.museum.upenn.edu/aemw/alalakh/idrimi/).

The statue of Idrimi (Figure 22), inscribed in Akkadian with an account of his life and achievements, informs us that after a seven-year stretch (exile?) living amongst the Ḫabiru in *Ammiya* (mountains above Byblos), and prior to ascending the throne at Alalakh (ca. 1450 BC), he built some ships for a nautical invasion of the land of Mukish (on the date, see Carre Gates 1981; Dietrich and Loretz 1981; Oller 1989: 412). As is apparent in much of the documentary record of the Levantine Late Bronze Age, naval battles and hostile coastal raids are not uncommon.

One of the earliest textual references to the types of goods traded during the LB is a stele commemorating the pharaoh Kamose's victory over the Hyksos (Canaanite)

Figure 22: *Statue of Idrimi, king of Alalakh in the fifteenth century BC. The front is inscribed (in Akkadian) with the account of Idrimi's life and achievements, including the building of ships for a naval raid on the land of Mukish. Height: 104.14cm; width: 48.26cm; Diameter: 59.69cm.* From Tell Atchana/Alalakh. British Museum, registration number 1939,0613.101. Jononmac46 / Wikimedia Commons.

rulers of Avaris (Seventeenth Dynasty, ca. 1600 BC) (see Table 1 below, for list of Egyptian texts discussed here). Kamose mentions the plunder taken from ships docked at this port complex: gold, lapis lazuli, silver, turquoise, metal weapons and a range of organic goods (*moringa* oil, incense, fat, honey and various types of wood), all produced in *Retenu, i.e.* the southern Levant (Habachi 1972; Redford 1997: 14). Tuthmosis III boasts in the annals of his fifth campaign to the Levant (Year 29 of his reign, ca. 1498-1474 BC) that he seized two ships, laden with male and female slaves, copper, lead, emery (?) and 'every good thing' (Breasted 1906.2: §§454-62). In the annals of his ninth campaign, Tuthmosis III relates how he supplied various ports he had captured with 'every good thing', this time including cedar ships from *Keftiu* (Crete), *Kpn* (Byblos) and *Sktw*, which were perhaps commercial carriers (Breasted 1906.2: §492). The dockyard annals of Tuthmosis III also mention these same three classes of (presumably) seagoing vessels, undergoing repair or being built in the Nile River harbour at Perunefer (*Prw nfr*) (Glanville 1931: 116, 121). Whereas the names of these ships may suggest their foreign origin (Glanville 1932: 22 n.56, 36; von Rüden 2015: 39), Säve-Söderbergh (1946: 43-45, 47) regarded them as Egyptian-built seagoing vessels, whilst Wachsmann (1998: 51-52) considered them to be 'Syro-Canaanite' ships.

In writing about an assumed 'Canaanite thalassocracy', Linder (1981: 40) argued that two Ugaritic texts (UT 319–KTU 4.81; UT 2085–KTU 4.366) represent a Canaanite 'catalogue of ships' whose crews included seafarers both skilled (captains, sailors, shipwrights) and unskilled (rowers, warriors) (Herdner 1963: 173-174; Virolleaud 1965: 109-110) (see Table 2 for list of Ugaritic texts discussed here). To these documents Linder also added (1) UT 2062 (KTU 2.47), a request from one Yadinu to the king of Ugarit for 150 ships (Virolleaud 1965: 88-89), and (2) a fragmentary Hittite document (Bo 2810) that mentions a grain-laden ship (but probably not the 'hundred ships' that Linder mentions—Singer 1999: 717-718, n. 385) (see Table 3 for list of Hittite texts). A very fragmentary Akkadian text from Ugarit also mentions 30 ships (RS 20.141b–Nougayrol *et al.* 1968: 107-108, no. 34) (see Table 4 for list of Akkadian texts). In another Akkadian letter, the king of Ugarit writes to an unnamed king of *Alašiya* (Cyprus), stating that his navy (and army) were engaged in the *Lukka*-land, and that seven 'enemy' ships had arrived in Ugarit, wreaking havoc in the town and countryside (RS 20.238—Nougayrol *et al.* 1968: 87-89, no. 24).

Text nos./name	Findspot	Subject	References
Kamose Second Stele	Karnak	Plunder of ships at Avaris	Habachi 1972
Tuthmosis III Annals-Yr. 5 campaign	Karnak	Seizing 2 Levantine ships	Breasted 1906.2: §§454-62
Tuthmosis III-Yr. 9	Karnak	Keftiu, Kpn, Sktw ships	Breasted 1906.2: §492
Tuthmosis III 'Dockyard Annals'		Keftiu, Kpn, Sktw ships	Glanville 1931: 116, 121

Table 1: *Ships and Seafaring in Egyptian Texts.*

Text nos.	Findspot	Subject	References
KTU 2.38–RS 18.031	Ugarit-palace (tablet kiln)	Royal Ugarit ship wrecked	Virolleaud 1965: 81-83
KTU 2.42+2.43–RS 18.113A+B	Ugarit-palace room 77	Alašiyan merchant at Ugarit to buy ships	Virolleaud 1965: 14-15; Knapp 1983
KTU 2.47–RS 18.148	Ugarit-palace (tablet kiln)	Yadinu requests 150 ships	Virolleaud 1965: 88-89
KTU 4.40–RS 8.279	Ugarit-lower city	list of seamen	Herdner 1963: 167-168
KTU 4.81–RS 11.779	Ugarit-palace	'catalogue of ships' in Maḥadu, with owners	Herdner 1963: 173-74; Linder 1981: 40
KTU 4.102–RS 11.857	Ugarit-palace entrance	list of Alašiya families	Herdner 1963: 168-169
KTU 4.125–RS 14.001	Ugarit-palace east archive	ships built at Ugarit?	Virolleaud 1957: 66-68
KTU 4.132–RS 15.004	Ugarit-palace east archive	Tyrian textiles imported to Ugarit	Virolleaud 1957: 144
KTU 4.149–RS 15.039	Ugarit-palace east archive	wine deliveries to a Hittite and an Alašiyan	Virolleaud 1957: 114-115; Monroe 2016: 83
KTU 4.247–RS 16.399	Ugarit-palace central archive	admin. list including 15 squid, 2000 sardines	Virolleaud 1957: 162-63
KTU 4.263–RS 17.049	Ugarit-palace east archive	list of *mkrm* (merchants)	Virolleaud 1957: 84
KTU 4.337– RS 18.024	Ugarit-palace (tablet kiln)	Ugarit supplies copper and tin to Beirut	Virolleaud 1965: 124-126
KTU 4.338–RS 18.025	Ugarit-palace (tablet kiln)	Byblos king sells/leases ships to Ugarit	Virolleaud 1965: 129-130; Monroe 2009: 110-115
KTU 4.352–RS 18.042	Ugarit-palace (tablet kiln)	oil for Abiramu, the Alašiyan	Virolleaud 1965: 117-118
KTU 4.366–RS 18.07	Ugarit-palace (tablet kiln)	'catalogue of ships'	Virolleaud 1965: 109-110
KTU 4.390–RS 18.119	Ugarit-palace	Alašiya ship inventory	Virolleaud 1965: 74; Knapp 1983
KTU 4.394–RS 18.132	Ugarit-palace (tablet kiln)	copper cargo lost at sea	Virolleaud 1965: 110
KTU 4.421–RS 18.291	Ugarit-palace debris	royal ships, *br* ship	Virolleaud 1965: 75
KTU 4.647–RS 19.126	Ugarit-south palace	Ugarit ship-captain/owner	Virolleaud 1965: 146

Table 2: *Ships and Seafaring in Ugaritic Texts (Ugarit).*

SEAFARING AND SEAFARERS IN THE BRONZE AGE EASTERN MEDITERRANEAN

Text nos./name	Findspot	Subject	References
Bo 2810	Boğazköy	grain-laden ship	Klengel 1974: 170-74
KBo 12.38	Boğazköy	Hittite fleet (?) vs. Alašiya	Otten 1963; Güterbock 1967
KUB 56.15	Boğazköy	Puduhepa's ritual by sea, at Izziya	de Roos 2007: 240-43; Gates 2013: 232, 234 n.4

Table 3: *Ships and Seafaring in Hittite Texts.*

Text nos.	Findspot	Subject	References
RS 16.126B+257+258	Ugarit	merchant representatives	Nougayrol 1955: 199-203
RS 16.238+254	Ugarit palace	Şinaranu–tax-free goods from Kabduri (Crete)	Nougayrol 1955: 107-108
RS 16.386	Ugarit palace	two Ugaritic merchants granted tax-free status	Nougayrol 1955: 165-166
RS 17.039 (424C+397B)	Ugarit	'harbour master'	Nougayrol 1956: 219-220
RS 17.130	Ugarit	merchants of Ura	Nougayrol 1956: 103-105
RS 17.133	Ugarit palace– south archive	ship wrecked in harbour; 'chief mariner'	Nougayrol 1956: 118-119
RS 17.146	Ugarit	royal merchants	Nougayrol 1956: 154-157
RS 17.341	Ugarit	Ugarit and Beirut relations	Nougayrol 1956: 161-163
RS 17.424C+397B	Ugarit	Tyre complaint *re* high Ugaritic custom taxes	Nougayrol 1956: 219
RS 17.465	Ugarit-Rašap-abu archive	'harbour master'	Nougayrol et al. 1968: 20-21, no. 13
RS 19.028	Ugarit	shipment of clothing and textiles: Ugarit to Byblos	Nougayrol 1970: 100, no. 126
RS 20.141b	Ugarit	30 ships	Nougayrol et al. 1968: 107-108, no. 34
RS 20.168	Ugarit–House of Rapanu	Ugarit and Alašiya oil shipment	Nougayrol et al. 1968: 80-83, no. 21
RS 20.212	Ugarit	large boat + crew to ship grain to Ura in Cilicia	Nougayrol et al. 1968: 105-107, no.33
RS 20.238	Ugarit	Ugarit and Alašiya; navy of Ugarit in Lukka land	Nougayrol et al. 1968: 87-89, no. 24
RS 26.158	Ugarit	boats, grain to Ura	Nougayrol et al. 1968: 323-324, no. 171
RS 34.145	Ugarit–bibliothè-que sud	Ugarit ships not to travel beyond Byblos, Sidon	Bordreuil 1991: 32-34, no.9
RS 34.147	Ugarit–bibliothè-que sud	14 Carchemish ships at Ugarit	Bordreuil 1991: 23-25, no. 5
RS 34.167+	Ugarit	Exchange of goods–Ugarit and Tyre	Bordreuil 1991: 57-61, no. 25
RS 94.2483	Ugarit–House of Urtenu	Ugaritic emissary to Tyre to check on royal ship	Lackenbacher & Malbran-Labat 2016: 109-110
RS 94.2523, RS 94.2530	Ugarit–House of Urtenu	King of Ugarit fails to send ships to Lukka	Lackenbacher & Malbran-Labat 2016: 25-30
BM 130739 (1939,0613.101)	Alalakh	Idrimi built ships to raid Mukish	Dietrich & Loretz 1981

Table 4: *Ships and Seafaring in Akkadian Texts.*

An Akkadian text found in Ugarit's 'bibliothèque sud' lists 14 unseaworthy ships of the king of Carchemish harboured in the port at Ugarit (RS 34.147—Bordreuil 1991: 23-25, no. 5). Another Akkadian letter from the same locus, sent from the king of Carchemish (as vassal and regional representative of the Hittite king) to the queen of Ugarit, indicates she should not allow her ships to sail any farther than Byblos and Sidon, *i.e.* not as far as Egypt (RS 34.145—Bordreuil 1991: 32-34, no. 9). The Hittites seem concerned to maintain a fleet of ships at Ugarit (Singer 2000: 22), perhaps because as a land-locked power they may not have had their own navy. In that respect, however, it may be added that in a Hittite document from Hattuša, the Hittite king Šuppiluliuma II states that '...the ships of *Alašiya* met me in battle three times' (KBo XII 38—Otten 1963; Güterbock 1967). At the very least, this document indicates that the Hittites either had or could commandeer a fleet of ships, like that known from Ugarit, and that both they and the state of *Alašiya* (Cyprus) had warships ('long boats'?) in their fleets.

In a related matter, in two Akkadian letters from Ugarit, the Hittite king (Šuppiluliuma II?) and an official (Penti-Šarruma) reprimand king 'Ammurapi of Ugarit for failing to send his ships to the *Hiyawa*-men who awaited them in the *Lukka*-land (RS 94.2523, RS 94.2530—Lackenbacher and Malbran-Labat 2005: 237-238; 2016: 25-31; see also Singer 2006: 251-258). Following Vita (1995: 159, n.2), others have suggested that Ugarit never possessed a military fleet and instead used commercial vessels in times of trouble. Given therefore the strategic commercial and military importance of Ugarit's fleet, Singer (1999: 659) observed that '... the Hittites insisted upon keeping a careful eye upon the movements of Ugarit's ships'. Emanuel (2016: 268) recently suggested that Ugarit might well have had a small military fleet used to defend its port(s) and coastal waters, and/or to escort merchantmen carrying valuable shipments to foreign ports.

Another possible motive for the Hittites to perpetuate a fleet in Ugarit is seen in an Akkadian royal letter, wherein the Hittite king charges the king of Ugarit with failing to provide a large ship and crew to transport 2000 measures of grain from Mukish (north Syria) to Ura (Cilicia) (RS 20.212—Nougayrol *et al.* 1968: 105-107, no. 33). Another very fragmentary Akkadian letter also mentions boats and grain for Ura (in Cilicia) but the context is unclear (RS 26.158—Nougayrol *et al.* 1968: 323-324, no. 171). Knapp and Manning (2016: 120-122) recently discussed several other passages from Ugaritic, Akkadian and Hittite texts related to grain shipments or a grain shortage, and there is no point in repeating them here (see also Singer 1999: 715-719).

One of the two 'catalogues' of ships (KTU 4.366) lists the owners of 11 *tkt* ('light') ships, whilst the other (KTU 4.81) records 12 *br* ('heavy') ships and four *tkt* ships in the harbour of Maḫadu (Minet el-Beidha—see below, *The Levant and Egypt, Ports and Harbours*). A royal ship and three *br* ships are listed in another, very brief and fragmentary Ugaritic text (KTU 4.421—Virolleaud 1965: 75). Linder (1970: 97-98) suggested that the *br* ship was a seagoing merchant vessel, the *tkt* a troop carrier (similarly, Xella 1982: 32-33); the *br* has also been defined as a 'barge' and *tkt* as 'type of boat' (del Olmo Lette and Sanmartin 2003: 236, 904). KTU 4.81 also names five men, who were probably the owners or captains of the ships. In line 2, we find a man named *Tptbʻl* (Shipti-baʻal) recorded beside a heavy ship. A person with the same name is listed in another text (KTU 4.102—Herdner 1963: 168-169; Vita 1997), a register of families who were somehow associated with *Alašiya* (Cyprus) but who lived in Ugarit (perhaps in a 'Cypriot quarter' of town—Monroe 2009: 247); these *Alašiyans* were engaged in many different occupations, including foreign exchange and purchases of wine and other commodities.

From the palace at Ugarit comes an inventory list of a ship from *Alašiya* in Atalligu (a harbour of Ugarit?) (KTU 4.390—Virolleaud 1965: 74). The list includes copper (or bronze?), various types of metal tools and *irgmn*, which may refer to 'purple dye' (van Soldt 1990: 344 n. 164; McGeough 2015: 90). It has been observed that this list of goods, sent from Cyprus to Ugarit, is not unlike the finds from the Cape Gelidonya shipwreck (Linder 1981: 37; Knapp 1983: 43). One small tablet from Ugarit notes the loss at sea ('aboard ship') of an allotment of copper, but its origin is not indicated (KTU 4. 394—Virolleaud 1965: 110). Another text from the palace (tablet kiln) noting likely traded goods lists 660 [jars] of oil for Abiramu the *Alašiyan*, 300 [jars] of oil for Abiramu the 'Egyptian', and a further 448 [jars of oil] for others (KTU 4.352—Virolleaud 1965: 117-118). Niqmaddu III, the last king of Ugarit during troubled times, sent a rather prosaic letter (in Akkadian) to the king of *Alašiya* concerning a shipment of oil for which the price was disputed (RS 20.168—Nougayrol *et al.* 1968: 80-83 no. 21, 695). We might also note here an administrative document listing wine deliveries to various people associated with the palace, including one jar for the Hittite at Maḥadu (Minet el-Beidha) and 'two jars as a gift' (*kdm mtḥ*) for the *Alašiyan* (KTU .149—Virollaud 1957: 114-115; Monroe 2016: 83).

Several documents from Ugarit, as well as the Amarna tablets, are concerned to varying extents with maritime cargoes (Monroe 2009: 75-80). The items of cargo cover a very wide spectrum, including but not limited to grain, wine, salt, oil and perfumed oil, metals (gold, silver, copper, tin), textiles, linen, wool (some purple-dyed), various types of wood (ebony, olive, boxwood), incense (myrrh), animals (horses, oxen), chariots, lapis lazuli and other precious stones, jewellery, ivory, glass, stone, and a range of organic goods and containers far too numerous to list here (but see Knapp 1991). In Ugaritic letter KTU 2.38 (Virolleaud 1965: 81-83), the king of Tyre writes to inform the king of Ugarit (neither king is named) that his ship (ships?—see Singer 1999: 672; Pardee 2003: 93-94; Monroe 2009: 98), which had been dispatched to Egypt, was/were wrecked in a bad storm near Tyre, and that the *rb tmtt* (a 'master of salvage'?) had been able to retrieve the grain cargo. The king of Tyre then took over, kept the grain (and some food/belongings?) and returned it all (to the crew?) (see discussions by Singer 1999: 672-673; Monroe 2009: 99). Finally, the king noted that the wrecked ship was now moored in Akko, 'stripped' (of its rigging?) or 'unloaded'. Vita (2017) has suggested that a newly published Akkadian letter sent from the king of Ugarit to the king of Sidon may refer to one outcome of this disaster (RS 94.2483—Lackenbacher and Malbran-Labat 2016: 109-110). In this letter, the king of Ugarit informed his Sidonian counterpart that he had sent an emissary to Tyre to check on a royal ship, and decided that the ship's captain should take charge of both the ship and its cargo; he then asked the Sidonian king for logistical support during his ships' journeys. As Vita (2017: 70) observes, both letters indicate that Ugarit maintained close diplomatic and economic relations with other kingdoms at Levantine ports farther south along the coast.

Such relations also seem evident in text KTU 4.338 (RS 18.025) which, despite the ambiguities in understanding the Ugaritic, most likely points to the sale or leasing of ships by the king of Byblos to Ugarit (Virolleaud 1965: 129-130, no. 106; Pardee 1975; for full discussion of variant translations and commentaries, see Monroe 2009: 110-115). If nothing else, this text points to close commercial ties between the two polities and suggests that Byblos also had a significant commercial fleet at its disposal (Vidal 2005: 295).

It is likely that some ships were built at Ugarit itself (*ḥrš anyt*; see KTU 4.125– RS 14.001). Both royal ships and privately-owned boats are documented at the site: KTU 4.421 (discussed above) mentions a 'ship of the king' (*anyt.mlk*) as well as three *br* boats, whilst KTU 2.38 (also noted above) refers to a royal ship wrecked near Tyre. By contrast, KTU 4.366 and KTU 4.81 (both discussed above) refer to private vessels, as does RS 17.133, discussed below; see also Sasson 1966: 134, 137; Monroe 2009: 94-97). KTU 4.647 (RS 19.126) also lists private persons who owned or chartered (mainly *br*) boats, including a man named *Prkl*, the 'captain of a ship' (*bʿl any*) owned by another man, *Abr*[m] (Virolleaud 1965: 146; Monroe 2009: 95, 160). Finally, as also noted above, the Canaanite 'catalogue of ships' (KTU 4.81, KTU 4.366), Yadinu's request to the king of Ugarit for 150 ships (KTU 2.47), and the Akkadian text (RS 20.238) mentioning that the royal ships of Ugarit were engaged in or against the *Lukka*-lands, all suggest that a substantial maritime fleet — commericial, military or otherwise — anchored in or otherwise used the harbours at Ugarit.

Commercial relationships amongst the seaports at Byblos, Sidon, Tyre, Beirut and Ugarit are well documented in the archives at Ugarit (Liverani 1979b: 1329-1331; Vidal 2005: 295). For example, RS 34.145 (discussed above) demonstrates that Ugaritic ships travelled to Byblos and Sidon (see also Belmonte 2002), whilst KTU 2.38 indicates that the king of Tyre assisted in the salvage of a royal ship wrecked near Tyre; in the recently published Akkadian text (RS 94.2483—Lackenbacher and Malbran-Labat 2016: 109-110), the king of Sidon is informed by his Ugaritic fellow-king that the latter had dispatched an emissary to Tyre to check on a royal ship, perhaps this very one. The Akkadian text RS 19.028 (Nougayrol 1970: 100) records a shipment of clothing and textiles (related to ship's sails?) from Ugarit to Byblos. In RS 17.424C+397B (Nougayrol 1956: 219), the king of Tyre complained to the *šākinu* ('prefect') of Ugarit about the high customs taxes his agents had to pay to Ugarit's harbour master (Arnaud 1996: 63 n.94 for the reading of [URU]*Ṣur*[KI] = Tyre). RS 34.167+175 (Bordreuil 1991: 57-61) registers the request of Aḫi-Milku of (the 'cape' of) Tyre for a shipment from Ugarit of 50 jars of (oil?), 30 silver shekels and one talent of copper; he proposed to send in return Tyrian purple-dyed wool and dried fish. Imports of Tyrian textiles to Ugarit is also attested in KTU 4.132 (RS 15.004) (Virolleaud 1957: 144; Vidal 2005: 295).

The only indisputable indicator of commercial relationships between Beirut and Ugarit is recorded in KTU 4.337 (RS 18.024—Virolleaud 1965: 124-126; Márquez Rowe 1992: 259-260), when Ugarit supplied copper and tin to the more southerly port. Another (Akkadian) text from Ugarit was initially interpreted as indicating a commercial conflict between Ugarit and its close neighbour Siyannu concerning a trade in 'wine' that also involved Beirut (RS 17.341—Nougayrol 1956: 161-163). Although this interpretation was long accepted (*e.g.* Singer 1999: 663 n.189, 669), the preferred reading of the logogram in question is no longer 'wine' but 'food and drink, supplies', which alters the earlier interpretation. The text is now understood to refer not to any supposed commercial 'war' over wine but rather to a diplomatic accusation by Ugarit against Siyannu for selling 'supplies' to individuals from Beirut (see Vidal 2005: 295-296 for discussion and further references).

One ship, belonging to a 'man of the land of Ugarit' (*i.e.* not the king), was wrecked at an unspecified port, possibly Minet el-Beidha, and evidently not by accident. In this Akkadian royal letter (RS 17.133—Nougayrol 1956: 118-119), the Hittite ruler (Queen Puduhepa?) decreed to Ammistamru II, king of Ugarit, that if the 'chief mariner' swore (an oath) confirming the wreckage of the ship and the loss of its cargo, then a man named Šukku, charged with the offence, would have to reimburse the owner for damages. Given that both the Hittite ruler and the king of Ugarit were involved, this must have been more than a local matter and one that involved a considerable amount of capital (Monroe 2009: 76, 179-180; see also Linder 1970: 49-50; Singer 1999: 661).

The Akkadian letters from Amarna (Moran 1992) also mention various types of ships and merchants involved in diverse maritime affairs. Most of these texts have been discussed in detail above (Chapter 2: *Maritime Matters and Materials—Social Aspects, Merchants, Mariners and Pirates*), and thus are listed here only in summary fashion.

- EA 39-40: two letters indicating that the king of *Alašiya* owned merchant ships (Moran 1992: 112-113). EA 39 states specifically that the *Alašiyan* king's own merchants were in Egypt, and that no claim should be made against them or the king's ship.
- EA 98, 101, 105, 149: letters that mention the men and ships of *Arwada*, the latter used to intercept other vessels at sea, to cut off maritime communications and to seize or blockade ports. In EA 98, the ships controlled or blockaded two ports to prevent the delivery of grain to Ṣumur. In EA 101, an unnamed writer (Rib-Adda?) asked the Egyptian pharaoh to seize the ships of *Arwada* to prevent them from attacking Byblos. In EA 105, the ships of *Arwada* intercepted three ships from Byblos at sea (Moran 1992: 171, 177-179). In EA 149, the men of *Arwada* assembled their ships and chariots for an attack upon Tyre (Moran 1992: 236-237).
- EA 113-114: Rib-Adda of Byblos informed pharaoh that his ships have been seized at sea, perhaps by a coalition involving Amurru, Tyre, Sidon and Beirut (Moran 1992: 188-189).
- EA 245: letter of Biridiya of Megiddo, in which a man named Surata captured Lab'ayu (of Megiddo) and intended to send him to Egypt 'in the hold of a ship' (Moran 1992: 299-300; Monroe 2009: 89).

The Amarna letters demonstrate that some Levantine coastal polities — Arwad, Byblos, Sidon, Tyre and Beirut amongst them — had at least a small fleet of ships that were used for military as well as commercial purposes. Here it is also worth recalling Hittite text CTH 105, in which the Hittite king demanded that Amurru should not allow the ships of *Ahhiyawa* (i.e., the merchants or goods involved) to go to Assyria, pointing to the Hittite military embargo against its current adversary, Assyria.

MERCHANTS AND MARINERS

Both private (or at least semi-independent) and royal merchants regulary plied their trade at Ugarit (see, amongst many others, Rainey 1963; Linder 1970, 1981; Astour 1972; Monroe 2009; Routledge and McGeough 2009; McGeough 2015: 90-94). Akkadian text RS 17.146 (Nougayrol 1956: 154-157), for example, mentions the *tamkāru ša mandatti ša šar Ugarit*, merchants who somehow worked under the mantle of the king of Ugarit (Sasson 1966: 134, translates 'tributary merchants to the king of Ugarit'; Monroe 2009: 76, translates 'royally-endowed merchants'). Liverani (1962: 83-86) understood the term to refer to members of the royal household and suggested such a relationship might apply to all merchants at Ugarit (similarly Rainey 1963). Astour (1972: 26 and *passim*) suggested that Ugarit's wealthiest merchants belonged to an elite class, the *maryannū*, and indeed three of them did (Yabninu, Rašap-abu, Abdi-Ḥagab). As Monroe (2009: 153) points out, however, there are several other well-known merchants (*e.g.* Ṣinaranu, Urtenu, Rapanu) who evidently were not *maryannū*. Monroe's (2009: 151-157) extended review of the literature on 'trader-state relations' at Ugarit (and the Near East more generally) also provides a useful summary; equally important, he concludes that both merchants and the state benefitted economically from a situation in which the king never fully controlled mercantile trading activities but almost always benefitted from them.

The king of Ugarit, moreover, exempted some merchants from paying taxes or duties. The best known and widely cited example is seen in an Akkadian text from Ugarit (RS 16.238+254—Nougayrol 1955: 107-108) dealing with the merchant Ṣinaranu. The king of Ugarit, Ammistamru II, declared that the goods on Ṣinaranu's ship — grain, beer and oil — arriving from Crete (*Kabduri*) were 'free from claim' (*i.e.* taxes) (for a recent translation and critical commentary citing earlier works, see Monroe 2009: 165-167). A related, but badly damaged text indicates that Ammistamru (II?) also granted the status of 'free and clear' (from taxes) to two other merchants who undertook trips to Egypt, Hatti and another, unknown place, *Zizaḫallima* (RS 16.386—Nougayrol 1955: 165-166; Monroe 2009: 164-165).

An Ugaritic letter sent to the king of Ugarit by a local official ('chief of the 100') seems intended to convince the king of Ugarit to permit some (presumably) Ugaritic merchants to sell ships to another merchant, arguably from *Alašiya* (KTU 2.42+2.43— Virolleaud 1965: 14-15). This text is fragmentary and difficult of interpretation, and the association with *Alašiya* is based on the appeal in the letter 'to all the gods of *Alašiya*' (Knapp 1983: 41). As a member of the Ugaritic bureaucracy, the writer may have solicited the gods of the merchant whose case he was mediating. For reasons unknown, a local official seems to have made himself the arbiter of this sale and sought to gain royal approval. The vessels specified as 'their ships' were evidently owned by Ugaritic merchants but their sale had to be authorised by the king of Ugarit. In other words, this text portrays a Cypriot merchant investing in ships offered for sale by Ugaritic merchants, but in so doing the former sought to obtain a royal seal of approval from the king of Ugarit (Knapp 1983: 43). The king of Ugarit may have had final authority over certain commercial matters, as well as the institutions involved in the state's economic welfare; this is also implied by the exemption the merchant Ṣinaranu enjoyed on the goods imported from Crete.

Various Ugaritic and Akkadian documents from Ugarit mention a 'ship's captain' (*b'l any*—KTU 4.647), a 'harbour master'/'overseer of the quay' (*wakil kāri*—RS 17.465; RS 17.039; Monroe 2009: 69), and possibly a trading corporation (*ḫubur*—Linder 1981: 34). The question of merchant organisations or 'cooperatives' at Ugarit is controversial and far from resolved (Astour 1972; Heltzer 1982: 152-154; Monroe 2009: 123-126, 278, 281-283). In a long Akkadian list of personnel at Ugarit (priests, advisors, bronzesmiths and others), one column is headed 'merchants', *i.e. tamkāru: bidaluma* (RS 16.126B+—Nougayrol 1955: 199-203). Once thought to point to an Ugaritic gloss for *tamkāru*, the term *bidaluma* (Ugaritic *bdl*) is now understood to mean 'representative' or 'deputy' (del Olmo Lete and Sanmartin 2003: 217; Monroe: 2009: 159-160, 163); this name-list within a list thus refers to people somehow representing merchants in the complex bureaucracy of the Ugaritic state.

Linder (1981: 35-36) regarded the 'merchants of Ura' (in Cilicia) as maritime traders who enjoyed a special status at Ugarit under Hittite oversight. The most informative text that sheds light on these traders is RS 17.130 (Nougayrol 1956: 103-105), which regulated their commercial activities in Ugarit seasonally, and forbade them from acquiring land or dwellings within the realm of Ugarit. Monroe (2009: 178-179, 194-196) presents various interpretations of several documents that mention these merchants, but concludes that only some of them were actually merchants working under the aegis of the Hittite king.

Ugaritic text KTU 4.40 (RS 8.279—Herdner 1963: 167-168) lists the names of three (?) ship's captains and several crewmen of ships from at least five localities within the realm of Ugarit (Linder 1970: 16-19; Dietrich and Loretz 1977; Hoftijzer and van Soldt 1998: 337). Ugaritic text KTU 4.263 (RS 17.049— Virolleaud 1957: 84) is a list of merchants (*mkrm*) followed by a list of people from Maḫadu; Monroe (2009: 162) has suggested plausibly that the last four names on the list (following the line that reads *mḫdym*) are those of merchants who resided in Maḫadu (Minet el-Beidha). Various ship owners, merchants, 'business men' and manufacturers — over 100 adult males —are recorded in several different texts as likely residents at Maḫadu (Astour 1970: 117-118).

With respect to seamen, in Akkadian letter RS 20.212 (Nougayrol *et al.* 1968: 105-107, no. 33), already noted above, the Hittite king asks the king of Ugarit to transport 2000 measures of grain from Mukish (north Syria) to Ura (Cilicia) in one large ship, along with a crew of mariners (*malaḫḫu*). Also noted earlier was an Akkadian letter (RS 17.133—Nougayrol 1956: 118-119) in which the Hittite king and the king of Ugarit dealt with a wrecked ship and the loss of its cargo, invoking the sworn testimony of the 'chief mariner' (*rab malaḫḫī*) (for full translation and discussion of the text, see Monroe 2009: 179-180).

To summarise: the documentary evidence indicates that both royal merchants and private entrepreneurs functioned within the commercial and diplomatic parameters of the Ugaritic polity, both sides enriching themselves in the process. At least on two separate occasions, the king of Ugarit freed certain merchants from paying duty on goods being imported to the town. Several wealthy merchants are known by name, and at least three of them — Urtenu, Rapanu, Rašap-abu — maintained their own archives that dealt not only with commercial but also other matters of family, state, legal and diplomatic importance. In RS 94.2406 (Bordreuil *et al.* 2012: 160), for example, an unnamed queen of Ugarit writes to Urtenu with instructions regarding how he should handle her affairs whilst she is away, travelling by ship to Anatolia. Sauvage and Pardee (2015) discuss details of the sea voyage, and the possible routes taken from the Cilician coast inland to the town of Adana, and thence to the final, unknown destination(s), *Sunnagara* and *'Unugi* (see the map in Sauvage and Pardee 2015: 248 fig. 3).

For most merchants and mariners, we know little beyond their personal names, if that. On at least one occasion, however, a Cypriot merchant sought to purchase ships offered for sale by his Ugaritic counterparts, but needed the approval of the king of Ugarit to do so. The close relationship between the rulers of Ugarit and *Alašiya* is indicated not only by the fact that the king of Ugarit refers to the Cypriot king as 'my father' (RS 20.238—Nougayrol *et al.* 1968: 87-89; Beckman, in Knapp 1996: 27), but also by two other Akkadian documents discussed above (RS 20.18, RSL 1; see Chapter 2—*Merchants, Mariners and Pirates*), evidently an exchange of letters warning the king of Ugarit to take protective measures against enemy ships sighted at sea. The documents from Ugarit also refer to a 'ship's captain' (*b'l any*), a 'harbour master' (*wakil kāri*), possibly a trading corporation (*ḫubur*), certainly a 'merchant's representative' (*tamkāru: bidaluma*) and a 'chief mariner' (*rab malaḫḫī*), but it is seldom clear how they functioned, or even if they held some 'rank' within the intricate bureaucracy of the Ugaritic polity. Based on Monroe's (2009: 171, fig. 5.1) scheme portraying the oversight of long-distance exchange at Ugarit, Figure 23 presents a rough outline of how this bureaucracy might have looked; whilst well grounded in the documentary evidence, it remains hypothetical.

In the following chapter (Chapter 6: *Seafaring, Seafarers and Seaborne Trade*), I return to consider all this documentary evidence of maritime matters in association with the archaeological, iconographic and spatial evidence related to ships, ports, MTCs, stone anchors and fishing equipment, which is presented next.

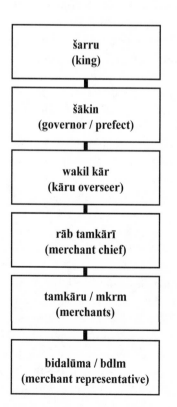

Figure 23: *Ugarit: administrative structure to oversee transactions of merchants and related personnel.* After Monroe 2009: 171, fig. 5.1. Drawing by Irini Katsouri.

THE LEVANT AND EGYPT

Unlike the situation in Anatolia and the Aegean, currently there are no actual Late Bronze Age (LB) shipwreck remains documented in the southeastern Mediterranean. At Hishuley Carmel, just south of Haifa off the southern Levantine coast, Galili *et al.* (2013) have reported a wreck deposit, dated to the LB (thirteenth century BC) on the basis of the copper and tin ingots found at the site (there are no remains of a ship). Elsewhere, the same authors claim to have identified four LB wreck deposits along a three-km stretch of beach south of Haifa (Galili *et al.* 2011); until it can be demonstrated that this was not the result of dumping, taphonomic or other factors, or until some evidence of an actual ship is found (see already Wachsmann 1998: 208-209), this claim seems less convincing.

Several coastal sites were instrumental in the movement of a great variety of goods during the LBA — from ores, metal and timber to maritime transport containers (MTCs) and many other types of pottery, to precious stones, ivory and organic goods, etc. These sites include, most prominently but not exclusively, the following:

- in Syria, Ugarit and its port, Minet el-Beidha, Tell Kazel and its port (Tabbat el-Hammam?) (Schaeffer 1932, 1933; Badre *et al.* 2005; Badre 2011; Jung 2006, 2011)
- in Lebanon, Byblos, Beirut, Sidon and Tyre (Badre 1998; Frost 2004; Belmonte 2002; Vidal 2005; Carayon *et al.* 2011)
- in Israel, Tel Akko, Tell Abu Hawam, Tel Nami, Jaffa and Tell el-'Ajjul (Raban 1987; Artzy 2005, 2006; Fischer 2000, 2002; Stewart 1974; Burke 2011; Burke *et al.* 2017)
- in Egypt, Marsa Matruh (White 2002a, 2002b); possibly Zawiyet Umm el-Rakham (Snape 2003).

Most Levantine port or harbour sites discussed in this chapter have already been noted at least briefly in the previous chapter on the Middle Bronze Age (MB). Here I present some of them in more detail, as LB evidence tends to be more plentiful (excepting sites in modern-day Lebanon) and more informative than that of the MB.

PORTS AND HARBOURS

The LB site at Ugarit (and its two main ports—Minet el-Beidha, Ras Ibn Hani) was situated at an interface between maritime and overland trading routes; it lay within a day's sail of Cilicia and Cyprus, as well as several, more southerly Levantine ports. As already demonstrated by the documentary evidence presented above, Ugarit served as a key intermediary between the Levant, Egypt and Mesopotamia, Anatolia and Cyprus, if not the Aegean world (Yon 2000; 2006: 136-171; Matthäus 2014). There, merchants and mariners met and exchanged raw materials, organic goods and finished products with their local and overseas counterparts (Courtois 1979; Knapp 1991: 35-41; Bell 2006, 2012). Ugarit's manifold commercial connections with the Mediterranean world, and the wealth that derived from such commerce, are evident in both material and textual sources (McGeough 2007, 2015; Monroe 2009).

Astour (1970: 113-116) suggested that the kingdom of Ugarit controlled a shoreline from Mt. Casius in the north to Tell Sukas in the south, but he focused on two sites indicated in the Ugaritic documents: *Rish* and *Mahdl Ma-a-ha-di*. The former may be identified only tentatively with Ras Ibn Hani. The latter, *Maḫadu*, is referred to in text KTU 4.81 (RS 11.779—see above, *The Documentary Record*). Overall, a minimum of 122 adult males in various professions are listed as residents at *Maḫadu* (Astour 1970: 117-118). Only one site qualifies as having such mercantile potential, and that is Minet el-Beidha, a natural, deepwater cove situated about one km from Ugarit, and largely protected from the winds by its orientation (Yon and Sauvage 2015: 81) (the site is shown above, in Figure 1). Schaeffer (1937: 140-141, fig. 7) reported a sea-wall made of ashlar headers at the site. In a storehouse at Minet el-Beidha, eighty Canaanite jars stood in ordered stacks (Schaeffer 1932: 3, pl. III.3) (Figure 24). Excavations have revealed not only storage rooms, but also large quantities of imported Cypriot pottery, MTCs, and buildings (perhaps shops) in which perfumes, alabaster flasks, bronze artefacts, ivory boxes and more were produced (Courtois 1979: 1283-1287; Yon 1997). This is not to discount the potential significance of Ras Ibn Hani, which may have been established in the thirteenth century BC by a member of the Ugaritic royal family as a rival maritime mercantile centre to Minet el-Beidha (Bounni 1991: 107).

Inland, at the highest point of the centre at Ugarit itself, stone anchors were deposited at the 'Temple of Ba'al' (Ṣapon), perhaps giving some credence to the suggestion that the anchors were offerings from sailors, and that the structure itself served as a landmark for ships and sailors (Frost 1991; Akkermans and Schwartz 2003: 338-339). Brody (1998: 95-96), however, argues that Ba'al Ṣapon's 'residence' was on Mount Ṣapon, just north of the site of Ugarit; the height of its summit and proximity to the sea would have made it both a landmark and navigational aid for maritime traffic using Ugarit's ports. At various times in the LB, ships from several Levantine ports (*e.g.* Beirut, Byblos, Tyre, Sidon), and from Cyprus (*Alašiya*), Crete (*Kabduri*) and Egypt, docked at its ports; seafaring merchants from these areas dealt with local merchants and officials, or with the king in specific cases (Astour 1973; Heltzer 1989: 12-13; Buchholz 1999; Monroe 2009: 171-189; see also above, *The Documentary Record*). Shipwrights at Ugarit may have built the town's fleet of ships (Linder 1981: 38, 40; Artzy 2003). Although Ugarit was at different times allied with either Hittite Anatolia or New Kingdom Egypt, documentary evidence shows that many surrounding towns and villages were dependent on the town and its port, whose wealth was based largely on maritime trade (Liverani 1962; Singer 1999).

Figure 24: *Minet el-Beidha, eighty Canaanite jars stacked in storehouse.* From Schaeffer 1932: pl. III.3.

The site of Tell Kazel, situated today some 3 km inland from the Syrian coast, is strategically located at the only pass between the mountain chains of the Lebanon–anti-Lebanon to the south and Gebel al-Ansariyeh to the north; it thus forms the main passage between inland Syria and the Mediterranean coast. It has been argued that Tell Kazel should be identified with the port town of Şumur (Dunand and Saliby 1957; Klengel 1984), a key LB centre in the kingdom of Amurru, which stretched east-west from the Orontes River to the Mediterranean, and north-south at least from Arwad to Tripoli (Moran 1992: 388; *cf.* Stieglitz 1991; for a more detailed breakdown of the still-controversial extent of the territory of Amurru, see Altman 2014: 13 n.13). Şumur is mentioned in Tuthmosis III's Annals and in the Amarna tablets (EA 98, 104, 105), the latter with reference to ships bound for the port and a naval blockade against it (Moran 1992: 171, 178-180; see above, Chapter 2—*Merchants, Mariners and Pirates*). Throughout the fourteenth and early thirteenth centuries BC, the Egyptians and Hittites struggled for control over Amurru, with victory finally passing to the Hittites after the epic battle at Kadesh (Van de Mieroop 2007: 36-40).

Excavations at Tell Kazel have produced a large number (over 4000 sherds—Capet 2006-07: 187) of imported Cypriot pottery — White Slip, Base-ring, Monochrome, White Shaved, etc. (Badre 2006: 67-71, 77, 80-82; 2011: 206-209, 211-212, 214) and significant amounts of Late Helladic (LH) IIIA and LH IIIB wares (Badre 2006: 71-74, 77-80, 82; 2011: 209-213, 214-216; Jung 2006, 2011). I leave aside here any discussion of the contentious origin(s) of two other wares found at the site: Handmade Burnished Ware (Capet 2006-07; Boileau *et al.* 2010) and 'Grey Ware' (Badre 2006: 87-88; 2011: 219), the latter defined elsewhere as being of 'Trojan', *i.e.* northwest Anatolian, origin (Allen 1991, 1994; *cf.* Boileau *et al.* 2010: 1686-1688). Mountjoy and Mommsen (2015) have recently assigned Cypriot origins to various vessels found at Tell Kazel, from a jug thought to originate in Sinda to a 'simple' style stirrup jar and piriform jar sherds from Kition/Hala Sultan Tekke or Palaipaphos.

Although neither the excavators nor the pottery specialists working at Tell Kazel report on any maritime transport containers at the site, Pedrazzi (2007: 368; 2010: 54) argued that fully preserved forms of her Type 4 Canaanite jars (dated to the very end of the LB) are common at Tell Kazel, which may even have been a centre for their production. Moreover, petrographic and chemical analyses (ICP-AES and ICP-MS — Inductively coupled plasma-atomic emission and plasma-mass spectroscopy) of Canaanite jar sherds from Kom Rabia (near Memphis, at the apex of the Nile Delta), revealed four distinctive compositional groups, the most northerly of which was the area around Tell Kazel and Tell Arqa (Ownby 2010: 178; Ownby and Bourriau 2009: 177-181; Ownby and Smith 2011). Finally, Late Cypriot *pithoi* (Groups IB1, II) have been found on shipwrecks and at several sites throughout the Aegean and eastern Mediterranean including, in Syria, at Tell Kazel and Ugarit as well as its port Minet el-Beidha (Pilides 2000: 48-51; Jeremy Rutter, pers. comm.). Whilst the primary purpose of these *pithoi* was storage, some may have served at times for the bulk transport of organic materials or liquids (Knapp and Demesticha 2017: 88-93).

Archaeological (as opposed to marine geomorphological) evidence from Late Bronze Age levels in the main coastal sites of the central Levant — Arwad, Byblos, Beirut, Sidon, Tyre — is far more sporadic and less well published (Sauvage 2012: 45-50). At Byblos, for example, coastal erosion may have destroyed any remains of the LB levels (Salles 1980: 66). By contrast, the fortified LB town at Beirut has been identified and published in a preliminary manner (Badre 2001-02). Based on several earlier studies by Frost (*e.g.* 1971, 1973, 1995), Altman (2014: 27) suggests that only Arwad, Tyre and Sidon had sizeable natural harbours during the LB period, and that the harbours at Byblos and Beirut may not have been adequate to accommodate large ships on a year-round basis.

From geomorphological evidence, it does seem clear that both Sidon and Tyre had pre-Phoenician proto-harbours (Marriner *et al.* 2006a, 2006b, 2008) as well as natural downwind embayments or coves north of their promontories that could have served as anchorages for small ships. Sidon had another potential anchorage on the small offshore island of Zire (see more detailed discussion above, Chapter 4: *Middle Bronze Age—The Levant and Egypt, Ports and Harbours, Levant*, and Figure 13). Beyond the geomorphological work and scattered textual references, however, the archaeological evidence from LB Sidon and Tyre remains limited. From the 'College site' at Sidon, Doumet-Serhal (2013) discusses pottery imports from the Aegean (Minoan, Mycenaean wares), Cyprus and Syria (also a metal 'torque'), as well as Egyptian pottery, alabaster and steatite vessels, miniature hematite and faience vessels, scarabs and a faience cylinder seal, arguing that Sidon was a prominent maritime centre. At Tyre, LB levels are known solely from Bikai's (1978) limited 15 sq m sounding at the site. Information on the maritime aspects of the 'Late Bronze Age reoccupation' of Tyre is based mainly on three burials with numerous Cypriot ceramic imports and a fishhook; the settlement is presumed to be nearby, but is said to have become and remained a 'manufacturing area' into the Iron Age (Bikai and Bikai 1987: 77; see also Badre 1992: 40-41). Finally, Sarepta — perhaps the most extensively excavated and well published coastal town in the central Levant — is well known for its Mycenaean (most frequent) and Cypriot imports (summarised in Bell 2005: 365-367; see also Koehl 1985: 142-147), as well as its maritime transport containers; we know virtually nothing, however, of its Bronze or Iron Age harbour facilities.

In the southern Levant, within the area of Haifa Bay and along the southern part of the Carmel Coast, three LB sites have been proposed as harbours or anchorages for receiving and/or transshipping goods: Tel Akko and Tell Abu Hawam (both situated on the bay) and Tel Nami (Artzy 2006, 2013) (Figure 25). At Tel Akko, the excavations conducted over many years present a very complex picture (*e.g.* Dothan 1976; Raban 1991; Artzy 2013: 11*-12*). Moreover, despite repeated and ongoing attempts by the various excavators to locate or define an anchorage or some part of it, nothing has been found at Tel Akko. Artzy (2013: 15*), however, notes: 'Recent studies have shown that Akko Bay extends to below the tell. It is proposed that an anchorage, based on the sea was used during the Bronze Age, although the question ... whether it was based on the River Na'aman's outlet, or the bay as it was in antiquity, is being presently researched ...'.

Figure 25: *Aerial photo showing location of Tel Akko and Tell Abu Hawam (both on Haifa Bay) and Tel Nami on the coast.* Courtesy of Michal Artzy.

The main, hard evidence adduced in support of Akko's role as a harbour or anchorage is imported ceramics. During the LB II period, for example, imports included Cypriot and Aegean-style wares, and other wares from Egypt and Anatolia (Artzy 2006: 50); at least two of the 'Aegean style' LH IIIC sherds from Akko analysed by NAA are regarded as Cypriot imports (Mountjoy and Mommsen 2015: 454 fig. 20, 457). In addition, in terms of maritime connections, it may be noted that in Area H (lower, northern sector of the tell), excavations revealed an 'altar' with ships engraved upon it (Artzy 2003: 233; see further below, under *Ships' Representations, Levant*).

In any case, Artzy (2006: 59-60) suggests — not unreasonably given the site's location on Haifa Bay and its later, indisputable role as a port (*e.g.* during the Crusader period, when it was known as Acre) — that Tel Akko served as a seaside centre for wider hinterland and related political interests. Along with two of its rulers (Surata, Satatna), Akko (*Akka*) is mentioned (largely in passing) in several Amarna tablets (EA 8, 88, 111, 232-235, 366—Moran 1992), and in Akkadian and Ugaritic texts from Ugarit. Intriguingly, petrographic analyses of three of the Akko Amarna tablets (EA 232, 234-235) indicates that their clay originated in the region of Beth Shan, far to the east in the Jordan river valley (Goren *et al.* 2004: 237-239). One of the Ugaritic texts (RS 18.031—KTU 2.38, discussed above), sent from the king of Tyre to the king of Ugarit, mentions Akko (*'ky*) as the site (port?) where an Ugaritic ship that had been wrecked in a storm was being unloaded ('stripped'—Monroe 2009: 98-99). Another, very fragmentary Ugaritic text (RS 11.832—KTU 4.94) *per se* does not mention Akko but indicates that a ship loaded with copper was 'lost'. In one of the Amarna letters (EA 245: 24-31), Surata (known from elsewhere in the Amarna correspondence as the 'mayor' of Akko) promised to send one Lab'ayu (of Shechem) to Egypt 'in the hold of a ship' (*a-na-yi*).

The site of Tell Abu Hawam is situated on the southern side of Haifa Bay (see Figure 25, above), on the estuary of the Nahal Qishon and just north of the Carmel Ridge, which protects it from prevailing southwesterly winds but equally hampers its access to overland routes. Such a location may have enhanced its role as a harbour or anchorage, ideal for accommodating maritime traffic but connected only with difficulty to inland trade routes (Artzy 2006: 46-47). Following a series of early, salvage excavations and later, follow-up work (Balensi 1985, 1988), Artzy (2006: 48-49, figs. 1-2; 2013: 10*; 2016: 98-100) undertook further salvage excavations at the site in 2001-2002, penetrating to a depth of about 1.5m below mean sea level (MSL). She interprets the geomorphological layers (river clay and sand), including changes in the soil attributed to flooding and sand silting, as part of an anchorage dated mainly to LB II (ca. 1350-1230 BC); some ceramic material from the late fifteenth-early fourteenth century BC, however, was also present. One wall 'element' dated to the LB was covered with mollusc shells, and so interpreted as having been underwater. Ballast stones found alongside the pottery in recent salvage excavations reportedly have multiple provenances, namely from the coastal areas of Cyprus, Anatolia and the northern Levant, as well as the Carmel coast (Yanklevitz 2007, cited by Artzy 2016: 103).

The site seems to have come to an end by the mid-thirteenth century BC (Artzy 2006: 48). The role of Tell Abu Hawam as an anchorage is, once again, largely argued on the basis of imported pottery: Cypriot wares (the majority), including White Slip, Base-ring I-II, Monochrome, White Shaved and Plain White Wheelmade Ware (both imported and local variants—Artzy 2016: 100-102, figs. 2-4); Aegean-style sherds of LH IIIA-B date (mainly LH IIIA2), comparable to those excavated by Hamilton, which originated in the Greek Argolid (Asaro and Perlman 1973: 215-216; French *et al.* 1993: 7-10). Whilst the number of Late Helladic sherds recovered in Hamilton's early excavations was such that some considered Tell Abu Hawam to be a Mycenaean 'emporium' (*e.g.* Harif 1974), in fact the Cypriot wares outnumber those from the Aegean by anywhere from 2:1 to 30:1, depending on who is counting (Van der Post 1991; Artzy 2016: 105).

Petrographic analyses of numerous Canaanite jars from the Uluburun shipwreck indicate they originated in the areas around Tell Abu Hawam and Haifa Bay (Goren 2013: 54–61); the same or a very similar origin has been assigned to other Canaanite jars found in Egypt (Serpico *et al.* 2003: 373). Artzy (2016: 100-102) also maintains that other MTCs from Tell Abu Hawam were divided into two major groups, one of Cypriot origin and the other of various local origins. At the very least, the large number of sherds from MTCs found at Tell Abu Hawam — including locally-produced ones — indicates that the site was intimately involved in maritime trade. Over 70 examples of Cretan Transport Stirrup Jars, another key MTC of the Late Bronze Age, have been found in the Levant, the majority at Tell Abu Hawam (Ben-Shlomo *et al.* 2011: 335-336, 340 table 1, and online appendix). Yasur-Landau (2010: 205-207) has also argued that Tell Abu Hawam was a major trading centre, a gateway community for foreign goods entering the southern Levant.

Artzy (2016: 107) now defines Tell Abu Hawam as a '… small, frontal shipping site with storage areas; it was likely too small for habitation or for industries such as ceramic production'. Nonetheless, she maintains that the Cypriot presence at the site points to a significant involvement in international trade, more than a simple transit harbour. Elsewhere, Artzy and Zagorski (2012: 3) suggested that the harbours at Tell Abu Hawam and Akko may have been involved in different networks of trade. The limited number of Egyptian imports and the diversity and preponderance of Cypriot pottery at Tell Abu Hawam may indicate that it functioned as part of a network serving the coastal Levant and the west (Cyprus, the Aegean, western Anatolia), whilst Akko's contacts may have been focused on Egypt.

The final site of this Haifa Bay/Carmel Coast trio, Tel Nami, is situated on a peninsula jutting some 150m into the sea, along the southern part of the coast (see Figure 25, above). This places Nami midway between the sites of Atlit and Dor, themselves both argued to have served as anchorages. The site has several components: the tell, with MB II remains; another sector some 70m to the east (Nami East), with both MB II and LB IIB remains; and a necropolis and 'sanctuary' in Nami East (Artzy 2013: 10*). Artzy (2006: 50) suggested that its position — near the estuary of the Nahal Me'arot — would have made it suitable for an anchorage, whilst the peculiar rock formation of the Carmel Ridge itself (ca. 4 km east and inland) has long been used as a locational point for seafarers. Moreover, in three different areas on the western side of the Carmel Ridge (along the Nahal Me'arot and Nahal Oren), various types of ships were engraved on the rock (Artzy 2003: 232-234, 235-236 figs. 4-6, 240-241, figs. 11-13); they are discussed below (*Ships' Representations, Levant*).

In Artzy's (2006: 51-52) view, Tel Nami served to connect the coast to its economic hinterland, and in particular to Megiddo, less than a day's walk distant. She notes that its short life span as a harbour or anchorage may have resulted from problems associated with silting and changes in the course of Nahal Me'arot, as well as from salinisation, since the site had only a limited agricultural hinterland. Once again, however, there are no physical remains of a harbour at Tel Nami, and its role as an international port rests mainly on the wealth of the metal goods and imported pottery found in the excavations, or perhaps on its role in the incense (*Pistacia* spp.) trade (Artzy 1994). As far as an actual anchorage is concerned, Artzy (2013: 11*) notes only that Y. Salmon is attempting '… to establish the exact anchorage of the site in the different periods of its activity, using geomorphological and geophysical methods'.

Tel Nami was first settled during the MB II period (ca. nineteenth century BC), then abandoned until LB IIB (thirteenth century BC), and finally destroyed early in the twelfth century BC (Artzy 1995; Marcus 1995). The imported pottery is mainly of Cypriot origin, although there are also some LH IIIB2 and 'simple style' wares as well. A selection of these LH wares was examined by NAA (unpublished work carried out by J. Yellin), which indicated that some were produced from Cypriot clays whilst others were of local (*i.e.* coastal Levantine) origin (Artzy 2006: 52). Some of the Cypriot juglets found at Tel Nami, for example, clearly originated on the island, whilst others of likely local manufacture have counterparts at Megiddo (Artzy 2006: 55).

With respect to all three possible port sites she discusses (Tel Nami, Tell Abu Hawam, Tel Akko), Artzy (2006: 59-60) argued that their use in slightly different time periods may be related to their individual agricultural hinterlands and regional access to terrestrial trade routes. For example, when Tell Abu Hawam went out of use in the thirteenth century BC, regional maritime trade may have shifted to Tel Akko. In turn, toward the very end of the LB, Tel Nami would have come into use as a port for the transhipment of goods (Artzy 1998: 441), perhaps bypassing earlier 'controls' exerted by either Tell Abu Hawam or Tel Akko (Sherratt 2016: 292). Tel Akko was the only one of these sites with both a presumed anchorage facility and an adequate agricultural hinterland. Artzy (2006: 45-46) also suggested that the material evidence from all these sites calls into question Egyptian written sources indicating that they were under Egypt's control; in her view, independent, dynamic trade networks may be seen at all three sites. She feels that they were not just way stations linking Egypt and Egyptian trade with the north, but also transshipment centres involved in local and long-distance exchange networks.

As already noted above (Chapter 4: *Middle Bronze Age—The Levant and Egypt, Ports and Harbours*), there is little doubt that Dor — also on the southern Carmel Coast and only a few km south of Tel Nami — could have served as a coastal station for maritime commerce and traffic sailing between points to the south, including Egypt, and other Canaanite towns or ports farther north. Even so, the lagoon at Dor is characterised by rocky reefs, shifting sandbars and a complex current that makes entering its anchorages a risky undertaking at any time (Cvikel *et al.* 2008: 201, 205). Moreover, as the excavators lament, 'The Late Bronze Age at Dor (ca. 1550-1200 BCE) is currently our biggest enigma' (Gilboa and Sharon 2008: 148); LB remains have only been encountered in the centre of the mound. The site may thus have been of limited extent during the LB period, at least in comparison with its Iron Age successor. Furthermore, a reassessment of the reputedly LB pottery found in earlier excavations (*e.g.* Raban 1987, 1993) has shown that this material dates no earlier than the eleventh century BC. Thus, even if the installations in the southern bay are of a maritime nature (as Raban argued), they can only be of early Iron Age date (Gilboa and Sharon 2008: 151). As indicated by the renowned eleventh century BC Egyptian Tale of Wenamun (Goedicke 1975), ships en route from Egypt to Byblos stopped over at Dor, which had become a bustling port by the early Iron Age. Indeed, this is demonstrated most dramatically in material terms, as Egyptian jar fragments of 21st Dynasty date have been found in virtually every Iron I locus at the site of Dor (Gilboa 2015: 251-253).

Some ten km south of Dor lay the site of Tel Mevorakh, where an isolated 'temple' was built during the LB period (Stern 1977, 1984). Although interpreted by its excavator as a shrine built and used by travellers along the coastal highway (Stern 1984: 36), Brody (1998: 57) suggests that it might also have been used by mariners. Although Mevorakh today lies over two km from the sea, in a pinch, boats travelling along the Nahal Tanninim might have reached the site from the Mediterranean (see the sketch map in Brody 1998: 154, fig. 56).

The antiquity as well as the significance of a port at Jaffa, situated on the south-central coast of modern-day Israel, has long been recognised. Indeed, Burke *et al.* (2017: 90) argue that 'Jaffa remains the primary Egyptian port north of Gaza and south of Byblos on the southern Levantine coast'. Its likely role as both a harbour and Egyptian fortress (or granary for the Egyptian army?) during the LB was recognised following Kaplan's excavations there during the 1950s and 1960s (summarised in Kaplan 1972). According to Burke (2011: 63), Jaffa's clearest advantages over other, southern coastal sites was a natural, deepwater anchorage along its western side and a natural breakwater formed by a ridge about 200m offshore from the western edge of the Bronze Age site. As yet, however, no geomorphological or palaeogeographical research has been undertaken to demonstrate the physical presence of such an anchorage or harbour.

Known as *Yapu* in the Amarna letters, Jaffa evidently served as an Egyptian 'granary' (*šunuti*—EA 294: 20), perhaps with an Egyptian official in residence (EA 138: 7) (Moran 1992: 221-223, 336-337). Another letter (EA 296: 33) notes that one Yaḫtiru (a local official?) was guarding the city gate of *Yapu* (Moran 1992: 338-339). Burke (2011: 68-70; Burke *et al.* 2017: 124-125) discusses other, Egyptian documentary references to Jaffa, in particular its conquest by Tuthmosis III, but none of these shed any direct light on its role as a harbour or maritime base (*cf.* Morris 2005: 138-139, n. 90, who suggests that Jaffa may have served as one of Egypt's *ḫtm*-bases, *i.e.* 'harbours'). At most, we might conclude from the written evidence that LB Jaffa was an Egyptian garrison town that also served as a granary; by virtue of its strategic location on the sea and with easy access to the interior, it could well have served as a harbour or stopping point for goods and soldiers moving inland and/or along the coast. Such a function also seems likely in light of imports from both the older and more recent excavations at Jaffa, including Cypriot wares (Bichrome Wheelmade, *pithoi*), Canaanite jars, Egyptian 'storage jars' and 'transport containers', a range of other Canaanite, Philistine and Egyptian vessels, scarabs, and much more (Burke *et al.* 2017: 92-98, 100 fig. 10, 103 fig. 14, 110-115).

The site of Tell el-ʿAjjul is situated about 3 km southwest of Gaza, on the north bank and near the outlet of the Wadi Gaza (Nahal Besor); today it lies some 2 km from the sea. ʿAjjul is often argued to be one of the richest archaeological sites in the southern Levant, the counterpart of Ugarit in the north (*e.g.* Sjöqvist 1940: 162-163; Oren 1997: 253-255, 279; Bergoffen 2001a: 145; for the ultimate maximalist view of the site, see Robertson 1999: 324-329, and *passim*). Both Stewart (1974: 9-14) and Fischer and Sadeq (2000: 211-213) provide reasonable summaries of the site, its dating (MB, LB), previous excavations and some of the wide array of imported goods at the site (especially Egyptian, Cypriot and Mycenaean pottery—for which see also Merrillees, in Stewart 1974: 86-111; Bergoffen 2001a, 2001b; Steel 2002; Fischer and Sadeq 2002). None of the published drawings of pottery from Tell el-ʿAjjul reveals any sign of maritime transport containers, whilst attempts to describe and inventory exhaustively Tell el-ʿAjjul's pottery types, decoration, motifs, etc. (*e.g.* Stewart 1974: *passim*; Bergoffen 2001a, 2001b) provide little useful information for any broader-based study.

Kempinski (1974) demonstrated beyond reasonable doubt that the ancient name of Tell el-ʿAjjul was Šaruhen (in ancient Egyptian and Hebrew texts). Its strategic location between Egypt and the southern Levantine coast has led to statements that it had '… a convenient ancient harbour which permitted small vessels to reach the city' (Fischer and Sadeq 2000: 213). Oren (1997: 255) claims to have identified an 'inner harbor'; the widening of the wadi bed would have allowed upstream navigation at Tell el-ʿAjjul, assuming that sea level was 1m higher than at present, enabling even seagoing vessels to sail through river outlets. Burke (2011: 63-64), however, argues that 'it is both unlikely and remains undemonstrated that ships could sail any distance up rivers such as the Ayalon and the Yarkon'. Moreover, the fact remains that there is no published physical evidence of such a harbour, nor has any geomorphological work yet been done in the region. Any discussion of the role of seafaring, maritime trade and exchange as it relates to Tell el-ʿAjjul is thus

Figure 26: *plan of the small port at Marsa Matruh, showing the location of Bates's Island, where the LB site is located.* Background figure by Google Earth Pro.

confined to the study of its imports and their provenance, not to any harbour or anchorage *per se*.

Turning to Egypt, in a remote location some 300 kms west of the Nile delta, along Egypt's Mediterranean coast, lay the small port of Marsa Matruh (White 2002a; 2002b) (Figure 26). Although there are no physical remnants of a built harbour, excavations on Bates's Island in LB levels produced several examples of maritime transport containers: Canaanite jars, Aegean transport stirrup jars and Cypriot *pithoi* (Russell, Hulin, in White 2002b: 8-15, 28-38). White (1986: 83-84; 2003: 75) maintains that Marsa Matruh served as an essential way station for merchants or sea traffic travelling between the Aegean, Egypt, the Levant and Cyprus (also Broodbank 2013: 403). Numerous ostrich eggshell fragments from the site, regarded as 'exotica' elsewhere in the eastern Mediterranean, point to the same conclusion (Conwell 1987; White 1999: 933-934).

Twenty-five km west of Marsa Matruh, and today situated about one km from the coast, lay the large fortified site of Zawiyet Umm el-Rakham (Snape 2003). Dated to the thirteenth century BC, the imported pottery from this site includes 15 whole and several fragmentary Canaanite jars, at least five coarse-ware Aegean transport stirrup jars (two with apparent Cypro-Minoan marks on their handles) and a range of Cypriot wares (Snape 2003: 67-69, figs. 3-6). White (2003: 77) questions the role of Umm el-Rakham as a trading post and suggests instead that the transport and storage containers found at the site represent provisions offloaded at Marsa Matruh and carried overland. The main significance of Marsa Matruh as a port, together with its possible role vis-à-vis Zawiyet Umm el-Rakham, lies in its unique location and its deep connectivity within broader Mediterranean exchange systems.

SHIPS' REPRESENTATIONS (LEVANT)

Amongst the remnants of the cuneiform archives in the 'Petit Palais' at Ugarit, the excavators recovered two small but largely preserved faïence scarabs; the context suggests they should be dated toward the end of the thirteenth century BC (Schaeffer 1962: 134 figs. 114-115, 147). The more readily understandable scarab shows a very schematic vessel with what the excavator thought was an Egyptian-type double central mast and sail, as well as the yard and stays (Schaeffer 1962: 134 fig. 114, left). Schaeffer compared it imaginatively with 'barques égyptiennes' (Schaeffer 1962: 134

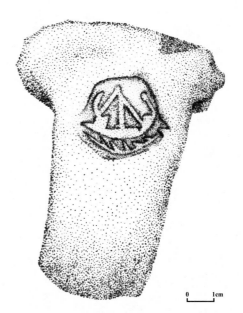

Figure 27: *Tell Tweini, handle of a Canaanite jar (?) with seal impression depicting a boat with sail and possible oars.* After Bretschneider and Van Lerberghe 2008: 38 fig. 39. Drawing by Irini Katsouri.

fig. 115). Basch (1987: 70), more soberly, saw only a single mast, and suggested that the strictly vertical prow and stern-posts resemble a model from Byblos dated to approximately the same period, *i.e.* towards the end of the Egyptian New Kingdom (Basch 1987: 67, fig. 122). Wachsmann (1998: 49) interprets the rigging of this highly-schematised ship somewhat differently, but agrees that it appears to represent a 'Syro-Canaanite' vessel. Frost (1991: 363-364) noted that both seals showed vessels with oars and sails, but that the apparent concavity of the keels seemed incompatible with oars; she suggested that whoever made the seal was not a seaman.

From Tell Tweini in Syria comes a tantalizing seal impression (on the handle of a vessel that may be a Canaanite jar) depicting a boat (galley?) with what appear to be both oars and a sail (Bretschneider and Van Lerberghe 2008: 33, 38 fig. 39) (Figure 27). Excavations in the 'cremation cemeteries' of Hama (Syria) uncovered a funerary urn with painted decoration, including the drawing of a ship; this object is dated by its context to ca. 1200-1075 BC, during the Hama F phase (Ingholt 1940: 69-84, pl. 22.2; Riis 1948: 200-202). The ship depicted has a long, upcurving hull that ends in a spur, above which the stem-post is surmounted by a bird-headed device (Wachsmann 1981: 205-206, fig. 20e; 1998: 174-176, fig. 8.19). Above the hull are a series of short vertical lines topped by a horizontal line, which Wachsmann (1981: 206; 1998: 175-176) thought could represent an open rowers' gallery. In Wachsmann's (1981: 213; 2013: 63-64) view, the Hama ship may be 'patterned after a Sea Peoples' ship', an interpretation that occasions no surprise since at least four of his ground-breaking studies (1981; 1997; 1998: 163-204; 2013) devote a great deal of attention to bird-headed iconography/devices and the ships of the 'sea peoples' (likewise Basch 1987: 66-69). Although I return to consider some of these points further below (*Ships' Representations–Egypt*), I leave aside (here and elsewhere) Wachsmann's compelling arguments regarding bird-headed iconography, but note that attempts to link such a design element to specific ethnic groups of the 'sea peoples' seem untenable. Such bird's head devices are quite common on ship depictions from central Europe and Italy through the Aegean to Egypt, a point that did not escape Wachsmann (1998: 177-197; see also Kristiansen 2016: 175-176, fig. 10.6).

I have already discussed above (*Middle Bronze Age–Ships' Representations*) two terracotta ship models excavated at Byblos (Dunand 1937, 1954; Wachsmann 1998: 52-54). And, as already noted, Basch (1987: 67, fig. 122) regarded one of these models as a typical 'Syrian' vessel and dated it to the time of the Egyptian New Kingdom. Wachsmann, whilst agreeing with the dating, argued that this model is of Egyptian 'travelling-ship' type (Wachsmann 1998: 52, figs. 3.16-3.17). The second terracotta model from Byblos is also usually seen as a 'Syrian' or Canaanite craft (*e.g.* Fevrier 1950: 135-136; Sasson 1966: 127), but Wachsmann (1998: 53-54, fig. 3.19) maintained that it is more akin to Egyptian boats dated to the earlier, First Intermediate period or the Middle Kingdom.

Moving to the southern Levant, a very schematic graffito incised on a pottery bowl fragment from Tell Abu Hawam, dated very generally to the LB II period, shows only the hull of a ship, perhaps a mast, and two quarter rudders trailing behind (Wachsmann 1998: 48-49, figs. 13.12-13). From Dor comes an ashlar stone with a ship's graffito, depicting what appears to be the vessel's hull and rigging (Wachsmann and Raveh 1984: 224, 228). Based on the type of rigging (boom-footed), Wachsmann (1998: 48) suggested a *terminus ante quem* of ca. 1200 BC. He regards both the Tell Abu Hawam and Dor graffiti as representations of 'Syro-Canaanite' ships.

By contrast, Wachsmann (2000: 135, fig. 6.30; 2013: 64, fig. 2.35) identified a very simple and highly stylised rendering of a ship engraved on a limestone seal from Beth Shemesh as a 'Helladic galley' (Keel 1994: 33 n.39, 34 fig. 20, and further refs.). The ship's hull is represented by a single line, above which are four lines interpreted as a rowers' gallery and below which are four shorter lines, perhaps the oars. The vessel appears to have a vertical stem and a curving stern. Two figures standing on the ship hold what may be large curving weapons, perhaps swords.

An 'altar' from Tel Akko dated around 1200 BC (based on its associated ceramics and find-spot, in a pit) is engraved with representations of ships (Artzy 1987: 75-77, figs. 1-2; 2003: 232-233, fig. 1) (Figure 28). Lying on the altar were three orange-sized stones on which were incised a small ship, a dolphin, a bird and another type of fish. On the altar itself, four further ships could be distinguished. The largest ship has a mast and (square?) sail, oars and two rudders or steering oars. Each of the four ship representations tends to accentuate the front of the ship with an inwardly curving 'fan', similar to those on ships represented at Kition in Cyprus (Basch and Artzy 1985: 324-325, figs. 1-2, 4-6, 8) (see further below, *Ships' Representations–Cyprus*). Artzy (1987: 80-81) identifies these 'fan' ships as round boats, and compares them (1) with what she regards as 'Syrian ships' known from representations in Egypt (Thebes, Abydos), and (2) with some Cypriot boat models of Iron Age date. Wachsmann (1998: 176) questioned the classification as a 'round ship' as well as the Egyptian comparisons. There are thus no indisputable comparanda, but the closest analogies are with the graffiti from Kition. Artzy (1987) once conjectured that those who used the altar and carved these representations were seafarers, perhaps the 'sea peoples' known as *Tjeker* or *Shardana*, although elsewhere she suggested they are probably independent merchants or mariners of

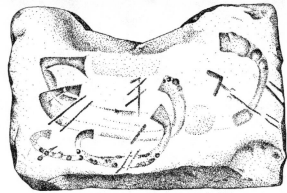

Figure 28: *An 'altar' from Tel Akko engraved with ships' representations.* From Artzy 2003: 233, fig. 1. Courtesy of Michal Artzy.

diverse origins (the Levant, Cyprus, the Aegean, Anatolia) who plied their trade along the coasts of the eastern Mediterranean (Artzy 1997; 2003: 245).

According to Artzy (2003: 232), three different areas in the Nahal Me'arot and Nahal Oren, on the west side of the Carmel Ridge, bear rock carvings with similar, 'fan'-type boats. On a 'pyramid-shaped' rock where the Nahal Me'arot passes through Carmel Ridge, some 3.5 kms inland from Tel Nami, is a 'composition' with numerous incised boats of various forms and sizes (Artzy 1998: 444-445, figs. 1-2). The most common style of boat is the 'fan' type noted at Akko and Kition, and the dating of these engravings is based on comparison with the ships' representations from those sites. Another vessel depicted is said to be of 'Aegean type' (although elsewhere attributed to the Neolithic—Wreschner 1971) and is compared to examples from sites in Boeotia (Greece), dated ca. 1200 BC, and from Egypt's Dakleh Oasis, dated to the late thirteenth-early twelfth century BC (Basch 1987: 142-145; 1994b: 20-21; 1997; Wachsmann 2013: 41-52; see further below—*Ships' Representations, Egypt*). A third type of ship has an outward-facing animal head on the prow (Artzy 1998: 445 fig. 4).

Excavations at Tel Miqne (Ekron) turned up a small (2.5x1 cm), dark red cylinder seal engraved with a crescent-shaped image of a ship, with hull, keel or deck, oars or a rowers' gallery (or ribs of the hull?), a mast close to midship and lines that may represent the rigging (Gittlen 2007: 25 fig. 1). The seal also shows two tree-like features and two apparently human forms. A similar style of masted ship with rigging

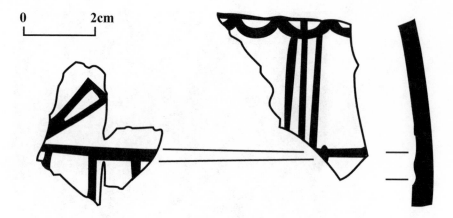

Figure 29: *Two sherds of a twelfth century BC Mycenaean krater from Tel Miqne (Israel), showing a sail, mast and halyards, below which are vertical lines that may indicate a rowers' gallery.* After Dothan and Zukerman 2004: 33 fig. 35:10. Drawing by Irini Katsouri.

(but with the human figures inside the ship) is seen on a Late Cypriot grey steatite cylinder seal from Dromolaxia on Cyprus (Kenna 1972: 643 fig. 86:42, 647).

From the same site (Tel Miqne), two sherds of what Emanuel (2016: 273, fig. 2a) defines as a twelfth century BC Philistine Monochrome krater depict 'a furled brailed sail', a mast and halyards, and vertical lines that may indicate the rowers' gallery (Dothan and Zukerman 2004: 33 fig. 35:10, 41 define the sherds as Late Helladic IIIC1) (Figure 29). Both Emanuel and Wachsmann (2013: 64) believe these sherds portray an example of the long-hulled, oared galley, but Wachsmann sees it as a 'Helladic galley' whilst Emanuel (2016: 271-274) regards the brailed sail, at least, to be Levantine in origin.

Here is should be clarified that two key developments in maritime technology, which emerged toward the end of the LB period, were a new type of vessel, the long-hulled oared galley, and a new type of rigging, the loose-footed, brailed sail, often with a top-mounted crow's nest (Emanuel 2016: 271). Vessels with all these features are depicted in the sea battle on the reliefs at Medinet Habu (see further below). The oared galley is usually considered to be of Aegean derivation (*e.g.* Wachsmann 1981: 209-210; Wedde 1999: 465), whilst the brailed sail and top-mounted crow's nest are thought to have originated along the Levantine coast (*e.g.* Wachsmann 1981: 214-216; 1998: 130-158; Vinson 1993: 137 and *passim*; Emanuel 2016: 277). Even so, because the transfer and widespread adoption of maritime technological features such as these were characteristic of the LB period (*e.g.* Monroe 2009: 37; Broodbank 2013: 464-465), we cannot assume that in every case where a galley is represented we are dealing with Mycenaean mariners, or 'sea peoples' for that matter (see discussion of the wooden boat model found at Gurob in Egypt, in the following section).

SHIPS' REPRESENTATIONS (EGYPT)

With the exception of the recently published ship's model from Gurob (Wachsmann 2013), I leave aside here any discussion of Egyptian New Kingdom wooden ship models, such as those found in the royal tombs of Thutmose III, Amenhotep II and Tutankhamun (in general, see Landström 1970: 98-110). Although fitted with rowers, cabins and landing planks, these models almost certainly represent ceremonial vessels of some sort (or pleasure boats for pharaoh's use?—Reisner 1913: xxvii-xxviii), not seagoing merchant vessels or warships, which are our concern here.

From a New Kingdom tomb in the Memphite necropolis at Saqqara in Egypt comes a relief drawing dated to the end of Egypt's XVIII Dynasty, *i.e.* the late fourteenth century BC (Capart 1931: 62, pl. 67; Millet 1987; Vinson 1993: 136 n.12, 136-139). In the views of both Vinson (1993: 137) and Emanuel (2016: 272), the relief may represent a Syrian (or 'Syro–Canaanite') ship. In the main scene, five men are unloading one of two ships (Vinson 1993: 136), evidently at an Egyptian port on the Nile (Nilotic fish and vegetation are seen in the upper register). Some of the men are handling what Vinson (1973: 137) termed 'unusually squat Canaanite amphoras', but he noted that 'The crudity of the relief … makes specific comparisons difficult'. That is indeed the case but Emanuel (2016: 272) does not hesitate to associate these vessels specifically with Canaanite jars belonging to Killebrew's 'Family 11, Form CA 22' (Killebrew 2007: 167, 172 fig. 4.6; see above, Figure 17.6), the most common MTC in the Bronze Age eastern Mediterranean (see further below—*Maritime Transport Containers*). Whilst Vinson (1973: 137) described the ship's sail as rather unusual, Emanuel (2016: 272) defines it unequivocally as a loose-footed sail; both seem to agree that the top-mounted crow's nest of the ship is of foreign derivation (likely Levantine), *e.g.* like those seen on the reliefs at Medinet Habu (see below).

From the tomb of Iniwia (Iniuia, Nia), also in the New Kingdom necropolis of Memphis at Saqqara, comes a relief block (now in the Cairo Museum) depicting three ships, from which pottery vessels (Canaanite jars?) are once again being offloaded (Landström 1970: 138-139, fig. 403; see also Schneider *et al.* 1993: 5). Wachsmann (1987: 9-11; 1998: 54-60, figs. 3.24, 3.29-30) maintained that that the ships in this relief drawing are 'hybrids', based partly on the type of 'stock scene' characteristic of the ships in the Theban tombs of Kenamun and Nebamun (see below), and partly on Hatshepsut's 'Punt ships'. The basket-like crow's nest, the *pithos* stowed in the bow of the ships and the (possible) Canaanite jars on both the Iniwia and Theban tomb reliefs tend to support the 'hybrid' hypothesis; at the same time these features indicate

Figure 30: *Drawing of a relief from the New Kingdom tomb of Iniwia at Saqqara depicting three ships, with pottery vessels (Canaanite jars?) shown in ship's hold and being offloaded from ship* From Wachsmann 1998: 59 fig. 3.30A. Courtesy of Shelley Wachsmann.

that the Iniwia ship is also a Levantine vessel (Figure 30). Wachsmann (1987: 11; 1998: 60), however, felt that '… the ships in the Iniwia relief never really existed'.

The naval battle between the Egyptians and certain groups of 'sea peoples' (*Peleset, Tjeker, Shekelesh, Denyen, Weshesh*) portrayed in the reliefs on the outer walls of the mortuary temple of Ramesses III at Medinet Habu (Theban necropolis) is well known and has been discussed at length in works treating the end of the LB period in the eastern Mediterranean (Figure 31) (for original text, see Breasted 1906.4: §64; for brief discussion and original image, see Nelson *et al.* 1930: 6, pls. 36-39). Wachsmann (1981; 1998: 166-175, fig. 8.1; 2000a: *passim* and fig. 6.1) has presented the nautical aspects of the ships (design, rigging, decorations) in admirable and perceptive detail, and one can read a great deal into what has been preserved (or not—Nelson 1929: 22) on these scenes. Those who associate the 'sea peoples' with 'piracy' have interpreted them rather generously (*e.g.* Jung 2009: 78-79, 83; Hitchcock and Maeir 2016: 246, 251; Emanuel 2016: *passim*; for fuller discussion, see above, Chapter 2—*Merchants, Mariners and Pirates*), but the historicity as well as the intended purpose of the reliefs have been assessed critically, and very differently, by a range of scholars — Egyptologists, archaeologists and Assyriologists (*e.g.* Lesko 1980; Cifola 1994; O'Connor 2000; Redford 2000: 7; Roberts 2009, 2014; Emanuel 2013; Middleton 2015; Ben-Dor Evian 2016). Whilst the ships of both the Egyptians and the 'sea peoples' are represented in the reliefs by only a single prototype, three types of Egyptian ships are listed in the accompanying inscription: *mnš, br* and *ꜥh3 (aha)*. Artzy (2003: 243) perhaps too hastily concluded that there is no correspondence between the written and the iconographic elements of the naval battle, and elsewhere even called into question the authenticity of the scene (Artzy 1987).

With respect to the ship types indicated in the inscription, Säve-Söderbergh (1946: 51, 58 fig. 12) published the Egyptian determinative for an *mnš* ship, and defined it as a seagoing vessel, occasionally involved in trade; in his view, it was a vessel of Egyptian type eventually adopted by Levantine peoples and so perhaps

Figure 31: *Relief drawing of naval battle from mortuary temple of Ramesses III at Medinet Habu.* Wikimedia commons.

SEAFARING AND SEAFARERS IN THE BRONZE AGE EASTERN MEDITERRANEAN

under pharaonic control. Wachsmann (1998: 47 and fig. 3.10), however, pointed out that the determinative for the *mnš* ship closely resembled ships depicted in two Theban tombs (those of Kenamun and Nebamun, discussed below), and argued that the ships are of a Levantine ('Syro-Canaanite') type that was later adopted by the Egyptians (see also Basch 1978: 99-109; Vinson 1993: 146-147; Monroe 2009: 73, n. 53, 225-226). According to Basch (1978), the *mnš* ship — as depicted in tomb paintings, reliefs and graffiti — had high stem and stern posts. The Papyrus Anastasi (IV 3, 10-11—Caminos 1954: 137-43) records an *mnš* ship arriving in Egypt from the land of *Kharu* (*i.e.* the Levant). In the Egyptian *Tale of Wenamun*, *br* appears to be the common word for 'ship'; in one passage (1,58–2,2), moreover, *br* and *mnš* seem to be used as synonyms (note that in Ugaritic, *br* simply refers to a 'large' ship, or barge—see further above, *The Documentary Record*). The *'h3* (*aha*) is well known as a 'fighting' ship and so might be expected in the scene of a naval battle.

The only 'nautical' weapon portrayed in the relief drawings from Medinet Habu is a four-hooked grapnel, thrown by Egyptians into the enemy ships (Wachsmann 1998: 317). Even so, Nelson (1929: 22), in discussing the painted parts of the reliefs that are now all largely worn away, noted that various details such as bow strings or lance shafts were partly carved and partly painted, which suggests that many of the original details of the naval scene, including weapons, may have been lost. Perhaps one salient point we can make about the Medinet Habu reliefs and inscriptions is that the fleet of Ramesses III was comprised at least in part of seagoing, sailing ships (with brailed sail), some of which (*br*) were originally merchant ships, likely of Levantine origin or design, others (*'h3*) likely Egyptian ships intended for use in naval skirmishes.

As to the 'sea peoples' ships from Medinet Habu, Wachsmann has repeatedly argued that they find their closest parallels in Aegean galleys portrayed in representations of Late Helladic and Greek Geometric warships (Wachsmann 1981; 1997; 1998: 172-196; 2000a; 2013: 33-40). In his view (Wachsmann 2000a: 121): 'The Sea Peoples' ship(s) at Medinet Habu so closely parallels what we know of Mycenaean galleys that in our present state of knowledge we cannot differentiate between their construction. Either the ships in use by the Sea Peoples were Mycenaean, or such ships were patterned closely on Mycenaean prototypes'. He also suggested that the prototype of the ships depicted at Medinet Habu may have been a *pentekonter*, *i.e.* a 'fifty-oared' galley (Wachsmann 1998: 174).

More recently, he has published a wheeled, wooden boat (and cart) model found in an early Iron Age tomb at Gurob in Egypt, arguing that it is an Aegean or 'sea peoples' ritual vessel, most likely the representation of a *pentekonter* (Wachsmann 2013: 202; see also Emanuel 2013: 18) (Figure 32). Ultimately, he suggests that this model, when paired with evidence from the Wilbour Papyrus for *Sherden* landholders living in the Fayyum, indicates that the tomb represents the burial of an individual *Sherden* or one of his descendants (Wachsmann 2013: 206): he thus implies some link between what he sees as an Aegean-type sailing vessel and one group of the 'sea peoples'. Even if it is broadly agreed that the Gurob ship-cart model evinces Aegean aspects in its design, there is no definitive link here between the Aegean world and the *Sherden* or any other group of 'sea peoples'. At most, as Emanuel (2016: 277) points out, 'if the galley model and the Sherden are in fact connected, this should be

Figure 32: *Wooden boat model from an early Iron Age tomb at Gurob in Egypt.* Photo by Shelley Wachsmann. Courtesy Petrie Museum of Egyptian Archaeology.

seen as evidence that these people were beneficiaries of the intense contact between cultures within the eastern Mediterranean's zones of transference'.

Wachsmann (2013: 41-52) discusses in detail a ship's graffito from the Dakleh Oasis, dated to the late thirteenth-early twelfth century BC, and already mentioned above in relation to the ships' carvings at Nahal Me'arot. Basch (1994b, 1997) had already identified the boat as being of Aegean type and identified its mariners as Libyans, thus attempting to make a link to the 'sea peoples' and their boats. Artzy (1998: 444) too argued that the most distinctive boat amongst these carvings was of 'Aegean type', and compared it to the Dakhleh Oasis graffito. The ship depicted is very schematic (Wachsmann 2013: 43 fig. 2.10), with a single line representing the hull, a sharply-angled sternpost rising from it (to the left) and one curving, nearly vertical quarter rudder descending from the sternpost. A vertical line amidships may represent a mast, which has a diagonal line running from it to the deck (Wachsmann 2013: 47-50, 203 regards this line as a large phallic symbol); to the right stands a horizontally bisected forecastle. Nine stick-like figures can be seen at different places on the ship, several with a distinct 'appendage' (long hair?) that trails from their head, with the forward-most figure also sporting a three-pronged device on his head (Basch 1997: 21 fig. 14; Wachsmann 2013: 48 fig. 2.18). Wachsmann (2013: 52) regards this highly stylised vessel as a 'Helladic galley', the headgear as possible plumed helmets, and the people as Mycenaeans, 'sea 'peoples or the Libyans (in this case, the *Tjemhu*).

From the tomb of Kenamun in Thebes (no. 162) comes what is probably the best known and most detailed representation of Levantine ('Syro-Canaanite') seagoing ships, eleven in total (Wachsmann 1998: 42-47). Kenamun was 'mayor of Thebes' during the reign of Amenhotep III (ca. 1408-1386 BC), and the scene depicts ships and merchants arriving at what is presumably the dock at Thebes. Whereas earlier scholars — Säve-Söderbergh (1946: 56-57) and Davies and Faulkner (1947: 41) — regarded the ships depicted in Kenamun's tomb to be of Egyptian origin and design, Wachsmann (1981: 214-216; 1998: 45) argued that these vessels are 'Syro-Canaanite', on the basis of the ships' rigging, mast, sail and crow's nest, as well as the hair, beards and clothing of the ships' crews (see also Vinson 1993: 137-138,

144-145). Moreover, in one well known register, an Egyptian official is engaged in a transaction with a 'Syrian' merchant who, along with at least three other men, are carrying Canaanite jars, the most widely traded MTC in the LB eastern Mediterranean (see Figure 5, above). From this scene, it seems evident that Levantine merchants and mariners engaged directly in trade with Egyptian merchants and/or shopkeepers who touted local goods in the port at Thebes.

In the somewhat earlier tomb of the physician Nebamun, dated to the reign of Amenhotep II (ca. 1445-1423 BC), a single, poorly preserved ship is depicted, whilst Nebamun himself is shown examining a Levantine (based on dress, hair style) merchant, whose wife stands beside him (Wachsmann 1998: 45-47, figs. 3.7-3.9; Säve-Söderbergh 1946: 54-56; 1957: 25-27, pl. 23). The style and rigging (such as it is) of the ship depicted is similar to those seen in Kenamun's tomb and the ship is thus argued to be another 'Syro-Canaanite' vessel. All these scenes from Theban reliefs, as well as those from the Memphite necropolis at Saqqara, suggest that the Egyptian state was well organised to receive foreigners and to administer overseas trade and related affairs, registering and unloading cargoes, arranging meetings with foreign traders or individuals (*i.e.* Nebamun), and in general overseeing all the bustling activity at dockside (Monroe 2009: 191-192).

MARITIME TRANSPORT CONTAINERS (MTCS)

As already noted in Chapter 4 (*Middle Bronze Age—The Levant and Egypt*), the Canaanite jar is the best known and most widely circulated MTC in the Bronze Age eastern Mediterranean. Examples from the Late Bronze Age have been described, categorised, classified and analysed extensively by art historians, archaeologists and science-based archaeologists ever since the pioneering work of Grace (1956), Amiran (1970: 139-142) and Parr (1973). As Amiran (1970: 140) noted in her well-known corpus of pottery from the southern Levant, the Canaanite jar was not valued or exchanged because of some intrinsic value attached to it, but rather for what it contained: 'These large jars were not worth loading on a ship, unless they were filled with oil or wine'. Knapp and Demesticha (2017: 46-66) recently presented the history of research, the typologies, analytical work (provenance studies, organic residues analysis–ORA) and known distribution of the Canaanite jar in the Aegean and eastern Mediterranean during the Bronze and early Iron Ages (see also Pedrazzi 2016; Cateloy 2016; Martin 2016). Because earlier work often listed only complete examples of Canaanite jars, or classified them as 'storage jars', it is impossible to quantify their numbers accurately within or beyond the eastern Mediterranean during the LB. Given the diversity of their contents as well as a shape and capacity (7-30 litres) that made them ideal for shipping, they became the MTC *par excellence* for LBA Mediterranean trade.

Given the extent of recently published work, here I only summarise what is currently known about the distribution, provenance and significance of both the Canaanite jar and Egyptian jar (on the latter, see also Knapp and Demesticha 2017: 66-70). Following Killebrew's (2007: 167-169, fig. 1: 1-3) typology, the angular-shouldered form CA 22 — Pedrazzi's (2007: 75-77, 87-90; 2016: 62-66) Type 5.4 — represents the most common type of MTC found in the LB eastern Mediterranean (see Figure 17.6 above). Variations of this type are shown being offloaded from ships on the Egyptian New Kingdom reliefs mentioned above (*Ships' Representations* — see *e.g.*

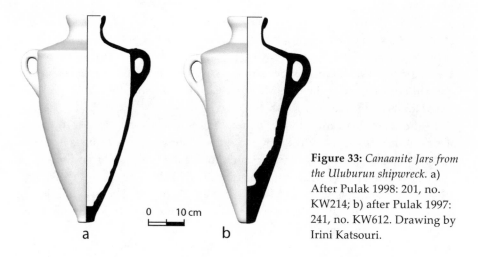

Figure 33: *Canaanite Jars from the Uluburun shipwreck.* a) After Pulak 1998: 201, no. KW214; b) after Pulak 1997: 241, no. KW612. Drawing by Irini Katsouri.

Davies and Faulkner 1947: 43, 45, pl. 8; Wachsmann 1998: 57-58, fig. 3.29); it is also represented by 80 physical examples found stacked in rows in a storeroom at Minet al-Beidha, the main port of Ugarit (Schaeffer 1932: 3, pl. 3.3) (see Figure 24 above). At least 150 examples are known from the Uluburun shipwreck (most recently Pulak 2008: 317-320, nos. 190a-b; 2010: 867), and a few more from the Cape Gelidonya shipwreck (Hennessy and Taylor, in Bass 1967: 122-123, fig. 132) (Figure 33).

Examples of form CA 22 are found in Cilicia, all along the Levantine coast (more commonly in Lebanon and Syria, but also at coastal sites in the south such as Deir el-Balah, Tell Abu Hawam and Tel Qasile—Killebrew 2007: 173, nn. 34-35); in northern Sinai, at sites along the 'Ways of Horus' (Oren 1987: 83-84, 95, 103); in Egypt at some 14 different sites (Ownby 2010: 90-92, fig. 3.40); at Wadi Gawasis on the Red Sea coast (Bard and Fattovich 2010: 9), and along western Egypt's coast at Marsa Matruh (Hulin, in White 2002b: 19-20, fig. 8.2, 39-42, figs. 8.12-8.14) and Zawiyet Umm el-Rakham (Snape 2003: 67; Snape and Wilson 2007: 58-68). Canaanite jars have been found at over 20 different sites in Cyprus (see Table 5, below), including at least 84 examples from Maa *Palaeokastro* (Hadjicosti 1988), and over 68 examples from renewed excavations at Pyla *Kokkinokremnos* (Georgiou 2014: 176, 186).

The array of analytical work — petrographic analysis, Neutron Activation Analysis (NAA), ORA — carried out on LB Canaanite jars presents a complex picture (Knapp and Demesticha 2017: 60-64). There is a variety of likely contents (wine, olive oil, pistacia resin) and numerous possible production centres, from the western Jezreel Valley and the Bay of Haifa all the way north to Syria if not Cilicia and on Cyprus (Raban 1980: 5-6; Sugerman 2000; Serpico *et al.* 2003; Serpico 2005; Smith *et al.* 2004; Killebrew 2007: 175-180; Ownby *et al.* 2014). ORA conducted on some Canaanite jars from Tell el-Amarna indicated that their contents included wine, oil and pistacia resin (Serpico and White 2000: 891-894; Stern *et al.* 2000). This seems to be corroborated by 'jar dockets' (hieratic inscriptions) occasionally inscribed on the exterior surfaces of the vessels (Serpico *et al.* 2003: 365-366, 373; Serpico and White 2000: 894). Such jar dockets also listed details of production dates, the type of goods to be transported and occasionally the names of the agents involved. From Deir el-Medina, more than 200 kms upstream from Amarna, some

| SEAFARING AND SEAFARERS IN THE BRONZE AGE EASTERN MEDITERRANEAN

30 jar dockets list the captains of the ships (*ḥrj mnš*) on which olive oil and resin (*snṯr*) were transported to Egypt (Bavay 2015: 130, 137).

ORA and petrographic analyses of Canaanite jars from both Memphis and Amarna showed that two of the six (petrographic) groups identified carried pistacia resin and two others oil (Bourriau *et al.* 2001: 143-144; Serpico *et al.* 2003: 369-372). Five Canaanite jars from the Uluburun shipwreck containing pistacia resin were made from a fabric similar to that of 40 Canaanite jars from Amarna containing resin (Ownby 2010: 83; see also Mills and White 1989; Stern *et al.* 2008; but *cf.* McGovern and Hall 2016, who re-analysed the resin samples from five Uluburun jars, and conclusively identified tartaric acid/tartrate, the biomarker of grape and wine, in two if not three samples). Petrographic and ORA on some Canaanite jars from Deir el-Medina also show that other products — olive oil (*nḥḥ*), moringa oil (*b3k*), *mrḥt* (vegetal oil or animal fat), honey — are associated with three distinct fabric groups (Bavay 2015: 129-132); one docket from a Deir el-Medina Canaanite jar refers to the 'honey of *ikaryti*' (Ugarit), which coincides precisely with the petrographic origin proposed for fabric group 4 at Deir el-Medina.

One final pattern bears emphasis. Preliminary petrographic analyses indicate that over 80% of the Canaanite jars recovered from the Uluburun shipwreck were made from sediments typical of the region around the Haifa Bay; a second group (14%) stems from the area between Tyre and Sidon in Lebanon (Pulak 2008: 317-318, n. 5; Goren 2013: 57). Some of the clays used to make the Canaanite jars found on the Uluburun shipwreck also seem to match those of Fabric Group 1 Canaanite jars from Amarna in Egypt (Bourriau *et al.* 2001); both have a common source around sites in the vicinity of Haifa Bay (Serpico *et al.* 2003: 369, 373; Pulak 2008: 319-320, and n. 5).

If such links between the fabric of a jar and the commodity it held, or amongst petrographic groups identified by different researchers working in different regions, could be established more widely, our understanding of the key role played by MTCs in the local economies of the LBA eastern Mediterranean would be greatly enhanced. More generally, these links could also be related to production and consumption patterns within the region.

Imports of Canaanite jars into Egypt probably began during the late Middle Kingdom, ca. 1800 BC (Aston 2004: 176) and eventually led to local imitations. By the onset of the Eighteenth Dynasty (ca. 1570 BC), wheelmade Egyptian jars (aka Egyptian amphorae) began to appear (Bourriau 2004: 80-81), becoming increasingly common throughout the New Kingdom and Ramesside periods (Wood 1987; Bourriau *et al.* 2000). The shape of these jars became increasingly narrow and angular, with (two) loop handles and a severely pointed base (Wood 1987: 79-81; see also Grace 1956: 88, 90), making it ideal for seaborne transport.

The shape of the New Kingdom Egyptian jar is similar to that of the Canaanite jar, and both types of vessel served similar functions—transport and storage. In terms of their distribution, Egyptian jars have been found on Cyprus (Hala Sultan Tekke, Pyla *Kokkinokremos* and Maa *Palaeokastro*—Peltenburg 1986: 165; Eriksson 1995: 203-204) and throughout the southern Levant, *e.g.* in tombs at Akko (Ben-Arieh and Edelstein 1977: fig. 10.9), Deir el-Balah (Dothan 1979: 14, 16) and Ashkelon, and at settlement or related contexts at Beth Shan, Megiddo and Ashkelon (Martin 2008; 2011: 73-77, figs. 38-39) (Figure 34). Farther afield, they have also been

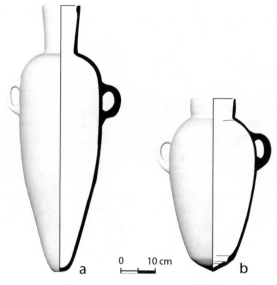

Figure 34: *Egyptian Amphorae.*
a) medium-large size, slender and
pointed type AM 1; b) smaller,
broad ovoid type AM 2.
a) After Martin 2011: pl. 45.2; b)
after Martin 2011: pl. 42.1.
Drawing by Irini Katsouri.

found at Kommos on Crete (Day *et al.* 2011: 518-519). Martin (2011: 253) states that these jars '… arrived in the southern Levant mainly by sea trade as shipping containers'. The hieratic inscriptions found on many of them suggest they were used to store or transport a variety of locally produced goods, most importantly wine but also beer, honey, milk, fats, meats, fowl, fish, grains, fruit, gum and incense (Wood 1987: 76 for refs; Tallet 1998; see also Lesko 1996: 220-228 for New Kingdom wine labels; Aston 2007 for honey).

Petrographic studies and NAA conducted on New Kingdom Egyptian jars have been contradictory. McGovern's (1997: 90-91) Instrumental NAA (INAA) on some Egyptian jars ('Marl D group') suggested an origin around Thebes, whereas petrographic studies indicated that they were most likely manufactured far downriver, near Memphis in the upper Nile Delta (Bourriau and Nicholson 1992; Bourriau *et al.* 2000: 17-18, 31-32). Fifteen Egyptian jars found at Kommos on Crete were analysed by thin-section petrography and INAA, and were found to match comparative marl fabrics from the region of Memphis (Day *et al.* 2011: 518-519, 550). Egyptian jars reveal a great deal of homogeneity in their composition, and thus perhaps reflect their origin at a single location over an extended period. If, as James (1996) and Murray (2000) have argued, the Nile Delta and Fayyum regions near Memphis were the principal vine-growing areas of ancient Egypt, and if these jars served at least in part to store or transport wine, it makes more economic sense to assume they were produced in the Memphite region, rather than around Thebes.

STONE ANCHORS, FISHING TACKLE AND FISH

Stone anchors of Bronze Age date abound in the eastern Mediterranean seabed, and are found on land at sites all along the Levantine coast, on Cyprus and in Egypt. I already noted above (Chapter 2: *Material Aspects—Stone Anchors, Fishing and Fishing Equipment*) the division of Mediterranean pierced stone anchors into three types: (1) sand anchors (with multiple holes); (2) weight-anchors (with a single hole); and (3) composite-anchors (with three holes) (Frost 1985: 283-284, fig. 1; see also Wachsmann 2000b: 816).

Frost (1982: 269) once observed that only weight-anchors are found in Early Bronze Age contexts on land; elsewhere, she noted that in earlier Bronze Age contexts at Byblos, no composite anchors are recorded, whereas at Late Bronze Age Kition on Cyprus, both weight-anchors and composite-anchors existed (Frost 1991: 367). Wachsmann (1998: 255) therefore suggested that because 'Composite- and weight-anchors are found together in Middle Bronze and Late Bronze Age contexts at Ugarit and Kition… the weight-anchor preceded the composite-anchor but continued in use alongside it'; it should be noted, however, that there are no MB contexts at Kition. Of equal interest, the thirteenth century BC (LB) Uluburun ship carried 24 weight-anchors, but no composite anchors (Pulak 1998: 216-217, fig. 25). Whatever the value of the standard three-fold typology, it bears repeating that dating stone anchors found in the sea (as opposed to those found on a shipwreck site) is a precarious undertaking. Moreover, Wachsmann (1998: 211-212) and others (Howitt-Marshall 2012: 109; Harpster 2013) have rightly pointed to several problems associated with identifying a wrecked ship's port of origin or 'ethnic' affiliation; at the same time, however, they suggest that a ship's anchors could, in some cases, provide more secure evidence. Indeed, Frost (1991: 367) stated forcefully: 'Goods are … no indication of the "nationality" of the vessels that carried them; stone-anchors are'.

In general, Frost (1963, 1970a, 1970b, 1985: 282) demonstrated clearly the crucial importance of stone anchors for understanding seaborne trade in the Mediterranean, and argued that ships of Cypriot and Levantine origin plied the sea-lanes of the eastern Mediterranean during the Late Bronze Age (Frost 1985; 1991: 370-371). Wachsmann's (1998: 265-273) very useful summary of published Bronze Age stone anchors has already been called upon above (Chapter 4: *Middle Bronze Age—The Levant and Egypt, Stone Anchors*) and I do so again here for some LB examples.

From Megadim in Israel comes a pair of anchors first identified as being of Egyptian origin, based on two hieroglyphic-like signs incised on them (Stieglitz 1972a). Wachsmann (1998: 265-266, 268 fig. 12.21-22) reconsidered these anchors, along with two further examples from Megadim (Galili and Raveh 1988), and maintained that their general shape indicates they are of 'Syro-Canaanite' origin. Other stone anchors from Dor and Kfar Samir (one each), Tell Abu Hawam (8 examples) and Tel Akko are cited, all possibly of LB date (Wachsmann 1998: 266-271, 268 fig. 12.23-27, with refs.). Several stone anchors of 'Byblian' type, but most likely of MB II date, have been recovered from the sea off the coast of Israel: 25 from the Carmel coast, 15 from Naveh Yam, two from the area around Dor, and two near Megadim (Galili 1985; Galili *et al.* 1994; Wachsmann 1998: 272-273, figs. 12.29-32). Of the 28 stone anchors found at Byblos itself (Frost 1969), most are weight-anchors tentatively dated to the MB, but at least nine examples were found in secondary use in post-MB strata (Wachsmann 1998: 271-272, fig. 12-28).

At Ugarit, under somewhat trying conditions in a 1963 visit to the site, Frost (1991: 356) recorded 29 pierced stone anchors 'from all areas of past excavation including Minet el-Beidha'; a further 14 anchors were recorded in 1986. Twenty-two of these 43 anchors were deposited in or around what is known as the 'Temple of Ba'al' (see above, Chapter 4: *Middle Bronze Age—The Levant and Egypt, Stone Anchors*), whilst another 15 came from various structures and tombs at Minet el-Beidha, 'where they are without any utilitarian maritime association' (Frost 1991: 356). Whereas Schaeffer (1978: 375) proposed a MB date (between about 1900 and 1780 BC) for all the anchors found around the 'Temple of Baal', Frost (1991: 356, 375-82) was more circumspect and frequently pointed to possible LB parallels, especially from Kition on Cyprus (which is entirely of LB date). She also confirmed a fifteenth-fourteenth century BC date for two anchors found beside the entrance to Tomb 36 in the *Ville Basse* at Ugarit (Frost 1991: 360-362, 382-383; see also Wachsmann 1998: 274 fig. 12.33:27-28), and for another 'weight-anchor' found in the *Palais Sud* (Frost 1991: 383). Of the Minet el-Beidha anchors, Frost (1991: 385-389) included 12 in her catalogue, dating eight of them specifically to the LB.

From the 'acropolis' at Ugarit come five stone weights shaped like miniature versions of a ship's anchor, some with extra piercings (Frost 1991: 365-366). There are also three examples of another type of stone weight, shaped like a quoit, *i.e.* circular in form with a hole in the middle; these may have served as sinkers, or as 'messengers' (dropped from the deck of a ship to disentangle a rope or other line). Although no fishing tackle has been preserved from Minet el-Beidha, Frost notes that accounts of the first two seasons (Schaeffer 1929, 1931) mention 'pierced pebbles' and 'curious pierced stelae' (the latter must be anchors). Other types of fishing tackle and three different kinds of shells were also recorded (Frost 1991: 366, 403, pl. IX:9-12, 404-405, pls. X-XI). One curious Ugaritic document records diverse types of merchandise, including 2000 sardines (*alpn*) and 15 squid (KTU 4.247—Dietrich *et al.* 1995: 308-309; Virolleaud 1957: 162-163, no. 128), both species that can be caught (netted) in the coastal zone (von Rüden 2015: 43).

With respect to fish, a cylinder seal from Alalakh, not far north of Ugarit in Syria, depicts an offering table with a fish, shown before a seated god (Collon 1975: 105-106, no. 96; pl. XLII shows several other seals with fish). Early excavations in Ugarit's harbour at Minet el-Beidha produced large amounts of crushed murex shells (Schaeffer 1929: 290, 293, 296), presumably for producing purple dye. Fish from the Nile have been found at LB Levantine coastal settlements such as Sarepta, Tel Akko, Tell Abu-Hawam, Tel Dor and Ashkelon, and at inland sites such as Megiddo, Lachish, Tel el-Wawayat, Timna and Tell al-Umayri (van Neer *et al.* 2004: 120; on shellfish remains at LB sites, see Reese *et al.* 1986: 82). Several different taxa of Mediterranean fish imports are also noted from Megiddo and Lachish, and sea bream from Tel el-Wawayat (van Neer *et al.* 2004: 134). At Marsa Matruh, various Mediterranean species (*e.g.* shark, grouper, sea bass, bream, tunny, mackerel, mullet) as well as shellfish (mainly *Monodonta, Patella, Murex trunculus*) have been documented (Reese and Rose 2002: 88-92, 95-101). Because such data have seldom been published in any detail, it is worth noting that more recent excavations at Timna's Site 34 (Early Iron Age) have uncovered a diverse array of fish bones — mullet (*Mugilidae sp.*), porgies (*Sparidae sp.*) and catfish (*Clariidae* sp.) — that most likely originated in the Mediterranean and arrived at Timna via long-distance trade with one or another of the coastal polities (Sapir-Hen and Ben-Yosef 2014: 781, 785; Ben-Yosef 2016: 178 fig. 9f; 180). Had earlier excavations taken such care with icthyofaunal data, or at least published them, we might be much better informed on this aspect of Mediterraenan seafaring.

CYPRUS

HARBOURS

There are no physical remains of formal built harbours on Bronze Age Cyprus (for a recent discussion, see Knapp 2014: 84-85). Nonetheless there are several indicators of suitable ports or anchorages on the island, at sites such as Maroni *Tsarroukas*, Tochni *Lakkia*, Enkomi, Kition and Hala Sultan Tekke *Vyzakia* (Manning and DeMita 1997; Manning 1998; Morhange *et al.* 2000; Manning *et al.* 2002; Crewe 2007; Brown 2013; Devillers *et al.* 2015; Andreou and Sewell 2015; Bony *et al.* 2016; Andreou *et al.* 2017). Cyprus's most important harbours throughout historical times were usually sited in bays or inlets on the southern and southeastern coasts, from Limassol in the south around to modern day Larnaca and Famagusta in the east (Georgiou 1997: 121). To the west of modern Limassol, the site of Kourion/Episkopi may also have served as a harbour, but thus far no material indicators of such have been found on land or in Kourion Bay. Farther west, along the coast below the Late Cypriot (LC) site of *Palaipaphos*, Howitt-Marshall (2012) conducted an underwater survey at Kouklia *Achni*, recording 120 stone anchors. Although this might suggest the existence of a 'proto-harbour' here during the Bronze Age, Iacovou (2008: 271) has proposed that the main harbour of *Palaipaphos* was most likely at the locality *Loures*.

From the very beginning of the Late Bronze Age, the site of Enkomi served as an *emporion*, receiving all manner of imported goods and specialised products: ivory, metals, cylinder seals, jewellery, Canaanite jars and Egyptian pottery, and much more (Courtois *et al.* 1986; Keswani 1989; Crewe 2007: 16-25; 2012: 232-234). Enkomi was only one day's sail from Syria or Cilicia, and to judge from its mortuary remains, archaeometallurgical installations and Cypro-Minoan texts (Ferrara 2012: 50-56 and *passim*; 2016: 229-232; Knapp 2013a: 427-432), the site functioned as a crucial nexus in the island's external trade, whether to the east or the west. Late Bronze Age Kition *Kathari*, likewise rich in imported products, lay within a large, semi-protected bay; ongoing geomorphological and related studies indicate that it may have been situated directly on a protected marine embayment that would have given it access to the sea via an inlet (Morhange *et al.* 2000; Devillers *et al.* 2015: 78; Bony *et al.* 2016; see also Collombier 1988: 43-44) (see Figure 6, above). In any case, Kition's role as a major coastal port and trading centre is not in doubt (Karageorghis and Demas 1985).

Early work by Gifford (1985) indicated that Bronze Age harbour facilities at Hala Sultan Tekke *Vyzakia* were most likely situated in the shelter of a coastal lagoon, with a navigable outlet to the sea. More recent geormorphological work (Devillers *et al.* 2015) has confirmed the formation of such a lagoon, and identified two possible natural channels along the eastern and southern edges of the lagoon through which maritime traffic could have passed during the Late Bronze Age. Ancient ports may also have existed in the hinterland west of Hala Sultan Tekke, along the southern coast at the mouth of the Tremithos and Pouzis rivers (Leonard 2000: 135-137; Coenaerts and Samaes 2015: 81; see also Ghilardi *et al.* 2015 on human-induced change along the Tremithos during the Late Chalcolithic).

Farther west along the south coast, at Maroni *Tsaroukkas*, imported pottery and stone anchors recovered during underwater survey indicate that this site also served as a Late Bronze Age anchorage (Manning *et al.* 2002: 113 fig. 6, 121-123). Some five km west of Maroni lies the eroding coastal site of Tochni *Lakkia,* quite likely another Late Bronze anchorage — perhaps serving as a coastal outlet for the site of Kalavasos *Ayios Dhimitrios* (Andreou and Sewell 2015; Andreou *et al.* 2017). The limited survey work conducted thus far at *Lakkia*, both on land and underwater, has produced a submerged circular stone feature (a well?), four possible net weights and a possible stone anchor (the last lost since discovery—Todd 2016: 327-328), several sherds of storage jars and *pithoi*, and one fragment of a Canaanite jar. In the southwest, survey and geophysical work carried out by the Palaipaphos Urban Landscape Project (Iacovou 2008: 271; 2012: 62 fig. 7.4, 64) suggest that the locality *Loures*, just east of the natural terrace where the Late Bronze Age site of *Palaipaphos* is located, may have been the inlet of that site's original harbour.

SHIPS' REPRESENTATIONS

In Area II at LBA Kition, ship graffiti were incised on the wall of 'Temple' 1 and on two limestone slabs found in 'Temple 4', dated to the twelfth-early eleventh centuries BC (Basch and Artzy 1985: 323-324, 329 figs. 1-2). On the southern façade of 'Temple' 1 are 19 engraved ships' graffiti (Figure 35), and four further 'scratchings' that may represent ships (Basch and Artzy 1985: 324-326, 330 fig. 3). In 'Temple' 4, the two clearest engravings (on limestone slabs) depict ships that the authors identify as 'round boats', one with a distinctive inward-curving 'fan' at its left extremity, like those already noted in the carved ships' representations at Tel Akko and the Nahal Me'arot (see above, *Ships' Representations, Levant*). At least three of the ships in Temple 1 also show this fan-like extremity. Basch and Artzy (1985: 326-327) suggest that one of these ships represents a 'long boat' (a warship), and that all of them show the prow on the left. Wachsmann (1998: 147-148) observed that these graffiti are badly weathered, and allow for multiple interpretations; he questions, for example, whether one ship ('P') might be facing right, and so what Basch and Artzy see as a ram might instead be a quarter rudder (Wachsmann 1998: 147 fig. 7.36, 357-358 n.108; 2013: 69, 72 fig. 2.44B). He also calls into question their identification as 'round boats', and suggests that the fan-like finial '…bears more than a passing resemblance to an inward-facing bird's head' (Wachsmann 1998: 148).

Another schematic ship graffito is engraved on a stele from Enkomi (Schaeffer 1952: 102-103, fig. 38, pl. 10; Basch 1987: 147-148, fig. 12), likely dated to the twelfth century BC, i.e. Late Cypriot (LC) LC III. Wachsmann (1998: 142-144, fig. 7.29) suggested this ship was facing right, and outfitted with a brailed rig and furled sail (also Emanuel 2016: 273). From Hala Sultan Tekke *Vyzakia* comes a further graffito carved on a limestone ashlar block of similar date (Öbrink 1979: 16-17 [N4007], 73 figs. 103-104) (Figure 36). Based on the shape of the ship's hull (like the Egyptian *mnš*-ship determinative) and its ending in a post like those depicted on the ships represented in the tombs of Nebamun and Kenamun (see above, *Ships' Representations, Egypt*), Wachsmann (1998: 49-50, fig. 3.14) maintained that this graffito portrays a 'Syro-Canaanite' ship. Because none of these representations seem intent on portraying nautical reality, it seems somewhat misleading to associate them

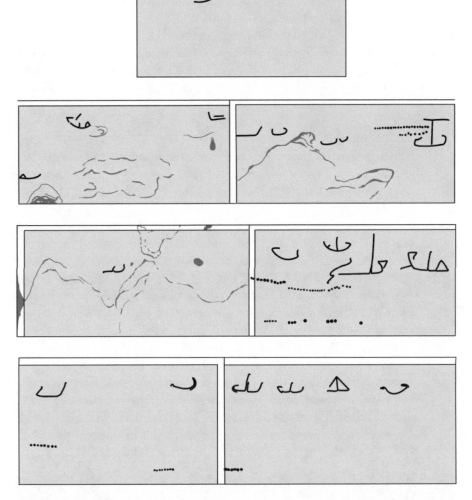

Figure 35: *Ships' graffiti on south wall of 'Temple 1' at Kition.* From Webb 1999: 302 fig. 94. Courtesy of Jennifer Webb.

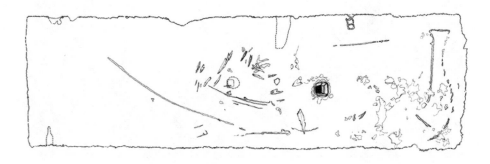

Figure 36: *Ship graffito from Hala Sultan Tekke Vyzakia, carved on a limestone ashlar block.* After Öbrink 1979: 73 fig. 103.

with specific kinds of ships or ethnicities (also Wachsmann 1998: 147-148). If Basch and Artzy (1985: 324-327; see also Wachsmann 1981: 206-207) are correct, these Cypriot engravings represent both 'round boats' and 'long boats', and may indicate that two different boat-building traditions existed on LBA Cyprus.

In addition to the four possible clay boat models dated to the Middle Cypriot period and noted in the previous chapter (*Middle Bronze Age—Cyprus, Ships' Representations*), several more are dated to the Late Cypriot (LC) period (some of the following are also listed in Knapp 2014: 82):

1. White Painted IV model from Kazaphani *Ayios Andronikos* (now in Cyprus Museum, Tomb 2 B, no. 377) with a deep hull and what appears to be a massive stern construction, perforated amidships with a circular socket for the mast (Göttlicher 1978: 37 and pl. 12, no. 167; Basch 1987: 71-72 figs. 138-141). Date: LC I-II, ca. 1600-1400 BC.

2. Plain White Handmade model from Maroni *Tsaroukkas* (A50), with lower half of hull missing, a striking stern (?) projection and two stubby horizontal ledges on either side amidships (Göttlicher 1978: 34, pl. 9, no.147; Basch 1987: 71, 73-74, figs. 143, 145; Wachsmann 1998: 63-66, figs. 4.6-4.7). Date: LC I-II, ca. 1600-1400 BC. (Figure 37a)

3. Plain White Handmade model from Maroni *Tsaroukkas* (A49), with a narrow, flattened bottom rising at both ends and a raised mast socket amidships (Göttlicher 1978: 34, pl. 9, no.146; Basch 1987: 71, 73 fig. 144; Wachsmann 1998: 64-66, figs. 4.8-4.9). Date: LC I-II, ca. 1600-1400 BC. (Figure 37b)

4. Boat model from tomb (?) at Enkomi *Ayios Iakovos* with symmetrical prow and stern, now in Musées Royaux d'Art et d'Histoire, Brussels, no. A1240 (gift of British Museum) (Basch 1987: 73-74, fig. 146; Westerberg 1983: 15, no. 9, fig. 9). Wachsmann (1998: 50-51, fig. 3.15) suggests this might be a 'Syro-Canaanite' ship. Date: LC I-II (?), ca. 1600-1400 BC.

Figure 37a, b: *Plain White Handmade ware boat models from Maroni Tsaroukkas. a) No. A50 (right, top, large); b) no. A49 (left, bottom, small).* © The Trustees of the British Museum, Reg. no. 1898,1201.121 (AN362832).

5. Boat model of unknown provenance, now in the Louvre, no. AM 636, made of light yellow clay, with crescent-shaped hull and stems rising above the ship's deck (Göttlicher 1978: 34, no. 145; Westerberg 1983: 15-16, no. 10, fig. 10). Date: LC I-II (?), ca. 1600-1400 BC.

6. Fragment of a model from Maroni Tomb 17 (British Museum GR 1898,12-1.146; BM C 694) in the form of a boat's hull and stern (?), with quarter rudder (?) angled downward; on the sides of the model are painted some Aegean design elements (boat with oars and quarter rudder[?], or part of a fish, scale pattern) (Johnson 1980: 23, no. 132, pl. XXV:132; Sewell 2015: 189, fig. 5). Date: Late Helladic (LH) IIIA2, ca. 1350 BC.

7. Fragment of a painted (brown), terracotta model from Maa *Palaeokastro*, with sharp end (keel?) and high prow decorated with painted horizontal lines and rows of 'festoons' (Karageorghis and Demas 1988: 120, 228, no. 691, pls. LXVI, CLXXXVI). Date: LC III, ca. 1200 BC.

8. Two fragments of a boat model from Sinda *Siri Dash*, on whitish-buff ceramic with bands painted in brownish-black (Furumark and Adelman 2003: 119, pl. 39 [pl.14]). Date: LC III tomb, ca. 1200 BC.

Wachsmann (1998: 64, 66, 328) suggests that models 1-3 may represent 'indigenous' Cypriot merchant ships, *i.e.* vessels that could have easily navigated the open sea (to these, we might add models 4-5 above). The date and type (*i.e.* boat or not) of the following clay models from Cyprus is uncertain:

9. Model found in the sea, near Amathus on the south coast, and now in a private collection in Cyprus, with apparent rounded hull, pointed stems and a mast-socket amidships (Westerberg 1983: 14-15, no. 8, fig. 8). Date: LC or Cypro-Geometric, ca. 1600-1050 BC.

10. Model found in the sea, probably near Amathus, and now in a private collection in Cyprus, made of rough red clay with slender hull, raised stern with small cabin, and 12 holes below ship's edge/deck/gunwale (Basch 1987: 254, 257 no. 554; Westerberg 1983: 16, no. 11, fig. 11). Date: LC (ca. 1600-1200 BC) or, more likely, Cypro-Archaic.

11. Terracotta model with bichrome decoration, of unknown provenance, and now in the Israel National Maritime Museum, with narrow crescent-shaped hull and high projecting, red- and black-painted stem- and stern-posts (Stieglitz 1972b; Göttlicher 1978: 31, pl. 7: 107; Wachsmann 1998: 152, fig. 7.51; 2013: 27, fig. 1.27). Date: mid-eleventh century BC (Westerberg 1983: 18-19, no. 17, dates this model to the Cypro-Geometric period).

Three Proto-White Painted *rhyta* (or *askoi*) from Lapithos are also regarded as ship models (Göttlicher 1978: 35, pl. 9:149; Basch and Artzy 1985: 334 figs. 11-12). Basch and Artzy (1985: 326) interpreted them as 'long ships' with a ram at the stem. Wachsmann (1998: 151-152, fig. 7.48, 187 fig. 8.47; 2013: 69, fig. 2.41) compared them to 'Mycenaean galleys' or 'warships', and argued that the ship was facing the opposite direction; thus the device regarded by Basch and Artzy as a ram was instead most likely a quarter rudder. In any case, these objects — like

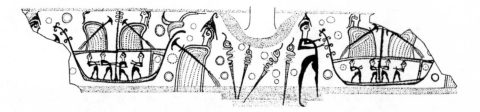

Figure 38: *Enkomi Late Helladic IIIB krater depicting two round boats, with warriors above deck and rowers (?) below.* After Sjöqvist 1940: fig. 20:3.

no. 11 above — most likely date to the Cypro-Geometric period, and thus fall beyond the temporal framework under discussion here. It may be noted, however, that 50 further, quite diverse ship models are known from early Iron Age Cyprus (Demesticha 2012: 81, cat. nos.78-79), which might indicate a growing Cypriot involvement in maritime ventures in the eastern Mediterranean.

A few further ships' representations are painted on pottery sherds. A krater of LH IIIB (LC II) date from Enkomi depicts what have been argued to be two round boats with armed men standing on their decks and smaller figures below deck (Sjöqvist 1940: fig. 20:3; Basch 1987: 147-148, fig. 312) (Figure 38). Three further sherds depicting bits of both people and ships do not add much to the scene (Karageorghis 1960: 146, pl. 10.7). Wachsmann (1998: 141-143, fig. 7.28; 2013: 76) discussed this scene in some detail, and suggested that the men below deck were rowers whilst the ships themselves were Mycenaean galleys that served a military, not a mercantile function, in this case a water-borne procession (see also Wedde 2000: 324, no. 644). Mountjoy (2005: 424 n. 6, pl. 97:d) has identified what she believes to be parts of boats painted on LH IIIC (middle) sherds from Enkomi (Dikaios 1969: pl. 72: 8; 1971: 593 no. 5549/3). One sherd shows a bird-head post decoration, the other depicts parts of two rowers and an arm, as well as an oar. Wachsmann (2013: 76, 79, fig. 2.50) believes these sherds may depict parts of two different ships, although this is pushing what is already a somewhat extravagant interpretation. Another, highly schematic boat is painted on the shoulder of a Proto-White Painted (LC III or Cypro-Geometric?) amphora from Vathyrkakas on the north coast; it shows two figures rowing or perhaps fishing, with two large fish depicted either side of the vessel (Westerberg 1983: 16-17, no.12, 86 fig. 12; Wachsmann 1998: 67). Finally, I note here a LC II-III (?) serpentine cylinder seal carved with a crescent-shaped, masted ship, perhaps showing a crow's nest (Cyprus Museum inventory no. N.40, but in private collection—Kenna 1967: 573, fig. 31; Westerberg 1983: 18 no. 16, 89 fig. 16). There are two human figures in the ship, one of whom seems to be manoeuvring a quarter rudder (Wachsmann 1998: 66-67, fig. 4.10).

MARITIME TRANSPORT CONTAINERS

In a recent publication (Knapp 2016), I discussed the presence of both locally produced and imported Canaanite jars (CJs), and Transport Stirrup Jars (TSJs), on LB Cyprus (see also Knapp and Demesticha 2017: 88-93). What follows, therefore, is a succinct summary of that investigation.

Enkomi [at least 20 from the 'Sanctuary of the Ingot god']	Dikaios 1971, Volume IIIa: pls. 65:10, 77:22-23; 120:11-12; 125:4; Courtois 1971: 248 fig. 89, 249, 251 fig. 91, 256 fig. 96; 1981: 37-38, fig. 15.3; Gunneweg et al. 1987; Mazar 1988; Åström 1991a; Crewe 2012: 232-234 (minimum count 31)
Arpera Mosphilos	Merrillees 1974: 54 fig. 35, 59; Crewe 2012: 229
Hala Sultan Tekke [at least 10,000 sherds-50 vessels?]	Åström et al. 1976: 15-16, pl. XVd; Åström 1991b; Fischer 1991; Åström 1989: 118 lists all refs. to Canaanite jars at Hala Sultan Tekke
Alassa Pano Mandilares	Hadjisavvas 1986: 67
Kalopsidha 'C', 'Gjerstad's house' [at least 26 examples]	Åström 1966: 9; Crewe 2010: 68, 2012: 232
Pyla Verghi	Grace 1956: 92 n. 22; Åström 1972: 261
Korovia Nitovikla	Crewe 2012: 232 ('significant quantities')
Galinoporni Tomb 1(?)	Crewe 2012: 230-231, fig. 2.5
Pyla Kokkinokremos [up to 100 vessels]	Karageorghis and Demas 1984: 51, pls. 37-38; Georgiou 2014
Kition	Karageorghis and Demas 1985: 279
Kouklia Palaipaphos	Maier and Karageorghis 1984: 54
Kouklia Evreti [at least 33?]	Jacobs 2016: 44-45, 50 fig. 21, 66-68
Kouklia Kaminia [Tomb VII: 1]	Jones 1986: 572, pl. 7.16
Maroni Vournes, Tsaroukkas [at least 4, and 1 in Tomb 15]	Cadogan et al. 2001: 77; Manning et al. 2002: 137-140; Manning et al. 2006: 478, table 2
Apliki Karamallos ['storage jars']	Du Plat Taylor 1952: 160-161 figs. 11.9, 12.4
Kalavasos village	Pearlman 1985: 167 fig. 2:1, 168 no. 1
Kalavasos Ayios Dhimitrios [11 examples catalogued; 1224 sherds in database; Alison South, pers. comm., October 2016]	South et al. 1989: 10, 107, 146, fig. 14, pl. 5:1070-1074; South 1983: 97, 109, pl. 15:3; South 1991: 135 fig. 2 (K-AD 1500); South 1997: 159, pl. 13:2; South 2008: 310, chart pl.63
Arediou Vouppes	Steel and Thomas 2008: 241, fig. 23; Steel and McCartney 2008: 14 table 1, 21
Myrtou Pigadhes ['Syrian jars']	Catling, in Du Plat Taylor 1957: 53-55, fig. 23: 318-320)

Table 5: *Canaanite Jars from Cyprus.*

Over 150 CJs, some with Cypro-Minoan or other, similar signs incised on their handles, have been found at 20 different sites on Cyprus (Table 5). Twenty-six of 84 examples found at Maa *Palaeokastro* were analysed petrographically and chemically (Jones and Vaughan 1988: 393): seven may have been produced in south central or western Cyprus. Similarly, some CJs excavated at Pyla *Kokkinokremos* may have been manufactured on the island (Georgiou 2014: 176, 186). An early NAA of several CJs from Hala Sultan Tekke indicated that some were locally produced, others imported from Syria or Cilicia (Raban 1980: 6, 146 table 5, 148 table 6). Three other CJ fragments from Hala Sultan Tekke recently analysed using lead isotope analysis and petrography may also represent local production (Renson *et al.* 2014). The new Swedish excavations at Hala Sultan Tekke continue to turn up further examples of CJs (*e.g.* Fischer and Bürge 2017: 54, 60, 84). Petrographic analysis likewise suggests that two Canaanite jars found at Kommos on Crete could have originated on the south coast of Cyprus (Day *et al.* 2011: 549 fig. 11:b, 551, 553). All these instances of possible local production tend to support Sherratt's (1998: 300-301 n. 15, 305) suggestion that some of the oils derived from pressing installations known at Late Cypriot sites such as Kalavasos *Ayios Dhimitrios*, Alassa *Pano Mandilares* and Maroni *Vournes* may have been exported in locally-made CJs, or perhaps in Group II or IB1 Cypriot *pithoi* (see further below). Andreou (2016: 163), in turn, has emphasized the importance of olive oil production at *Ayios Dhimitrios* for both intra-island and external exchange. The possibility that some CJs were manufactured locally on Cyprus also gains interest in light of Papyrus Anastasi IV, 15.1-5, which records the export of two kinds of oil (*dft* and *ynb*) from Cyprus (Ockinga, in Knapp 1996: 48).

Some 110 TSJs have been recovered on Cyprus, mainly from the coastal sites of Hala Sultan Tekke *Vyzakia*, Enkomi, Kition and Episkopi *Bamboula*. Of those analysed petrographically and/or chemically, most were produced in central, southern or western Crete. One TSJ, evidently inscribed before firing with a sign of the Cypro-Minoan script, was found in a Late Cypriot IIC context at Kourion (Episkopi) *Bamboula*; once again, petrographic analysis indicates it is likely of west Cretan origin (Palaima *et al.* 1984: 68-69).

TSJs inscribed with Cypro-Minoan signs form an interesting class of their own, not least the last-mentioned case of a typical Cretan vessel produced on Crete but marked with a Cypro-Minoan sign and excavated on Cyprus. Day (1999: 68) suggested that TSJs inscribed with Cypro-Minoan may indicate that they were re-used, possibly on Cyprus or perhaps when filled with new contents for re-shipment. Hirschfeld (1996: 291-293) has argued that all vessels inscribed *after firing* with Cypro-Minoan signs were either shipped to or through Cyprus, or else must have been handled by people familiar with the Cypriot marking system (Cypriot traders in the view of van Wijngaarden 2002: 275-277). It is also worth noting that four of ten inscribed TSJs found on the

Figure 39: *Transport Stirrup Jar, Late Minoan III. From Episkopi Bamboula, Cyprus, 'Site D', tomb 50.* © Trustees of the British Museum, Reg. no. 1896,0201.265.

Uluburun shipwreck, of both Aegean and uncertain origin, had Cypro-Minoan signs incised on their handles after firing (Haskell *et al.* 2011: 130). Merchants or customs officials in receiving ports may have marked certain vessels to keep track of offloaded items of cargo, as was customary in later periods (Arnaud 2011a: 66), but that doesn't help to explain the Kourion vessel, if it was indeed incised before firing. Some of the medium-sized TSJs made in the Argolid (Greece) and incised with Cypro-Minoan signs may be regarded as 'branded' (Bevan 2010), *i.e.* marked out for the Cypriot market, just as the blistered surface of copper ingots may have marked out those objects as Cypriot products. Catling and Karageorghis (1960: 121) long ago observed that the octopus motif seen on several TSJs found on Cyprus might have served as a 'trademark' for Cretan products (Figure 39).

Based on criteria established by Knapp and Demesticha (2017: 42), in particular that any vessel defined as an MTC should have been designed or used repeatedly (not just occasionally) to move bulk organic cargo over long distances by sea, only one native Cypriot vessel — the *pithos* — shows at least some characteristic components. The medium-sized Group II *pithos* (Keswani 2009: 111, table 2) could have been used to transport liquids or other produce, although Group IB1 examples also have a reasonable balance between portability and volume (Pilides 2000: 49; Keswani 2009: 107-112, fig. 1, tables 1-2). Both Group IB1 and Group II vessels have medium heights (50-65cm) but Group IB1 vessels lack the restricted rim/mouth, crucial for MTCs. Chemical and petrographic analyses of some *pithoi* verify they were produced on Cyprus (*e.g.* Jones and Day 1987: 262; Xenophontos *et al.*, in Pilides 2000: 167-182; Tomlinson *et al.* 2010: 218), and Keswani (2009) maintains that they were produced in regional centres.

Group II *pithoi* have a wide distribution in the LB Mediterranean, from Egypt and the Levant through the Aegean and west to Sicily and Sardinia; they have also been found on the Cape Iria and Uluburun shipwrecks (Pilides 2000: 48-51, with refs.; Knapp and Demesticha 2017: 90) (Figure 40). Pulak (2008: 296) suggests that some of the ten examples found on the Uluburun shipwreck may have been

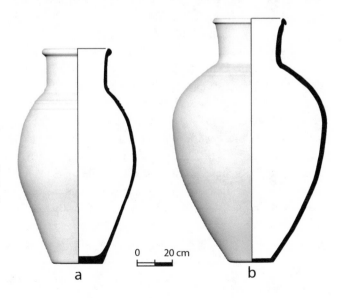

Figure 40: *Cypriot Group II pithoi; a) Cape Iria wreck; b. Uluburun wreck.* a) After Pennas et al. 1995: 12, fig. 8c, no. A5; b) after Pulak 1997: 242, fig. 10, no. KW255. Drawing by Irini Katsouri.

used as transport containers for liquids, pomegranates, possibly figs and other commodities. At least three of the ten Cypriot *pithoi* from Uluburun were used to transport pottery vessels (Hirschfeld 2011: 120). Of the 15 Cypriot *pithoi* recorded at Marsa Matruh (coastal western Egypt), all but one belonged to Group I (largely IB1); the single exception is a Group II *pithos* (Hulin, in White 2002b: 28-29).

Although some 200 *pithoi* with seal impressions have been recorded on Cyprus (Smith 2007, 2012; Keswani 2009: 119-121), these impressions do not provide any useful information about the contents or specific uses of these vessels. *Pithoi* clearly were 'multi-task' vessels and thus it is only possible to suggest that the Cypriot Group IB1 and II examples may have served occasionally for the bulk transport of organic goods, less commonly if ever for liquids. The main purpose of these vessels was for storage, and most types are simply too large, or of the wrong form, to serve as MTCs. Whilst a couple of the Cypriot *pithoi* found on the Uluburun shipwreck seem to have been used to transport pomegranates and possibly figs, no analytical work (*e.g.* ORA) exists to indicate what other contents may have been involved.

The people of Cyprus imported and used both CJs and TSJs and seem to have produced some CJs. There is no doubt that the ships and merchants of LB Cyprus were engaged in maritime trade within the eastern Mediterranean, and may also have played some role as middlemen in commercial activities (Knapp 2014), not least through the production, handling and transport of MTCs. The fact that diverse Cypriot goods, including Group II *pithoi*, have been found on five of the eight known MB-LB shipwrecks also points to a Cypriot role in the international exchanges that were so prevalent during the Late Bronze Age.

STONE ANCHORS

In a series of publications, Honor Frost (1963, 1970a, 1970b, 1985: 282) emphasized the significance of stone anchors in the Mediterranean and on Cyprus, pointing out that diagnostic examples found in the sea ought to be dated in accordance with findings of similar types recovered in stratified land excavations. Stone anchors have been recorded at several Late Bronze Age Cypriot coastal sites, both on land and in the sea, *e.g.* at Hala Sultan Tekke *Vyzakia*, Kition and Maroni *Tsaroukkas* (Frost 1970a; 1985; McCaslin 1980: 21-22; Manning *et al.* 2002: 111-118, 123-143), and possibly at Tochni *Lakkia* (Todd 2016: 328). McCaslin's (1980: 21-31) corpus of anchors found on Cypriot sites was supplemented by Frost (1983, 1985, 1991), who also discussed the role and significance of stone anchors for Cypriot and Levantine maritime trade. More recently, Howitt-Marshall (2012: 111) carried out underwater survey at Kouklia *Achni* — some 2.5 km south of the LC site of *Palaipaphos*) — and recorded 120 stone anchors of uncertain date (Figure 41).

Turning to the actual finds (and findspots) on Cyprus, nearly 150 anchors were recovered in the 'temple precinct' at Kition ('Temples' 1, 4, 5), in diverse contexts — *e.g.* used as corner stones and paving stones, or in foundation courses, on thresholds and in five wells (Frost 1985: 294-295; 1991: 359-60). There is a range of shapes, and Frost (1985: 293) suggested that one type — a composite anchor with a rounded, triangular shape — might be native to Kition and its region. Thin section analyses indicated that all but three of the Kition anchors were made from local stone (Frost 1985: 287-288, 290-291). One anchor from Temple 2 has a Cypro-Minoan sign (Frost 1985: 293, 297

Figure 41: *Kouklia Achni, satellite image showing points where 120 stone anchors were recorded.* From Howitt-Marshall 2012: 110 fig. 7.5. Courtesy of Duncan Howitt-Marshall.

fig. 4:7), similar to signs engraved on two anchors from Hala Sultan Tekke (Nikolaou and Catling 1968: 228-229, pl. 34b; Frost 1970a: 14-15, fig. 1.1, 1.3), leading to further speculation that all such inscribed anchors might be of Cypriot origin.

Frost (1970a: 14-17) published four additional stone anchors from Hala Sultan Tekke, and others have been excavated in habitation levels as well as in tombs at the site (*e.g.* Hult 1977; Öbrink 1979: 19-20; McCaslin 1980: 21-22). Åström and Svensson (2007) listed 41 stone anchors from Areas 8 and 22 at Hala Sultan Tekke, and the most recent excavations continue to produce further examples of stone anchors, *e.g.* three weight anchors re-used as building elements, and one composite type found in a pit (*e.g.* Blattner 2013; Fischer and Burge 2015: 34-35, fig. 9a-9b) (Figure 42). In the region nearby, 26 further anchors of uncertain date were recovered from Cape Kiti (McCaslin 1978); farther distant, five other anchors have been recorded from the sea around Capes Pyla and Greco (McCaslin 1980: 26).

Along Cyprus's south coast, 35 stone anchors were recorded during underwater survey just off the coast from the LB site of Maroni *Tsaroukkas*; these comprised 22 weight, 10 composite and three broken stone anchor types (Manning *et al.* 2002: 111-118, figs. 5-12) (Figure 43). Sewell (2015: 188 and fig. 1) illustrates what is presumably one of the composite (3-hole) stone anchors, still *in situ*. Ten further weight anchors were recovered from settlement and mortuary contexts at *Tsaroukkas* (Manning *et al.* 2002: 114 and table 1, 116 fig. 10). The underwater area ('Site 1'), which extended over 300 m into the sea and where some 75 examples of contemporary local and imported pottery were found, may well have served as a Late Cypriot anchorage (see the reconstruction in Manning *et al.* 2002: 113

Figure 42: *Hala Sultan Tekke Vyzakia, Stratum 2 (ca. 1200 BC): stone anchors re-used in wall of a domestic structure.* Courtesy of Peter M. Fischer.

Figure 43: *Maroni Tsaroukkas composite stone anchor, in situ on seabed, with concretion cleared from two of three holes.* Inventory no. TSBS.037. Courtesy of Sturt W. Manning.

fig. 6, 121-123. Howitt-Marshall's (2012: 111) underwater survey at Kouklia *Achni* recorded 120 stone anchors — 96 of weight type and 24 of composite type (see Figure 41, above).

Basch (1978: 118, 119 figs. 32–33, 120–121) identified a stone anchor of typical Cypriot shape (three-hole, composite with rounded, triangular shape) amongst architectural fragments from the precinct around the Temple of Amun at Karnak in Egypt; despite the shape, however, it was shown to be made of local stone. There is no simple explanation for this anomaly, despite some imaginative attempts, all of which assume it is an *ex voto* 'sacred anchor', somehow made and deposited on the site by Cypriot seafarers during the eleventh century BC (*e.g.* Frost 1979: 155-157 and fig. 4; Wachsmann 1998: 62, 281 fig. 12.44; 2013: 183).

Wachsmann (1998: 273, n. 82) cites a 'Byblian'-type anchor from 'Cape Lara, on the southeast tip of Cyprus' (citing Frost 1970c: 60, who mentions 'Lara Point' at 'the south eastern extremity of Cyprus'). However, the only location named Lara on the island is Lara Beach, a promontory at the southern end of the Akamas peninsula in western Cyprus. Since Frost also states that Lara Point '… is marked in the *Mediterranean Pilot* as the landfall for modern ships coming from the Aegean', it makes more sense to see 'Lara Point' as Lara Beach, although no other anchors have been reported anywhere in this area. Finally, a weight anchor very similar in shape to LB examples was uncovered in a Cypro-Archaic II (ca. 650-550 BC) context at Kition *Bamboula* (Frost 1982: 265-266); its context — placed against the southern wall of a courtyard to the 'sanctuary' — seems secure, even if it remains possible that the anchor itself might date from an earlier period.

MINIATURE ANCHORS, FISHING TACKLE AND FISH

With the exception of some earlier work by Honor Frost (cited below), studies of fishing gear and related material culture — hooks, net weights, sinkers or spears — tend to be rare, and even the bones of fish are seldom recorded systematically. Comparatively speaking, work in the Aegean tends to outpace that on Cyprus and in the eastern Mediterranean generally (*e.g.* Rose 1994; Powell 1996; Mylona 2003, 2014, 2016). Even so, there is some useful evidence published from three Cypriot sites — Kition, Enkomi and especially Hala Sultan Tekke (Lindqvist 2016).

From Kition, six 'miniature anchors' were found in the vicinity of 'Temple 1', three in workshops attached to this structure and others in disturbed contexts nearby (Frost 1985: 310, fig. 11:10-12; 312, fig. 12:9-11). Frost (1985: 319-320; 1991: 365-366) argues that these objects may be line-weights for set long-line fishing, which uses a string of baited hooks held on the bottom by the rough stone weights. Two quite similar, one-holed miniature anchors were found in a well at Enkomi, one with what may be Cypro-Minoan signs, the other with a simple cross engraved on it (Dikaios 1969-71: 205, 891 nos. 4039/1, 6319/2, pl. 150:1, 5). Frost (1991: 360, 366) suggests that these miniatures were used 'for anchoring fishing tackle', and she notes six more miniature examples (unpublished) from the site. Other fishing weights, fishhooks and a conch shell found on Floors I-III of Area I at Kition (Karageorghis and Demas 1985: pls. XXI, XXV, XXXII) led Frost (1991: 366) to suggest the structures in question might have been 'fishermen's houses'.

In early excavations at Hala Sultan Tekke, a bronze trident that may have served as a spear for fishing was found amongst grave goods in Tomb 23 (Åström *et al.* 1983: 174 n. 1231, 179) (see above, Figure 7). Åström (1986: 14-16, figs. 17, 24) also noted the presence of stone and lead net weights as well as bones from a variety of fish. Lindqvist (2016: 243-244, table 1) has now compiled a list of all types of fish recorded in the various excavations at Hala Sultan Tekke: grouper, wreckfish (stone bass), sea bass, meagre, brown meagre or shi drum, red mullet, grey mullet, gilthead (bream), black sea bream, parrotfish, Nile perch, tope shark, ray/skate, tunny (?) and barracuda. Some of these are deep sea fish (*e.g.* seabass, wreckfish, meagre, grouper, shark and ray) and were probably caught with hook and line, whilst other, smaller types of fish (*e.g.* gilthead, black sea bream, grey mullet) may have been netted closer to the shore. Finds of carp and grey mullet are also reported from Apliki (Du Plat Taylor 1952: 167).

Two medium-sized, barbed, bronze hooks were found in recent excavations at Hala Sultan Tekke (Fischer 2011: 79, 83 fig. 17); their size suggests they were used to catch larger fish at sea. Fischer and Bürge (2016: 36-37, 46) also list five lead fishing net weights, one from an interior room, the other two from what seems to be an external courtyard. From earlier excavations at the site, Lindqvist (2016: 240-241) notes three possible lead and 35 possible stone net weights (pierced or with worked channels); all but one was found lying together in a single room (Öbrink 1979: 44-45, N6019). Lindqvist (2016: 241) also suggests that two elliptically-shaped stones found amongst a group of clay loomweights may be net weights (Fischer and Bürge 2014 [Appendix 6]: 100, 102 fig. 41).

Figure 44: *Crushed murex shells (about 25 kg) from Area 6 West, Stratum I at Hala Sultan Tekke.* After Fischer and Bürge 2016: 37 fig. 5. Courtesy of Peter M. Fischer.

SEAFARING AND SEAFARERS IN THE BRONZE AGE EASTERN MEDITERRANEAN

It is also worth noting that recent excavations Hala Sultan Tekke have uncovered over 25 kg of crushed murex shells in an open space near the lead net weight finds (Fischer and Bürge 2016: 37 fig. 5, 51) (Figure 44), and close to a basin with evidence of purple colouring in it (Fischer and Bürge 2014: 65, 67 fig. 8). Another related find is a White Painted 'pictorial style' krater depicting a fish (Fischer and Bürge 2015: 36, 37 fig. 11:5). Finally, recent fieldwork at MC I-LC I Erimi *Laonin tou Porakou*, an inland site situated some 6 km from the south-central coast of Cyprus, has produced 26 marine shell fragments from five unique species (Bombardieri 2017: 321). Dietary use of the shells is excluded by the excavators, which suggests they were probably used as beads and pendants, *i.e.* for ornamental puposes.

ANATOLIA

HARBOURS

Whether or not one regards Troy as a 'hub of trade', the longevity of the site, its size and its position '… on the edge of the Bronze Age urban world, and at a gateway to the territories beyond, gave it a particular prominence in the skein of Bronze Age economic relations' (Easton *et al.* 2002: 101-102). Its position on a key maritime passageway and likely 'choke point', as well as its diverse imports (at least in the Early Bronze Age) certainly suggest that the site of Troy would have had a harbour, but is there any physical evidence for it?

Following earlier work by other German scholars (*e.g.* Brückner 1912; Dörpfeld 1925), Korfmann (1986a) presented an eloquent and detailed argument — based on Ottoman historical sources as well as climatological and meteorological data — that Beşik Bay, an embayment some 8 kms southwest of Troy (Hisarlık), could have served as the harbour for Troy during both the third and second millennia BC. Open and unhindered by reefs, this bay is rather shallow with sandy beaches; it would not have lent itself readily to the construction of a built harbour, and could only have accommodated small, shallow-draft ships that would have been hauled onto the beach. Regarding the association of Hisarlık with Troy and the Trojan War, Korfmann (1986a: 13) concluded: 'Homer's geographical description … not only conveys a remarkably accurate impression of the Troad in general, but also provides a concrete description of Beşik Bay as the harbour and encampment of the Greek troops'. Excavations at nearby Beşik-Yassıtepe uncovered a cemetery with many *pithos* burials and good evidence for international connections (especially with the Mycenaean world) but no signs of anything associated with a harbour (Korfmann 1986b; 1990 [and earlier reports in *Archäologischer Anzeiger*]; Basedow 2000).

In his polemical reaction to Korfmann's views on Troy and its alleged harbour at Beşik Bay, Kolb (2004) argued that (1) Troy VI could not have been a hub of commercial trade; (2) the cemetery at Beşik Bay did not necessarily belong to a harbour settlement and nor were Mycenaeans buried there (see also Basedow 2002: 469); (3) the reconstruction of the 'lower city' with a 'defensive ditch' (or moat) and 'palisade' encircling it is inconsistent if not unfounded; and (4) there is no evidence to support the assumption that Beşik Bay served as Troy's harbour. In their response to Kolb's paper, Jablonka and Rose (2004) essentially reject his 'minimalist view' of Bronze Age trade and economics, and argue that the excavations conducted by Korfmann make untenable much of Kolb's argument. Their only passing reference to a possible harbour is the comment that Troy itself or Beşik Bay could be reached by ships arriving from either the Mediterranean or the Black Sea (Jablonka and Rose 2004: 626).

What does related paleogeographic and geomorphological research add to this picture? Brückner *et al.* (2005: 99-100, and fig. 3) present a convenient summary of the different outcomes of two research projects closely associated with Korfmann's excavations at Troy. Kraft *et al.* (1982; 2003: 166) effectively conclude that their geological investigation and paleogeographic reconstructions tally with Homer's description of Trojan topography, whilst Kayan's (1991, 1995; Kayan *et al.* 2003) geomorphological work indicates that after the Early Bronze Age, progradation of the entire plain of the Scamander (Karamenderes) valley (to the northwest of Hisarlık) increasingly became covered with swamps and could never have served as a viable harbour in the Late Bronze Age.

To summarise radically these two rather complex field endeavours using diverse techniques: both projects mapped the palaeoenvironmental context of Troy and the surrounding region over the past six millennia in the attempt to identify any areas that might have served as harbours for Troy. Around 7000 years ago, the sea — in the form of 'Troia Bay', now the Scamander (Karamenderes) alluvial plains to the north and northwest that open onto the Dardanelles Strait — extended as far inland as the mound of Hissarlik. By the third millennium BC (Troy I, II), sedimentation and a slight lowering of sea level meant that the settlement was situated on a level plain near the water's edge (Kayan 1995: 221 fig. 8, 230). By the end of the Bronze Age (ca. 1200 BC), however, alluviation resulted in the coastline retreating even farther northward, and the coastal configuration — to both the north and west — came to resemble that of today (Kraft *et al.* 2003: 164-165, fig. 5).

Kayan (1995: 231) suggested that as the coast retreated north, it is possible that some 'convenient sites' along the eastern shore of 'Troia Bay' were used as civil or military harbours; along the western shore, however, there was no geomophological evidence to indicate that three 'natural indentations' (Yeniköy, Kesik, Kumtepe) were ever used as Bronze Age harbour sites. I leave aside here any discussion of Zangger's (1992) attempt to link the alluvial plains around Troy to the mythical site of Atlantis; Kayan (1991: 232-233) provides a thorough geomorphological critique. Finally, this same programme of paleogeographic research indicated that although the plain behind (east of) Beşik Bay formed a marine embayment during times of higher sea level, there was no evidence to indicate it was ever used as a major harbour (Kayan 1991; 1995: 220-221). Thus neither project produced any evidence for an actual harbour, either around the LB site of Troy itself or to its southwest at Beşik Bay.

As already noted earlier (Chapter 3: *Early Bronze Age—Anatolia, Ports and Harbours*), the site of Çeşme–Bağlararası at the far western point of the Urla Peninsula, just across the strait from the Aegean island of Chios, is said to have been 'an important harbour settlement from at least the EBA onwards' (Sahoğlu 2015: 593). The following is based on Sahoğlu's (2015) recent overview of the site. The later, MB and LB levels at this site reflect a typical west Anatolian settlement of the second millennium BC: Level 2b is seen to be contemporary with Middle Minoan (MM) III (ca. 1800-1675 BC) on Crete, with an indigenous material culture but including small amounts of imported Minoan and 'Minoanising' finds as well as domestic structures and a possible workshop for wine production. After a severe earthquake, Level 2a represents a short period of occupation with the same cultural elements. In the Level 1 phase (no architecture, numerous pits), contemporary with Late Minoan (LM) IA (ca. 1675-1600 BC), various pits include local wares, more Minoan and 'Minoanising' pottery and Minoan loomweights, as well as bone and other organic remains. Ceramic finds reflect the local character of the site with a growing amount of imported pottery from the Cyclades, Crete and the east Aegean islands as well as from other Anatolian sites. Following Level 1, further pits of LB date (fourteenth-thirteenth centuries BC) contained local west Anatolian and grey wares as well as imported and locally produced Mycenaean pottery. As was the case with the pits of Level 1, no architectural elements were preserved.

Beyond noting that the location of Çeşme–Bağlararası represents 'one of the most favourable harbouring areas in the Aegean and [was] continuously used for this purpose for thousands of years' (Sahoğlu 2015: 606), there is little evidence beyond Minoan and Cycladic imports, or the mention of 'Minoan seafarers', to confirm that this was the case. Whilst the location almost demands that this site would have served as a harbour settlement and may have been 'one of the most important gateways between Anatolia and the Aegean during this period' (Sahoğlu 2015: 607), there are still no physical remains of a harbour.

Similarly, rich finds of Mycenaean pottery at nearby Liman Tepe (about 50 km east of Çeşme) indicate that it continued to be a key maritime centre during the Late Bronze Age. Aykurt and Erkanel (2017: 61-63, figs. 2-3) report that although LBA deposits 'from secure stratigraphical contexts' have been identified at Liman Tepe, the remains have been badly damaged by post-Bronze Age activity. Artzy (2009: 14) suggested that the Bronze Age harbour at Liman Tepe/Klazomenai was rubble-built (of 'Aegean' type?), but beyond the two moles of mid-first millennium BC date (Votruba *et al.* 2016: 672), there is still no physical evidence of a Bronze Age port at the site.

Another 50 km northeast of Liman Tepe (and 10 km inland from the modern coastal town of İzmir) lies the settlement of Panaztepe in the Gediz (Hermos) river basin. Panaztepe was continuously inhabited from the end of the Early Bronze Age to the Classical period, and is thought to have been an island settlement during prehistoric periods. Three different areas have been excavated at Panaztepe: the 'acropolis', the 'seaport city' (Çınardalı-Karaaslan 2008) and the 'necropolis' (Erkanal-Öktü 2008). Several *tholos* tombs at the site have been taken as indicators of Mycenaean influence; burial goods included Mycenaean pottery alongside local wares, as well as a rich array of glass artefacts (Çınardalı-Karaaslan 2012). An ashlar building within the settlement produced more Mycenaean pottery (Kelder 2004-05: 56). In the light of such evidence, Panaztepe is also argued to have been a port city, but like all the other sites in the region around the modern Bay of İzmir, there is still no physical evidence of the harbour.

Some 200 km south of the Bay of İzmir on the west Anatolian coast lies the site of Miletos, situated near the mouth of the Maeander River (Büyük Menderes). According to Greaves (2002: 12), the site was endowed with four natural harbours, and three are

Figure 45: *Theatre at Miletos (Roman).* Ken and Nyetta / Wikimedia Commons.

known by name: the Lion Harbour (Hellenistic), the Theatre Harbour and another harbour to the east of Humei Tepe (in the northeast, site of the later Roman baths). All these features are now silted in (with sediment from the Maeander River) but their configuration is apparent in a GIS simulation of the city (Greaves 1999: 61, fig. 2; see also Brückner 1998: 251; 2003: 129 fig. 4). The so-called Theatre Harbour (named after a Roman period structure along the northern shore) (Figure 45) was probably Miletos's most important harbour and the focus of Bronze Age settlement (Kleiner 1968; Greaves 2002: 13); it was protected from potentially strong westerly winds by the nearby island of Lade. Whilst the site was separated from the interior by high mountains, the Maeander River valley provided access to the Anatolian heartland; readily accessible by sea, it was ideally situated for maritime trade and communications.

Much of what is known about the MB and LB settlement comes from the area around the later 'Temple of Athena' and the Theatre Harbour site (Greaves 2002: 48). From at least the beginning of the Bronze Age, the settlement was situated on an island or small peninsula (not the larger peninsula on which the later city was established) (Brückner 2003: 128 fig. 3, 130), and thus mainly surrounded by the sea. Of the Middle and Late Bronze Age levels excavated at the site, the earliest and subsequent levels (Miletos III-IV) were already heavily influenced by Minoan material culture (Raymond 2005), whilst the later settlement (Miletos V-VI) displays strong Mycenaean influences (Niemeier 2005: 3-13). The main architectural feature of Level VI, however, was a defensive wall in the northernmost part of the excavated area, of apparent Hittite type or at least influence (Niemeier 2005: 12, 20, col. pl. 1).

Palaeogeographical fieldwork and extensive coring indicate that, by the beginning of the Bronze Age, the (Milesian) peninsula where Miletos is located consisted of two major islands, one made up of Humei (Home) Tepe and Kale Tepe, the other in the area of the 'Temple of Athena' (Brückner 2003: 129 and fig. 4, 141). This situation evidently continued into the second millennium BC, although by this time the island may already have been connected to the mainland by a sand bar (tombolo). Despite all this work the case remains, once again, that there is still no physical evidence of an actual Bronze Age harbour.

Along the southern, Mediterranean coast of Anatolia lies the site of Kinet Höyük, in eastern Cilicia, today situated just over 0.5 km from the sea (Figure 46). From the Early Bronze Age up to at least the first century BC, a river estuary on the

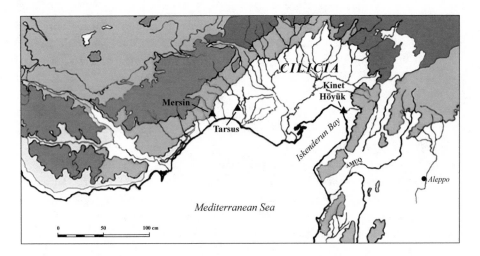

Figure 46: *Map of Cilicia showing the location of the site and possible harbour of Kinet Höyük.* After Gates 2103: 224 fig. 1. Drawing by Irini Katsouri.

mound's southern flank and a shallow bay to the north would have provided suitable harbours (Beach and Luzadder-Beach 2008; Gates 2013: 223-224). Configured like a promontory, the mound is oriented westward, toward the sea; to the north, soundings in the surrounding fields have identified structures that may have been situated along or faced the seaside during the site's settlement history. According to Gates (2013: 224), winds do not reach into the back of the Bay of Iskenderun, off which the site is located, a key factor that could have provided shelter for ships visiting the port.

Even with all these favourable locational factors, however, there is still no evidence of an actual harbour at Kinet Höyük, only a suite of local, LB central Anatolian ('Hittite') wares and 'cult' objects, and imported pottery including LB examples of Canaanite jars, now occasionally stamped with Hittite seals (Gates 2013: 229-233, figs. 14-17). The site also boasts a range of Cypriot pottery dating from MB II up to the end of the LB: White Painted, Black-on-Red, Bichrome, Monochrome, White Slip I-II, Base-ring I-II, White Shaved wares are all represented (Kozal 2016: 54; see also Gates 2013: 227 fig. 8). Although several sites in and around Cilicia have remains of MB-LB Cypriot pottery, only Kinet Höyük offers the evidence in a controlled chronological and contextual sequence. Gates (2013: 232, 234 n.4, following Forlanini 2001: 553-557), suggests that Kinet Höyük might be identified with the LB place-name *Izziya*, where the Hittite queen Puduhepa (wife of Hattušili III) is said to have carried out a ritual by the sea (KUB 56.15—de Roos 2007: 240-243). Gates (2013: 223) emphasizes that before the work at Kinet Höyük, '… not a single Bronze Age seaport had been investigated on Turkey's entire Mediterranean coast'.

SHIPWRECKS

The two best-known shipwrecks of the LB are those found at Uluburun and Cape Gelidonya off the southern, Mediterranean coast of Anatolia. These ships, it must be borne in mind, are not necessarily 'Anatolian' in origin, and the home port of the Uluburun ship has been argued to be almost anywhere except Anatolia (see further below). Nonetheless, the excavation of the Uluburun shipwreck has produced what is perhaps the most significant body of material evidence for seafaring and seafarers in the Mediterranean, the 'quintessential artefact [of] all Late Bronze Age cultures captured in transit' (Monroe 2011: 93). It also provides potential indicators of a maritime route for the transport of raw materials, manufactured goods and 'exotica' within and beyond the eastern Mediterranean (Bass *et al.* 1989; Pulak 1988, 1998, 2008, 2010).

Its most prominent cargo consists of raw materials, notably some ten tons of copper (350 ingots, 317 of them in the typical 'oxhide' shape) and about one ton of tin ingots in various shapes, but primarily 'oxhide' (Pulak 2000; 2009). Amongst the other raw materials were 175 discoid glass ingots (mainly cobalt blue or turquoise in colour) (Figure 47), ivory (hippopotamus teeth and one elephant tusk), over two dozen African ebony logs and terebinth resin, the last found in over half of the approximately 150 Canaanite jars on board (Pulak 2008: 293-295). In addition to the Canaanite jars, other manufactured goods include some 150 pieces of diverse types of Cypriot pottery stacked in large *pithoi*, copper-alloy and tin metal vessels, intact and scrap gold and silver jewellery, faience and glass beads, various containers made of ivory and boxwood (Figure 48), and three ostrich eggshells (Pulak 2008: 296-297, 330-333). The shipwreck has been dated to the last quarter of the fourteenth century BC on the basis of (1) a golden scarab of Nefertiti, wife of the pharaoh Akhenaten, who ruled ca. 1353-1336 BC, thus giving a *terminus post quem* (Weinstein 2008: 358); (2) synchronisms between the Late Helladic IIIA2 pottery found on board the ship and the reign of Akhenaten (Bachhuber 2007: 347, with full refs.); and (3) dendrochronological dating (very end of the fourteenth century BC) of a piece of dunnage or firewood carried on board (Pulak 1998: 213-214).

Regarding the maritime route of this vessel, there is some consensus — largely driven by the excavator's opinion (*e.g.* Pulak 2008: 299-300; 2010: 870-872) — that the Uluburun ship sailed from the southern Levant (Carmel coast) northward

Figure 47: *Glass ingots from the Uluburun shipwreck.* Courtesy of Cemal Pulak, Institute of Nautical Archaeology.

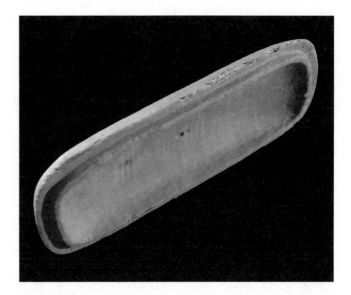

Figure 48: *Boxwood lid from an ovoid box/container; from the Uluburun shipwreck.* Courtesy of Cemal Pulak, Institute of Nautical Archaeology.

along the coast and then westward along southern coastal Anatolia, with an intended destination in the Aegean (see, *e.g.* Bachhuber 2006; Yon and Sauvage 2015: 95-96; Zangani 2016: 232-234, the last with interesting counter arguments). This conviction has gained strength through various scientific analyses. Cucchi (2008), for example, argued that the mandible of a 'stowaway' house mouse found amongst the ship's copper ingots originated along the north Syrian coast, perhaps at Ugarit's port Minet el-Beidha. Optical mineralogy conducted on the pottery and stone anchors recovered from the wreck led Goren (2013: 56-59) to conclude that the galley wares and some 80% of the Canaanite jars — as well as all 24 stone anchors — originated along the Carmel coast in the southern Levant.

More recently, Rich *et al.*'s (2016: 517) strontium isotope analysis of the wood from the Uluburun ship's hull and keel (?) reveals no match with any of the cedar forests they sampled (central-northern Lebanon, southern Anatolia, Cyprus). Nonetheless, the cedar samples from the shipwreck are so uniform that they must have come from a single site/area. Rich *et al.* (2016) note two likely forest areas: the south and central Amanus in Anatolia, and the Syrian Coastal Range, near Ugarit. Given that Ugarit was one of the most prominent LB trading centres, they suggest that cedars from the latter region may eventually prove to be the source of the ship's building material (also Goren 2013: 58-59). This falls in line with their observation that the overlapping distributions of four tree species (*C. libani, Tamarix sp., Quercus cerris, Q. coccifera*) associated with the assemblage of wood from the Uluburun wreck point to a locale between southeastern Turkey and Lebanon (Liphschitz and Pulak 2008: 74; Liphschitz 2012).

Few scholars have considered how Cyprus might fit into the ship's itinerary (*cf.* Monroe 2011: 92). Of course, nobody doubts the Cypriot origin of the ten tons of copper ingots (Pulak 2000: 147-150), by far the heaviest component of the cargo, or of the Cypriot fine wares stacked in Cypriot *pithoi*. Some have suggested the possibility of a Cypriot origin for the Uluburun ship (*e.g.* Hulin, in White 2002b: 173-174; Muhly 2011: 44; Broodbank 2013: 402). Whilst not discounting a Cypriot origin, Cline and Yasur-Landau (2007) argue that the ship most likely sailed from a single port in Egypt or north Syria (*i.e.* Ugarit) but had been commissioned (and the raw materials in the cargo paid for) by one or more Aegean polities. In a variation on this theme, Goren's (2013: 60) imaginative scenario portrays the ship, Canaanite in origin, being loaded in Egypt with raw materials as well as precious goods and sent to the Aegean to secure an Egypto-Aegean alliance against the Hittites.

It is difficult to imagine a scenario in which an Egyptian port (certainly not Thebes, far up the Nile, which is implied by Cline and Yasur-Landau's [2007: 130-131, and fig. 1] argument) or even the international port at Ugarit would make the necessary investment to stockpile all the raw materials found on the Uluburun wreck, in the hope of an 'order' from the distant Aegean world. Bloedow (2005) has even suggested the Uluburun ship was blown off course as it set sail from Ugarit to Egypt (*cf.* Bachhuber 2006: 359, n.176; Cline and Yasur-Landau 2007: 132). All these attempts to establish the possible origins and route of the Uluburun ship seem to involve special pleading, and make little economic sense: what experienced, sea-wise merchant or prestige-conscious ruler would arrange to send 10 tons of copper ingots over 100 km eastward (to Ugarit) or 600 km southward to Egypt — the latter not an easy venture in itself — if it were ultimately destined for the Aegean, well over 400 km to the west (at its nearest point, Rhodes)? Cline (2015: 214) rightly adds (somewhat in contradiction of his own, earlier argument—Cline and Yasur-Landau 2007) that 'sending ships back and forth would have involved risk factors such as piracy, ... as well as weather and other environmental factors'. Monroe (2009: 15) pointedly suggests that most such arguments, like the ship itself, are 'lost at sea': 'There is nothing immediately linking the wreck to a particular kingdom, palace, people or city'.

Ward (2010a: 155–156) reasonably points out that the finds represent the output of nine or ten cultures with multiple origins, and concludes that the Uluburun ship exemplifies 'directional trade' by some of the most 'conspicuous consumers' of the LB era. In Monroe's (2011: 91-95) view, it is the role of merchants, not 'consumers', that must be considered in any scenario involving the maritime networks of the LB, including that of the Uluburun ship. Accepting the difficulties in attributing any specific cultural association or 'ethnic' identity to a (Bronze Age) shipwreck (*e.g.* Wachsmann 1998: 330; Howitt-Marshall 2012: 109; Harpster 2013: 610), Monroe (2011: 94) adds that the 'conclusive origins for the material and people of the Uluburun venture may never be knowable'. The kind of ambiguity seen in this case may relate less to interpretation (or preservation for that matter) than to 'accurate readings of a maritime past lived in maritime, liminal, and semiperipheral conditions'. Monroe suggests we should consider instead a small, unstructured, maritime *communitas* that answered the demands of outfitting and manning a merchantman like the Uluburun ship, including not just 'Syro-Canaanite' merchants with their balance-pan weights and cultic rituals (Pulak 2000; 2008: 340-341; Brody 1998: 68, 100) but also Mycenaeans, whether merchants or mercenaries (Pulak 2005). All the evidence called upon to support one or another viewpoint, one or several potential itineraries, is thus by its nature ambiguous, an intentional response to the 'liminal', risk-ridden conditions of the international maritime trade networks of the LB period in which merchants and mariners had to function. In short, we can speculate endlessly about the maritime route followed by the Uluburun ship before it sunk along the coast of southwest Anatolia, but it might be more productive to think about the mechanisms of exchange that brought it there.

Of the eight known shipwrecks from the Bronze Age eastern Mediterranean and Aegean, only those at Uluburun and Cape Gelidonya preserve any wooden remains of the actual ships. The shipwreck excavated at Cape Gelidonya is estimated to have been 10-12 m in length (Bass 1967: 49-50; Hirschfeld and Bass 2013: 102), although Bass (2013: 67) now estimates its length at 16 m. Its cargo included more than one ton of metal and includes one of the best surviving assemblages of LB metalworking tools; it may be described generally as an itinerant bronzesmiths's stock-in-trade (Bass 1967: 163-164). The primary cargo consisted of copper ingots and ingot fragments and some heavily corroded products identified as tin ingots. There were 34 'oxhide' ingots, 20 complete or nearly complete bun ingots (plus nine half-ingots and other fragments) and 19 'slab' ingots (Bass 1967: 52-83). Whilst an early lead isotope analysis of a single piece of lead from the wreck pointed vaguely to an eastern Mediterranean ore source (Brill, in Bass 1967: 170), more recent work has demonstrated that most of the 'oxhide' and all the bun ingots are consistent with production from Cypriot ores (Gale and Stos-Gale 1992: 94, 95 fig. 24; Stos 2009: 170-172, fig. 3).

As Bass (1967: 113-117, 119-120) hinted long ago, the metal types, castings and scrap metal from the wreck have parallels in various Cypriot and Aegean hoards; in turn, Knapp *et al.* (1988: 237-239) suggested their equivalence to a 'founder's hoard' (as opposed to a 'merchant's hoard', which might characterise the metals found on the Uluburun shipwreck). In Bass's (1967: 117-121) view, most of the fragmentary bronzes — agricultural tools, axes and adzes, spearheads, knives, vessels and tripod stands, needles and awls, bracelets and rings — found on the Gelidonya shipwreck were of Levantine type, made by 'Near Eastern smiths' both on Cyprus and in the Levant. Equally it could be argued that the close parallels between the ship's bronzes, Levantine bronzes and such bronzes as have been found in Cypriot hoards were the result of a *koine* of metalworking traditions within the LB eastern Mediterranean (Muhly 1982: 254-256; Knapp *et al.* 1988: 239).

Based on comparative analyses of the finds and three radiocarbon dates, Bass (1967: 164-168) originally suggested the Gelidonya ship, carrying a cargo that was 'picked up in Cyprus', sunk ca. 1200 BC en route to the Aegean (on the controversy over this dating, *i.e.* late thirteenth or early twelfth century BC, see Giveon 1985; Catling 1986). Bass (1967: 164) regarded this vessel as 'Syrian' in origin, at once a 'Phoenician merchantman' as well as a 'tinker', *i.e.* an itinerant smithy equipped to conduct business anywhere in the eastern Mediterranean. Others tended to agree that it was the ship of an itinerant tinker, if not necessarily Syrian or a merchantman (*e.g.* Linder 1972; Muhly *et al.* 1977: 361; Knapp *et al.* 1988: 237, 239; Peachey 1997: 84; Gestoso Singer 2010: 272). Bass's identification was based on various personal objects recovered from what was identified as the cabin area of the wreck: a 'Syrian' cylinder seal, Syro-Palestinian imitations of Egyptian scarabs (but *cf.* Giveon 1985), balance-pan weights, stone maceheads and mortars, a lamp, etc. The pottery included five (pieces of) Canaanite jars, four or more (Aegean) transport stirrup jars (one of two analysed was possibly produced on Crete), two Cypriot (Plain White Wheelmade) jugs, a Base-ring II or Bucchero jug and at least one Cypriot *pithos*, and some fragmentary Mycenaean pottery (Hennessy and du Plat Taylor 1967: 122-125).

Brief revisits to the site in the 1980s and 1990s produced more metal (balance-pan weights, a bull's head protome, bronze knives and a spit, ingot fragments, further scrap), two Mycenaean stirrup jars (LH IIIB), a (Cypriot) *pithos* base, and a one-hole ('weight') stone anchor (Bass 2010: 802: 2013: 62-67, figs. 2, 5-8). Recent petrographic analyses have indicated that some of the lamps, the *pithos* and a stirrup jar, as well as the stone anchor, are of Cypriot origin (Yuval Goren, pers. comm., 20 May 2017). As a result, Bass (2010: 802; 2013: 70) would now allow that the Gelidonya wreck itself was more likely Cypriot than Levantine in origin. Such a conclusion, or at least various counter-conclusions, were evident to several other scholars long ago (*e.g.* Cadogan 1969; Muhly *et al.* 1977: 361-362).

Whilst the size and technological sophistication of the main cargo aboard the Uluburun ship (copper, tin and glass ingots; Canaanite Jars) point to 'bulk' trade aimed at a 'palatial' consumer, other cargo items might suggest a more 'private' level of trade (*e.g.* ivory, African blackwood, amber, gold, silver and tin scrap metal). By contrast, the Gelidonya wreck almost certainly represents the craft of a 'private', itinerant smith repairing, recycling or trading metals. It is worth reiterating here that speculations regarding the origins of either the Cape Gelidonya or Uluburun shipwrecks represent artificial, modern constructs developed to substantiate scholarly positions on the ethnic associations of the ships ('Canaanite', 'Phoenician', 'Mycenaean') or even their likely destinations (Harpster 2013). Wherever they were headed, their capsizing and eventual excavation have provided archaeologists with some of the most valuable evidence we have for understanding LB trade and seafaring.

SHIPS' REPRESENTATIONS

The most prominent ship depicted from Late Bronze Age Anatolia is on a LH IIIC krater from Bademgediği Tepesi (Meriç and Mountjoy 2002; Mountjoy 2011: 486, fig. 3, centre, bottom) (Figure 49). According to Wachsmann (2013: 74-75, 77 fig. 247), the scene depicts two antithetical ships, although only the one on the left has been published. The vessel faces right, as do the warriors standing above what may be a group of oarsmen, which may point to the existence of a partial ship's deck. To the right of both the oarsmen and the warriors is a stem-post with horizontal bands terminating in what may be a 'bird-head device'. The warriors clearly sport spiked helmets whilst those of the oarsmen are too vague to describe; Wachsmann (2013: 75), however, has no hesitation in interpreting both

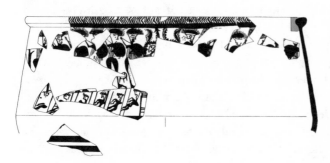

Figure 49: *Bademgediği Tepesi, Turkey, LH IIIC krater depicting warriors standing (on a ship's deck?) above what appears to be a group of oarsmen.* After Mountjoy 2011: 486, fig. 3, centre, bottom. Courtesy of Penelope Mountjoy.

as 'feathered helmets' like those worn by some of the 'sea peoples' on Egyptian monuments (Ben-Dor Evian 2016: 159 and n.40 defines those who wear such helmets as 'reed-capped warriors'). In Wachsmann's (2013: 74) view, '… this is our clearest two-dimensional representation of rowers plying their oars below deck level from an open rowers' gallery intersected with vertical stanchions'. In Mountjoy's (2011: 487) view, the scene on the Bademgediği Tepesi krater most likely portrays a sea battle, with the warriors on deck preparing to board another ship.

From LB levels at Liman Tepe, Aykurt and Erkanal (2017) report on a small body sherd (possibly from a LH IIIC krater) depicting a figure they believe to be an oarsman (Figure 50). The figure faces left and holds an object, possibly an oar, in his right hand; part of his knee can also be seen, which would indicate he is in a sitting position. The figure has spiked hair or perhaps wears a 'hedgehog'-type helmet. There is a thick horizontal line over his head, above which appear the legs of another figure that faces to the right, *i.e.* in the opposite direction of the oarsman. Although this is a very small sherd, its similarity to the scene depicted on the Bademgediği Tepesi vessel is striking, and Aykurt and Erkanal (2017: 62-66, figs. 4-5) regard it in the same way, *i.e.* an oarsman on the lower deck and a naval warrior on the deck above.

From a disturbed layer west of the 'Temple of Athena' at Miletos comes an unstratified LH IIIC sherd, likely of local clay, depicting two very schematic boats with oars, and a third set of oars that no doubt belongs to another boat (Mountjoy 2006: 114, 115 fig. 5:10). Several other LH IIIC sherds from western Anatolian sites (Troy, Miletos, Yeniköy) depict fish or dolphins, perhaps not suprising in coastal or near-coastal sites that would have exploited marine resources or engaged in trade with the Aegean world. For example, from Çine-Tepecik, inland from Miletos on the edge of a valley that forms the southern branch of the Maeander River system, the rim of another krater preserves the figure of what appears to be a warrior standing on the deck of a ship (Günel and Herbordt 2014: 4-5, figs. 3-5).

Compared to all other known ship's representations from the LB eastern Mediterranean, those on the so-called 'Flotilla Fresco' from the Cycladic island of Thera stand apart (amongst the vast literature, see Morgan 1998; Wachsmann 1998: 87-97; Strasser 2010; Strasser and Chapin 2014). This wall painting depicts 14 seacraft; seven of the larger vessels cross an expanse of water with a rocky headland and, in the background, one or perhaps two towns. Most of the large ships are richly adorned and

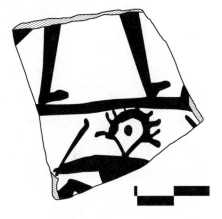

Figure 50: *Liman Tepe, Turkey, sherd (from a LH III krater?) depicting a figure with spiked hair, holding what may be an oar and standing beneath a line that may represent a ship's deck, with another figure above, as on the Bademgediği Tepe krater.* After Aykurt and Erkanal 2017: 65 fig. 5. Drawing by Irini Katsouri.

manned by crews, a captain and some (elite?) passengers. Most ships are propelled by oars, but at least one reveals a (largely reconstructed) sail, unfurled and at half-mast; Morgan (1998: 121) identifies this as a cargo ship. Wachsmann (1998: 90) notes that the shape of the Theran ships' hulls is typically Minoan. Dated to the Late Cycladic I period (ca. 1600 BC), this wall painting provides a superb snapshot of Mediterranean oared and sailing vessels — surely 'Cycladic' in origin — that should be borne in mind when trying to assess the meanings of the images discussed above.

STONE ANCHORS AND FISHING EQUIPMENT

As already noted above (Chapter 4: *Middle Bronze Age—Anatolia, Shipwrecks and Stone Anchors*), the Museum of Underwater Archaeology at Bodrum, Turkey has on exhibit several (unpublished) stone anchors, both composite- and weight-anchors, but they remain unpublished and their date is uncertain (see Figure 21, above). Wachsmann (1998: 274) is probably correct to observe that 'We know nothing of stone anchors used by Late Bronze Age Anatolian seafarers', even if we then have to assume that such seafarers existed. Nonetheless, two of the best-known shipwrecks of the Late Bronze Age were found just off the coast of south-southwestern Anatolia, and one of them packed a very impressive assemblage of anchors.

The Uluburun ship carried 24 stone anchors — 22 large examples all made from coastal sandstone, and two smaller, limestone examples (Wachsmann 1998: 281-285) (Figure 51). The full suite of anchors is of the single-hole, 'weight' type, with shapes varying from trapezoidal to more triangular; at least six of them have squared holes at the narrower end for an anchor cable or hawser. Collectively, these anchors weigh some 3.3 tons and represent the largest group of anchors ever found with a shipwreck (Pulak 2008: 306, and fig. 100 for a trapezoidal example) . The large number of anchors suggests that they were either unreliable or expendable, *i.e.* they might frequently have been lost at sea, or else had to be cut loose in an emergency (Wachsmann 1998: 283; Pulak 2008: 306). Amongst the parallels cited for these anchors are examples from the port sites of Kition on Cyprus, and Ugarit/ Minet el-Beidha and Byblos in the Levant (Pulak 2008: 306, with further refs.). As already noted, Goren's (2013: 56-59) petrographic analyses led him to conclude that all 24 Uluburun anchors were produced from stone originating along the Carmel coast of the southern Levant. On this basis, Pulak (2008: 307; 2010: 870, 874) concluded that a coastal port such as Tell Abu Hawam, in the general area between Israel's northern coast and southernmost coastal Lebanon, may have been the point of origin for the Uluburun ship's fateful trip, if not its home port.

Only a single anchor has ever been found in association with the Cape Gelidonya shipwreck (Pulak and Rogers 1994). During the original excavations, no anchors were recovered, only a 'triangular, pierced stone' that lay beyond the main area of the finds (Bass 1967: 28 fig. 10, 44-45, fig. 37). A revisit to the area of the wreck in 1994, however, produced a very heavy (219 kg) sandstone anchor, similar to but larger than those found on the Uluburun ship (Wachsmann 1998: 283, 285 fig. 12.48c; Bass 2013: 66-67, fig. 8). As already noted, petrographic analysis of this anchor indicates that it is of Cypriot origin (Bass 2013: 70; Yuval Goren, pers. comm., 20 May 2017).

Figure 51: *Stone weight anchor (one of two 'small'-sized anchors) from the Uluburun shipwreck.* Find number: KW4418. Courtesy of Cemal Pulak, Institute of Nautical Archaeology.

A few pieces of fishing equipment — copper alloy fishhooks, lead fishnet weights — have been recovered from the LB shipwreck at Uluburun (Yalçin *et al.* 2005: 628-629, nos. 184-185). There is also some limited information on fishing gear from the Gelidonya wreek, but it must be reiterated that both of these shipwrecks, and thus the fishing paraphernalia found amongst their remains, are not necessarily 'Anatolian' in origin. The finds from Gelidonya include what were identified as two line or net sinkers made of stone (du Plat Taylor, in Bass 1967: 128-129, figs. 137-138), 18 lead net weights, one conical weight and a lead line sinker (Bass 1967: 131-132, fig. 139). In addition, several fish vertebrae and other smaller fish bones were recovered, although Bass (1967: 133-134, fig. 144. 163) tends to dismiss them as the remnants of a meal. As emphasized earlier, it is still rare to find any systematic recording of fishing gear like the sinkers and weights, not to mention the fish bones, like those recovered from the excavation of the Cape Gelidonya shipwreck. One exception is the fish and mollusc remains from Kilise Tepe, some 40 km from the Mediterranean coast in southern Anatolia, where several freshwater and marine taxa have been recorded (van Neer and Waelkens 2007: 608 table 41; Debruyne 2017). It is to the credit of the excavators at these sites, and the care they took in the field as well as in the full, final publication of their sites, that even this level of information exists.

CHAPTER 6

SEAFARING, SEAFARERS AND SEABORNE TRADE

A DIACHRONIC OVERVIEW: EARLY—LATE BRONZE AGES

In this section, I summarise the material and documentary evidence discussed and referenced at length in the preceding three chapters (Chapters 3-5). At the same time, I begin to address some of the questions raised in the introduction to this volume:

- who might have built the ships with which Bronze Age maritime trade was conducted?
- who captained or sailed them, *i.e.* who was involved in these early maritime ventures?
- which ports and harbours were the most propitious for ships, merchants and maritime trade?

EARLY BRONZE AGE

Material evidence for 'the business of seafaring' during the Early Bronze Age in the eastern Mediterranean is thin, whether on the ground or under the sea. Beyond the northern shores of the Red Sea, harbours or anchorages may be postulated but none have been securely identified. Shipwrecks of the third millennium BC have yet to be discovered. The main types of archaeological evidence for maritime connectivity during the third millennium BC are ships' representations, maritime transport containers (MTCs) from the central-southern Levant and Egypt, and the considerable numbers of goods exchanged (ores, metals, metal implements and weapons, other types of pottery beyond MTCs, certain types of stone).

Most ship representations only demonstrate the early use of the sail within Egypt or else indicate an early and unexpected Egyptian presence in the Sinai peninsula. Even the apparently seaworthy ships depicted in Egyptian Fifth Dynasty contexts at Abusir and Saqqara cannot be used to argue for any notable level of Egyptian shipping in the southeastern Mediterranean (a point made long ago, if somewhat obliquely, by Ward 1963: 41-45). In the southern Levant, the very fragmentary incised boat representations on pottery sherds from Megiddo, as well as a miniature clay boat model from Tel Erani, seem to depict riverine craft. Documentary evidence is limited to the mention of 'Byblos ships' (*kbnt*), some passages of the Egyptian pharaoh Sneferu (ca. 2600 BC) referring to enigmatic ships of 50m length, and the 'autobiography' of a Sixth Dynasty court official (Uni) who might have used seagoing ships in naval battles waged along the southern Levantine coast. Stone anchors, in other times and places a solid indicator of seaborne ships and maritime activity, turn up mainly as pictorial representations (in the reliefs of Sahure and Unas), whereas actual stone anchors have been found only in Old Kingdom tombs at Abusir and Saqqara, and in likely EB contexts at Byblos (nine examples in all). Of the other 'Bronze Age' anchors known from coastal sites in the southern Levant, none can be assigned definitively to the EB.

Of course, the evidence for maritime contacts between Egypt and the Levant during the Early Bronze Age is firmly established (*e.g.* Marcus 2002; various papers in van den Brink and Levy 2002; Sowada 2009). Wengrow (2006: 150) suggests that such ventures may have been conducted at the elite level, *i.e.* through direct contacts between restricted groups who could mobilise the local production of commodities in demand — cedar wood, metals, MTCs carrying oil, wine or resins — on an increasingly greater scale (see also Marfoe 1987: 27). Egyptian stone vessels inscribed with royal names, found in Byblos as well as in Ebla, demonstrate further elite exchanges between these two regions (Bevan 2007; see also Sparks 2003: 48). In nodal harbours such as that at Byblos, which likely facilitated Egyptian-Levantine interconnections, some people had established the means to control imports and exports as well as the transhipment and redistribution of various goods, thus facilitating inland trade as well (Marfoe 1987: 34-35).

Elsewhere in the eastern Mediterranean, evidence for seafaring and/or a 'maritime consciousness' is largely missing from the archaeological record. The relevant material data from Cyprus and Anatolia are mainly metallurgical or ceramic (not MTCs) in nature. Likely imports to Cyprus include raw materials (copper, tin), metal tools and weapons, pottery, faience and shell beads, and gypsum vessels; exports include pottery, and copper (artefacts made from ores consistent with Cypriot production) found in Anatolia, Jordan and the Aegean. We can only speculate on the trade mechanisms involved in this exchange, but the main point worth emphasizing about Cyprus (and the Cyclades or eastern Aegean for that matter) is that all goods and materials had to be moved by sea.

The role of Anatolia in EB trade and seafaring is based upon the appearance after about 2500 BC of a suite of material features — tin bronzes, wheelmade pottery in new shapes, monumental fortifications — throughout western and southern Anatolia, the eastern Aegean islands and the Cyclades, and in parts of mainland Greece. Such features have been interpreted as part an 'international' maritime and terrestrial trading system based in Anatolia (the Anatolian Trade Network—ATN) (see Figure 10, above). The Bronze Age settlement at Liman Tepe on the Bay of İzmir in west central Anatolia is ideally situated for a harbour or anchorage, and its interregional maritime links are evident throughout most of the Early Bronze Age. Even so, beyond some much later remains (two moles dated to the mid-first millennium BC), there is no geophysical or material evidence for a Bronze Age harbour at this site.

Although the evidence at our disposal is therefore more suggestive than definitive, it can still be argued that —within the eastern Mediterranean — seagoing, sailing ships emerged earliest in Egypt and the southern Levant, by the mid-third millennium BC. Despite the evidently seaworthy ships depicted in Fifth Dynasty representations, Egypt appears to have had an ambiguous relationship with the Mediterranean (unlike its involvement in the Red Sea region). Moreover, the ships that made the Byblos run (*kbnt*) were most likely of Levantine origin (Ward 2010b: 43; Sauvage 2012: 234-235), even if one Sixth Dynasty inscription mentions the return to Egypt of the corpse of a man who oversaw the construction of 'Byblos ships' somewhere in the Levant (Strudwick 2005: 335; von Rüden 2015: 38). Thus we may suggest, on present evidence, that early maritime ventures between Egypt and the Levant involved ships built in the Levant and manned by Levantine merchants and mariners.

Some of the best evidence for seaborne trade is represented by the EB IB–III Levantine MTCs, which were almost certainly designed and produced under the aegis of potters and merchants (if not winemakers) to transport liquid or other organic goods to Egypt in newer, larger sailing vessels. Some Levantine communities like Ugarit, Byblos, Tyre, Jaffa or Ashkelon must have established anchorages (or improved upon 'natural' harbours that existed along their coastlines) and invested in the new sailing technology. Based on a range of metallurgical, ceramic and stone raw materials and finished goods exchanged between the southern Levant, Cyprus, Anatolia and the Cyclades, the technology of seagoing, sailing ships seems to have spread north and west during the course of the third millennium BC.

All materials exchanged during the third millennium BC must be considered within the context of the ATN and other, associated exchange systems, whether international or local (*e.g.*, Cycladic, Cypriot) in scale. Whereas Şahoğlu (2005: 352) maintains that seaborne traders from the İzmir region in coastal central Anatolia played a key role in maritime exchange between Anatolia and the Aegean islands, Knappett and Nikolakopoulou (2014: 28-30; also Broodbank 2000: 211-246) emphasize the central role of the Cyclades themselves in Aegean-Anatolian interaction. Trade within and through the Cycladic islands thus most likely involved local people and communities (as may be the case also for Cyprus—Webb *et al.* 2006). Nonetheless, it seems reasonable to assume that, during the Early Bronze Age, Anatolia may well have served as an exchange intermediary between the Levant and Mesopotamia to the east, and the Balkans and Aegean to the west (Massa and Şahoğlu 2015: 67-69). Although Anatolia's maritime connections are thus not in doubt, like most other regions of the Early Bronze Age eastern Mediterranean it offers limited material evidence of seafaring and seafarers. That picture persists for the most part during the subsequent, Middle Bronze Age, but changes dramatically in the Late Bronze Age.

MIDDLE BRONZE AGE

Documentary evidence related to seafaring and seafarers during the Middle Bronze Age remains quite limited, stems primarily from Egypt and pertains more to the Red Sea than to the Mediterranean. For example, several ostraca or stele from the Wadi Gawasis refer to the Twelfth Dynasty rulers Amenemhet II, III and IV, whilst the tale of *The Shipwrecked Sailor* mentions a large ship sailing in the Red Sea. One, partly preserved late Twelfth Dynasty text from El-Lisht (Papyrus Lythgoe) refers to an Egyptian travelling to the Levant and includes mention of a *kbnt* ('Byblos ship'). Most relevant are the court records of the Twelfth Dynasty pharaoh Amenemhet II, preserved on some inscribed granite blocks from Mit Rahina (Memphis); these include what Marcus (2007: 154) terms a 'cargo manifest' listing a variety of raw materials, organic products and finished goods transferred to Egypt, most likely from several Levantine ports. To this extent, it seems that the maritime trade routes established between Egypt and the Levant during the EB continued to develop further in the MB.

Although there are still no actual shipwrecks known from MB Egypt and the Levant, a considerable range of evidence (presented in Chapter 4) indicates that maritime trade was expanding both in scope and spatial scale in the eastern Mediterranean — involving Egypt, the Levant, Anatolia and the Aegean. This evidence includes (1) the intricate and enigmatic ships' representations from Abydos; (2) Cretan oval-mouthed amphorae and the quantities of Canaanite jars recovered in the elaborate harbour complex at Tell ed-Dab'a; (3) the Mit Rahina inscription and its implications for Levantine-Egyptian trade; (4) stone anchors found along the Levantine coast and cedars (for ship-building?) exported from Lebanon; and (5) the emergence or development of a series of likely proto-harbours along the Levantine coast, extending into the Egyptian Delta (*e.g.* Ugarit, Byblos, Beirut, Tyre, Sidon, Akko, Jaffa, Tell el-'Ajjul, Tell ed-Dab'a). A proposed Egyptian maritime expedition against Ura in Cilicia and Cyprus — as noted in the Mit Rahina inscription — seems at best equivocal, and decidedly controversial (Altenmüller and Moussa 1991: 35, n.24; Quack 1996: 79-80; Marcus 2007: 144-148). As Marcus (2007: 176) notes, however, 'significant material wealth' flowed into Egypt from the north, which may have spurred seafaring ventures and encouraged further investments in developing Levantine ports and coastal settlements, all signs of an expanding maritime consciousness in the region.

Nonetheless, beyond the expansive pictures painted by the Mit Rahina inscription and the excavations at Tell ed-Dab'a ('Venice on the Nile'—Marcus 2006, 2007), and despite an apparent 'explosion of urban life' throughout the Levant (Broodbank 2013: 362-365), the evidence for similar levels of expansion in maritime transport and trade, 'port power', seafaring or even actual ships remains more sporadic than systematic. We may assume that seafaring people from Levantine coastal ports (and possibly from the Aegean) continued to build ships and transport organic products such as wine, oil and resins to Egypt, but the elaborate harbour complex at Tell ed-Dab'a and all the imported goods found there, as well as the elaborate ships' representations from Abydos, indicate that we cannot rule out Egyptian involvement in these martime trading ventures.

Current evidence of maritime-related activities from MB Cyprus is less compelling but nonetheless demonstrates that the island was not isolated from the surrounding Mediterranean world. The four known ship models (if such they are) may indicate no more than an awareness of the sea that surrounds the island. Although one may question the significance or indeed even the presence of more than a few scattered examples of maritime transport containers on Cyprus, an array of other evidence — imported pottery, metals and metal products of all kinds, faience, alabaster — from Crete, the Levant, Anatolia and Egypt indicates that the island was somehow involved in interregional trade during the MC period.

Amongst an array of archaeological sites that show Cyprus's copper sulphide orebodies were now being exploited (Knapp 2013a: 298-302), work at MC I (ca. 1900 BC) Ambelikou *Aletri* provides solid evidence for copper extraction from deep mining shafts (Merrillees 1984; Webb and Frankel 2013: 25-30). Textual evidence, moreover, indicates that someone on the island had the capacity to ship copper ore overseas (to Crete, Syria), unless one argues that foreign merchants and traders somehow addressed this demand for Cypriot copper. Even if we accept the notion that the islanders themselves were producing and transporting copper and other goods at this time, there is as yet no archaeological evidence for the ships that would have been involved in such mercantile enterprises. The limited number of imports, whether the 'approximately 25' I have identified (Knapp 2013b: 24) or ten-fold that amount (Webb 2016: 62-63), adds up to no more than a few imports per year, even if they all seem to have been destined for north coast sites, especially Lapithos (the only site that lies near the coast). In short, the scale of Cyprus's overseas trade must be seen in context: clearly international trade was making inroads into the island and the notion of 'distance and the exotic' must have had some impact. But the question remains whether Cypriot communities, merchants or mariners were themselves actively involved, and if so, to what extent.

Turning to Anatolia, a new shipwreck dated to the early second millennium BC has been reported at Hisarönü, near Bodrum, but remains unpublished. Beyond that, the cargo of a late MB shipwreck at Sheytan Deresi has a few ceramic vessels that might be designated as maritime transport containers; their generally coarse, homogenous fabric, however, suggests a more utilitarian type of vessel, one that may have served as a transport container for locally traded goods or more simply as a container for storage of those goods. The most detailed study of the ceramic material from the wreck deposit suggests that the ship itself was a small vessel (*i.e.* less than 10m in length) involved in coastal trading (*i.e.* cabotage) that sunk not far from its point of origin. There are no ships' representations with which we might compare it, nor any stone anchors from which we might speculate on its capacity. Imports at Liman Tepe, along the western coast of Anatolia, indicate that it continued to be an important regional centre during the MB, although there is still no physical evidence there of a contemporary harbour. The same holds true for the MB levels at Çeşme-Bağlararası, where close interactions with the Aegean are attested. The only other likely port, at Kinet Höyük on the Bay of Iskenderun, dates to the very end of the MB, as its few Canaanite jars also attest. The number and type of Cypriot imports seem impressive but, given their late MC or early LC dates, perhaps not surprising, as that brings us to the verge of an era in which all aspects Mediterranean maritime trade and seafaring enterprises increase exponentially, and are evident in both material and documentary evidence. Many people had by now developed a maritime consciousness and increasingly were 'working' the sea (*i.e.* making a living from travelling on it or exploiting its resources).

LATE BRONZE AGE

Documentary evidence related to seafaring and seafarers during the Late Bronze Age is voluminous compared to earlier periods, but stems primarily from two sites: Ugarit in Syria and Tell el-Amarna in Egypt. The evidence from Ugarit is rich and rewarding, but only if it is considered comprehensively, something that often eludes archaeologists who call upon it. Moreover, when trying to determine the significance of Levantine seafaring and seafarers in the LB, it must be borne in mind that what holds true for Ugarit may not apply to Byblos, Beirut, Sidon, Tyre and other coastal Canaanite polities (Bell 2016: 93; but *cf.* Sherratt 2016: 293). Nonetheless, the multifaceted, intricate and often personal relationships evident in the texts from Ugarit provide an unparalleled view into the practices of LB Levantine merchants, and into the constraints and affordances that characterised and sustained their actions. Although we know little beyond the personal names of most merchants and seafarers, some of the wealthiest merchants (*e.g.* Urtenu, Rapanu, Rašap-abu) maintained their own personal archives, which treat all manner of commercial, diplomatic, legal and family matters. During the LB, the primary role of Levantine merchants, mariners and ship owners or captains in the business of seafaring throughout the eastern Mediterranean seems beyond doubt.

Both state-sponsored and private merchants functioned at Ugarit, and on occasion the king exempted some merchants from paying duty on imported goods. The texts also indicate a close relationship between the rulers of Ugarit and Cyprus (*Alašiya*). Both Akkadian and Ugaritic documents from the site mention other maritime personnel or groups: a 'ship's captain', a 'harbour master', a 'merchant's representative' and a 'chief mariner', although it is far from clear just how they functioned, and who was responsible to whom, within Ugarit's politico-economic bureaucracy (see Figure 23, above).

The documentary evidence also makes it clear that Levantine port towns like Ugarit, Arwad, Beirut, Byblos, Tyre, Sidon and Jaffa were intricately linked into the commercial networks that distributed, or facilitated the distribution of, a wide range of raw materials, organic goods, finished products and exotica between and beyond the other polities of the eastern Mediterranean: Egypt, Anatolia and Cyprus. Other sites not mentioned in the texts — *e.g.* Tell Kazel, Sarepta, Tell Abu Hawam, Tel Nami — arguably were involved at some level in these same networks. It is equally evident that naval encounters and coastal raids were widespread along the Levantine coast, and that these maritime states were thus not only in commercial contact but also in military conflict with one another, some calling upon the Egyptian pharaoh for support, others relying upon the intervention of the Hittite state.

Bearing in mind the source of much of this material (*i.e.* Ugarit), there is little doubt that the ships anchored at Ugarit's harbours — some under the mantle of the king, some not, and whether used for commercial or military purposes or both — comprised a fleet (or fleets) of exceptional size for a Bronze Age polity, evidently larger than those that anchored at other Levantine ports. Based on documents from both Ugarit and Hittite Anatolia, it is also evident that the Hittites made an effort, at least during the centuries between 1400-1200 BC, to provide some level of protection for ships that frequented Ugarit's harbours. Like the Egyptians, the Hittites felt it advantageous not to interfere unduly in Ugarit's maritime commerce (see also Sherratt 2016: 292). Despite all this, and although it's clear that LB Levantine merchants and mariners had mastered the art of seafaring along maritime routes within the eastern Mediterranean and beyond (i.e., at least to Crete and mainland Greece if not the central Mediterranean), there were (1) too many powerful and influential polities (coastal or inland), and (2) too many harbours throughout the international arena of the eastern Mediterranean — both factors indicating how uncontrollable maritime trade actually was — to sustain any notion of an exclusive, dominant, 'Canaanite thalassocracy' (Sasson 1966; Linder 1981; *cf.* Knapp 1993; Lambrou-Phillipson 1993).

The Akkadian letters from Amarna make reference to various types of ships, merchants and several Levantine coastal polities — *e.g.* Arwad, Beirut, Byblos, Sidon, Tyre and Akko — that maintained ships used for military and/ or commercial purposes. Most of these texts were discussed above (Chapter 2— *Merchants, Mariners and Pirates*), where it was emphasized that not only is there no term in contemporary Akkadian, Ugaritic and Hittite documents that can be equated with either 'pirates' or 'piracy', but also that there is no indisputable link between the vast range of material culture linked to LB piracy and what has been termed a 'culture of piracy' (Hitchcock and Maeir 2016: 247, 259). On the one hand, the terms 'pirates' and 'piracy' should only be used in a qualified manner, at least during this time period. On the other hand, based on all the maritime peoples and activities mentioned in LB documents, it is crucial to emphasize that land-based polities — even those like Ugarit that may have had a sizeable 'navy' — were at a loss to contain the commando-like raids that took coastal towns and ports by surprise, with the perpetrators often sacking or destroying them. Thus we might better refer to these groups as 'coastal raiders', not 'pirates'.

With the possible exception of a thirteenth century BC wreck deposit at Hishuley Carmel just off the Levantine coast near Haifa (Galili *et al.* 2013), no LB shipwrecks are yet known from the southeastern Mediterranean. Nonetheless, documentary evidence mentions a royal ship that was wrecked near Tyre (KTU 2.38), whilst another non-royal ship, from Ugarit, was wrecked at an unspecified port (RS 17.133).

Documentary and material evidence alike make it clear that a great variety of mineral, organic, manufactured and 'exotic' goods moved to or through several Levantine and Mediterranean Egyptian ports, most notably Ugarit, Byblos, Sidon, Tyre, Tel Akko, Tell Abu Hawam, Tel Nami, Tell el-'Ajjul and Marsa Matruh (if not Zawiyet Umm el-Rakham). Along with the documentary evidence, excavations at Ugarit and its ports have produced a wealth of evidence on LB maritime trade: *e.g.* large quantities of imported Cypriot and Aegean pottery, maritime transport containers (and a storage room to hold them, at Minet el-Beidha—see Figure 24, above), Egyptian alabaster, Syrian (or African) ivory, and a mould for making copper oxhide ingots (at Ras Ibn Hani—Lagarce *et al.* 1983: 278 fig. 15, 279, 284-285), which can only have been produced using imported copper. Tell Kazel likewise contained large amounts of imported Cypriot and Aegean pottery as well as some 'Grey Ware' that most likely originated in northwest Anatolia. Perhaps Kazel was another major LB emporium, but its presumed harbour (Tabbat el-Hammam, some 3 km distant on the coast) seems to be exclusively Iron Age in date. Relevant archaeological evidence from most of the main coastal sites of the central Levant — Byblos, Beirut, Sidon, Tyre — is more sporadic, although the site of Sarepta, with its high concentration of Mycenaean pottery, stands out (Bell 2005: 365-367).

Some key port sites of the southernmost Levant — *e.g.* Tel Akko, Tell Abu Hawam, Tel Nami, Jaffa, Tell el-'Ajjul — offer a treasure trove of diverse information on LB Mediterranean maritime trade, especially the quantities of imported Cypriot and Aegean pottery (Tell Abu Hawam, Tel Nami) and other wares from Egypt and Anatolia (Tel Akko). If it was the case that Tel Akko focused its external trade efforts on Egypt (Artzy and Zagorski 2012: 3), Tell Abu Hawam and Tel Nami may have served wider, Mediterranean networks of trade. Artzy (2006: 59-60), moreover, has suggested that these three sites might have flourished at slightly different times: Tell Abu Hawam until the thirteenth century BC, when regional maritime trade may have shifted to Tel Akko and, toward the very end of the LB, to Tel Nami. In her view, independent traders involved in both local and long-distance trade may have operated out of all three sites (Artzy 2006: 45-46). Although LB evidence from Dor is still limited, that is not the case for Jaffa, whose diverse imports — Cypriot wares, maritime transport containers (Canaanite and Egyptian), Canaanite, Philistine and Egyptian pottery and scarabs — indicate that it too served as a key harbour or transshipment point, especially with respect to Egypt (Burke *et al.* 2017). Tell el-'Ajjul's role as a port also seems evident from the diversity of imported goods at the site, in particular the range of pottery from Egypt, Cyprus and the Aegean.

In Egypt, the bright star of Mediterranean interconnections at Avaris (Tell ed-Dab'a) in the eastern Nile Delta dimmed significantly after its conquest by the Theban king Ahmose in the latter half of the sixteenth century BC. Although its citadel with a palatial precinct, famed in textual evidence as the river port of Perunefer (Bietak 2005), flourished until the early fifteenth century BC, no longer did it function as 'Venice on the Nile'. The 'dockyard annals' of Tuthmosis III, moreover, indicate that at least some of the ships docked at Perunefer were of Byblian or Cretan, not Egyptian origin. On present evidence, the most significant 'Egyptian' anchorage for Mediterranean maritime interaction lies far west of the Nile Delta, at Marsa Matruh. With abundant evidence of maritime transport containers (Canaanite jars, Aegean transport stirrup jars, Cypriot *pithoi*), as well as widely-prized ostrich eggshell fragments, Marsa Matruh most likely functioned as a way station for maritime traffic travelling from the Aegean, Cyprus and the Levant. The large fortified site of Zawiyet Umm el-Rakham, some 25 km west of Marsa Matruh, also has imported maritime transport containers from the Levant and the Aegean as well as a range of Cypriot wares. However, its location, today about one km inland from the coast, calls into question its role as a port, and suggests that its imported wares may have been offloaded at Marsa Matruh and transported overland to the site.

Representations of ships, most very schematic in style, are found widely throughout Levantine coastal sites, from north to south: on faience scarabs from Ugarit and a funerary urn from Hama; in the form of terracotta boat models from Byblos, and ships' graffiti from Tell Abu Hawam, Dor and Beth Shemesh; on an 'altar' from Tel Akko engraved with ship representations and carvings with 'fan'-type boats similar to those from rock carvings on the Carmel Ridge; and on a cylinder seal and two (Philistine ware) pottery sherds from Tel Miqne. Despite the schematic style, the frequency and widespread distribution of these reliefs suggest that the Canaanites had a deep experience and detailed knowledge of navigation.

From the Memphite necropolis at Saqqara in Egypt, two tombs display relief drawings of what are most likely Levantine ships; in both scenes, maritime transport containers (schematised Canaanite jars) are being offloaded from the ships. The famous reliefs from the mortuary temple of Ramesses III at Medinet Habu depict both Egyptian and 'sea peoples' ships (the latter often argued to be Aegean 'galleys'—*e.g.* Wachsmann 1998: 172-196; 2013: 33-40). Based on both the reliefs and accompanying inscriptions, the Egyptian fleet seems to have been made up of sailing ships, some merchant ships of Levantine design, and other, native Egyptian ships purposely built for naval battles. Although Wachsmann (2013) regards the wooden boat model from Gurob in Egypt as an Aegean galley, it seems equally likely that any similarities between the various kinds of ship concerned may simply reflect the technological standard of the time, as well as the intense interaction amongst all the maritime players in the LB eastern Mediterranean. From Thebes, the tombs of Nebamun and Kenamun both have reliefs depicting what are probably Levantine ('Syro-Canaanite') seagoing ships. Whereas the Nebamun relief shows only one poorly preserved ship, that of Kenamun portrays 11 detailed ships' representations, and in one register Canaanite jars are again depicted being offloaded from a ship.

Even if it proves to be the case that all these representations depict ships that are of Levantine (or Aegean) origin, at the same time it is clear from the Punt reliefs at Deir el-Bahri (see, conveniently, Wachsmann 1998: 18-21, figs. 2.15-2.18) that the Egyptians were capable of building seagoing vessels, at least for voyages on the Red Sea. Nonetheless, despite all the pharaonic raids into, if not conquest of, large areas of the southern-central Levant during the Eighteenth and Nineteenth Dynasties, with respect to matters such as sailing, navigating, trading or even fishing, one might well conclude that the Egyptians had little interest in the Mediterranean Sea (von Rüden 2015: 38-42).

The juxtaposition of Levantine ships from Egyptian tomb reliefs depicting Canaanite jars, together with the storage-room deposit of some 80 such vessels at Minet el-Beidha, signals the importance of maritime transport containers in LB seaborne trade (see also Knapp and Demesticha 2017). Their contents included olive and other oils (and/or animal fat), pistacia resin, wine and honey. Their presence at LB sites throughout Cyprus, Cilicia and the Levant, in Egypt and along the north African coast, on the Uluburun and Cape Gelidonya shipwrecks, and throughout the Aegean (Rutter 2014), marks them out as key material factors in the bulk transport of Mediterranean goods during this international era. Analytical studies on LB Canaanite jars indicate that they were produced at various sites along the Levantine coast, from the Bay of Haifa northward, perhaps in Cilicia, and even on Cyprus.

The shape of the New Kingdom Egyptian jar was very similar to that of the Canaanite jar, making it ideal for seaborne transport and/or storage. Egyptian jars have been found throughout the southern Levant and on Cyprus and Crete. Hieratic inscriptions on some of them indicate they served to store or transport wine, honey, meats, fish and fowl, grains and fruits, and incense. Analytical work regarding their composition points to a high degree of homogeneity in production, and we can assume such jars were produced in the region around Memphis and the Nile Delta, rather than around Thebes.

Stone anchors of Bronze Age date are found at coastal sites all along the Levantine littoral, as well as in Egypt and on Cyprus. The most coherent and securely dated group of stone anchors are the 24 weight-anchors recovered during the excavation of the LB Uluburun shipwreck (Pulak 1998: 216-217, fig. 25) (see further below, and Figure 51, above). More difficult to date precisely are the 43 stone anchors recorded at Ugarit and its port Minet el-Beidha; both MB and LB parallels have been cited. Other types of gear related to fishing and found at Ugarit and/or Minet el-Bediha include stone weights shaped like miniature anchors and quoits (perhaps sinkers, or 'messengers), 'pierced pebbles' of unknown function, other types of fishing tackle and shells. Finally, fish that originated in the Nile have been found at LB coastal and inland settlements throughout the southern Levant, whilst several different types of Mediterranean fish and shellfish have a more limited distribution (*i.e.* Megiddo, Lachish and Tel el-Wawayat). This is an odd pattern and probably reflects little more than the vagaries of archaeological excavation, or the lack of attention paid to certain types of materials or small finds, as well as to ichthyofaunal data.

Turning to LB Cyprus, once again there is no material evidence of formal, built harbours, but several sites must have served as ports for the shipment or receipt of goods. Foremost amongst them are Maroni *Tsarroukas*, Enkomi, Kition, Hala Sultan Tekke *Vyzakia* and (most likely) Tochni *Lakkia*; Kourion Bay and an undetermined area near Kouklia *Palaipaphos* probably had port facilities too. Ship representations abound on LB Cyprus, and include ship graffiti (Kition, Enkomi, Hala Sultan Tekke *Vyzakia*), at least eight terracotta boat models (mostly from coastal sites—Enkomi, Maroni, Maa *Palaeokastro*), a few further ships painted on LH IIIB and IIIC pottery sherds from Enkomi, and an unprovenanced serpentine cylinder seal carved with a masted ship.

Cyprus imported and used both Canaanite jars (CJs) and Transport Stirrup Jars (TSJs), and may well have produced some of the former. Over 150 CJs, imported and locally made, are known from 20 different sites on Cyprus, whilst 110 TSJs (manufactured on Crete) have been found on the island, mainly at coastal sites. Locally produced Group II *pithoi* may also have been used to transport liquids or other produce, but their main purpose was for storage. Such *pithoi* have been found widely distributed at sites in the LB Mediterranean, and on the Cape Iria and Uluburun shipwrecks. It seems clear that Cypriot merchants played some role as middlemen in maritime commerce within the eastern Mediterraenan (Knapp 2014), not least through the production, use, shipment or transhipment of these MTCs, if not other pottery wares (most notably, Late Helladic wares from the Aegean). The fact that diverse Cypriot goods, including Group II *pithoi*, have been found on five of the eight known shipwrecks in the prehistoric eastern Mediterranean, also points to a significant Cypriot role in the international exchanges that characterised the Late Bronze Age.

Hundreds of stone anchors have been found on Cyprus, some 250 of them at LB coastal sites (Kition, Hala Sultan Tekke, Maroni). These anchors have a range of shapes, but one type (composite, rounded and triangular shape) may be native to Kition; thin section analyses indicated that all but three of 150 anchors found at the site were locally made. In Wachsmann's (1998: 328) compelling view, the large numbers of stone anchors found on Cypriot land sites, along with a range of other evidence, suggests that seafaring was an important enterprise on LB Cyprus, and that the ships and merchants of the island likely played a key role as middlemen in exchange relations between Egypt, the Levant and the Aegean.

Miniature anchors found at Kition may have been used as line-weights in set long-line fishing, or for anchoring fishing tackle; other fishing weights and fishhooks have also been recovered at Kition. Further evidence for fishing-related activities comes from Hala Sultan Tekke. The fishing gear and related materials, as well as the abundant ichthyological data from the site (Lindqvist 2016), point to both coastal and offshore fishing, whilst the two types of net weights (lead, stone) may indicate two different types of net used for in-shore fishing. The generally larger-sized fish that dominate the remains from Hala Sultan Tekke point to deep sea fishing.

Turning to Anatolia, there is as yet no physical evidence of the actual harbour facilities at LB sites such as Troy (or Beşik Bay), Çeşme–Bağlararası, Panaztepe, Liman Tepe, Miletos and Kinet Höyük. However, given their strategic locations and the wide range of imported goods from the Aegean, Cyprus or the Levant found in excavations at these sites, it is clear that ports such as these, if not others along the western and at least some parts of the southern coasts of Anatolia, served the needs of Mediterranean merchants, mariners and ships of the 'international' Late Bronze Age, from at least the mid-second millennium BC onward.

Schematic but beguiling ships' representations are seen on sherds of LH IIIC kraters from western coastal Anatolia, at Bademgediği Tepesi (two antithetical ships, oarsmen and 'warriors'), Liman Tepe (similar to the Bademgediği sherd but showing only a likely oarsman), Çine-Tepecik (mariner standing on the deck of a ship) and Miletos (two very schematic boats with oars, and a third set of oars). Although it has been suggested that that the Bademgediği Tepesi krater portrays 'warriors' on the deck of a ship battling or preparing to board another ship, this cannot be demonstrated conclusively, especially when compared, for example, to the battle and boarding scenes on a classical, Attic black-figured *kylix* portraying two ships — a small, two-level, oared vessel, with sails raised (a 'pirate' ship), and a taller merchantman, with sails furled (and about to be boarded) (Morrison and Williams 1968: 109, pls. 10, 20a).

There is some limited information on fishing gear from the Gelidonya wreck (stone and lead line or net sinkers, net weights) as well as several fish vertebrae, and some freshwater and marine fish and mollusc remains from Kilise Tepe, far to the east in southern Anatolia. Although several stone anchors (both composite- and weight types) are known from LB Anatolia, most remain unpublished and cannot be dated. The notable exception is the 24, single-hole ('weight') stone anchors, totalling over three tons, known from the Uluburun shipwreck. These anchors reveal a suite of different shapes, varying from trapezoidal to triangular (see Figure 51 above), and have known parallels at Kition on Cyprus, and at Minet el-Beidha and Byblos in the Levant. Petrographic analysis, however, indicates that the stone from which all the Uluburun anchors were made originated along the Carmel coast of the southern Levant. By contrast, the single anchor recovered from the Cape Gelidonya shipwreck was most likely made of stone native to Cyprus.

The most dramatic and informative material evidence yet found related to maritime seafaring, seafarers and ships in the LB eastern Mediterranean comes from the excavations of the two Late Bronze shipwrecks found along the southern coast of Anatolia — Cape Gelidonya and Uluburun, whatever their origin may have been. Although speculation is rife about the home ports of these ships (Levant, Egypt, Cyprus), the maritime route(s) they followed and their destinations (Aegean, Anatolia, Cyprus), of all eight known Bronze Age wreck deposits only these two preserve any wooden remains of the actual ships. We can infer reasonably that the Uluburun ship was a bulk cargo carrier involved in long-distance trade, whilst the Cape Gelidonya ship served as a 'tinker' carrying a more 'general', much smaller cargo. Indeed, Sherratt and Sherratt (1991: 372–374) long ago suggested that the systems involved in Mediterranean maritime trade during the LB had at least two different components: (1) 'heavily capitalised' large ships with significant capacities carrying major 'bulk' cargoes and sailing long-distance, international routes marked by major ports or emporia; and (2) largely independent boats of smaller size and more limited capacities sailing short distances (not necessarily local) over opportunistic routes, not always with a final destination in mind.

Given this encapsulated, diachronic overview of ships, seafarers and the business of seafaring in the Bronze Age eastern Mediterranean, what can be said about the various trade networks and routes of exchange followed by ships and seaman on the Mediterranean? This is an exercise in possibilities rather than certainties.

NETWORKS AND ROUTES OF EXCHANGE

In this section, I also consider further such issues as:

- the origins and emergence of early trade networks and maritime ventures
- social aspects of seafaring, the relationship different peoples had with the sea
- 'seascapes', voyaging, mobility, connectivity.

Various material features — *e.g.* port facilities or anchorages, coastal settlements, zones of maritime transport (see below), the origin and provenance of maritime transport containers — enable archaeologists to gain a fuller understanding of seafaring, if not seascapes and the ideology of the sea. Seafaring not only reduced the 'tyranny' of distance, but also, at least in certain instances, helped to build and bolster the power and influence of coastal towns and ports. Centralised polities like Late Bronze Age Ugarit and Cyprus, or New Kingdom Egypt, invested heavily in, and came to rely upon, maritime transport to develop trading networks and naval ventures, and to project or stabilise power relations (Marcus 2002: 411-412).

To develop maritime networks of exchange, it was essential for land-based polities to support people (merchants, sailors, tinkers) who were motivated to travel, and to promote the 'technologies of mobility' (boats, sails, port facilities) and socioeconomic institutions (the 'palace', merchant organisations) that assisted them (Kristiansen 2016: 156). The resulting 'cognitive geographies' meant that distance, dangers and destinations became more familiar to the traveller, and made far-away worlds seem smaller, more accessible. The world of merchants, sailors, tinkers or 'pirates' was one in which travellers had to go beyond known borders, and try to engage with liminal or distant places and things (Monroe 2011), all the while earning a profit or at least making a living — working the sea. If we wish to gain insights into ancient seascapes or a maritime consciousness, it is essential to engage some of these social, economic, symbolic and liminal aspects of maritime space, using the imaginary eyes and ears of mariners or merchants to envisage or portray coastal features, harbour installations, merchant or fishing fleets, and the types of trade or mechanisms of exchange involved.

Panagiotopoulos (2011: 38-39) has suggested that cabotage ('small-scale coastal trade') was the main form of maritime interconnectedness at the regional level, '… the only possibility for acquiring the indispensable means of subsistence'. Similarly, Horden and Purcell (2000: 145, 365, 368–369) maintain that local or regional, coastal-oriented trade, from port to port, in search of markets, was a key aspect of Mediterranean connectivity. On a broader, interregional level, however, highly specialised merchants, emissaries and sailors — who were engaged in long-distance maritime trade and were supported or sponsored by elites and state-level institutions — formed the basis of (a more narrowly focused) maritime connectivity. For example, the remains of the Uluburun shipwreck, by far the best material witness of LB trade in the Mediterranean, represents the highest level of elite-sponsored connectivity, one we may term 'grand cabotage'.

On the one hand, then, we can see a high degree of maritime connectivity by the time of the Late Bronze Age in the eastern Mediterranean, characterised by well organised, long-distance maritime expeditions ('grand cabotage') and by smaller-scale, coastal oriented trade ventures between a succession of ports and capes (cabotage). On the other hand, an array of material and/or documentary evidence from various earlier and contemporary periods of the Bronze Age, alongside what is by now a significant corpus of analytical data (*e.g.* McGovern 2000; Mommsen *et al.* 2002; Serpico 2005; Hartung 2014; Hartung *et al.* 2015; Mountjoy and Mommsen 2015; Knapp and Demesticha 2017) suggests that seaborne trade within the eastern Mediterranean was complex and multi-dimensional, always changing: it involved local as well as 'state' control, entrepreneurial ventures like tramping, and state-level gift exchange (Sherratt and Sherratt 1991, 1998; Knapp and Cherry 1994: 126-151; Panagiotopoulos 2012). Moreover, we should recall Arnaud's (2005: 118-121) observation that it is necessary not only to distinguish between long-distance trade and cabotage, but also to realise that the rule was to combine the two. Because routes of travel tended to be composite and segmented, cabotage was not the only way to sail, and the journey may not always have been from port-to-port but rather, for example, from landmark to landmark (capes, estuaries, islands).

Multiple webs of communication, transport and exchange linked several regions of the eastern Mediterranean during the Bronze Age; these involved various vectors of trade, for example Tartaron's (2013: 186, table 6.1) local ('coastscape'), small worlds, regional and interregional spheres of interaction. Commercial, sociopolitical and ideological interests are deeply entangled in these vectors of trade, regardless of the exchange mechanism involved. Equally important from a maritime perspective are the likely routes of seaborne trade.

Based to some extent on known shipwreck sites, Wachsmann (2000b: 811-815, fig. 7) outlined several possible Bronze Age sea routes in the eastern Mediterranean, providing detailed (if now somewhat dated) references:

1. Levantine coast, from Egypt to Ugarit, from the earliest stages of the Bronze Age
2. continuation of the Levantine route to Cilicia and southern coast of Anatolia
3. from north Syria to/from Aegean via Cyprus, or along the southern coast of Anatolia and thence via Rhodes
4. from north Syria to Cyprus, then southward to Egypt and/or Marsa Matruh (the only 'natural' harbour between Tobruk and Alexandria)
5. southeast from Crete to Egypt and/or Marsa Matruh, but probably not vice-versa (see also Knapp 1981: 267-269; but *cf.* Barcat 2015).

Based on the trade in Mycenaean pottery and some limited written evidence, Hirschfeld (2009) discussed possible sea routes between the Aegean, Cyprus and the Levant. Whilst evidence from Linear B documents is slim, relevant cuneiform texts from the Levant (mainly Ugarit), as already noted above, never cite direct communications with the Aegean and only mention one case of indirect contact, that concerning the merchant Ṣinaranu (Monroe 2009: 165-167). The two documents regarding ships of Ugarit sailing to Lukka and referring to the *Hiyawa*-men (Singer 2006: 251-258) are only relevant here if *Hiyawa = Ahhiyawa*, and if *Ahhiyawa*, in turn, is equivalent to 'Achaia' (*i.e.* the Aegean).

With respect to Mycenaean pottery found on Cyprus and in the Levant, Hirschfeld follows Hankey (1967) and Mee (2008: 377), suggesting that cargoes from the Aegean may have been offloaded in Cypriot ports, and transhipped to Levantine ports by Cypriot middlemen. Mee (2008: 377), notably, mentions that whilst over 3000 Aegean vessels have been found in some 90 Levantine sites, the amount of Cypriot pottery at the same sites greatly outnumbers them. Hirschfeld (1996; 2000: 183-184) herself has argued that Cypro-Minoan signs incised on some Mycenaean transport containers indicate they reached the Levant via Cyprus or through the intercession of Cypriot merchants. Finally, based on earlier work by Steel (1999, 2002) and Bell (2005), Hirschfeld suggests four possible routes/modes of trade that brought Aegean pottery to the Levant:

1. direct exports to Sarepta
2. targeted exports to Ugarit
3. secondary distribution (via Cyprus) to Ugarit and most of Canaan, and
4. an incidental link to southern Levantine sites, where Egyptian practices prevailed.

Concerning a 'return trade', Levantine pottery, notably Canaanite jars, travelled from the Levant to the Aegean, but the mechanism of exchange is uncertain: Hirschfeld (2009: 289) suggests that some of these vessels may have originated on Cyprus rather than the Levant. Finally, regarding a 'special relationship' between Cyprus and Tiryns, she cites Maran's (2004) study, which suggested that certain people from Tiryns may have adopted not only materials but also ideas perhaps directly from the Levant or else via Cyprus (see also Brysbaert and Vetters 2013). On the basis of her case studies (Mycenaean chariot kraters in the Levant, Mycenaean pottery from Tell el-'Ajjul and Sarepta, the special relationship with Tiryns), and in line with my own comments above, Hirschfeld (2009: 291) suggests that Levantine-Aegean interactions should not be defined in terms of 'monolithic blocks', as the evidence suggests that several alternative routes were involved, used by different LB Levantine communities. She avoided the issue raised by Bass (1998) about the involvement of 'Mycenaeans' in this trade. Whereas Bass denied any role on the part of the Mycenaeans (but not Minoans) in Levantine-Aegean trade relations, Hirschfeld (2009: 291) only notes how people from 'the diverse communities that inhabited the eastern Mediterranean littoral in the Late Bronze Age' forged the multiple connections she discusses.

More recently, and as already mentioned, Tartaron (2013: 185–203, 186 table 6.1) has proposed a framework for interpreting Late Bronze Age Aegean maritime connections and for enhancing our understanding of maritime landscapes. He outlines four different 'spheres of interaction' as well as the chronological, geographic and material scales that characterise them:

1. coastscape
2. maritime small world
3. regional (or intracultural) and
4. interregional (or intercultural)

In his framework, the entire Aegean was a 'regional' sphere, comprising many small worlds, such as the Saronic Gulf, the southeastern Aegean and Miletos, and the Bay of Volos (Tartaron 2013: 213–284).

If we turn to the (qualitative) evidence presented in this study to ponder some possible maritime small worlds or regional interaction spheres in the eastern Mediterranean, there are at least six possibilities:

1. Egypt and the central-southern Levant
2. Levantine coastal ports (south to north)
3. the Levant and Cyprus
4. Cyprus and Egypt
5. northern Levant and southern coastal Anatolia (and Cyprus)
6. western coastal Anatolia and the Aegean

It must be emphasized that the boundaries of these small worlds cannot be drawn easily on a map, and the distinctions between them vary over time and in geographic orientation (Horden and Purcell 2000: 523). Traffic between Egypt and the Levant was common if not intensive throughout much of the Bronze Age, and the coastal current (Hamad *et al.* 2006) certainly facilitated northbound maritime traffic, whether Egyptian or Levantine. With respect to travel time, there are no contemporary (*i.e.* Bronze Age) accounts that mention sailing along the Levantine coast to Egypt or vice-versa. Some later records, however, may be of interest: for example, the eleventh-century-AD letters from Geniza indicate that it could take up to four days (unfavourable conditions) to travel south from Akko to the northeastern Nile Delta (near modern Port Said); up to eight days from Alexandria north to Tripoli in Lebanon; and seven days from the area near Port Said north to Ashkelon (Whitewright 2011: 13). Marfoe (1987: 26-27) estimated that a (Early Bronze Age) trip from Egypt to Byblos — given favourable westerly winds and the northerly current — would have taken six days; a return trip from the Carmel coast, with less favourable winds and a counter-current, would have taken at least eight-ten days. According to the calculations of Marcus (2007: 145-146, and n.23), the ships recorded in the Mit Rahina inscription (Middle Bronze Age) sailed to the Levant early in the summer and did not return until the autumn. Clearly a multitude of social, commercial and other factors, beyond the actual trip, might come into play. Nonetheless, if the southeastern Levant (say central-southern Lebanon to Ashkelon or even Gaza) were regarded as one small world and the Nile Delta as another, then this sphere of interaction was prominent throughout the Bronze Age (Stager 2001: 625).

To the north and northwest of Egypt, travel on the Mediterranean would have taken sailing ships beyond the sight of land, where the winds and currents are not favourable for northwesterly travel (Manning and Hulin 2005: 276-278, and fig. 11.1). In this region, therefore, the sea may have served as a barrier between Egypt and Cyprus, or beyond, to Anatolia and the Aegean. By the Late Bronze Age, however, it is possible that mariners may have been crossing the open sea (northward) between Egypt and Cyprus, and perhaps beyond Cyprus, to the Aegean (Cline 1987). At the very least, it seems clear that Cypriot and/or Aegean ships sailed southward to landing or stopping points from the Cyrenaica eastward (*e.g.* Knapp 1981; Portugali and Knapp 1985; Cline 1987; Wachsman 1998: 297-299; Phillips 2008; Barcat 2015).

As a wide range of material as well as specific documentary evidence from Ugarit attests, the port cities of the Levantine coast must have formed another small world, one with several important harbours (*e.g.*, Ugarit, Byblos, Tyre, Akko, Jaffa, Ashkelon), involved in both local as well as regional if not interregional trade. One way or another, or perhaps in more ways than one, the island of Cyprus — or at least its eastern and southeastern port towns — was also closely linked to this maritime interaction sphere. In terms of wind speed and direction, Safadi (2016: 354, and fig. 5) suggests that there are no particular dangers to open sea crossings from Cyprus to the Levantine coast, or vice versa. Bar-Yosef Mayer *et al.* (2015: 416 fig. 1, 426-429), however, caution that seasonal winds vary, and may make the east-west (*i.e.* Levant-Cyprus) crossing difficult, particularly when sailing northwest (*e.g.* from Beirut to Cape Greco, or Limassol). More favourable winds would have accompanied vessels sailing directly westward, *e.g.* from Latakia (near Ugarit) to Famagusta Bay (Enkomi region). The return passage from Cyprus to the east or southeast would have been relatively easy, and could be completed within two days (Bar-Yosef Mayer *et al.* 2015: 29). Indeed,

Strabo (*Geography* 14.6.3) recorded the distance from Kition to Beirut as 1500 stadia, the equivalent of two days plus one night at sea.

The northernmost Levantine ports, and certainly Ugarit, were linked somehow to the coast of Cilicia which, along with Lycia and Pamphylia, may have comprised another small world. Arnaud (2005: 220–221) estimates that return travel between several of the ports or capes along Anatolia's southern coast took no more than one day. In regional terms, both the northern Levantine-Cilician (*e.g.* Kinet Höyük, Ura) and Lycian coastal ports would have been linked to the (intervisible) north coast of Cyprus, and thence to the entire island. Favourable wind conditions during most months of the year made the crossing from southern coastal Anatolia to Cyprus quick (within one day) and reasonably safe (Bar-Yosef Mayer *et al.* 2015: 427, 428). Unsurprisingly, Cyprus may well have been involved in two if not three eastern Mediterranean regional or small-world interaction spheres: Egypt and the central-southern Levant, the Levantine coastal ports more generally, and the southern coast of Anatolia.

Another, not so small maritime world may have existed along western coastal Anatolia, with quite early maritime connections extending especially into the Cyclades (Şahoğlu 2005; Kouka 2009a, 2016) and the Aegean (Stos-Gale and Gale 2003; Stos-Gale 2015), if not farther afield, *e.g.* to Cyprus and the southern Levant (Philip *et al.* 2003; Webb *et al.* 2006). The interregional maritime links of sites like Troy and Liman Tepe are evident throughout the Bronze Age. Close maritime contacts between both Liman Tepe and Çeşme-Bağlararası with the central and southern Aegean seem to intensify from the Early Bronze Age onward (Şahoğlu 2015; Erkanal and Şahoğlu 2016; Kouka 2016); rich finds of Mycenaean pottery signal their roles as key maritime centres in the Late Bronze Age. Although seaborne traders from the İzmir region in coastal central Anatolia thus almost certainly played a key role in maritime exchanges between Anatolia and the Aegean islands (Şahoğlu 2005: 352), the Cyclades themselves should not be regarded simply as passive recipients in Aegean-Anatolian interaction.

As Hirschfeld (2009: 286) pointed out, in proposing these various routes and modes of maritime interconnections, we still lack a fundamental physical map (showing currents, winds, landmarks, visibility of shorelines, harbours, water sources) that might help us better to define more viable sea routes in the Bronze Age eastern Mediterranean. Such a map, of course, could never be decisive but rather should be regarded as '…a description of the board on which the game is played and the pieces which each player has been dealt …' (Sherratt and Sherratt 1998: 330). Horden and Purcell (2000: 172), moreover, argued that at least from the second millennium BC onwards, people moved around the Mediterranean in 'patterns of interaction too various and detailed to be called 'routes'. The notion of 'fixed' or static shipping lanes traversing the Bronze Age Mediterranean is probably misleading, and the reality was probably '… a myriad possible combinations, of routes within routes, differing each time by the accidents of wind, current and mariners' preferences for safe harbours, anchorages and markets' (Vella 2004: 48; see also Horden and Purcell 2000: 137-143).

Having examined, albeit all too generally, the nature of seafaring networks and possible routes of exchange that linked various people and lands in the Bronze Age eastern Mediterranean, I turn finally to consider the impact of seafaring and maritime trade on the Bronze Age polities and economies of the region.

SEAFARING, SEAFARERS AND BRONZE AGE POLITIES

In this section, I consider further some other issues raised in the introduction:

- the impact of distance and the exotic upon peoples' identities and ideologies
- the identities of ships' captains or merchants, sailors and raiders
- how maritime trade transformed politico-economic institutions throughtout the Bronze Age eastern Mediterranean.

Developing the maritime knowledge and experience — part of the 'maritime consciousness' — that made it possible to link consumers with producers was a lengthy process (Horden and Purcell 2000: 125-127); prehistoric archaeologists have access to this process primarily through the types of material and documentary evidence presented in this volume. Based on a wealth of later Mediterranean historical evidence, however, we might also venture to say that securing such knowledge must have proceeded sequentially, from port to port or anchorage to anchorage, and that some mariners — like those on the Cape Gelidonya and Uluburun ships — did not always reach their intended destination. Others, of course, like the fleet of 11 Levantine merchant ships shown at a seaside dock in the tomb of Kenamun at Thebes (Egypt), seem to have succeeded in grand fashion.

Human predators as well as natural factors (wind, waves, climate, reefs and shoals) presented a series of obstacles to mariners, whether along coastal routes (Pryor 1988: 15; Beresford 2013: 63-90) or in ventures to and from prominent but 'distant' islands (Braudel 1972/1: 150). Outbound and return routes were not necessarily the same, and involved different winds and currents that were not always predictable; in later periods, such ventures have been termed 'travelling bazaars' (Braudel 1972/1: 107). In modelling wind speed and direction, and wave heights for some 20 Bronze-Iron Age Levantine harbour sites, Safadi (2016) was able to show that sites such as Sidon, Beirut, Byblos and especially Tyre enjoyed a significant level of protection and accessibility — a 'natural maritime predisposition' — that enabled them to engage in local and regional scales of interaction. Walsh (2014: 67) proposed that the 'agency' of winds and currents impacted not only on the economies of coastal and island polities that exploited the sea but also on their social structure.

Some archaeological 'things' were also imbued with agency, or at least with what may be said to be a 'biography'. Such objects are not just tokens or surrogates for human acts or activities, but rather act as material agents in their own right (see, amongst many others, Kopytoff 1986; Gosden 2005; Knappett and Malafouris 2008; Hodder 2012; Olsen *et al.* 2012; Witmore 2014). In the present case, we might think of the life-journeys of various Transport Stirrup Jars (TSJs) made in the Aegean and marked out for the Cypriot market — with incised Cypro-Minoan signs, or with the (Cretan) octopus motif (Catling and Karageorghis (1960: 121). In general, however, it can be argued that agency or intentionality are best applied to matter by a thinking subject (Knapp 2018).

Seafaring people exploited terrestrial as well as marine resources, transporting and trading raw materials, staple foods and manufactured goods: in many cases, their ventures helped to establish, secure and/or legitimise certain states and kingdoms whose livelihood depended on the sea — *e.g.* those along the Levantine coast during the Middle and Late Bronze Ages, or others along the Cypriot coast during the Late Bronze Age, or perhaps those at Liman Tepe or Çeşme-Bağlararası on the west-central coast of Anatolia throughout the Bronze Age. Seafaring was a normal, everyday practice in such communities, and the ability to travel to distant places and return with foreign goods, unfamiliar things or knowledge of far-away places brought renown to those who undertook such ventures.

At times, of course, these same ventures subjected merchants and travellers to taxation or other import duties at the quayside. The motivation of some mariners or merchants was primarily economic, *i.e.* to secure access to raw materials (especially metals) and finished products (*e.g.* maritime transport containers and their contents) in demand. Detailed studies of MTCs, in fact, offer insights into the large-scale transport of goods during the course of the Bronze Age, and into the role of certain Levantine, Cypriot or Aegean polities that depended on seaborne trade and people with maritime skills (Demesticha and Knapp 2016). Such seafaring practices contributed significantly to mobility and connectivity in the eastern Mediterranean Bronze Age.

Throughout the third millennium BC, ships under sail and new port facilities along the Levantine coast (*e.g.* Byblos, Ugarit), if not the western coast of Anatolia (*e.g.* Troy, Liman Tepe, Çeşme-Bağlararası), spurred maritime interconnections that were emerging in the eastern Mediterranean. This increase in seaborne traffic, along with a growing demand for metals, organic goods (olive oil, wine) and exotica, came to be key factors in new networks of long-distance maritime trade, which became even more pronounced during the Middle and especially the Late Bronze Age. After about 1600 BC, the 'proto-harbours' of earlier periods functioned as entry ports for people, goods and ideas coming from afar; they became key centres of regional and interregional trade (Broodbank 2013: 358, 413, estimates some 40-50 such centres operated within the LB eastern Mediterranean).

Physical evidence for Bronze Age ports or harbours, however, is quite limited: a few underwater or marine geomorphological explorations (*e.g.* Tyre, Sidon, Hala Sultan Tekke); land-based excavations in sectors of coastal sites thought to have served as ports or anchorages (*e.g.* Minet el-Beidha, Tel Akko, Kition); the presence of stone anchors; and a few pictorial representations of ships and sailors. Such representations, typically drawn by unskilled artisans, tend to be schematic if not unrealistic. Even so, many of them stem from high-status, 'ritual' or 'symbolic' contexts (*e.g.* 'altars', mortuary 'temples') (Broodbank 2010: 253). Thus they have the potential to inform us about the key role that merchants and seamen played in exceptional circumstances as well as in everyday maritime practices. The latter is notably the case with the images from the Egyptian tomb of Kenamun at Thebes, or the tomb in the Memphite necropolis at Saqqara, where workers are shown unloading goods, including what may be Canaanite jars, from merchant ships moored at seaside.

Despite the lack of evidence for built harbours in the Bronze Age, both material and documentary evidence demonstrates that various coastal and island polities in the eastern Mediterranean increasingly gained political if not ideological prominence. This is notably the case for sites or polities — like *e.g.* Tell ed-Dabʿa in Egypt, Ugarit in Syria, or Enkomi on Cyprus — whose populations included merchants or mariners with sufficient seafaring knowledge as well as an economic base that enabled them to develop and establish maritime trading ventures. By the end of the Bronze Age (late thirteenth-early twelfth centuries BC), however, several of these closely interconnected ports were disrupted, abandoned or destroyed (*e.g.* Troy, Ugarit, Tell Tweini, Tel Akko, Ashkelon, several coastal sites on Cyprus, Marsa Matruh in Egypt). The highly centralised and economic interdependencies amongst many of the state-level polities that supported and sanctioned these ports and harbours were shattered, along with the maritime networks and high-risk ventures perpetrated by eastern Mediterranean merchants, mariners and 'pirates' (Broodbank 2014: 53; Monroe 2015: 7-8).

Our knowledge of the seamen and merchants involved in maritime trade in the eastern Mediterranean is somewhat limited for the Early-Middle Bronze Ages. Moreover, the best documentary source for Middle Bronze Age merchants stems from the cuneiform records found at the Assyrian colony of Kanesh in central Anatolia, which deals with overland trade (most recently, Larsen 2015). Nonetheless it would seem that the third millennium BC witnessed a transformation in navigational prowess — the era of 'the Mediterranean's first true argonauts' (Broodbank 2010: 253-254) — and the meanings of seaborne travel, as well as in the movement of high-value prestige goods and materials that were often available only on islands, coasts or peninsulae. We might assume, for example, that Levantine merchants, or at least ships' captains, commanded the 'Byblos ships' (*kbnt*) and their cargoes of cedar (following Ward 2010b: 43; Sauvage 2012: 234-235), but this may not hold true for ships that the pharaoh Sneferu (ca. 2600 BC) or the Sixth Dynasty official Uni dispatched to the Levantine coast. Likewise, the EB IA–III Levantine MTCs (ledge- and loop-handled jars; 'shale-derived' vessels; 'metallic' or 'combed' ware) used to transport liquid or other organic goods (olive oil, wine) to Egypt must have travelled from ports like Byblos, Tyre or Ashkelon in ships captained by Levantine merchants or mariners (and/or those who produced the goods). Finally, if we accept the notion of an Anatolian Trade Network and other, associated exchange systems (Şahoğlu 2005), then we must also accept that seaborne traders played a key role in maritime trade between Anatolia and the Aegean islands, possibly also with Cyprus and the Levant (see also Marfoe 1987: 34-35, on major reorientations in EB Levantine and Syro-Anatolian trading relationships).

During the second millennium BC, the eastern Mediterranean along with the Aegean and eastern north Africa became 'a single zone of maritime trade and innovation' (Broodbank 2010: 256). With respect to the Middle Bronze Age, the Papyrus Lythgoe mentions a *kbnt* ('Byblos ship'), which may suggest an Egyptian travelling to the Levant (Simpson 1960). One court record of the Twelfth Dynasty pharaoh Amenemhet II from Mit Rahina, Memphis (Altenmüller and Moussa 1991: 14-16) mentions two 'transport ships' returning to Egypt from the Levant laden with a variety of goods (raw materials, organic products, finished goods) that plausibly may have involved an Egyptian merchant.

Maritime transport containers — the earliest versions of the Canaanite jar as well as Minoan oval-mouthed amphorae — have been recovered in excavations at the harbour complex around the site of Tell ed-Dab'a in the eastern Nile delta (at least eight other Egyptian sites have produced MB Canaanite jar fragments—Ownby 2010: 88-90). A range of different types of (late) Middle Cypriot pottery has also been unearthed at Tell ed-Dabʿa (Maguire 2009), at a time not long after documentary evidence from Mari and Babylon refers to the import of copper from *Alašiya* (Knapp 2008: 307-308). Tell ed-Dabʿa clearly served as a vital nexus in eastern Mediterranean trade, and so must have embraced merchants both domestic and foreign. Ships sailing to or from Egypt may have anchored at any number of Levantine ports (*e.g.* Ashkelon, Jaffa, Tel Nami, Sidon, Tyre, Beirut, Tell Arqa, Tell Tweini, Ugarit) to acquire raw materials or finished products, as the Mit Rahina inscription suggests. In sum, maritime exchanges between Egypt, the Levant, Cyprus and Anatolia clearly escalated during the MB, demonstrating that merchants or shippers, if not the rulers of those polities, realised the commercial value of exploiting and trading various raw materials and commodities in demand.

During the Late Bronze Age, shipping seems to have become more diverse as brail rigs were introduced in the eastern Mediterranean, facilitating travel to windward (Wachsmann 1998: 251-254; 2000b: 803; Wedde 2000: 85-87; Broodbank 2013: 464). Likewise the keel was a major LB innovation that must have made a huge impact on sailing — stiffening the hull, better supporting the mast and generally helping to stabilise the ship (Monroe 2015: 16 n.10; see also Broodbank 2013: 374). Lighter galleys ('long ships') came to be used for naval engagements whilst other craft ('merchantmen') were used for mercantile undertakings, including coastal trading and tramping. The cost of of such developments in sailing technology would have required substantial investments in labour, materials and wealth (Monroe 2007; 2011). The development of these new types of ships may be correlated broadly with increases in socio-economic complexity, and an intensified demand for bulk goods or exotic materials from afar, all of which were almost certainly inititated by state-level polities (Broodbank 2010: 256; see also Sherratt and Sherratt 2001: 21). The archives of LB Ugarit indicate that its merchants sponsored shipping ventures of their own as well as in cooperation with the state.

Documentary evidence referring to the merchants that dwelt in or operated out of Ugarit and its ports (Ras Ibn Hani and Minet el-Beidha–*Maḥadu*) is extensive (see *e.g.* Astour 1972; Heltzer 1978, 1982; Singer 1999; Schloen 2001; Bell 2012). Recent research by Monroe (*e.g.* 2009, 2015) has set a new standard in studies concerning these merchants (Akkadian *tamkāru*, generally). In general, these documents indicate that most merchants did not belong to a single social, economic or ethnic group: some travelled in caravans or lived aboard ships, others lived in the harbour town or community where they worked, whether at home or abroad. Some were members of the elite (financiers, creditors), others held state or civic offices, and still others, the wealthiest, were those who conducted business for the state and were paid in silver — the *tamkāru ša šarri*, literally 'merchants of the king' (Monroe 2009: 282).

Wealthy Ugaritic merchants like Urtenu, Yabninu, Rapanu and Rašap-Abu lived in elaborate houses, used their homes to store goods, maintained documentary archives of their diverse — often metallurgical — transactions (as well as seals to identify themselves or their goods), and involved their families in various aspects of production and exchange (Monroe 2009: 240, 283; Bell 2012: 182-184). McGeough (2015: 93-94) notes various commercial, royal, diplomatic and even ritual activities and transactions of the merchants Yabninu and Urtenu. The geographic extent of non-royal, elite activities — which was one primary means of conveying international goods to and from Ugarit (McGeough 2015: 91) — stretched from the Aegean, Cyprus and inner Anatolia in the west, to Egypt in the south and upper Mesopotamia in the east (Bell 2012: 184 and table 19.1; Broodbank 2013: 395 and fig. 8.39).

Cuneiform records from Ugarit also indicate that independent merchants (*mkrm, bdlm, mzrǧlm*—Astour 1972) invested in ships and cargoes like the one that sank at Uluburun. They, or other commercial agents like them, also invested in ventures on behalf of the king of Ugarit (Monroe 2009: 181-189; 2011: 91-95; see also Liverani 1979a; Knapp 1991: 48); some (*tamkāru ša mandatti*) may have been involved in collecting tribute. Shipments that involved the crown at Ugarit, whether imports or exports, required royal as well as merchant capital, but especially merchant expertise (Monroe 2011: 94). Thus the role of the king (or the state) in maritime trade at Ugarit seems to have been indirect, or 'symbiotic' (Monroe 2011: 94), and was typically overseen by a 'prefect' (*šākinu*). Rather than maintaining a fleet of vessels to undertake trading expeditions, the crown sought — to various degrees — to invest in and tax merchants and commerce. Even foreign merchants who operated in Ugarit's harbours, sometimes as temporary residents (Rainey 1963; Astour 1981: 25), might be assessed duties in silver (Astour 1972: 17). The harbour community itself (*kāru* in Akkadian) provided an optimal solution to the problem of where to locate foreign, especially maritime merchants and traders, who lived a 'liminal' existence between the sea and the port, and who were often regarded by locals with the typical mistrust of the 'other' (Monroe 2009: 280).

The system overall had a complex administrative structure to oversee the transactions of merchants and other, related personnel: a 'governor' or 'prefect' (*šākin*), a 'master of payments' (*b'l mšlm*), a 'harbour master' (*wakil kāri*), a 'master of ships' (*b'l any*), a 'chief of merchants' (*rāb tamkāri*) and a 'merchant representative' (*bdlm/bidāluma*) (Monroe 2007: 14; 2009: 164-173, 171 fig. 5.1) (see Figure 23, above). One frequently cited example of such transactions concerns the local merchant Ṣinaranu, whose goods (grain, beer and oil from Crete) were exempted from any taxes or claims by the king of Ugarit (Monroe 2009: 165-167). The ships themselves might be owned privately, or by the crown, or by a temple, as documents from Ugarit, Egypt and Assyria demonstrate (Monroe 2009: 94-100). Seaborne trading ventures out of Ugarit were financed by various means: royal grants, endowments, familial relations, loans and cooperatives (Monroe 2009: 105-115). Whilst kings and higher officials couched their trading relations and negotiations in terms of gift exchange, merchants and other officials operated on a more obviously entrepreneurial, profit-making basis.

Of course, all this begs the difficult question of how much we can extrapolate from the documentary record of Ugarit to the wider eastern Mediterranean world. The archives of Ugarit mention various types of commercial relationships it had with Byblos, Sidon, Tyre and Beirut: *e.g.* the high customs taxes levied by Ugarit's harbour master, the Ugaritic ships docked at Byblos or Sidon, the shipment of clothing and textiles from Ugarit to Byblos, or the exchange of other goods between Tyre or Beirut and Ugarit. The cuneiform letters from Amarna in Egypt not only reveal competition and various commercial alliances amongst Levantine port towns (Altman 2014), but also indicate that some of these coastal polities had at least a small fleet of ships used for commercial purposes (*e.g.* king of *Alašiya* owned merchant ships) and others employed in naval encounters (*e.g.* the raiding or blockading of coastal sites, the plundering or interception of ships at sea). Ships from *Keftiu* (the Aegean?) brought timber, ivory and precious or semi-precious stones to Egypt; some accounts from an Egyptian naval yard, dated to the reign of Amenhotep II, indicate that *Keftiu* ships were either built or repaired in Egypt (Strange 1980: 74-75, 96-98). Whilst the situation in Egypt seems to have been more centralised (Monroe 2009: 189-192; Zingarelli 2010), for the rest — Cyprus, Anatolia and the Levantine coast more generally — there is no simple answer at this time, and our knowledge must be extrapolated from the goods we know to have been exchanged between various regions or polities.

Given the positive correlation between trade and piracy, and the economic lure of the former, we must also factor into the discussion the possible role of pirates. As argued above (Chapter 2—*Merchants, Mariners and Pirates*), the material evidence for pirates and piracy is equivocal at best, but documentary reveals that groups such as the *Šikila*, the *Lukki*, the men of *Arwada* and possibly the *Ahhiyawa* or *miši* were engaged in what could be regarded as piratic activities. These included naval battles (the Hittites and *Alašiya*, the 'sea peoples' and the Egyptians), the interception of ships at sea (ships of Ugarit vs the *Lukka*-lands, ships of *Arwada*, Amurru or Beirut vs Byblian ships), the seizure of goods from ships at sea (Wenamun and the *Tjeker*), the raiding of coastal ports or blockades of them (involving sites such as Ugarit, Byblos and Ṣumur, Cypriot coastal sites, the Aegean island of Lesbos/*Lazpa*), and the seizing of captives (from Cyprus by a Hittite vassal, from Lesbos by an Anatolian renegade). Such seaborne raiders clearly were skilled in navigation, had access to reliable information concerning exchange networks and were beyond the control of any of the Late Bronze Age coastal polities with whom they came into frequent conflict.

What about the port towns and the actual sea routes used (see also the previous section—*Networks and Routes of Exchange*)? Each port would have formed the centre of its own network and, directly or indirectly and to differing extents, also would have been linked to larger networks. Under the Roman Empire, port towns held markets (*emporion* and *agora*) and provided various other services, not least crucial commercial information on trade, exchange networks and the organisation of diasporas (Arnaud 2016: 126-127). These ports served as 'urban centres of consumption' and more or less framed the parameters of maritime trade; the extent to which port towns were integrated into larger-scale networks defined the hierarchy of the ports and the networks to which they belonged (Arnaud 2016: 166).

For the Bronze Age, we lack the level of detailed information on which such an interpretation might be based, but it is clear from the material and documentary evidence available that several ports served as key nodes in the exchange networks that operated in the eastern Mediterranean during the Late Bronze Age, if not already in the Middle Bronze Age: *e.g.* Troy, Liman Tepe, Ugarit, Byblos, Tyre, Sidon, Akko, Tell Abu Hawam, Jaffa, Asheklon, Tell ed-Dab'a, Marsa Matruh, Enkomi, Kition, Hala Sultan Tekke and Maroni. In Sherratt's (2016: 293) view, sites such as Tyre and Sidon (to which we might add Liman Tepe, Arwad and Marsa Matruh), located on offshore or estuarine islands or promontories, were established primarily for mercantile reasons. Moreover, following the battle of Kadesh in the early thirteenth century BC, Sherratt suggests that these coastal towns effectively may have wound up in 'no-man's land'. No longer under the aegis of either the Egyptians or the Hittites, politico-economic power in such polities came to reside in the hands of maritime mercantile elites.

On Cyprus, the rapid development and expansion of 'urban' coastal or near-coastal sites during the Late Bronze Age has also been interpreted as the result of economic control by mercantile elites and the expansion of overseas trade (*e.g.* Merrillees 1992; Manning and DeMita 1997; Peltenburg 2012a, 2012b; Sherratt 2016: 293). Peltenburg (2012a), for example, suggested that the new commercial, coastal centres on Cyprus required an institution like that of Levantine mercantile elites to conduct its foreign relations and to engage effectively in international maritime commerce. I have critiqued such views elsewhere at some length (*e.g.* Knapp 2013: 437-447), and maintain that the single unified polity that emerged on Cyprus by the fourteenth century BC exercised broad control over copper production and exchange, in and of itself probably more than adequate to explain the key role the island played in seaborne trade at this time (but *cf.* Andreou 2016).

To summarise: certain Levantine port towns and Cypriot coastal polities, owing at least in part to their geographic position, probably had fleets of commercial — if not naval — vessels (both 'heavily capitalised' large ships and smaller independent boats) that were intimately interconnected in the commercial networks that underpinned maritime trade in the LB eastern Mediterranean. We can assume with some justification that these ships were built locally, and captained by local mariners and/or merchants; various texts from Ugarit strongly support such a suggestion. Anatolia's role in maritime commerce seems to have stemmed largely from its western (Aegean) rather than its southern (Mediterranean) coast, but port locations in both regions must also have been linked into wider networks; the extent to which local merchants or mariners may have been involved, however, remains unknown. The case of Egypt is more enigmatic. Pharaonic Egypt was clearly a major political player in the region, and probably was an important driver of connectivity, given its resources and demands, its active involvement in the Levant (Panagiotopoulos 2011: 37) and its hostile attitude towards the Hittites. Certainly Egypt was capable of building seaworthy ships and conducting trade on the Red Sea, but it appears to have had a more ambiguous relationship with the Mediterranean. Egyptian ships must have ventured into the Mediterranean, alongside those from the Levant and Cyprus, but none of them seems to have dominated any aspect of maritime mobility or connectivity during the Late Bronze Age. Throughout the Bronze Age and into the early Iron Age, the Mediterranean remained '… a free-for-all zone for anyone with the skill, daring and funds to set out upon it' (Broodbank 2013a: 394).

CHAPTER 7

CONCLUSIONS

Beyond a mastery of materials and tools, early maritime technology was a harnessing of the elements. Seafarers commanded unseen forces of buoyancy, current, and wind to move large cargoes over great distances, profiting their masters and themselves in the bargain. While technologies have changed, the key economic principle of the ship has remained the same, namely making the water and wind pay much of the transport costs. The history of shipping is usually written with an economic orientation, marked by increases in the size of vessels, efficiency of construction methods, and how far and fast ships could voyage. It is also a history with plenty of gray areas, such as the Bronze Age (Monroe 2007: 13).

The Bronze Age is indeed a 'gray area' when it comes to our understanding of seafaring, seafarers and the ships they sailed in the eastern Mediterranean. The sources are many and diverse, but divulge their meanings only grudgingly, especially during earlier periods and in certain areas, like Anatolia or Cyprus.

Already by the Early Bronze Age, maritime ventures had taken on new meanings and importance: speed, distant travel, the movement of various commodities or materials in demand that promoted status at home and established social and economic 'credentials' abroad (Broodbank 2010: 253-254). Increasingly throughout the third millennium BC, trade and connectivity between peoples became seaborne and was facilitated by ships using the sail, bringing more speed and higher capacities to maritime transport (Broodbank 2014: 51-52). On land, much of this traffic was handled by new entrepôts along the Levantine coast, most prominently at Byblos and Ugarit, perhaps also at Tyre and Ashkelon. Thus the 'long third millennium' BC witnessed the emergence of *voyaging*, pushing the boundaries of what was possible for these seafarers and their ships in terms of distance and the unknown, or even making possible seaborne raids to acquire status, wealth and power.

The Middle Bronze Age saw further developments in seafaring, maritime interconnections and the infrastructure (anchorages, harbours) necessary to support them. Maritime journeys came to be favoured over land-based ventures because they allowed the lower cost, higher volume exchange of goods such as metals. Although we lack the physical evidence to demonstrate likely developments in boat technology, it must be assumed that strong advantages accrued to those who had the material resources (and funds) to construct ships that were able to navigate successfully under difficult conditions, carry larger cargoes and accommodate specialist mariners or weapon-wielding warriors such as those seen on the later (end of the Late Bronze Age) kraters from Bademgediği Tepesi (Anatolia) and Kynos (Greece) (see also Earle *et al.* 2015: 649 for Bronze Age Europe).

By the Late Bronze Age, all such developments in maritime transport and connectivity reached their peak, involving several different peoples and polities in multiple networks of economic and social exchange. Specialised personnel such as merchants, craftsmen, oil/wine producers, naval 'warriors' and other state functionaries fuelled the growth of regional and interregional trade in low volume, high status wealth items ('exotica'), and high volume goods such as metals and maritime transport containers (and the wine, oil, resin etc. within them), transforming societies and politico-economic institutions throughout the LB eastern Mediterranean. Not all the polities involved were necessarily on an equal footing, in either economic or technological terms: Levantine coastal ports like Ugarit, Byblos or Tyre, their Cypriot counterparts at Enkomi, Kition or Maroni, and Tell ed-Dabʻa in the northeastern Egyptian Delta, all seem to have excelled in their maritime capacities and capabilities.

Many of the questions raised at the outset of this volume remain only partly answered. The origins of earliest trade networks in the Bronze Age Mediterranean lie deep in the Neolithic (*e.g.* Robb and Farr 2005; Broodbank 2006; Leppard 2014b), but by the Early Bronze Age they are most evident in, or more accurately between, the central-southern Levant and Egypt. The trade in metals is fully evident by the mid-late third millennium BC, not least through the Anatolian Trade Network and the maritime exchanges between Anatolia, the Cyclades, Crete, Cyprus and the southern Levant (*e.g.* Philip *et al.* 2003; Stos-Gale and Gale 2003; Şahoğlu 2005; 2011; Webb *et al.* 2006). Of course, wherever Cypriot copper was shipped during the EB, it also went by sea (Stos-Gale 2015: 111-113, table 1).

It is less straightforward to identify who was involved in these early maritime ventures, at least before the Late Bronze Age, when cuneiform and Egyptian documents illuminate some of the diverse activities of the Levantine merchants who were involved in multiple and complex mechanisms of exchange, and the small worlds in which they were conducted. A range of material and (limited) documentary evidence indicates that Cyprus too was intimately linked into the LB trading systems that operated in the eastern Mediterranean; its merchants and mariners may well have served as middlemen, at least in Aegean-Levantine commerce. Except for its western (Aegean) coast, the case for Anatolia is less clear, perhaps because the Hittites were more involved in overland trade with polities to the east than in maritime trade with the Mediterranean. And the Egyptians, fully capable of building seagoing vessels, and powerful enough to maintain their influence in — if not control over — many areas of the southern through central Levant, seem to have taken little interest in maritime enterprises on the Mediterranean Sea.

Regarding the question of who might have built or captained the ships of the Bronze Age eastern Mediterranean, Idrimi — king of Alalakh in the mid-fifteenth century BC —tells us that he built some ships for a naval-based invasion of the land of Mukish (Oller 1989; see also Figure 22 above). The somewhat later texts from Ugarit refer to ships' and harbour personnel, possibly even a traders' corporation. Contemporary ships' representations from Egypt (*e.g.* those of Kenamun and Nebamun at Thebes) are best interpreted as depicting Levantine merchants and mariners engaged directly in trade or other types of social relations with Egyptian merchants, shopkeepers or physicians. From the LB Levant, there are many, highly schematic ships' representations portrayed on a variety of materials; however, only the two sherds from a twelfth century BC Philistine Monochrome krater reveal enough detail to indicate that it is a galley, and even then it is disputed whether it represents an Aegean or a Levantine type.

From earlier periods, the Egyptian Fifth Dynasty relief fragments from the temple of Sahure at Abusir (12 ships) depict what may be a shipment of Levantine jugs (the relief from the causeway of Unas at Saqqara shows only a more generic cargo of pottery vessels), whilst the extensive 'tableau' of some 120 diverse drawings of (presumably) pharaonic watercraft dating from the reign of the Twelfth Dynasty pharaoh Senwosret III (ca. 1889-1836 BC) have yet to be assessed in iconographic terms: certainly there are sailing vessels amongst them and it seems safe to assume that these are representations of Egyptian ships captained and crewed by Egyptians (see Figure 15, above). The same holds true for a wall painting from a Middle Kingdom tomb at Beni Hassan depicting two ships under sail, towing a funerary barge.

The large numbers of ships' graffiti and boat models from LB Cyprus are suggestive of a local tradition in building boats, but they have variously been interpreted as 'Syro-Canaanite' or 'Mycenaean' vessels. At best, this seems misleading and it it probably safer to assume that the Cypriot engravings, at least, depict both 'round' and 'long' boats, which may point to two different boat-building traditions (Basch and Artzy 1985: 324-327; Wachsmann 1981: 206-207). Moreover, one of the Amarna letters (EA 39) makes it clear that the king of *Alašiya* had dispatched his own merchants on his own ship to Egypt: 'No one making a claim in your [i.e. the pharaoh's] name is to approach *my* merchants or *my* ship' (Moran 1992: 112, emphasis added*).* The most prominent ship depictions from LB Anatolia (Bademgediği Tepesi, Liman Tepe, Çine-Tepecik) are all on sherds of Late Helladic IIIC kraters and so beg the question of whether the oarsmen and warriors depicted on them are intended to represent Aegean or local people.

Thus we may suggest that the ships of the Bronze Age eastern Mediterranean were built and sailed by people from Levantine coastal ports, Egypt and Cyprus. Documentary evidence states clearly that a Levantine king (Idrimi) built ships, and that the king of *Alašiya* not only owned ships but sent his merchants to Egypt on one or more of them. Although one might conclude reasonably that these ships were captained by Cypriotes, one can always cite modern counter-analogies to undermine such assumptions. Bass (1998: 188), for example, pointed out the complexities of ownership, captaincy and cargo on a modern shipwreck (quoting from *Newsweek* magazine): 'The Sea Empress was owned by a Norwegian, registered in Cyprus, managed from Scotland, chartered by the French, crewed by Russians, flew a Liberian flag and carried an American cargo'.

Stone anchors too have proved to be crucial indicators of seafaring and various aspects of maritime trade in the Bronze Age eastern Mediterranean. Frost (1985; 1991: 370-371), for example, based on her studies of anchors from Kition on Cyprus and Ugarit, argued that Cypriot and Levantine ships were amongst the largest vessels plying the sea-lanes in the Late Bronze Age eastern Mediterranean. Equally informative is the information to be derived from maritime transport containers, whose design facilitated movement by sea and whose readily recognisable shapes established the commercial credibility of those responsible for their movement. Their production within local Levantine, Cypriot and Egyptian communities of practice, and their subsequent widespread distribution to other lands, contributed to the increasingly large-scale transport of goods that depended on seafaring and seaborne trade.

Merchants, mariners and monarchs alike capitalised on new maritime opportunities to foster autonomy, generate wealth and establish power in multiple Bronze Age societies. The merchants themselves had to deal not only with the crown and royal court but also with specific maritime personnel, from governors and harbour masters to entrepreneurs and liminal agents like Artzy's (1997) 'nomads of the sea'. The maritime expertise of such people allowed them a certain degree of economic adaptability, shifting from independent ventures of (coastal) trade, to more official undertakings, to piracy, as the broader economic or political situation demanded (Monroe 2011: 94). Indeed, there is little reason to doubt that some of them — whether we define them as maritime nomads, 'sea peoples' or pirates — may have been merchants at one time or another themselves.

The archaeology of transport and travel involves the study of communications: on land, such lines of communication may be preserved by roads or paths or walls (Gibson 2007), but at sea they are much less tangible. Shipwrecks or isolated wreck deposits are seldom encountered, especially of Bronze Age date; and the movements of ships, as indicated by their wrecks, may have no relation to their origins and intended course, or even to a frequently travelled route (Parker 2001: 25). By contrast, classical sources often name the city — e.g. Alexandria, Adramyttion or Carpathus — from which a ship came as part of its identity. The epitaph of one ship's master buried in Rome says that he commanded an 'Alexandrian ship' (Arnaud 2016: 139). Even with epigraphic or other types of documentary evidence, however, the distinction between the 'nationality' of ships and that of their owners is not always clear. Attempts to determine the ultimate origin(s) or ethnic alliances of ancient shipwrecks or even boat builders are problematic on several grounds. Speculating on the destination of a shipwreck is even more hazardous. In discussing ports of the Roman period, for example, Morillo *et al.* (2016: 276) point out that whilst the region of origin of a ship's main cargo may be identified with some degree of precision, that is not the case for the ship's ultimate destination, especially given the diversity of possible sea routes, or the existence of ports where goods were transhipped or redistributed.

In the case of the LB wreck at Uluburun off the south coast of Turkey, existing interpretations concerning its origin represent modern constructs developed to suggest not only the identity of the ship ('Canaanite', 'Mycenaean') but also its likely destination (the Aegean, Egypt). Monroe's (2009: 234-238) 'ethnic' analysis of personal items found on the Uluburun wreck indicates that the crew could have included people of multiple origins: Kassite, Assyrian, Mitannian, Hittite, Mesopotamian, Levantine, Cypriot and Aegean. Ward (2010a: 155-156) also pointed out that nine or ten cultures are represented by the finds from Uluburun: the substantial Cypriot cargo, 24 Levantine-type anchors, diverse raw materials as well as 'luxury' finished goods (gold, silver, ivory, cobalt, tin, amber, ostrich eggs) with multiple origins, and more.

Westerdahl (1994: 267) would argue that assigning specific geographic names to a 'culture' might present no problem, but assigning an ethnic label is at best spurious. Ship-building, at least, is not essentially ethnic in character, and for prehistoric and even protohistoric shipping, we simply do not know most of the possible permutations of ownership, sponsorship or 'nationality'. Such ambiguity may relate less to interpretation or preservation than to '... accurate readings of a maritime past lived in maritime, liminal, and semi-peripheral conditions' (Monroe 2011: 94).

Be that as it may, once a ship arrived in port, it may have been welcomed or registered but equally may have become subject to taxes and duties (for an example from fifth century BC Egypt, see Yardeni 1994). The attempt to control access to a ship and its goods by land-based rulers thus may be expected, but is not always borne out by written records, as was the case at LB Ugarit on the northern Levantine coast (Monroe 2009: 94-100, 165-166). Even if coastal polities and their rulers did not level direct charges on goods, they sought to control the information, experience or knowledge of the merchants, mariners or immigrants who had arrived from distant shores (Parker 2001: 37).

Ports may also be seen as liminal 'thresholds', where different maritime peoples met and exchanged goods, resources or ideas unavailable elsewhere (Monroe 2011: 90, 96). Westerdahl (2005: 3) regards them more metaphorically as geographic points of contention between an ordered land and the chaotic sea. In this study, I have treated ports and harbours as hubs of connectivity and mobility, links between diverse land and sea trading routes where ships are docked, sheltered and/ or repaired, where people met, and where goods and ideas from near and far were exchanged, redistributed, reformulated and re-appropriated. Amongst the most propitious ports and 'proto-harbours' of the Bronze Age were the following: in the Levant, Ugarit (Minet el-Beidha), Tyre, Sidon, Tel Akko and Ashkelon; in Egypt Tell ed-Dab'a and Marsa Matruh; on Cyprus, Enkomi, Hala Sultan Tekke, Kition and Maroni. Although there are virtually no physical remains of these Bronze Age harbour facilities, ongoing geomorphological explorations are at least clarifying some of the possibilities, whilst some relief sculpture or tomb paintings (*e.g.* the tomb of Kenamun at Thebes) illustrate nicely how they facilitated maritime transport, travel and trade during the Bronze Age.

Indeed, Bronze Age eastern Mediterranean ships' representations — in all their variety and quality — are suggestive of the key role that seafaring and seafarers played in everyday social and economic practices. Representational art not only depicts the ships and people who sailed them but also various types of fish and shells, highlighting the links between fishing and seafaring as well as maritime trade. Marine shells, of course, are also significant because they might be used for multiple purposes, particularly for personal display. In turn, fishing can show the different ways that people used the sea (*e.g.* inshore vs. deep-sea fishing), or even the extent of their seafaring skills. Fish and other marine resources undoubtedly made an important contribution to the mixed economies that formed the basis of most Bronze Age Mediterranean societies.

FINAL WORDS

The study of the maritime aspects of Mediterranean archaeology is nothing new, but examining issues of fluidity, mobility and connectivity upon and *via* the sea is a product of the twenty-first century (*e.g.* Horden and Purcell 2000; Broodbank 2006, 2010; Knapp 2008; van Dommelen and Knapp 2010; van Dommelen 2014; Kiriatzi and Knappett 2017; Russell 2017; Russell and Knapp 2017). Examining maritime mobility and connnectivity involves foregrounding change through time, on different analytical scales, employing distinctive methodologies and mediating between them; the points of contact as well as the level of connectivity will have changed constantly (Horden and Purcell 2000: 172). Procuring foreign goods and raw materials represents one impetus for maritime connectivity, but another, equally important impetus was to create or maintain the social relationships upon which such exchanges relied. This is the social domain of seafaring and maritime interaction — the relationships people had with the sea, which have all too often been ignored (Farr 2006: 89). Maritime interaction involves communication, and a better understanding of prehistoric exchange involves the evaluation of social resources as well as the identification of natural or mineral resources. Maritime interaction not only motivated politico-economic development and facilitated human mobility, it also transformed social structures and modified individual human actions.

Diverse mechanisms propelled the elaborate commercial networks and interaction spheres of the Bronze Age Mediterranean, and dictated the nature and intensity of Mediterranean connectivity. In order to advance our understanding of seafaring, seafarers and maritime connectivity in the Bronze Age Mediterranean, where all is fluidity and 'mutability' (Morris 2003: 38), we will need to gauge better the extent of mariners' mental maps—their maritime consciousness, which helped them direct their ships in familiar waters, under predictable weather conditions, to known ports and anchorages; all this and more represents the business of seafaring. We should also aim to quantify as fully as possible the frequency and types of goods exchanged amongst the small maritime worlds of the Mediterranean. And, finally, to establish a more holistic and realistic approach, we must continue to develop network analyses (*e.g.* Knappett 2013; Leidwanger *et al.* 2014; Leidwanger 2017) and refine them with models that take into account wind speed, direction and seasonality, sea currents and wave actions (*e.g.* Bar-Yosef Mayer *et al.* 2015; Safadi 2016).

On islands, all along coastal shores, at river mouths and tidal flats, and *via* marine currents, the sea provides a means of contact between inhabited communities and serves as a key focus of human life, rituals and ideology. People socialise and spiritualise these seascapes through local knowledge and lived experience, and they often mark both land and sea in ways that leave material traces (Cooney 2003: 323-324). The sea itself does not, and by its nature cannot, represent a palimpsest of human activity. Unlike a landscape, whose surface preserves in diverse ways a record of past or present activities, the seascape is a surface of flows and change, and the history of the sea is one that involves movement, mobility, transport and mutability.

Whilst seafaring facilitated the transport of goods and materials, it also afforded the movement of people and the exchange of ideas — a way of traversing maritime space, connecting people and communicating knowledge over the sea and amongst different lands. Seafaring increased the spatial and cognitive range of migrants, mariners, merchants and colonists, and facilitated the development of maritime (coastal or island) states and kingdoms. Ships crossed borders, real or imaginary, and engaged with the unknown, their seaman and captains in search of good fortune as well as renown (Kristiansen 2004: 111). Ships' crews had to be mobilised, whether for building the vessel or for sailing it, and the ship itself had to be equipped with food, goods and people, an investment that — especially by the Late Bronze Age — was only possible for a king, or a wealthy merchant, or perhaps an enterprising 'pirate'. Sailing ships and developing harbours offered to various people the opportunity to travel afar, and thus to enhance their status and wealth, if not that of the polities they regarded as their own.

The transformative power of maritime space has shaped sociocultural practices and facilitated long-distance trade; it has instigated new exchange systems and sparked trade diasporas; and it has fuelled the exploitation and/or colonisation of lands near and far, bringing people together for good or ill (Monroe 2011: 95-96). The evidence presented in this study is often ambiguous, or inadequate, or both. As is ever the case in archaeology, our views and understandings of Mediterranean Bronze Age seafaring and seafarers will change as new finds emerge, or as new interpretations of older materials appear. There was never any doubt that the Levantine coast (and in particular its Late Bronze Age polities and peoples) had the widest array of evidence to offer, but one aim of this study was to pull together a much broader panorama of related materials, from the entire eastern Mediterranean, and throughout the Bronze Age. To pull all that evidence together, however, and to present it coherently, has been a real challenge; the present effort should be regarded only as the beginning, not the end of this story.

REFERENCES

ANCIENT SOURCES
Thucydides:
C.F. Smith
1928   *History of the Peloponnesian War* I-II. Revised ed. Cambridge, Massachusetts: Harvard University Press.
Appian:
1912   *Appian: Roman History* II. Loeb Classical Library 3. Cambridge, Massachusetts: Harvard University Press.

ABBREVATIONS
CTH: Laroche, E. 1971. *Catalogue des textes hittites.* Études et commentaires 75. Paris: Klincksieck. Supplements in *Revue Hittite et Asianique* 30 (1972) 94-133, and *Revue Hittite et Asianique* 33 (1975) 68-71.

EA: El-Amarna — with reference to the numbering of the texts (letters) in Moran 1992

KBo: Keilschrifttexte aus Boğazköy. Berlin: Wissenschaftliche Veröffentlichungen der Deutschen Orient-Gesellschaft.

KTU: Die Keilalphabetischen Texte aus Ugarit. Neukirchen-Vluyn: Kevelair.

KUB: Keilschrift Urkunden aus Boghazköy. Berlin: Institut für Orientforschung.

RS: Ras Shamra — prefix for field numbers of tablets and other registered finds of the French Archaeological Mission to Ras Shamra (Ugarit).

REFERENCES
Åström, P.
1966   *Excavations at Kalopsidha and Ayios Iakovos in Cyprus.* Studies in Mediterranean Archaeology 2. Lund: P. Åström's Förlag.
1972   *The Swedish Cyprus Expedition* IV: 1C. *The Late Cypriote Bronze Age. Architecture and Pottery.* Lund: Swedish Cyprus Expedition.
1986   Hala Sultan Tekke–an international harbour town of the Late Cypriote Bronze Age. *Opuscula Atheniensia* 16: 7-17.

1991a   Problems of definition of local and imported fabrics of Late Cypriot Canaanite ware. In J.A. Barlow, D. Bolger and B. Kling (eds), *Cypriot Ceramics: Reading the Prehistoric Record*. University Museum Monograph 74: 67-72. Philadelphia: University Museum, University of Pennsylvania.

1991b   Canaanite jars from Hala Sultan Tekke. In N.H. Gale (ed.), *Bronze Age Trade in the Mediterranean*. Studies in Mediterranean Archaeology 90: 149-151. Göteborg: P. Åström's Förlag.

Åström, P. (with collaborators)

1989   *Hala Sultan Tekke* 9: *Trenches 1972-1987*. Studies in Mediterranean Archaeology 45.9. Göteborg: P. Åström's Förlag.

Åström, P., D.M. Bailey and V. Karageorghis

1976   *Hala Sultan Tekke* 1: *Excavations 1897-1971*. Studies in Mediterranean Archaeology 45.1. Göteborg: P. Åström's Förlag.

Åström, P., E. Åström, A. Hatziantoniou, K. Niklasson and U. Öbrink

1983   *Hala Sultan Tekke* 8. *Excavations 1971-1979*. Studies in Mediterranean Archaeology 45.8. Göteborg: P. Åström's Förlag.

Åström, P., and B. Svensson

2007   Stone anchors. In P. Åström and K. Nys (eds), *Hala Sultan Tekke* 12: *Tomb 24, Stone Anchors, Faunal Remains, and Pottery Provenance*. Studies in Mediterranean Archaeology 45(12): 31-49. Sävedalen: P. Åström's Förlag.

Abdelhamid, S.

2013   Against the throw-away-mentality: the reuse of amphoras in ancient maritime transport. In H.P. Hahn and H. Weiss (eds), *Mobility, Meaning and the Transformations of Things*, 91-106. Oxford: Oxbow.

Abulafia, D.

2014   Mediterranean 'prehistory'. In P. Horden and S. Kinoshita (eds), *A Companion to Mediterranean History*, 139-153. Chichester: John Wiley & Sons.

Adams, J.

2001   Ships and boats as archaeological source material. *World Archaeology* 32: 292-310.

Agouridis, C.

2011   The Late Bronze Age shipwreck off the islet of Modi (Poros). *Skyllis* 11(2): 25-34.

Ahrens, A.

2015   Objects from afar—the distribution of Egyptian imports in the northern Levant: parameters for ascertaining the character of diplomatic contacts between Egypt and the Levant during the Bronze Age. In B. Eder and R. Pruzsinszky (eds), *Policies of Exchange: Political Systems and Modes of Interaction in the Aegean and the Near East in the 2nd Millennium B.C.E.* Oriental and European Archaeology 2: 141-156. Vienna: Österreichische Akademie der Wissenschaften.

Akar, M.

2006   The MBII Building at Kinet Höyük: The Levantine Palace Tradition in Eastern Cilicia. Unpublished MA dissertation, Graduate School of Social Sciences, Middle East Technical University, Ankara, Turkey.

Akkermans, P.M.M.G., and G.M. Schwartz

2003   *The Archaeology of Syria: From Complex Hunter-Gatherers to Early Urban Societies (ca. 16,000-300 BC)*. Cambridge: Cambridge University Press.

Allen, S.H.

1991   Northwest Anatolian Grey Wares in the Late Bronze Age: Analysis and Distribution in the Eastern Mediterranean. Unpublished PhD dissertation, Brown University, Providence, Rhode Island.

1994   Trojan grey ware at Tell Miqne-Ekron. *Bulletin of the American Schools of Oriental Research* 293: 39-51.

Al-Maqdissi, M.

2013   From Tell Sianu to Qatna: some common features of inland Syrian and Levantine cities in the second millennium BC. In J. Aruz, S.B. Graf and Y. Rakic (eds), *Cultures in Contact: From Mesopotamia to the Mediterranean in the Second Millennium BC*, 74-83. New York: Metropolitan Museum of Art.

Al-Maqdissi, M., J. Bretschneider, P. Degryse, H. Hameeuw, D. Kaniewski, E. Paulissen, S. Van Simaeys and K. Can Lerberghe

2007   Environmental changes in the Jebleh Plain (Syria): geophysical, geomorphological, palynological, archaeological and historical research. *Res Antiquae* 4: 3-10.

Alpözen, O.

1983   The Bodrum Museum of Underwater Archaeology. *Museum* 35: 61-63.

Altenmüller, H., and A.M. Moussa

1991   Die Inschrift Amenemhets II aus dem Ptah-Tempel von Memphis: ein Vorbericht. *Studien zur Altägyptischen Kultur* 18: 1-48.

Altman, A.

2014   The struggle among the Lebanese port-cities to control seaborne trade in the mid-fourteenth century BCE. *Ugarit-Forschungen* 45: 11-33.

Álvarez-Ossorio Rivas, A.

2013   La piratería en Cilicia durante la Antigüedad: el paisaje como factor desencadenante de la práctica de la piratería por los indígenas y los foráneos. In N. Jaspert and S. Kolditz (eds), *Seerarub in Mittelmeerraum: Piraterie, Korsarentum und Maritime Gewalt von der Antike bis zur Neuzeit*. Mittelmeerstudien 3: 155-173. Paderborn, Germany: Wilhelm Fink/ Ferdinand Schöningh.

Amiran, R.

1970   *Ancient Pottery of the Holy Land*. New Brunswick, New Jersey: Rutgers University Press.

Anderson, A.

2010   The origins and development of seafaring: towards a global approach. In A. Anderson, J. Barrett and K. Boyle (eds), *The Global Origins and Development of Seafaring*, 3-16. Cambridge: McDonald Institute for Archaeological Research.

Andreou, G.M.

2016   Understanding the rural economy of Late Bronze Age Cyprus: a diachronic perspective from the Vasilikos valley. *Journal of Mediterranean Archaeology* 29: 143-172.

Andreou, G.M., and D.A. Sewell

2015   Tochni *Lakkia* revealed: reconsidering settlement pattens in the Vasilikos and Maroni valleys, Cyprus. In H. Matthäus, B. Morstadt and C. Vonhoff (eds), *PoCA (Postgraduate Cypriot Archaeology) 2012*, 198-219. Newcastle upon Tyne, UK: Cambridge Scholars Publishing.

Andreou, G.M., R. Optiz, S.W. Manning, K.D. Fisher, D.A. Sewell, A. Georgiou and T. Urban

2017   Integrated methods for understanding and monitoring the loss of coastal archaeological sites: the case of Tochni-*Lakkia*, south-central Cyprus. *Journal of Archaeological Science, Reports* 12: 197-208.

Angelopoulou, A.

2008   The 'Kastri Group': evidence from Korfari ton Amygdalion (Panormos) Naxos, Dhaskalio Keros and Akrotiri Thera. In N. Brodie, J. Doole, G. Gavalas and C. Renfrew (eds), *Horizon: A Colloquium on the Prehistory of the Cyclades*, 149-164. Cambridge: McDonald Institute for Archaeological Research.

Araque Gonzalez, R.

2014   Social organization in Nuragic Sardinia: cultural progress without 'elites'? *Cambridge Archaeological Journal* 24: 141-161.

Arnaud, D.

1996   Études sur Alalah et Ougarit à l'age du Bronze récent. *Studi Micenei ed Egeo-Anatolici* 37: 47-65.

Arnaud, P.

2005   *Les routes de la navigation antique. Itinéraires en Méditerranée*. Paris: Errance.

2011a   Ancient sailing-routes and trade patterns: the impact of human factors. In D. Robinson and A. Wilson (eds), *Maritime Archaeology and Ancient Trade in the Mediterranean*. Oxford Centre for Maritime Archaeology, Monograph 6: 61-80. Oxford: Centre for Maritime Archaeology.

2011b   La mer dans la construction Grecque de l'image du monde. In J. Santos Yanguas and B. Díaz Ariño (eds), *Los Griegos y el Mar*, 129-153. Vitoria-Gasteiz: Universidad del País Vasco, Servicio Editorial = Euskal Herriko Unibertsitatea, Argitalpen Zerbitzua.

2016   Cities and maritime trade under the Roman empire. In C. Schäfer (ed.), *Connecting the Ancient World. Mediterranean Shipping, Maritime Networks and their Impact*. Pharos: Studien zur griechisch-römischen Antike 35: 117-171. Rahden/Westfallen: Verlag Marie Leidorf.

Arnold, D.

1988   *The Pyramid of Senwosret I*. New York: Metropolitan Museum of Art.

Arnold, D., F. Arnold and S. Allen

1995   Canaanite imports at Lisht, the Middle Kingdom capital of Egypt. *Ägypten und Levante* 5: 13-32.

Artzy, M.

1985   Merchandise and merchantmen: on ships and shipping in the Late Bronze Age Levant. In Th. Papadopoullos and S. Chatzestylli (eds), *Acts of the Second International Cyprological Congress*, 135-140. Nicosia: A.G. Leventis.

1987 On boats and sea peoples. *Bulletin of the American Schools of Oriental Research* 266: 75-84.

1988 Development of war/fighting boats of the IInd millennium B.C. in the eastern Mediterranean. *Report of the Department of Antiquities, Cyprus*: 181-186.

1994 Incense, camels and collared rim jars: desert trade routes and maritime outlets in the second millennium. *Oxford Journal of Archaeology* 13: 121-147.

1995 Nami: a second millennium international maritime trading center in the Mediterranean. In S. Gitin (ed.), *Recent Excavations in Israel: A View to the West*. Archaeological Institute of America, Colloquia and Conference Papers 1: 17-40. Dubuque, Iowa: Kendall/Hunt.

1997 Nomads of the sea. In S. Swiny, R. Hohlfelder, and H.W. Swiny (eds), *Res Maritimae: Cyprus and the Eastern Mediterranean from Prehistory through Late Antiquity*. Cyprus American Archaeological Research Institute, Monograph 1: 1-16. Atlanta, Georgia: Scholars Press.

1998 Routes, trade, boats and 'nomads of the sea'. In S. Gitin, A. Mazar and E. Stern (eds), *Mediterranean Peoples in Transition: Thirteenth to Tenth Centuries BCE*, 439-448. Jerusalem: Israel Exploration Society.

1999 Carved ship graffiti – an ancient ritual? In H. Tzalas (ed.), *Tropis V: Fifth International Symposium on Ship Construction in Antiquity*, 21-29. Athens: Hellenic Institute for the Preservation of Nautical Tradition.

2003 Mariners and their boats at the end of the Late Bronze Age and the beginning of the Iron Age in the eastern Mediterranean. *Tel Aviv* 30: 232-246.

2005 Emporia on the Carmel coast? Tel Akko, Tel Abu Hawam and Tel Nami of the Late Bronze Age. In R. Laffineur and E. Greco (eds), *Emporia: Aegeans in the Central and Eastern Mediterranean*. Aegaeum 25 (1): 355-361. Liège, Austin: Université de Liège, University of Texas at Austin.

2006 The Carmel coast during the second part of the Late Bronze Age: a center for eastern Mediterranean transshipping. *Bulletin of the American Schools of Oriental Research* 343: 45-64.

2009 Liman Tepe underwater excavations: a retrospective. *Recanati Institute for Maritime Studies News* 35: 11-15.

2013 The importance of the anchorages of the Carmel Coast in the trade networks during the Late Bronze period. *Michmanim* 24: 7*-24*.

2016 Distributers and shippers: Cyprus and the Late Bronze II Tell Abu Hawam anchorage. In S. Demesticha and A.B. Knapp (eds), *Maritime Transport Containers in the Bronze–Iron Age Aegean and Eastern Mediterranean*. Studies in Mediterranean Archaeology and Literature, PB 183: 97-110. Uppsala: Åströms Förlag.

Artzy, M., and S. Zagorski

2012 Cypriot 'Mycenaean' IIIB imported to the Levant. In M. Gruber, S. Aḥituv, G. Lehmann and Z.Talshir (eds), *All the Wisdom of the East: Studies in Near Eastern Archaeology and History in Honor of Eliezer D. Oren*. Orbis Biblicus et Orientalis 255: 1-11. Fribourg and Göttingen: Academic Press, Vandenhoeck and Ruprecht.

Asaro, F., and I. Perlman

1973   Provenience studies of Mycenaean pottery employing Neutron Activation Analysis. In V. Karageorghis (ed.), *Acts of the International Archaeological Symposium: The Mycenaeans in the Eastern Mediterranean*, 213-224. Nicosia: Cypriot Department of Antiquities.

Aston, D.

2004   Amphorae in New Kingdom Egpyt. *Ägypten und Levante* 14: 175-213.

2007   A taste of honey: *mnt-* and *mdqt-*vessels in the late Eighteenth Dynasty. In T. Schneider and K. Szpakowska (eds), *Egyptian Stories: A British Egyptological Tribute to Alan B. Lloyd on the Occasion of his Retirement.* Alter Orient und Altes Testament 347: 13-31. Münster: Ugarit Verlag.

Astour, M.C.

1970   Ma'hadu, the harbor of Ugarit. *Journal of the Economic and Social History of the Orient* 13: 113-127.

1972   The merchant class of Ugarit. In D.O. Edzard (ed.), *Gesellschaftsklassen im Alten Zweistromland und in den angrenzenden Gebieten.* Rencontre Assyriologique Internationale 18. Abhandlungen der Bayerische Akademie der Wissenschaften 75: 11-26. Munich: Bayerische Akademie der Wissenschaften.

1973   Ugarit and the Aegean. In H.A. Hoffner, Jr. (ed.), *Orient and Occident.* Alter Orient und Altes Testament 22: 17-27. Neukirchen-Vluyn: Verlag Butzon and Bercker.

1981   Ugarit and the great powers. In G.D. Young (ed.), *Ugarit in Retrospect*, 3-29. Winona Lake, Indiana: Eisenbrauns.

Aykurt, A., and H. Erkanal

2017   A Late Bronze Age ship from Liman Tepe with reference to the Late Bronze Age ship from Izmir/Bademgediği Tepesi and Kos/Seraglio. *Oxford Journal of Archaeology* 36: 61-70.

Bachhuber, C.

2006   Aegean interest on the Uluburun ship. *American Journal of Archaeology* 110: 345-363.

2014   The Anatolian context of Philia material culture in Cyprus. In A. B. Knapp and P. van Dommelen (eds), *The Cambridge Prehistory of the Bronze and Iron Age Mediterranean*, 139-156. New York: Cambridge University Press.

Backman, C.R.

2014   Piracy. In P. Horden and S. Kinoshita (eds), *A Companion to Mediterranean History*, 170-183. Chichester: John Wiley & Sons.

Bader, B.

2011   Traces of foreign settlers in the archaeological record of Tell el-Dab'a. In K. Duistermaat and I. Regulski (eds), *Intercultural Contacts in the Ancient Mediterranean.* Orientalia Lovaniensia Analecta 202: 137-158. Louvain: Peeters.

Badre, L.

1992   Canaanite Tyre. In M. Sharp Joukowsky (ed.), *The Heritage of Tyre: Essays on the History, Archaeology, and Preservation of Tyre*, 37-42. Dubuque, Iowa: Kendall Hunt.

1998   Late Bronze and Iron Age imported pottery from the archaeological excavations of urban Beirut. In V. Karageorghis and N. C. Stampolidis (eds), *Eastern Mediterranean, Cyprus-Dodecanese-Crete 16th-6th Centuries B.C.*, 73-86. Athens: University of Crete and Leventis Foundation.

1997   Arwad. In E.M. Meyers (ed.), *The Oxford Encyclopedia of Archaeology in the Near East*, 218-219. Oxford: Oxford University Press.

2001-02 The Bronze Age of Beirut: major results. *ARAM* 13-14: 1-26.

2006   Tell Kazel-Simyra: a contribution to a relative chronological history in the eastern Mediterranean during the Late Bronze Age. *Bulletin of the American Schools of Oriental Research* 343: 65-95.

2011   Cultural interconnections in the eastern Mediterranean: evidence from Tell Kazel in the Late Bronze Age. In K. Duistermaat and I. Regulski (eds), *Intercultural Contacts in the Ancient Mediterranean*. Orientalia Lovaniensia Analecta 202: 205-223. Louvain: Peeters.

Badre, L., M.-C. Boileau, R. Jung and H. Mommsen

2005   The provenance of Aegean- and Syrian-type pottery found at Tell Kazel (Syria). *Ägypten und Levante* 15: 15-47.

Badreshany, K., and H. Genz

2009   Pottery production on the northern Lebanese coast during the Early Bronze Age II—III: the petrographic analysis of the ceramics from Tell Fadous-Kfarabida. *Bulletin of the American Schools of Oriental Research* 355: 51-83.

Bailey, G., and N. Milner

2002   Coastal hunter-gatherers and social evolution: marginal or central? *Before Farming* 3-4(1): 129-150.

Balensi, J.

1985   Revisiting Tell Abu Hawam. *Bulletin of the American Schools of Oriental Research* 257: 65-74.

1988   Tell Abu Hawam: un cas exceptionnel? In M. Heltzer and E. Lipinski (eds), *Society and Economy in the Eastern Mediterranean (c.1500-1000 BC)*. Orientalia Lovaniensia Analecta 23: 305-311. Louvain: Peeters.

Ballard, R.D., L.E. Stager, D. Master, D. Yoerger, D. Mindell, L.L. Whitcomb, H. Singh and D. Piechota

2002   Iron Age shipwrecks in deep water off Ashkelon, Israel. *American Journal of Archaeology* 106: 151-168.

Balthazar, J. Weinstein

1990   *Copper and Bronze Working in Early through Middle Bronze Age Cyprus*. Studies in Mediterranean Archaeology and Literature, Pocket-book 84. Göteborg: P. Åström's Förlag.

Barber, I.

2003   Sea, land and fish: spatial relationships and the archaeology of south island Maori fishing. *World Archaeology* 35: 3434-448.

Barcat, D.

2015   Une route maritime directe entre la Crète et l'Afrique? In D. Lefèvre Novaro, L. Martzolff and M. Ghilardi (eds), *Géosciences, archéologie et histoire en Crète de l'âge du bronze récent à la époque archäique*, 341-351. Padova and Torino: Aldo Ausilio Editore e Bottega d'Erasmo.

Bard, K.A., and R. Fattovich

2010   Spatial use of the Twelfth Dynasty harbor at Mersa/Wadi Gawasis for the seafaring expeditions to Punt. *Journal of Ancient Egyptian Interconnections* 2(3): 1-13.

2011   The Middle Kingdom Red Sea harbor at Mersa/Wadi Gawasis. *Journal of the American Research Center in Egypt* 47: 105-129.

2015   Mersa/Wadi Gawasis and ancient Egyptian maritime trade in the Red Sea. *Near Eastern Archaeology* 78: 4-11.

Bar-Yosef Mayer, D.E.

2002   Egyptian-Canaanite interaction during the fourth and third millennia BCE: the shell connection. In E.C.M. van den Brink and T. E. Levy (eds), *Egypt and the Levant: Interrelations from the 4th through the Early 3rd Millennium BC*, 129-135. London: Leicester University Press.

Bar-Yosef Mayer, D., Y. Kahanov, J. Roskin and H. Gildor

2015   Neolithic voyages to Cyprus: wind patterns, routes, and mechanisms. *Journal of Island and Coastal Archaeology* 10: 412-435.

Bar-Yosef Mayer, D., C. Bonsall and A.M. Choyke (eds)

2017   *Not Just for Show: The Archaeology of Beads, Beadwork and Personal Ornaments.* Oxford: Oxbow.

Basch, L.

1978   Le navire *mnš* et autres notes de voyages en Égypte. *Mariner's Mirror* 64: 99-123.

1987   *Le Musée Imaginaire de la Marine Antique.* Athens: Institut Hellénique pour la préservation de la tradition nautique.

1994a   Some remarks on the use of stone anchors and pierced stones in Egypt. *International Journal of Nautical Archaeology* 23: 219–227.

1994b   Un navire grec en Egypte à l'époque d'Ulysse. *Neptunia* 195: 19-26.

1997   Une représentation de navire de type égéen dans l'oasis de Dakhleh (Égypte) vers 1200 av. J.-C. In S. Swiny, R. Hohlfelder and H.W. Swiny (eds), *Res Maritimae: Cyprus and the Eastern Mediterranean from Prehistory through Late Antiquity.* Cyprus American Archaeological Research Institute, Monograph 1: 17-29. Atlanta, Georgia: Scholars Press.

Basch, L, and M. Artzy

1985   Ship graffiti at Kition. Appendix II in V. Karageorghis and M. Demas, *Excavations at Kition* V(1): 322-336. Nicosia: Department of Antiquities, Cyprus.

Basedow, M.A.

2000   *Beşik-Tepe: das spätbronzezeitliche Gräberfeld.* Studia Troica Monographien 1. Mainz am Rhein: Verlag Philipp von Zabern.

Bass, G.F.

1967   *Cape Gelidonya: A Bronze Age Shipwreck.* Transactions of American Philosophical Society 57.8. Philadelphia: American Philosophical Society.

1973   Cape Gelidonya and Bronze Age maritime trade. In H.A. Hoffner (ed.), *Orient and Occident.* Alter Orient und Altes Testament 22: 29-38. Kevelaer: Verlag Butzon und Bercker.

1976   Sheytan Deresi: preliminary report. *International Journal of Nautical Archaeology and Underwater Investigation* 5: 293-303.

1998   Sailing between the Aegean and the Orient in the second millennium BC. In E.H. Cline and D. Harris-Cline (eds), *The Aegean and the Orient in the Second Millennium*. Aegaeum 18: 183-191. Liège: Université de Liège.

2010   Cape Gelidonya shipwreck. In E.H. Cline (ed.), *The Oxford Handbook of the Bronze Age Aegean*, 797-803. Oxford: Oxford University Press.

2013   Cape Gelidonya redux. In J. Aruz, S.B. Graf and Y. Rakic (eds), *Cultures in Contact: From Mesopotamia to the Mediterranean in the Second Millennium BC*, 62-71. New York: Metropolitan Museum of Art.

Bass, G.F., C. Pulak, D. Collon and J. Weinstein

1989   The Bronze Age shipwreck at Ulu Burun: the 1986 campaign. *American Journal of Archaeology* 93: 1-29.

Bassiakos, Y., and T. Tselios

2012   On the cessation of local copper production in the Aegean in the 2nd millennium BC. In V. Kassianidou and G. Papasavvas (eds), *Eastern Mediterranean Metallurgy and Metalwork in the Second Millennium BC*, 151-161. Oxford: Oxbow.

Bavay, L.

2015   Canaanite jars and jar sealings from Deir el-Medina: scattered evidence of Egypt's economic relations with the Levant during the New Kingdom. In B. Eder and R. Pruzsinszky (eds), *Policies of Exchange: Political Systems and Modes of Interaction in the Aegean and the Near East in the 2nd Millennium B.C.E.* Oriental and European Archaeology 2:129-140. Vienna: Österreichische Akademie der Wissenschaften.

Beach, T.P., and S. Luzadder-Beach

2008   Geoarchaeology and aggradation around Kinet Höyük, an archaeological mound in the eastern Mediterranean, Turkey. *Geomorphology* 101: 416-428.

Beckman, G., T. Bryce and E. Cline

2011   *The Ahhiyawa Texts*. Writings from the Ancient World 28. Atlanta, Georgia: Society for Biblical Literature.

Bekker-Nielsen, T. (ed.)

2005   *Ancient Fishing and Fish Processing in the Black Sea Region*. Black Sea Studies 2. Aarhus: Aarhus University Press.

Bell, C.

2005   Wheels within wheels? A view of Mycenaean trade from the Levantine emporia. In R. Laffineur and E. Greco (eds), *Emporia: Aegeans in the Central and Eastern Mediterranean*. Aegaeum 25 (1): 363-370. Liège, Austin: Université de Liège, University of Texas at Austin.

2006   *The Evolution of Long Distance Trading Relationships across the LBA/Iron Age Transition on the North Levantine Coast*. British Archaeological Reports: International Series 1574. Oxford: Archeopress.

2012   The merchants of Ugarit: oligarchs of the Late Bronze Age trade in metals? In V. Kassianidou and G. Papasavvas (eds), *Eastern Mediterranean Metallurgy and Metalwork in the Second Millennium BC*, 180-187. Oxford: Oxbow.

2016   Phoenician trade: the first 300 years. In J.C. Moreno García (ed.), *Dynamics of Production in the Ancient Near East*, 91-105. Oxford: Oxbow Books.

Belmonte, J.A.

2002   Presencia sidonia en los circuitos comerciales del Bronce Final. *Rivista di Studi Fenici* 30: 3-18.

Ben-Arieh, S., and G. Edelstein

1977   *Tombs Near the Persian Garden*. 'Atiqot 12. Jerusalem: Israel Exploration Society.

Ben-Dor, I.

1950   A Middle Bronze-Age temple at Nahariya. *Quarterly of the Department of Antiquities in Palestine* 14: 1-41.

Ben-Dor Evian, S.

2016   The battles between Ramesses III and the 'Sea-Peoples'. When, where and who? An iconic analysis of the Egyptian reliefs. *Zeitschrift zur Ägyptischen Sprache* 143: 151-168.

2017   Ramesses III and the 'Sea-Peoples': towards a new Philistine paradigm. *Oxford Journal of Archaeology* 36: 267-285.

Ben-Shlomo, D., E. Nodarou and J.B. Rutter

2011   Transport stirrup jars from the southern Levant: new light on commodity exchange in the eastern Mediterranean. *American Journal of Archaeology* 115: 329-353.

Ben-Yosef, E.

2016   Back to Solomon's era: results of the first excavations at "Slaves' Hill" (Site 34, Timna, Israel). *Bulletin of the American Schools of Oriental Research* 376: 169-198.

Beresford, J.

2013   *The Ancient Sailing Season*. Mnemosyne Supplements. History and Archaeology of Cassical Antiquity 351. Leiden, Boston: Brill.

Bergoffen, C.

2001a   The Proto White Slip and White Slip I pottery from Tell el-Ajjul. In V. Karageorghis (ed.), *The White Slip Ware of Late Bronze Age Cyprus*. Österreichische Akademie der Wissenschaften, Denkschriften der Gesamtakademie 20: 145-155. Vienna: Verlag der Österreichische Akademie der Wissenschaften.

2001b   The Base-ring pottery from Tell el-'Ajjul. In P. Åström (ed.), *The Chronology of Base-ring Ware and Bichrome Wheel-made Ware*. Konferenser 54: 31-50. Stockholm: Royal Academy of Letters, History and Antiquities.

Bevan, A.

2007   *Stone Vessels and Values in the Bronze Age Mediterranean*. Cambridge: Cambridge University Press.

2010   Making and marking relationships: Bronze Age brandings and Mediterranean commodities. In A. Bevan and D. Wengrow (eds), *Commodities of Cultural Branding*, 35-85. Walnut Creek, California: Left Coast Press.

2014   Mediterranean containerization. *Current Anthropology* 55: 387-418.

Bietak, M.

1996   *Avaris: The Capital of the Hyksos. Recent Excavations at Tell el'Dab'a*. London: British Museum Press.

2005   The Tuthmoside stronghold of Perunefer. *Egyptian Archaeology* 26: 13-17.

2008   Tell el-Dab'a in the Nile Delta. In J. Aruz, K. Benzel and J.M. Evans (eds), *Beyond Babylon: Art, Trade, and Diplomacy in the Second Millennium BC*, 110-112. New York: Metropolitan Museum of Art.

2010   Minoan presence in the pharaonic naval base of Peru-nefer. In O. Krzyszkowska (ed.), *Cretan Offerings: Studies in Honour of Peter Warren*. British School at Athens Studies 18: 11-24. Athens: British School at Athens.

2013   The impact of Minoan art on Egypt and the Levant: a glimpse of palatial art from the naval base of Peru-Nefer at Avaris. In J. Aruz, S.B. Graf and Y. Rakic (eds), *Cultures in Contact: From Mesopotamia to the Mediterranean in the Second Millennium BC*, 188-199. New York: Metropolitan Museum of Art.

Bietak, M., and N. Marinatos

2001   Avaris (Tell el-Dab'a) and the Minoan world. In A. Karetsou, M. Andreadaki-Vlazaki and N. Papadakis (eds), *Crete–Egypt: Three Millennia of Cultural Contacts*, 40–44. Heraklion, Crete: Hellenic Ministry of Culture.

Bikai, P.M.

1978   *The Pottery of Tyre*. Warminster: Aris and Phillips.

Bikai, P.M., and P.M. Bikai

1987   Tyre at the end of the twentieth century. *Berytus* 35: 67-83.

Blackman, D.

1982   Ancient harbors in the Mediterranean. Parts 1, 2. *International Journal of Nautical Archaeology and Underwater Exploration* 11: 79-104, 185-211.

2011   Minoan shipsheds *Skyllis* 11(2): 4-11.

2013   Research and investigation of ancient shipsheds In D. Blackman, B. Rankov, K. Baika, H. Gerding and J. Pakkanen, *Shipsheds of the Ancient Mediterranean*, 4-15. Cambridge: Cambridge University Press.

Blackman, D., B. Rankov, K. Baika, H. Gerding and J. Pakkanen

2013   *Shipsheds of the Ancient Mediterranean*. Cambridge: Cambridge University Press.

Blattner, D.M.

2013   Appendix 5: Three Late Bronze Age stone anchors from 2012. In P.M. Fischer and T. Bürge, 'The new Swedish Cyprus Expedition 2012: excavations at Hala Sultan Tekke'. *Opuscula* 6: 74-76.

Bloedow, E.

2005   Aspects of trade in the Late Bronze Age Mediterranean: what was the ultimate destination of the Uluburun ship? In R. Laffineur and E. Greco (eds), *Emporia: Aegeans in the Central and Eastern Mediterranean*. Aegaeum 25 (1): 335-341. Liège, Austin: Université de Liège, University of Texas at Austin.

Blue, L.K.

1997   Cyprus and Cilicia: the typology and palaeogeography of second millennium harbours. In S. Swiny, R. Hohlfelder and H. W. Swiny (eds), *Res Maritimae: Cyprus and the Eastern Mediterranean from Prehistory through the Roman Period*. Cyprus American Archaeological Research Institute, Monograph 1: 31-44. Atlanta: ASOR/Scholars Press.

Boileau, M.-C., L. Badre, E. Capet, R. Jung and H. Mommsen

2010   Foreign ceramic tradition, local clays: the Handmade Burnished Ware of Tell Kazel (Syria). *Journal of Archaeological Science* 37: 1678–1689.

Bolger, D.

2013   A matter of choice: Cypriot interactions with the Levantine mainland during the late 4th–3rd millennium BC. *Levant* 45: 1-18.

Bombardieri, L.

2017   *Erimi-Laonin tou Porakou: A Middle Bronze Age Community in Cyprus. Excavations 2008-2014*. Studies in Mediterranean Archaeology 145. Uppsala: Åström Editions.

Bonn-Muller, E.

2010   First Minoan shipwreck. *Archaeology* 63(1): 44.

Bono, S.

2013   Pirateria, guerra e schiavitù nella storia del Mediterraneo. In N. Jaspert and S. Kolditz (eds), *Seeraub in Mittelmeerraum: Piraterie, Korsarentum und Maritime Gewalt von der Antike bis zur Neuzeit*. Mittelmeerstudien 3: 39-46. Paderborn, Germany: Wilhelm Fink/Ferdinand Schöningh.

Bony, G., N. Carayon, C. Flaux, N. Marriner, C. Morhange and S. Fourrier

2016   Évolution paléoenvironnementale de la baie de Kition: mise en évidence d'un possible environnement portuaire (Larnaca, Chypre). In C. Sanchez and M.-P. Jézégou (eds), *Les ports dans l'espace méditerranéen antique: Narbonne et les systèmes portuaires fluvio-lagunaires*. Revue Archéologique de Narbonnaise, Supplément 44: 369-379. Montpellier-Lattes: Éditions de l'Association de la Revue archéologique de Narbonnaise.

Bordreuil, P. (ed.)

1991   *Une bibliothéque au sud de la ville. Les textes de la 34e campagne*. Ras Shamra-Ougarit 7. Paris: Éditions Recherche sur les Civilisations.

Bordreuil, P., J. and E. Lagarce, A. Bounni and N. Saliby

1984   Les découvertes archéologiques et épigraphiques de Ras Ibn Hani (Syrie) en 1983: un lot d'archivs administratives. *Académie des Inscriptions et Belles-Lettres: Comptes-Rendus des Séances* (Avril-June): 393-438.

Bordreuil, P., D. Pardee and R. Hawley

2012   *Une bibliothèque au sud de la ville 3. Textes 1994-2002 en cunéiforme alphabétique de la maison d'Ourtenou*. Ras Shamra-Ougarit 18. Lyon: Publications de la Maison de l'Orient et de la Méditerranée.

Bounni, A.

1991   La Syrie, Chypre et l'Égée d'après les fouilles de Ras ibn Hani. In V. Karageorghis (ed.), *Proceedings of an International Symposium: The Civilizations of the Aegean and Their Diffusion in Cyprus and the Eastern Mediterranean, 2000-600 BC*, 105-110. Larnaca: Pierides Foundation.

Bourriau, J.D.

1990   Canaanite jars from New Kingdom deposits at Memphis, Kom Rabi'a. In A. Eitan, R. Gophna and M. Kochavi (eds), *Ruth Amiran Volume*. Eretz Israel 21: 18*-26*. Jerusalem: Israel Exploration Society.

2004   The beginnings of amphora production in Egypt. In J. Bourriau and J. Phillips (eds), *Invention and Innovation: The Social Context of Technological Change* 2. *Egypt, the Aegean and the Near East, 1650-1550 BC*, 78-95. Oxford: Oxbow.

2010   *Survey of Memphis* IV. *Kom Rabia: The New Kingdom Pottery*. Excavation Memoir 93. London: Egypt Exploration Society.

Bourriau, J.D., and P.T. Nicholson

1992   Marl clay pottery fabrics of the New Kingdom from Memphis, Saqqara and Amarna. *Journal of Egyptian Archaeology* 78: 29-91.

Bourriau, J.D., L. M. V. Smith and P. T. Nicholson

2000   *New Kingdom Pottery Fabrics: Nile Clay and Mixed Nile/Marl Clay Fabrics from Memphis and Amarna*. Egyptian Exploration Society, Occasional Publication 14. London: Egyptian Exploration Society.

Bourriau, J., L. Smith and M. Serpico

2001   The provenance of Canaanite amphorae found at Memphis and Amarna in the New Kingdom. In A. Shortland (ed.), *The Social Context of Technological Change in Egypt and the Near East, 1650-1550 BC*, 113-146. Oxford: Oxbow.

Bowen, R.L.

1960   Egypt's earliest sailing ships. *Antiquity* 34: 117-131.

Braudel, F.

1972   *The Mediterranean and the Mediterranean World in the Age of Philip II*. 2 volumes. New York: Harper and Row.

1982   *Civilization and Capitalism, 15th-18th Century*. Volume 2: *The Wheels of Commerce*. New York: Harper and Row.

Braun, E.

2011   Early interactions between people of the Nile Valley and the southern Levant. In E. Teeter (ed.), *Before the Pyramids: The Origins of Egyptian Civilization*. Oriental Institute Publications 33: 105-122. Chicago: Oriental Institute, University of Chicago.

Braun, E., and E.C.M. van den Brink

2008   Appraising south Levantine-Egyptian interactions: recent discoveries from Israel and Egypt. In B. Midant-Reynes and Y. Tristant (eds), *Egypt at its Origin* 2. Orientalia Lovaniensia Analecta 172: 643-688. Louvain: Peeters.

Breasted, J.R.

1906   *Ancient Records of Egypt*. 5 Volumes. Chicago: University of Chicago Press.

Bretschneider, J., and K. Van Lerberghe

2008   Tell Tweini, ancient Gibala, between 2600 BCE and 333 BCE. In J. Bretschneider and K. Van Lerberghe (eds), *In Search of Gibala: An Archaeological and Historical Study Based on Eight Seasons of Excavations at Tell Tweini (Syria) in the A and C Fields (1999–2007)*. Aula Orientalis, Supplementa 24: 11-68. Barcelona: Sabadell, Editorial AUSA.

Bretschneider, J., G. Jans and A.-S. Van Vyve

2014   Once upon a tell in the east: Tell Tweini through the ages. *Ugarit-Forschungen* 45: 347-371.

Brewer, D.J., and R.F. Friedman

1989   *Fish and Fishing in Ancient Egypt.* The Natural History of Egypt 2. Warminster: Aris and Phillips.

Brinker, C.

2011   'Are you serious? Are you joking?' Wenamun's misfortune at Dor in its ancient Near Eastern legal context. In J. Mynárová (ed.), *Egypt and the Near East–The Crossroads*, 89-101. Prague: Charles University, Czech Institute of Egyptology.

Brody, A.

1998   *"Each Man Cried Out to His God": The Specialized Religion of Canaanite and Phoenician Seafarers.* Harvard Semitic Monographs 58. Atlanta, Georgia: Scholars Press.

Broodbank, C.

1993   Ulysses without sails: trade, distance, knowledge and power in the early Cyclades. *World Archaeology* 24: 315-331.

2000   *An Island Archaeology of the Early Cyclades.* Cambridge: Cambridge University Press.

2006   The origins and development of Mediterranean maritime activity. *Journal of Mediterranean Archaeology* 19: 199-230.

2009   The Mediterranean and its hinterland. In B. Cunliffe, C. Gosden and R. Joyce (eds), *The Oxford Handbook of Archaeology*, 677-722. Oxford: Oxford University Press.

2010   'Ships a-sail from over the rim of the sea': voyaging, sailing and the making of Mediterranean societies c. 3500-800 BC. In A. Anderson, J. Barrett and K. Boyle (eds), *The Global Origins and Development of Seafaring*, 249-264. Cambridge: McDonald Institute for Archaeological Research.

2013   *The Making of the Middle Sea: A History of the Mediterranean From the Beginning to the Emergence of the Classical World.* London: Thames and Hudson.

2014   Mediterranean 'prehistory'. In P. Horden and S. Kinoshita (eds), *A Companion to Mediterranean History*, 45-58. Chichester: John Wiley & Sons.

Brown, M.

2013   Waterways and the political geography of southeast Cyprus in the second millennium BC. *Annual of the British School at Athens* 108: 121-136.

2017   Landscape and settlement in Late Bronze Age Cyprus: investigations at Pyla Kokkinokremos, 2007–2009. *Palestine Exploration Quarterly* 149: 274-294.

Brückner, A.

1912   Das Schlachtfeld vor Troja. *Archäologischer Anzeiger* 1912: 616-633.

Brückner, H.

1998   Coastal research and geoarchaeology in the Mediterranean region. In D.H. Kelletat (ed.), *German Geographic and Coastal Research—The Past Decade*, 235-258. Tübingen: Institute for Scientific Co-operation and Committee for the Federal Republic of Germany for the International Geographic Union.

2003 Delta evolution and culture—aspects of geoarchaeological research in Miletos and Priene. In G.A. Wagner, E. Pernicka and H.-P. Uerpmann (eds), *Troia and the Troad: Scientific Approaches*, 121-142. Berlin: Springer Verlag.

Brückner, H., M. Müllenhoff, M. Handl and K. van der Borg

2002 Holocene landscape evolution of the Büyük Menderes alluvial plain in the environs of Myous and Priene (western Anatolia, Turkey). *Zeitschrift für Geomorphologie* 127: 47-65.

Brückner, H., A. Vött, A. Schriever and M. Handl

2005 Holocene delta progradation in the eastern Mediterranean–case studies in their historical context. *Méditerranée* 104: 95-106.

Brunton, G., and G. Caton-Thompson

1928 *The Badarian Civilisation and Predynastic Remains Near Badari*. London: British School of Archaeology in Egypt and B. Quaritch.

Bryce, T.R.

2005 *The Kingdom of the Hittites*. Oxford: Oxford University Press.

2016 The land of Hiyawa (Que) revisited. *Anatolian Studies* 66: 67-79.

Brysbaert, A., and M. Vetters

2013 A moving story about exotica: objects' long-distance production chains and associated identities at Tiryns, Greece. *Opuscula* 6: 175-210.

Buchholz, H.-G.

1999 *Ugarit, Zypern und Agäis: Kulturbezeihungen im zweiten Jahrtausend v. Chr.* Alter Orient und Altes Testament 261. Munster: Ugarit-Verlag.

Burke, A.A.

2011 Early Jaffa: from the Bronze Age to the Persian period. In M. Pielstocker and A.A. Burke (eds), *The History and Archaeology of Jaffa* 1. Jaffa Cultural Heritage Project 1. Monumenta Archaeologica 26: 63-78. Los Angeles: Cotsen Institute of Archaeology, UCLA.

Burke, A.A., M. Pielstocker, A. Karoll, G.A. Pierce, K. Kowalski, N. Ben-Marzouk, J.C. Damm, A.J. Daneilson, H.D. Fessler, B. Kaufman, K.V.L. Pierce, F. Höflmayer, B.N. Damiata and M. Dee

2017 Excavations of the New Kingdom fortress in Jaffa, 2011-2014: traces of resistance to Egyptian rule in Canaan. *American Journal of Archaeology* 121: 85-133.

Cadogan, G.

1969 Review of G.F. Bass, *Cape Gelidonya: A Bronze Age Shipwreck* (Philadelphia, 1967), in *Journal of Hellenic Studies* 89: 187-189.

Cadogan, G., E. Herscher, P. Russell and S.W. Manning

2001 Maroni-*Vournes*: a long White Slip sequence and its chronology. In V. Karageorghis (ed.), *The White Slip Ware of Late Bronze Age Cyprus*. Österreichische Akademie der Wissenschaften, Denkschriften der Gesamtakademie, Band 20. Contributions to the Chronology of the Eastern Mediterranean 2: 75-88. Vienna: Verlag der Österreichische Akademie der Wissenschaften.

Caminos, R.A.

1954 *Late Egyptian Miscellanies*. Brown Egyptological Studies 1. London: Oxford University Press.

Capart, J.

1931   *Documents pour servir à l'étude de l'art égyptien*, vol. 2. Paris: Les Éditions du Pégase.

Capet, E.

2006-07 Les peuples des céramiques 'barbares' à Tell Kazel (Syrie). *Scripta Mediterranea* 27-28: 209-244.

Caraher, W., R. Scott Moore, J. S. Noller and D. Pettegrew

2005   The Pyla-*Koutsoupetria* Archaeological Project: first preliminary report (2003-2004 seasons). *Report of the Department of Antiquities, Cyprus*: 245-267.

Caraher, W., R. Scott Moore and D. Pettegrew

2014   *Pyla-Koutsopetria* 1: *Archaeological Survey of an Ancient Coastal Town.* American Schools of Oriental Research, Archaeological Reports 21. Boston: American Schools of Oriental Research.

Carayon, N.

2012-13 Les ports Phéniciens du Liban, milieux naturels, organisation spatiale et infrastructures. *Archaeology and History in Lebanon* 36-37: 1-137.

Carayon, N., N. Marriner and C. Morhange

2011   Geoarchaeology of Byblos, Tyre, Sidon and Beirut. *Rivista di Studi Fenici* 39: 45-55.

Carayon, N., C. Morhange and N. Marriner

2011-12 Sidon's ancient harbour: natural characteristics and hazards. *Archaeology and History in Lebanon* 34-35: 433-459.

Carmona, P., and J.M. Ruiz

2008   Geoarchaeological study of the Phoenician cemetery of Tyre-al Bass (Lebanon) and geomorphological evolution of a tombolo. *Geoarchaeology* 23: 334-350.

Carre Gates, M.-H.

1981   *Alalakh Levels VI and V: A Chronological Reassessment.* Syro-Mesopotamian Studies 4.2. Malibu, California: Undena Publications.

Cateloy, C.

2016   Trade and capacity studies in the eastern Mediterranean: the first Levantine trade amphorae. In S. Demesticha and A.B. Knapp (eds), *Maritime Transport Containers in the Bronze–Iron Age Aegean and Eastern Mediterranean.* Studies in Mediterranean Archaeology and Literature, PB 183: 39-55. Uppsala, Sweden: Åströms Förlag.

Catling, H.W.

1986   The date of the Cape Gelidonya shipwreck and Cypriot bronzework. *Report of the Department of Antiquities, Cyprus*: 68-71.

Catling, H.W., and V. Karageorghis

1960   Minoika in Cyprus. *Annual of British School at Athens* 55: 108-127.

Catling, H.W., and J.A. MacGillivray

1983   An Early Cypriot II vase from the palace at Knossos. *Annual of the British School at Athens* 78: 1-8.

Catsambis, A.

2008   The Bronze Age Shipwreck at Sheytan Deresi. Unpublished MA thesis, Department of Anthropology, Texas A&M University, College Station, Texas.

Caubet, A., V. Karageorghis and M. Yon

1981   *Les Antiquités de Chypre*. Tome 1: *Age du Bronze*. Notes et Documents des Musées de France 2. Paris: Réunion des Musées Nationaux.

Cesarano, D.A.

2008   Mycenaean Corsairs. A Reassessment of Late Helladic II Piracy. Unpublished MA thesis, University of Delaware.

Chehab, M.

1969   Noms de personalités égyptiennes découvertes au Liban. *Bulletin du Musée de Beyrouth* 22: 1-47.

Cherry, J.F., and T.P. Leppard

2015   Experimental archaeology and the earliest seagoing: the limitations of inference. *World Archaeology* 47: 740-755.

Cifola, B.

1994   The role of the Sea Peoples and the end of the Late Bronze Age: a reassessment of textual and archaeological evidence. *Orientis Antiqui Miscellanea* 1: 1-23.

Çınardalı-Karaaslan, N.

2008   Recent investigations at Panaztepe harbour town. In A. Erkanal-Öktü, S. Günel and U. Deniz (eds), *Batı Anadolu ve Doğu Akdeniz Geç Tunç Çağı Kültürleri Üzerine Yeni Araştırmalar*, 57–68. Ankara: Hacettepe Üniversitesi.

2012   The east Mediterranean Late Bronze Age glass trade within the context of the Panaztepe finds. *Oxford Journal of Archaeology* 31: 121-141.

Clark, P. U., J.X. Mitrovica, G.A. Milne and M. Tamisiea

2002   Sea-level fingerprinting as a direct test for the source of global Meltwater Pulse 1A. *Science* 295: 2438–2441.

Cline, E.H.

1987   Amenhotep III and the Aegean: a reassessment of Egypto-Aegean relations in the 14th century B.C. *Orientalia* 56: 1-36.

1991   A possible Hittite embargo against the Mycenaeans. *Historia* 40: 1-9.

2014   *1177 B.C. The Year Civilization Collapsed*. Princeton: Princeton University Press.

2015   Preliminary thoughts on abundance vs. scarcity in the ancient world: competition vs. cooperation in Late Bronze Age trade across the Aegean and eastern Mediterranean. In B. Eder and R. Pruzsinszky (eds), *Policies of Exchange: Political Systems and Modes of Interaction in the Aegean and the Near East in the 2nd Millennium B.C.E.* Oriental and European Archaeology 2: 209-219. Vienna: Österreichische Akademie der Wissenschaften.

Cline, E.H., and A. Yasur-Landau

2007   Musings from a distant shore: the nature and destination of the Uluburun ship and its cargo. *Tel Aviv* 34: 125-141.

Coenaerts, J., and M. Samaes

2015   Beyond rise, peak and fall: towards an interpretation of site organisation in south-east Cyprus during the Late Bronze Age. In A. Jacobs and P. Cosyns (eds), *POCA 2008. Cypriot Material Culture Studies: From Picrolite Carving to Poskynitaria Analysis*, 65-89. Brussels: Brussels University Press.

Cohen-Weinberger, A., and Y. Goren

2004   Levantine-Egyptian interactions during the 12th to the 15th dynasties based on the petrography of Canaanite pottery from Tell el-Dab'a. *Ägypten und Levante* 14: 69-100.

Collombier, A.M.

1988   Harbour or harbours of Kition on southeastern coastal Cyprus. In A. Raban (ed.), *Archaeology of Coastal Changes*. British Archaeological Reports, International Series 404: 35-46. Oxford: British Archaeological Reports.

Collon, D.

1975   *The Seal Impressions from Tell Atchana/Alalakh*. Alter Orient und Altes Testament 27. Neukirchen-Vluyn: Neukirchener Verlag.

Conwell, D.

1987   On ostrich eggs and Libyans. *Expedition* 29(3): 29-34.

Cook, J.M.

1984   The topography of the plain of Troy. In L. Foxhall and J.K. Davies (eds), *The Trojan War: Its Historicity and Context*, 163-172. Bristol: Bristol Classical Press.

Cooney, G.

2003   Introduction: seeing land from the sea. *World Archaeology* 35: 323-328.

Courtois, J.-C.

1971   Le sanctuaire du dieu au lingot d'Enkomi-Alasia. In C.F. A. Schaeffer (ed.), *Alasia* I. Mission Archéologique d'Alasia 4: 151-362. Paris: Klincksieck.

1979   Ras Shamra: archéologie. In H. Cazelles and A. Feuillet (eds), *Supplément au Dictionnaire de la Bible*, 1126-1295. Paris: Ane.

Courtois, J.- C., J. Lagarce et E. Lagarce

1986   *Enkomi et le Bronze Récent à Chypre*. Nicosia: Leventis Foundation.

Crewe, L.

2007   *Early Enkomi. Regionalism, Trade and Society at the Beginning of the Late Bronze Age on Cyprus*. British Archaeological Reports, International Series 1706. Oxford: Archaeopress.

2010   Rethinking Kalopsidha: from specialisation to state marginalisation. In D. Bolger and L.C. Maguire (eds), *The Development of Pre-State Communities in the Ancient Near East*. BANEA Publication Series 2: 63-71. Oxford: Oxbow.

2012   Beyond copper: commodities and values in Middle Bronze Cypro-Levantine exchanges. *Oxford Journal of Archaeology* 31: 225-243.

2015a   Plain wares and urban identities in Late Bronze Age Cyprus. In C. Glatz (ed.), *Plain Pottery Traditions of the Eastern Mediterranean and Near East: Production, Use, and Social Significance*. Publications of the Institute of Archaeology, University College London 67: 115-134. Walnut Creek, California: Left Coast Press.

2015b   Expanding and shrinking networks of interaction: Cyprus 2200 BC. In H. Meller, H.W. Arz, R. Jung und R. Risch(eds), *2200 BC—ein Klimasturz al Ursache für den Zerfall der Alten Welt?* Tagungen des Landesmuseum für Vorgeschichte Halle 12(1): 131-148. Halle, Germany: Landesmuseum für Vorgeschichte.

Cucchi, T.

2008   Uluburun shipwreck stowaway house mouse: molar shape analysis and indirect clues about the vessel's last journey. *Journal of Archaeological Science* 35: 2953-2959.

Cunliffe, B.

2001   *Facing the Ocean: The Atlantic and its People.* Oxford: Oxford University Press.

Cvikel, D., Y. Kahanov, H. Goren, E. Boaretto and K. Raveh

2008   Napoleon Bonaparte's adventure in Tantura lagoon: historical and archaeological evidence. *Israel Exploration Journal* 58: 199-218.

Czarnowicz, M.

2011   Between core and periphery-early contacts between Egypt and the southern Levant in light of excavations at Tell el-Farkha, eastern Nile Delta. In J. Mynárová (ed.), *Egypt and the Near East—The Crossroads*, 117-138. Prague: Charles University, Czech Institute of Egyptology.

2012   Southern Levantine imports and imitations. In M. Chlodnicki, K.M. Cialowicz and M. Mączyńska (eds), *Tell el-Farkha* I: *Excavations 1998–2011*, 245-266. Poznań, Poland: Poznań Archaeological Museum.

Czerny, E.

1998   Zur Keramik von 'Ezbet Rushdi (Stand Mai 1997). *Ägypten und Levante* 8: 41-46.

Dalfes, H.N. , G. Kukla, and H. Weiss (eds)

1997   *Third Millennium BC Climate Change and Old World Collapse.* NATO Science Affairs Division ASI Series, Volume 149. Springer Verlag: Berlin.

D'Andrea, M.

2014   Middle Bronze I cult places in northern Palestine and Transjordan: original features and external influences. In S. Pizzimenti and L. Roman (eds), *šime ummiānka: Studi in onore di Paolo Matthiae in occasione del suo 75° compleanno offerti dall'ultima generazione di allievi.* Contributi e Materialidi Archeologia Orientale 16: 39-71. Rome: Università di Roma, Dipartimento di Scienze dell'Antichità.

Davaras, C., and P.P. Betancourt

2004   *Hagia Photia Cemetery* I: *The Tomb Groups and Architecture.* Institute for Aegean Prehistory, Prehistory Monograph 14. Philadelphia: Institute for Aegean Prehistory Academic Press.

Davies, N. De G., and R.O. Faulkner

1947   A Syrian trading venture to Egypt. *Journal of Egyptian Archaeology* 33: 40-46.

Day, P.M.

1999   Petrographic analysis of ceramics from the shipwreck at Point Iria. In W. Phelps, Y. Lolos and Y. Vichos (eds), *The Point Iria Wreck: Interconnections in the Mediterranean ca. 1200 BC*, 59-75. Athens: Hellenic Institute of Marine Archaeology.

Day, P.M., J.B. Rutter, P.S. Quinn and V. Kilikoglou

2011   A world of goods: transport jars and commodity exchange at the Late Bronze Age harbor of Kommos, Crete. *Hesperia* 80: 511-558.

Debruyne, S.

2017   Section 12: The molluscs. In J. Postgate (ed.), *Kilise Tepe Excavations* 2. *Excavations at Kilise Tepe 2007-2011: The Late Bronze and Iron Ages.* Online only: https://doi.org/10.17863/CAM.10146 (last checked 17 July 2017).

del Olmo Lete, G., and J. Sanmartin

2003   *A Dictionary of the Ugaritic Language in the Alphabetic Tradition.* 2 vols. Second revised edition. Leiden, Boston: Brill.

Demesticha, S.

2012   Harbours, navigation and sea trade. In D. Pilides and N. Papadimitriou (eds), *Ancient Cyprus: Cultures in Dialogue*, 80-83. Nicosia: Department of Antiquities, Cyprus.

2017   Appendix: volumetric analysis and capacity measurements of selected MTCs. In A.B. Knapp and S. Demesticha, *Mediterranean Connections: Maritime Transport Containers and Seaborne Trade in the Bronze and Early Iron Ages*, 172-184. London, New York: Routledge.

Demesticha, S., and A.B. Knapp (eds)

2016   *Maritime Transport Containers in the Bronze–Iron Age Aegean and Eastern Mediterranean.* Studies in Mediterranean Archaeology and Literature, PB 183. Uppsala, Sweden: Åströms Förlag.

Demesticha, S., D. Skarlatos and A. Neophytou

2014   The 4th-century B.C. shipwreck at Mazotos, Cyprus: new techniques and methodologies in the 3D mapping of shipwreck excavations. *Journal of Field Archaeology* 39: 134-150.

de Miroschedji, P.

2002   The socio-political dynamics of Egyptian-Canaanite interaction in the Early Bronze Age. In E.C.M. van den Brink and T.E. Levy (eds), *Egypt and the Levant: Interrelations from the 4th through the Early 3rd Millennium BC*, 39-57. London: Leicester University Press.

2012   Egypt and southern Canaan in the third millennium BCE: Uni's Asiatic campaigns revisited. In M. Gruber, S. Ahituv, G. Lehmann and Z. Talshir (eds), *All the Wisdom of the East: Studies in Near Eastern Archaeology and History in Honor of Eliezer D. Oren.* Orbis Biblicus et Orientalis 255: 265-292. Fribourg and Göttingen: Academic Press, Vandenhoeck and Ruprecht.

2014   The southern Levant (Cisjordan) during the Early Bronze Age. In M.L. Steiner and A.E. Killebrew (eds), *The Oxford Handbook of the Archaeology of the Levant c. 8000-332 BCE*, 307-329. Oxford: Oxford University Press.

de Roos, J.

2007   *Hittite Votive Texts.* Leiden: Nederlands Instituut voor het Nabije Oosten.

de Souza, P.

1999   *Piracy in the Graeco-Roman World.* Cambridge: Cambridge University Press.

Der Manuelian, P.

1992   Interpreting 'The Shipwrecked Sailor'. In I. Gamer-Wallert and W. Helck (eds), *Festschrift für Emma Brunner-Traut*, 223-233. Tübingen: Attempto Verlag.

Deszö, T., and A. Vér

2013   Assyrians and Greeks: the nature of contacts in the 9th-7th centuries BC. *Acta Antiqua Hungaricae* 53: 325-359.

Devecchi, E.

2010   Amurru between Hatti, Assyria, and Ahhiyawa. Discussing a recent hypothesis. *Zeitschrift für Assyriologie* 100: 242-56.

Devillers, B., M. Brown and C. Morhange

2015   Paleo-environmental evolution of the Larnaca Salt Lakes (Cyprus) and the relationship to second millennium BC settlement. *Journal of Archaeological Science, Report* 1: 73-80.

Dickinson, O.T.P.K.

2006   *The Aegean from Bronze Age to Iron Age: Continuity and Change between the Eighth and Twelfth Centuries BC*. London: Routledge.

Dietrich, M., and O. Loretz

1977   Eine Matrosenliste aus Ugarit (KTU 4.40). Zu ug. *ġr* 'Gesamtheit' und *ġr* ON. *Ugarit-Forschungen* 9: 332-333.

1981   Die Inschrift des Königs Idrimi von Alalaḫ. *Ugarit-Forschungen* 13: 201-278.

Dietrich, M., O. Loretz and J. Sanmartin

1976   *Die Keilalphabetischen Texte aus Ugarit*. Alter Orient und Altes Testament 24.1. Neukirchen-Vluyn: Kevelair.

1995   *The Cuneiform Alphabetic Texts from Ugarit, Ras Ibn Hani and Other Places*. 2nd ed. Abhandlungen zur Literatur Alt-Syrien-Palästinas und Mesoptamiens 8. Münster: Ugarit-Verlag.

Dikaios, P.

1969-1971 *Enkomi. Excavations 1948-1958*. 3 Volumes. Mainz-am-Rhein: Philip von Zabern.

Dimopoulou-Rethemiotaki, N., D.E. Wilson and P.M. Day

2007   The earlier prepalatial settlement of Poros-Katsambas: craft production and exchange at the harbour town of Knossos. In P.M. Day and R.P.C. Doonan (eds), *Metallurgy in the Bronze Age Aegean*. Sheffield Studies in Aegean Archaeology 7: 84-97. Oxford: Oxbow.

Dörpfeld, W.

1925   Das Schiffslager der Griechen vor Troja. In H. Mötefindt (ed.), *Studien zur vorgeschichtlichen Archäologie. Alfred Götze zu seinem 60. Geburtstage*, 115-121. Leipzig: C. Kobitzsch.

Dothan, M.

1976   Akko: interim excavation report. First season 1973/74. *Bulletin of the American Schools of Oriental Research* 224: 1-48.

Dothan, T.

1979   *Excavations at the Cemetery of Deir el-Balah*. Qedem 10. Jerusalem: Institute of Archaeology, Hebrew University.

Dothan, T., and A. Zukerman

2004   A preliminary study of the Mycenaean IIIC:1 pottery assemblages from Tel Miqne-Ekron and Ashdod. *Bulletin of the American Schools of Oriental Research* 333: 1-54.

Doumet-Serhal, C.

2003   Sidon–British Museum excavations 1998–2003. *Archaeology and History of Lebanon* 18: 2-19.

2013   Tracing Sidon's Mediterranean networks in the second millennium BC: receiving, transmitting, and assimilating. Twelve years of British Museum excavations. In J. Aruz, S.B. Graf and Y. Rakic (eds), *Cultures in Contact: From Mesopotamia to the Mediterranean in the Second Millennium BC*, 132-141. New York: Metropolitan Museum of Art.

Dunand, M.

1937   *Fouilles de Byblos* 1: *1936-1952*. Paris: Maisonneuve.

1954   *Fouilles de Byblos* 2: *1933-1938*. Paris: Maisonneuve.

Dunand, M., and N. Saliby

1957   A la recherche de Simyra. *Annales Archéologiques de Syrie* 7: 3-16.

Du Plat Taylor, J.

1952   A Late Bronze Age settlement at Apliki, Cyprus. *Antiquaries Journal* 32: 133-167.

1957   *Myrtou-Pighades: A Late Bronze Age Sanctuary in Cyprus*. Oxford: Ashmolean Museum.

Earle, T.K., J. Ling, C. Uhnér, S. Stos-Gale and L. Melheim

2015   The political economy and metal trade in Bronze Age Europe: understanding regional variability in terms of comparative advantages and articulations. *European Journal of Archaeology* 18: 633-657.

Easton, D.F., J.D. Hawkins, A.G. Sherratt and E.S. Sherratt

2002   Troy in recent perspective. *Anatolian Studies* 52: 75-109.

Efe, T.

2002   The interaction between cultural/political entities and metalworking in western Anatolia during the Chalcolithic and Early Bronze Ages. In Ü. Yalçin (ed.), *Anatolian Metal* II. Der Anschnitt, Beiheft 15: 49-65. Bochum: Deutsches Bergbau-Museum.

2007   The theories of the 'Great Caravan Route' between Cilicia and Troy: the Early Bronze Age III period in inland western Anatolia. *Anatolian Studies* 57: 47-64.

Emanuel, J.P.

2013   'Srdn from the sea': the arrival, integration, and acculturation of a 'Sea People'. *Journal of Ancient Egyptian Interconnections* 5: 14-27.

2015   Sailing from periphery to core in the Late Bronze Age eastern Mediterranean. In J. Mynárová, P. Onderka and P. Pavuk (eds), *There and Back Again– The Crossroads* II, 163-179. Prague: Charles University, Czech Institute of Egyptology.

2016   Maritime worlds collide: agents of transference and the metastasis of seaborne threats at the end of the Bronze Age. *Palestine Exploration Quarterly* 148: 265-280.

Eriksson, K.

1995   Egyptian amphorae from Late Cypriot contexts in Cyprus. In S. Bourke and J.-P. Descoeudres (eds), *Trade, Contact, and the Movement of People in the Eastern Mediterranean*. Mediterranean Archaeology, Supplement 3: 199-205. Sydney: Department of Archaeology, University of Sydney.

Erkanal, H.

2008   Liman Tepe: a new light on the prehistoric Aegean cultures. In H. Erkanal, H. Hauptmann, V. Şahoğlu and R. Tuncel (eds), *The Aegean in the Neolithic, Chalcolithic and Early Bronze Age*. Ankara University Research Center for Maritime Archaeology, Publication 1: 179-190. Ankara: Ankara University.

Erkanal, H., and V. Şahoğlu

2016   Liman Tepe, an Early Bronze Age trade center in western Anatolia: recent investigations. In E. Pernicka, S. Ünlüsoy and S.W.E. Blum (eds), *Early Bronze Age Troy: Chronology, Cultural Development and Interregional Contacts*. Studia Troica Monographien 8: 157-166. Bonn: Verlag Dr Rudolf Habelt GmbH.

Erkanal-Öktü, A.

2008   The Late Bronze Age cemeteries of Panaztepe. In A. Erkanal-Öktü, S. Günel and U. Deniz (eds), *Batı Anadolu ve Doğu Akdeniz Geç Tunç Çağı Kültürleri Üzerine Yeni Araştırmalar*, 70-90. Ankara: Hacettepe Üniversitesi.

Ersoy, Y.

2004   Klazomenai: 900–500 B.C. History and settlement evidence. In A. Moustaka, E. Skarlatidou, M. C. Tzannes and Y. Ersoy (eds), *Klazomenai, Teos and Abdera: Metropoleis and Colony*, 43-76. Thessaloniki: University Studio Press.

Esse, D.

1991   *Subsistence, Trade, and Social Change in Early Bronze Age Palestine*. Studies in Ancient Oriental Civilization 50. Chicago: Oriental Institute, University of Chicago.

Farr, R.H.

2006   Seafaring as social action. *Journal of Maritime Archaeology* 1: 85-99.

Fattovich, R.

2012   Egypt's trade with Punt: new discoveries on the Red Sea coast. *British Museum Studies in Ancient Egypt and Sudan* 18: 1-59.

Faulkner, R.

1940   Egyptian seagoing ships. *Journal of Egyptian Archaeology* 26: 3-9.

Ferrara, S.

2012   *Cypro Minoan Inscriptions* 1: *Analysis*. Oxford: Oxford University Press.

2016   Writing away: mobility and versatility of scribes at the end of the Late Bronze Age. *Oxford Journal of Archaeology* 35: 227–245.

Février, J.-G.

1950   L'ancienne marine phénicienne et les découvertes récentes. *La Nouvelle Clio* 2: 128-143.

Fischer, P.M.

1991   Canaanite pottery from Hala Sultan Tekke: traditional classication and micro colour analysis (MCA). In J. Barlow, D. Bolger, and B. Kling (eds), *Cypriot Ceramics: Reading the Prehistoric Record*. University Museum Monograph 74: 73-80. Philadelphia: University Museum, University of Pennsylvania.

2011   The new Swedish Cyprus Expedition 2010: excavations at Dromolaxia Vizatzia/Hala Sultan Tekke. *Opuscula* 4: 69-98.

Fischer, P.M., and T. Bürge

2014   The new Swedish Cyprus Expedition 2013: excavations at Hala Sultan Tekke. *Opuscula* 7: 61-106.

2015   The new Swedish Cyprus Expedition 2014: excavations at Hala Sultan Tekke. *Opuscula* 8: 27-79.

2016   The new Swedish Cyprus Expedition 2015: excavations at Hala Sultan Tekke. *Opuscula* 9: 33-58.

Fischer, P.M., and M. Sadeq

2000   Tell el-'Ajjul 1999. A joint Palestinian-Swedish field project: first season preliminary report. *Ägypten und Levante* 10: 211-226.

2002   Tell el-'Ajjul 2000: second season preliminary report. *Ägypten und Levante* 12: 109-153.

Flatman, J.

2003   Cultural biographies, cognitive landscapes and dirty old bits of boat: 'theory' in maritime archaeology. *International Journal of Nautical Archaeology* 32: 143-157.

Flemming, N.C.

1983   Survival of submerged lithic and Bronze Age artefact sites: a review of case histories. In P. Masters and N. Flemming (eds), *Quaternary Coastlines and Maritime Archaeology*, 135-173. London: Academic Press.

Forlanini, M.

2001   Quelques notes sur la géographie historique de la Cilicie. In É. Jean, A. M. Dinçol and S. Durugönül (eds), *La Cilicie: Espaces et pouvoirs locaux (2e millénaire av. J.-C.–4e siècle ap. J.-C.)*, 553-563. Istanbul: de Boccard.

Forstner-Müller, I.

2009   Providing a map of Avaris. *Egyptian Archaeology* 34: 10-13.

Foster, H.

2015   *Bad New Days: Art, Criticism, Emergency*. London: Verso Books.

Frankel, D.

1974   A Middle Cypriot vessel with modelled figures from Politiko, *Lambertis. Report of the Department of Antiquities, Cyprus*: 43-50.

Frankel, D., and J.M. Webb

1996   *Marki Alonia: An Early and Middle Bronze Age Town in Cyprus. Excavations 1990-1994*. Studies in Mediterranean Archaeology 123(1). Jonsered: P. Åström's Förlag.

French, E.B., S.M.A. Hoffman and V.J. Robinson

1993   Wace and Blegen: some introductory thoughts and a case study. Appendix: Neutron Activation groupings of imported material from Tell Abu Hawam. In C. Zerner, P. Zerner and J. Winder (eds), *Wace and Blegen: Pottery as Evidence for Trade in the Aegean Bronze Age 1939-1989*, 3-10. Amsterdam: J.C. Gieben.

Frost, H.

1963   From rope to chain: on the development of the anchor in the Mediterranean. *Mariner's Mirror* 49: 1-20.

1969   The stone anchors of Byblos. *Mélanges de l'Université Saint-Joseph, Beyrouth* 45: 425-442.

1970a   Some Cypriot stone anchors from land sites and from the sea. *Report of the Department of Antiquities, Cyprus*: 14-24.

1970b   Bronze Age stone anchors from the eastern Mediterranean. *Mariner's Mirror* 56: 377-394.

1970c   Stone-anchors as indicators of early trade routes. In M. Mollat (ed.), *Sociétés et compagnies de commerce en Orient et dans l'océan Indien: actes du huitième colloque international d'histoire maritime*, 55-61. Paris: Jean Touzot.

1971   Recent observations on the submerged harbourworks at Tyre. *Bulletin du Musée de Beyrouth* 24: 103-111.

1972   Ancient harbours and anchorages in the eastern Mediterranean. In *Underwater Archaeology: A Nascent Discipline*. Museums and Monuments 13: 95-114. London and Paris: UNESCO.

1973   The offshore island harbours at Sidon and other Phoenician sites in the light of new evidence. *International Journal of Nautical Archaeology and Underwater Exploration* 2: 75-94.

1976   When is a wreck not a wreck? *International Journal of Nautical Archaeology and Underwater Exploration* 5: 101-105.

1979   Egypt and stone anchors: some recent discoveries. *Mariner's Mirror* 65: 137-161.

1982   Stone anchors as clues to Bronze Age trade routes. *Thracia Pontica* I. *Premier Symposium International: La Mer Noire et le Monde Mediterranéen*, 280-289. Sofia: Centre d'Histoire Maritime et d'Archéologie Sous-Marine, Institute de Thracologie de l'Academie Bulgare des Sciences.

1982   The birth of the stocked anchor and the maximum size of early ships: thoughts prompted by discoveries at Kition *Bamboula*, Cyprus. *Mariner's Mirror* 68: 263-273.

1983   Note on three fragmentary anchors from the Palaepaphos *Skales* tombs. In V. Karageorghis, *Palaepaphos-Skales: An Iron Age Cemetery in Cyprus*. Alt-Paphos 3: 433-434. Constanz: Universitätsverlag.

1985   The Kition anchors. Appendix I in V. Karageorghis and M. Demas, *Excavations at Kition* V(1): 281-321. Nicosia: Department of Antiquities, Cyprus.

1988-89 Marine prospection at Byblos. *Bulletin d'archéologie et d'architecure Libanaises* 3: 21-33.

1991   Anchors sacred and profane. Ugarit-Ras Shamra, 1986: the stone anchors revised and compared. In M. Yon (ed.), *Ras Shamra-Ougarit* 6: *Arts et Industries de la Pierre*, 355-408. Paris: Editions Recherchés sur les Civilisations/ADPF.

1995   Harbours and proto-harbours: early Levantine engineering. In V. Karageorghis and D. Michaelides (eds), *Cyprus and the Sea*, 1-22. Nicosia: University of Cyprus, Cyprus Ports Authority.

1996   Ports, cairns and anchors. A Pharaonic outlet on the Red Sea. *Topoi* 6: 869–890.

2004   Byblos and the sea. In C. Doumet-Serhal (ed.), *Decade: A Decade of Archaeology and History in the Lebanon*, 316-347. Beirut: Lebanese British Friends of the National Museum.

Furumark, A., and C. Adelman

2003   *Swedish Excavations at Sinda, Cyprus: Excavations Conducted by Arne Furumark, 1947-1948*. Skrifter Utgivna av Svenska Institutet i Athen 50. Stockholm: Swedish Institute in Athens.

Gabrielsen, V.

2013   Warfare, statehood and piracy in the Greek world. In N. Jaspert and S. Kolditz (eds), *Seerarub in Mittelmeerraum: Piraterie, Korsarentum und Maritime Gewalt von der Antike bis zur Neuzeit*. Mittelmeerstudien 3: 133-153. Paderborn, Germany: Wilhelm Fink/Ferdinand Schöningh.

Gale, N.H., and Z.A. Stos-Gale

1992   Lead isotope studies in the Aegean. In A.M. Pollard (ed.), *New Developments in Archaeological Science. Proceedings of the British Academy* 77: 63-108. London: British Academy.

Galili, E.

1985   A group of stone anchors from Newe-Yam. *International Journal of Nautical Archaeology* 14: 143-153

Galili, E., and K. Raveh

1988   Stone anchors with carvings from the sea off Megadim. *Sefunim* 7: 41-47.

Galili, E., J. Sharvit and M. Artzy

1994   Reconsidering Byblian and Egyptian stone anchors using numerical methods: new finds from the Israeli coast. *International Journal of Nautical Archaeology* 23: 93–107.

Galili, E., N. Gale and B. Rosen

2011   Bronze Age metal cargoes off the Israeli coast. *Skyllis* 11(2): 64-73.

Galili, E., N. Gale and B. Rosen

2013   A Late Bronze Age shipwreck with a metal cargo from Hishuley Carmel, Israel. *International Journal of Nautical Archaeology* 42: 2-23.

Galvin, P.R.

1999   *Patterns of Pillage. A Geography of Caribbean-based Piracy in Spanish America, 1536-1718*. American University Studies 25 (Geography 5). New York: Peter Lang.

Gamble, G.

2003   *Timewalkers: The Prehistory of Global Colonization*. Stroud, England: Sutton Publishing.

Gander, M.

2012   Ahhiyawa–Hiyawa–Que: gibt es Evidenz für die Anwesenheit von Griechen in Kilikien am Übergang von der Bronze zur Eisenheit? *Studi Micenei ed Egeo-Anatolici* 54: 281-309.

Gates, M.-H.

2011   Maritime business in the Bronze Age eastern Mediterranean: the view from its ports. In K. Duistermaat and I. Regulski (eds), *Intercultural Contacts in the Ancient Mediterranean*. Orientalia Lovaniensia Analecta 202: 381-394. Louvain: Peeters.

2013   The Hittite seaport Izziya at Late Bronze Age Kinet Höyük (Cilicia). *Near Eastern Archaeology* 76: 223-234.

Gell, A.

1998   *Art and Agency: An Anthropological Theory*. New York: Oxford University Press.

Georgiou, A.

2014   Appendix III: the Canaanite jars. In V. Karageorghis and A. Kanta, *Pyla-Kokkinokremos: A Late 13th Century BC Fortified Settlement in Cyprus. Excavations 2010-2011*. Studies in Mediterranean Archaeology 141: 175-187. Uppsala, Sweden: Åström Editions.

Georgiou, H.

1997   Seafaring, trade routes, and the emergence of the Bronze Age: urban centers in the eastern Mediterranean. In S. Swiny, R. Hohlfelder and H.W. Swiny (eds), *Res Maritimae: Cyprus and the Eastern Mediterranean from Prehistory through the Roman Period*. Cyprus American Archaeological Research Institute, Monograph 1: 117-124. Atlanta, Georgia: ASOR/Scholars Press.

Gestoso Singer, G. N.

2010   Forms of payment in the Amarna Age and in the Uluburun and Cape Gelidonya shipwrecks. *Ugarit-Forschungen* 42: 261-278.

Ghilardi, M., S. Cordier, J.-M. Carozza, D. Psomiadis, J. Guilaine, Z. Zomeni, F. Demory, D. Delanghe-Sabatier, M.A. Vella, G. Bony and C. Morhange

2015   The Holocene fluvial history of the Tremithos river (south central Cyprus) and its linkage to archaeological records. *Environmental Archaeology* 20: 184-201.

Giardino, C., G.E. Gigante and S. Ridolfe

2003   Archeometallurgical studies. Appendix 8.1. In S. Swiny, G. Rapp and E. Herscher (eds), *Sotira Kaminoudhia: An Early Bronze Age Site in Cyprus*. American Schools of Oriental Research, Archaeological Reports 8. Cyprus American Archaeological Research Institute, Monograph 4: 385-396. Boston: American Schools of Oriental Research.

Gibson, E.

2007   The archaeology of movement in a Mediterranean landscape. *Journal of Mediterranean Archaeology* 20: 61-87.

Gilan, A.

2013   Pirates in the Mediterranean—a view from the Bronze Age. In N. Jaspert and S. Kolditz (eds), *Seerraub in Mittelmeerraum: Piraterie, Korsarentum und Maritime Gewalt von der Antike bis zur Neuzeit*. Mittelmeerstudien 3: 49-66. Paderborn, Germany: Wilhelm Fink/Ferdinand Schöningh.

Gilboa, A.

2015   Dor and Egypt in the Early Iron Age: an archaeological perspective of (part of) the Wenamun report. *Ägypten und Levante* 25: 247-274.

Gilboa, A., and I. Sharon

2008   Between the Carmel and the sea: Tel Dor's Iron Age reconsidered. *Near Eastern Archaeology* 71: 146-170.

Gilboa, A., P. Waiman-Barak and R. Jones

2015   On the origin of Iron Age Phoenician ceramics at Kommos, Crete: regional and diachronic perspectives across the Bronze to Iron Age transition. *Bulletin of the American Schools of Oriental Research* 374: 75-102.

Gittlen, B.M.

2007   Sailing up to Ekron: a nautical seal from Tel Miqne-Ekron. In S.W. Crawford, A. Ben-Tor, J.P. Dessel, W.G. Dever, A. Mazar and J. Aviram (eds), *'Up to the Gates of Ekron': Essays on the Archaeology and History of the Eastern Mediterranean in Honor of Seymour Gitin*, 25-28. Jerusalem: Albright Institute of Archaeological Research, Israel Exploration Society.

Giveon, R.

1985   Dating the Cape Gelidonya shipwreck. *Anatolian Studies* 35: 99-102.

Gjerstad, E.

1926   *Studies on Prehistoric Cyprus*. Uppsala: Uppsala Universitets Arsskrift.

1960   Pottery types: Cypro-Geometric to Cypro-Classical. *Opuscula Atheniensia* 3: 105-122.

Glanville, S.R.K.

1931   Record of the royal dockyard of the time of Tuthmosis III: Papyrus British Museum 10056 (part 1). *Zeitschrift für Ägyptische Sprache und Altertumskunde* 66: 105-121.

1932   Record of the royal dockyard of the time of Tuthmosis III: Papyrus British Museum 10056 (part 2). *Zeitschrift für Ägyptische Sprache und Altertumskunde* 68: 7-41.

Goedicke, H.

1975   *The Report of Wenamun*. Baltimore: Johns Hopkins University Press.

Goitein, S. D.

1967   *A Mediterranean Society*. Volume 1: *Economic Foundations*. Berkeley: University of California Press.

Goldman, H.

1956   *Excavations at Gözlü Kule, Tarsus* II. Princeton: Princeton University Press.

Gophna, R.

2002   Elusive anchorage points along the Israel littoral and the Egyptian-Canaanite maritime route during the Early Bronze Age I. In E.C.M. van den Brink and T. E. Levy (eds), *Egypt and the Levant: Interrelations from the 4th through the Early 3rd Millennium BC*, 418-421. London: Leicester University Press.

Gophna, R., and N. Liphschitz

1996   The Ashkelon Trough settlements in the Early Bronze Age I: new evidence of maritime trade. *Tel Aviv* 23: 143-153.

Goren, Y.

2013   International exchange during the late second millennium BC: microarchaeological study of finds from the Uluburun ship. In J. Aruz, S.B. Graf and Y. Rakic (eds), *Cultures in Contact: From Mesopotamia to the Mediterranean in the Second Millennium BC*, 54-61. New York: Metropolitan Museum of Art.

Gosden, C.

2005   What do objects want? *Journal of Archaeological Method and Theory* 12: 193-211.

Göttlicher, A.

1978   *Materialien für ein Korpus der Schiffsmodelle im Altertum*. Mainz-am-Rhein: Arbeitskreis Historische Schiffbau e.V.

Grace, V.

1940   A Cypriote tomb and Minoan evidence for its date. *American Journal of Archaeology* 44: 10-52.

1956   The Canaanite jar. In S. Weinberg (ed.), *The Aegean and the Near East: Studies Presented to Hetty Goldman*, 80-109. Locust Valley, New York: J.J. Augustin.

Grandet, P.

1994   *Le Papyrus Harris I (BM 9999)*. 2 vols. Bibliothèque d'étude 109.1. Cairo: Institut français d'archéologie orientale du Caire.

Greaves, A.M.

1999   The shifting focus of settlement at Miletos. In P. Flensted-Jensen (ed.), *Copenhagen Polis Centre, Papers* 5. Historia Einzelschriften 138: 57-72. Copenhagen: Royal Danish Academy.

2002   *Miletos: A History*. Routledge: London.

Greenberg, R., and E. Eisenberg

2002   Egypt, Bet Yerah and early Canaanite urbanization. In E.C.M. van den Brink and T. E. Levy (eds), *Egypt and the Levant: Interrelations from the 4th through the Early 3rd Millennium BC*, 213-222. London: Leicester University Press.

Greenberg, R., and N. Porat

1996   A third millennium Levantine pottery production center: typology, petrography, and provenance of the Metallic Ware of northern Israel and adjacent regions. *Bulletin of the American Schools of Oriental Research* 301: 5-24.

Greene E.S., J. Leidwanger and H.A. Özdas

2011   Two early Archaic shipwrecks at Kekova Adası and Kepçe Burnu, Turkey. *International Journal of Nautical Archaeology* 40: 60–68.

2013   Expanding contacts and collapsing distances in early Cypro-Archaic trade: three case studies of shipwrecks of the Turkish coast. In M. Lawall and J. Lund (eds), *The Transport Amphorae and Trade of Cyprus*, 21-34. Aarhus: Aarhus University Press.

Griffiths, D.
2011-12 Petrographic analysis of Tell el-Yahudiyeh ceramics. *Archaeology and History in the Lebanon* 34-35: 154-162.

Günel, S., and S. Herbordt
2014 Mykenische Kraterfragmente mit figürlichen Darstellungen und ein Siegelabdruck eines hethitischen Prinzen aus der spätbronzezeitlichen Siedlung von Çine-Tepecik. *Archäologischer Anzeiger* 2014/1: 1-14.

Güterbock, H. G.
1967 The Hittite conquest of Cyprus reconsidered. *Journal of Near Eastern Studies* 26: 73-81

Gunneweg, J., I. Perlman and F. Asaro
1987 A Canaanite jar from Enkomi. *Israel Exploration Journal* 37: 168-172.

Habachi, L.
1972 *The Second Stele of Kamose and His Struggle against the Hyksos Ruler and His Capital*. Abhandlungen des Deutschen Archäologischen Instituts in Kairo, Ägyptologisches Reihe 8. Glückstadt: Augustin.

Hadjicosti, M.
1988 'Canaanite' jars from Maa-*Palaeokastro*. In V. Karageorghis and M. Demas, *Excavations at Maa-Palaeokastro 1979-1986*, 340-385. Nicosia: Cyprus Department of Antiquties.

Hadjidaki, E.
2004 A possible Minoan harbor on south Crete. In L.P. Day, M.S. Mook and J.D. Muhly (eds), *Crete Beyond the Palaces: Proceedings of the Crete 2000 Conference*. Institute for Aegean Prehistory, Prehistory Monographs 10: 53-60. Philadelphia: Institute for Aegean Prehistory Academic Press.

Hadjidaki, E., and P.P. Betancourt
2005-06 A Minoan shipwreck off Pseira island, east Crete. Preliminary report. *Eulimene* 6-7: 79-96.

Hadjisavvas, S.
1986 Alassa. A new Late Cypriote site. *Report of the Department of Antiquities, Cyprus*: 62-67.

Haggi, A.
2006 Phoenician Atlit and its newly-excavated harbour: a reassessment. *Tel Aviv* 33: 43-60.

Haggi, A., and M. Artzy
2007 The harbor of Atlit in northern Canaanite/Phoenician context. *Near Eastern Archaeology* 70(2): 75-84.

Hamad, N., C. Millot and I. Taupier-Letage
2006 The surface circulation in the eastern basin of the Mediterranean Sea. *Scientia Marina* 70: 457-503.

Hankey, V.
1967 Mycenaean pottery in the Middle East: notes on finds since 1951. *Annual of the British School at Athens* 62: 107-147.

Hansen, M.H.

1997   Emporion: a study of the use and meaning of the term in the archaic and classical periods. In T.H. Nielsen (ed.), *Yet More Studies in the Ancient Greek Polis*. Historia Einzelschriften 17: 83-105. Stuttgart: Franz Steiner Verlag.

Harif, A.

1974   A Mycenaean building at Tell Abu Hawam in Palestine. *Palestine Exploration Quarterly* 106: 83-90.

Harpster, M.

2013   Shipwreck identity, methodology, and nautical archaeology. *Journal of Archaeological Method and Theory* 20: 588-622.

Hartung, U.

2002   Imported jars from Cemetery U at Abydos and the relations between Egypt and Canaan in predynastic times. In E.C.M. van den Brink and T. E. Levy (eds), *Egypt and the Levant: Interrelations from the 4th through the Early 3rd Millennium BC*, 437-449. London: Leicester University Press.

2014   Interconnections between the Nile valley and the southern Levant in the 4th millennium BC. In F. Höflmayer and R. Eichmann (eds), *Egypt and the Southern Levant during the Early Bronze Age: C14, Chronology, Connections*. Orient-Archäologie 31: 107-133. Rahden/Westfalen: Verlag Marie Leidorf.

Hartung, U., E.C. Köhler, V. Müller and M.F. Ownby

2015   Imported pottery from Abydos: a new petrographic perspective. *Ägypten und Levante* 25: 295-333.

Haskell, H.W., R.E. Jones, P.M. Day and J.T. Killen

2011   *Transport Stirrup Jars of the Bronze Age Aegean and East Mediterranean*. Philadelphia, Pennsylvania: Institute for Aegean Prehistory Academic Press.

Hawkins, J.D.

1995   *The Hieroglyphic Inscription of the Sacred Pool Complex at Hattusa (Südburg)*. Studien zu den Boğazkoy-Texten, Beiheft 3. Wiesbaden: Harrossowitz.

Helck, W.

1986   Wenamun. *Lexicon der Ägyptologie* 6: 1215-1217. Wiesbaden: Harrassowitz.

Helms, M. W.

1988   *Ulysses' Sail: An Ethnographic Odyssey of Power, Knowledge, and Geographical Distance*. Princeton: Princeton University Press.

Heltzer, M.

1978   *Goods, Prices and the Organization of Trade at Ugarit*. Wiesbaden: Harrassowitz.

1982   *The Internal Organization of the Kingdom of Ugarit*. Wiesbaden: Harrassowitz.

1989   The trade of Crete and Cyprus with Syria and Mesopotamia, and their eastern tin-sources in the XVIII-XVII centuries B.C. *Minos* 24: 7-28.

Hennessy, J.B., K. Eriksson and I. Kehrberg

1988   *Ayia Paraskevi and Vasilia: Excavations by the Late J.R. Stewart*. Studies in Mediterranean Archaeology 82. Göteborg: P. Åström's Förlag.

Hennessy, J.B., and J. du Plat Taylor

1967   The pottery. In G. Bass, *Cape Gelidonya: A Bronze Age Shipwreck*. Transactions of the American Philosophical Society 57(8): 122-125. Philadelphia: American Philosophical Society.

Herdner, A.

1963   *Corpus des Tablettes en Cuneiformes Alphabetiques.* Mission de Ras Shamra 10. Paris: Klincksieck.

Hirschfeld, N.

1996   Cypriots in the Mycenaean Aegean. In E. DeMiro, L. Godart and A. Sacconi (eds), *Atti e Memorie del Secondo Congresso Internazionale di Micenologia, Roma-Napoli, 14-20 Ottobre 1991.* 2 volumes. Incunabula Graeca 98 (1): 289-297. Rome: Gruppo Editoriale Internazionale.

2000   Marked Late Bronze Age pottery from the kingdom of Ugarit. In M. Yon, V. Karageorghis and N. Hirschfeld, *Céramiques mycéniennes d'Ougarit.* Ras Shamra-Ougarit 13: 163-200. Paris, Nicosia: ADPF, Leventis Foundation.

2011   The Cypriot ceramic cargo of the Uluburun shipwreck. In W. Gauß, M. Lindblom, R.A.K. Smith and J.C. Wright (eds), *Our Cups Are Full: Pottery and Society in the Aegean Bronze Age: Papers Presented to Jeremy B. Rutter on the Occasion of his 65th Birthday.* British Archaeological Reports, International Series 2227: 115-120. Oxford: Archaeopress.

Hirschfeld, N., and G.F. Bass

2013   Return to Cape Gelidonya. *Pasiphae* 7: 99-104.

Hitchcock, L.A., and A. M. Maeir

2014   Yo-ho, yo-ho, a seren's life for me! *World Archaeology* 46: 624-640.

2016   A pirate's life for me: the maritime culture of the Sea Peoples. *Palestine Exploration Quarterly* 148: 245-264.

2018   Fifteen men on a dead seren's chest: yo ho ho and a krater of wine. In A. Batmaz, G. Bedianashvili, A. Michaelewicz and A. Robinson (eds), *Context and Connection: Essays on the Archaeology of the Ancient Near East in Honour of Antonio Sagona.* Orientalia Lovaniensia Analecta 268: 147-159. Leuven: Peeters.

Höckmann, O.

2001   The Kynos sea-fighters: exception or rule? In H. Tzalas (ed.), *Tropis VI: Proceedings of the Sixth International Symposium on Ship Construction in Antiquity,* 223-234. Athens: Hellenic Institute for the Preservation of the Nautical Tradition.

Hodder, I.A.

1990   *The Domestication of Europe: Structure and Contingency in Neolithic Societies.* Oxford: Blackwell.

2012   *Entangled: An Archaeology of the Relationships between Humans and Things.* Oxford: Wiley-Blackwell.

Hoftijzer, J., and W.H. Van Soldt

1998   Texts from Ugarit pertaining to seafaring. In S. Wachsmann, *Seagoing Ships and Seamanship in the Bronze Age Levant,* 333-344. College Station: Texas A&M University Press.

Holmes, Y.L.

1978   The messengers of the Amarna letters. *Journal of the American Oriental Society* 95: 376-381.

Horden, P., and N. Purcell

2000   *The Corrupting Sea: A Study of Mediterranean History.* Oxford: Blackwell.

Howitt-Marshall, D.

2012   The anchorage site at Kouklia *Achni*, southwest Cyprus: problems and perspectives. In A. Georgiou (ed.), *Cyprus An Island Culture: Society and Social Relations from the Bronze Age to the Venetian Period*, 104-121. Oxford: Oxbow Books.

Howitt-Marshall, D., and C. Runnels

2016   Middle Pleistocene sea-crossings in the eastern Mediterranean? *Journal of Anthropological Archaeology* 42: 140-153.

Hult, G.

1977   Stone anchors in Area 8. In P. Åström, G. Hult and M. Strandberg Olofsson (eds), *Hala Sultan Tekke 3: Excavations 1972*. Studies in Mediterranean Archaeology 45(3): 147-149. Göteborg: P. Åström's Förlag.

Iacovou, M.

2008   'The Palaepaphos Urban Landscape Project': theoretical background and preliminary report 2006-2007. *Report of the Department of Antiquities Cyprus*: 263-289.

2012   From regional gateway to Cypriot kingdom. Copper deposits and copper routes in the chora of Paphos. In V. Kassianidou and G. Papasavvas (eds), *Eastern Mediterranean Metallurgy and Metalwork in the Second Millennium BC*, 58-69. Oxford: Oxbow.

Ingholt, H.

1940   *Rapport préliminaire sur sept campagnes de fouilles à Hama en Syrie (1932-38)*. Det Kongelige Danske Videnskabernes Selskab. Archaeologisk-kunsthistoriske Meddelelser 1, no. 3. Copenhagen: Det Kongelige Danske Videnskabernes Selskab.

Jablonka, P., and C. Brian Rose

2004   Late Bronze Age Troy: a response to Frank Kolb. *American Journal of Archaeology* 108: 615-630.

Jacobs, A.

2016   The Plain and Canaanite wares. In C. von Rüden, A. Georgiou, A. Jacobs and P. Halstead, *Feasting, Craft and Depositional Practice in Late Bronze Age Palaepaphos. The Well Fillings of Evreti*. Bochumer Forschungen zur Ur- und Frühgeschichtlichen Archäologie 8: 39-70. Rahden-Westfallen, Germany: Verlag Marie Leidorf GmbH.

James, T.G.H.

1996   The earliest history of wine and its importance in ancient Egypt. In P.E McGovern, S.J. Fleming and S.H. Katz (eds), *The Origins and Ancient History of Wine*. Food and Nutrition in History and Anthropology 11: 197-213. Philadelphia: Gordon and Breach.

Jaspert, N., and S. Kolditz (eds)

2013   *Seerraub in Mittelmeerraum: Piraterie, Korsarentum und Maritime Gewalt von der Antike bis zur Neuzeit*. Mittelmeerstudien 3. Paderborn, Germany: Wilhelm Fink/ Ferdinand Schöningh.

Johnson, J.

1980   *Maroni de Chypre*. Studies in Mediterranean Archaeology 59. Göteborg: P. Åström's Förlag.

Jones, R.E.

1986   *Greek and Cypriot Pottery: A Review of Scientific Studies*. British School at Athens, Fitch Laboratory, Occasional Paper 1. Athens: British School at Athens.

Jones, R.E., and P. Day

1987   Aegean-type pottery on Sardinia: identification of imports and local imitations by chemical analysis. In M.S. Balmuth (ed.), *Nurgaic Sardinia and the Mycenaean World*. Studies in Sardinian Archaeology 3. British Archaeological Reports International Series 387: 257-269. Oxford: British Archaeological Reports.

Jones, R.E., and S.J. Vaughan

1988   Part 2: A study of some 'Canaanite' jar fragments from Maa-*Palaeokastro* by petrographic and chemical analysis. In V. Karageorghis and M. Demas, *Excavations at Maa-Palaeokastro 1979-1986*, 386-398. Nicosia: Cyprus Department of Antiquties.

Jung, R.

2006   Die mykenische Keramik von Tell Kazel (Syrien). *Damaszener Mitteilungen* 15: 147-218.

2009   Pirates of the Aegean: Italy – the east Aegean – Cyprus at the end of the second millennium BC. In V. Karageorghis and O. Kouka (eds), *Cypus and the East Aegean: Intercultural Contacts from 3000 to 500 BC*, 72-93. Nicosia: Leventis Foundation.

2011   Mycenaean vending cups in Syria? Thoughts about the unpainted Mycenaean pottery from Tell Kazel. In W. Gauß, M. Lindblom, R.A.K. Smith and J.C. Wright (eds), *Our Cups Are Full: Pottery and Society in the Aegean Bronze Age: Papers Presented to Jeremy B. Rutter on the Occasion of his 65th Birthday*. British Archaeological Reports, International Series 2227: 121-132. Oxford: Archaeopress.

Jung, R., and M. Mehofer

2005-06 A sword of Naue II type from Ugarit and the historical significance of Italian-type weaponry in the eastern Mediterranean. *Aegean Archaeology* 8: 111-135.

Jung, R., and B. Weninger

2015   Archaeological and environmental impact of the 4.2 ka cal BP event in the central and eastern Mediterranean. In H. Meller, H.W. Arz, R. Jung und R. Risch(eds), *2200 BC — ein Klimasturz al Ursache für den Zerfall der Alten Welt?* Tagungen des Landesmuseum für Vorgeschichte Halle 12(1): 205-234. Halle, Germany: Landesmuseum für Vorgeschichte.

Kantor, H.J.

1992   The relative chronology of Egypt and its foreign correlations before the First Intermediate Period. In R.W. Ehrich (ed.), *Chronologies in Old World Archaeology* (3rd ed.) I: 3-21; II: 2-45. Chicago: University of Chicago Press.

Kaplan, J.

1972   The archaeology and history of Tel Aviv-Jaffa. *Biblical Archaeologist* 35(3): 65-95.

Karageorghis, V.

1960   Supplementary notes on the Mycenaean vases from the Swedish Tombs at Enkomi. *Opuscula Atheniensia* 3: 135-153.

1998   Mycenaean defensive outposts in the Aegean and Cyprus: some comparisons. In E.H. Cline and D. Harris-Cline (eds), *The Aegean and the Orient in the Second Millennium*. Aegaeum 18: 127-136. Liège: Université de Liège.

Karageorghis, V., and M. Demas

1984   *Pyla*-Kokkinokremos: *A Late 13th Century B.C. Fortified Settlement in Cyprus*. Nicosia: Department of Antiquities.

1985   *Excavations at Kition* V, Parts 1, 2. *The Pre-Phoenician Levels*. Nicosia: Department of Antiquities, Cyprus.

Karyda, E.

2016   Sailing from coast to coast: cabotage on the Cypriot south coast. In R. Maguire and J. Chick (eds), *Approaching Cyprus*, 78-95. Newcaste-upon-Tyne: Cambridge Scholars Publishing.

Kayafa, M., S. Stos-Gale and N. Gale

2000   The circulation of copper in the Early Bronze Age in mainland Greece: the lead isotope evidence from Lerna, Lithares and Tsoungiza. In C.F. Pare (ed.), *Metals Make the World Go Round: The Supply and Circulation of Metals in Bronze Age Europe*, 39-55. Oxford: Oxbow.

Kayan, I.

1990   Late Holocene geomorphic evolution of the Besige-Troy area (NW Anatolia) and the environment of prehistoric man. In S. Bottema, G. Entjes-Nieborg, and W. van Zeist (eds), *Man's Role in the Shaping of the Eastern Mediterranean Landscape*, 69-70. Rotterdam, Holland and Brookfield, Massachusetts: A.A. Balkema.

1991   Holocene geomorphic evolution of the Besik Plain and changing environment of ancient man. *Studia Troica* 1: 79-92.

1995   The Troia Bay and supposed harbour sites in the Bronze Age. *Studia Troica* 5: 211-235.

Kayan, I., E. Öner, L. Uncu, B. Hocaoğlu and S. Vardar

2003   Geoarchaeological interpretations of the 'Troian bay'. In G.A. Wagner, E. Pernicka and H.-P. Uerpmann (eds), *Troia and the Troad: Scientific Approaches*, 379-401. Berlin: Springer Verlag.

Keel, O.

1994   Philistine 'anchor' seals. *Israel Exploration Journal* 44: 21-35.

Kelder, J.M.

2004-05 Mycenaeans in western Anatolia. *Talanta* 36-37: 49-85.

Kempinski, A.

1974   Tell el-'Ajjul–Beth-Aglayim or Sharuhen? *Israel Exploration Journal* 24: 145-152.

Kenna, V.E.G.

1972   Glyptic. In L. and P. Åström, *The Late Cypriote Bronze Age: Other Arts and Crafts*. Swedish Cyprus Expedition IV, 1D: 623-674. Lund: Swedish Cyprus Expedition.

Keswani, P. S.

1989 Dimensions of social hierarchy in Late Bronze Age Cyprus: an analysis of the mortuary data from Enkomi. *Journal of Mediterranean Archaeology* 2: 49-86.

2004 *Mortuary Ritual and Society in Bronze Age Cyprus*. Monographs in Mediterranean Archaeology 9. London: Equinox.

2009 Exploring regional variation in Late Cypriot II-III pithoi: perspectives from Alassa and Kalavasos. In I. Hein (ed.), *The Formation of Cyprus in the 2nd Millennium BC. Studies in Regionalism during the Middle and Late Bronze Ages*. Österreichische Akademie Der Wissenschaften, Denkschriften Der Gesamtakademie 52: 107-125. Wein: Österreichische Akademie Der Wissenschaften.

Killebrew, A.

2007 The Canaanite storage jar revisited. In S.W. Crawford, A. Ben-Tor, J.P. Dessel, W.G. Dever, A. Mazar and J. Aviram (eds), *"Up to the Gates of Ekron": Essays on the Archaeology and History of the Eastern Mediterranean in Honor of Seymour Gitin*, 166-188. Jerusalem: Albright institute of Archaeological Research, Israel Exploration Society.

Kiriatzi, E., and C. Knappett (eds)

2017 *Human Mobility and Technological Transfer in the Prehistoric Mediterranean*. Cambridge: Cambridge University Press.

Kitchen, K.A.

1983 *Ramesside Inscriptions. Historical and Biographical*. Volume 5. Oxford: Blackwell.

1996 *Ramesside Inscriptions, Translated and Annotated. Translations* Volume 2. Oxford: Wiley-Blackwell.

Klengel, H.

1974 'Hungersjahre' in Hatti. *Altorientalische Forschungen* 1: 165-174.

1984 Sumar/Simyra und die Eleutheros-Ebene in der Geschichte Syriens. *Klio* 66: 5-18.

Knapp, A.B.

1981 The Thera frescoes and the question of Aegean contact with Libya during the Late Bronze Age. *Journal of Mediterranean Anthropology and Archaeology* 1: 249-279.

1983 An Alashiyan merchant at Ugarit. *Tel Aviv* 10: 38-45.

1991 Spice, drugs, grain and grog: organic goods in Bronze Age eastern Mediterranean trade. In N.H. Gale (ed.), *Bronze Age Trade in the Mediterranean*. Studies in Mediterranean Archaeology 90: 21-68. Göteborg: P. Åström's Förlag.

1992 Bronze Age Mediterranean island cultures and the ancient Near East. *Biblical Archaeologist* 55(3): 112-128.

1993 Thalassocracies in Bronze Age eastern Mediterranean trade: making and breaking a myth. *World Archaeology* 24: 332-347.

1994 Emergence, development and decline on Bronze Age Cyprus. In C. Mathers and S. Stoddart (eds), *Development and Decline in the Mediterranean Bronze Age*. Sheffield Archaeological Monograph 8: 271-304. Sheffield: John Collis Publications.

1996   (ed.) *Near Eastern and Aegean Texts from the Third to the First Millennia BC*. Sources for the History of Cyprus II (edited by P.W. Wallace and A.G. Orphanides). Altamont, New York: Greece/Cyprus Research Center.

1997   Mediterranean maritime landscapes: transport, trade and society on Late Bronze Age Cyprus. In S. Swiny, R. Hohlfelder and H.W. Swiny (eds), *Res Maritimae: Cyprus and the Eastern Mediterranean from Prehistory through the Roman Period*. Cyprus American Archaeological Research Institute, Monograph 1: 153-162. Atlanta, Georgia: ASOR/Scholars Press.

2006   Orientalisation and prehistoric Cyprus: the social life of Oriental goods. In C. Riva and N. Vella (eds), *Debating Orientalisation: Multidisciplinary Approaches to Change in the Ancient Mediterranean*. Monographs in Mediterranean Archaeology 10: 48-65. London: Equinox.

2008   *Prehistoric and Protohistoric Cyprus: Identity, Insularity and Connectivity*. Oxford: Oxford University Press.

2013a   *The Archaeology of Cyprus: From Earliest Prehistory through the Bronze Age*. Cambridge: Cambridge University Press.

2013b   Revolution within evolution: the emergence of a 'secondary state' on Protohistoric Bronze Age Cyprus. *Levant* 45: 19-44.

2014   Seafaring and seafarers: the case for Late Bronze Age Cyprus. In J.M. Webb (ed.), *Structure, Measurement and Meaning: Insights into the Prehistory of Cyprus. Studies on Prehistoric Cyprus in Honour of David Frankel*. Studies in Mediterranean Archaeology 143: 79-93. Uppsala: Åström Editions.

2016   Maritime transport containers and Bronze Age Cyprus. In G. Bourogiannis and C. Mühlenbock (eds), *Ancient Cyprus Today: Museum Collections and New Research*. Studies in Mediterranean Archaeology and Literature PB 184: 249-259. Uppsala: Åström Editions.

2018   The way things are.... In A.R. Knodell and T.P. Leppard (eds), *Regional Approaches to Society and Complexity*. Monographs in Mediterranean Archaeology 15: 288-309. Sheffield: Equinox.

Knapp, A.B., and J.F. Cherry

1994   *Provenience Studies and Bronze Age Cyprus: Production, Exchange, and Politico-Economic Change*. Monographs in World Archaeology 21. Madison, Wisconsin: Prehistory Press.

Knapp, A.B., and S. Demesticha

2017   *Mediterranean Connections: Maritime Transport Containers and Seaborne Trade in the Bronze and Early Iron Ages*. London, New York: Routledge.

Knapp, A.B., and S.W. Manning

2016   Crisis in context: the end of the Late Bronze Age in the eastern Mediterranean. *American Journal of Archaeology* 120: 99-149.

Knapp, A.B., J.D. Muhly and P.M. Muhly

1988   To hoard is human: the metal deposits of LC IIC-LC III. *Report of the Department of Antiquities, Cyprus*: 233-262.

Knappett, C. (ed.)

2013   *Network Analysis in Archaeology: New Approaches to Regional Interaction*. Oxford: Oxford University Press.

Knappett, C., and L. Malafouris (eds)

2008   *Material Agency: Towards a Non-Anthropocentric Approach*. New York: Springer.

Knappett, C., and I. Nikolakopoulou

2014   Inside out? Materiality and connectivity in the Aegean archipelago. In A. B. Knapp and P. van Dommelen (eds), *The Cambridge Prehistory of the Bronze and Iron Age Mediterranean*, 25-39. New York: Cambridge University Press.

Knoblauch, C.

2010   Preliminary report on the Early Bronze Age III pottery from contexts of the 6th Dynasty in the Abydos middle cemetery. *Ägypten und Levante* 20: 243-261.

Koehl, R.

1985   *Sarepta* III: *The Imported Bronze and Iron Age Wares of Area II,X*. Publications de l'Université Libanaise 2. Beirut: Publications de l'Université Libanaise, Section des Études Archéologiques.

Köhler, C.E., and M. Ownby

2011   Levantine imports and their imitations from Helwan. *Ägypten und Levante* 21: 31-46.

Kolb, F.

2004   Troy VI: a trading center and commercial city? *American Journal of Archaeology* 108: 577-613.

Kopanias, K.

2017   Mercenaries or refugees? The evidence from the inscriptions of Merneptah on the 'sea peoples'. *Journal of Greek Archaeology* 2: 119-134.

Kopetzky, K.

2008   The MB IIB-corpus of the Hyksos period at Tell el-Dabʿa. In M. Bietak and E. Czerny (eds), *The Bronze Age in the Lebanon: Studies on the Archaeology and Chronology of Lebanon, Syria and Egypt*. Denkschriften der Gesamtakademie 50. Contributions to the Chronology of the Eastern Mediterranean 17: 195-242. Wein: Österreichische Akademie Der Wissenschaften.

Kopytoff, I.

1986   The cultural biography of things: commoditization as process. In A. Appadurai (ed.), *The Social Life of Things: Commodities in Cultural Perspective*, 64-91. Cambridge: Cambridge University Press.

Korfmann, M.

1986a   Troy: topography and navigation. In M. Mellink (ed.), *Troy and the Trojan War*, 1-16. Bryn Mawr, Pennsylvania: Bryn Mawr College.

1986b   Beşik-Tepe: new evidence for the period of the Trojan sixth and seventh settlements. In M. Mellink (ed.), *Troy and the Trojan War*, 17-28. Bryn Mawr, Pennsylvania: Bryn Mawr College.

1990   Beşik-Tepe.Vorbericht über die Ergebnisse der Arbeiten von 1987 und 1988. *Archäologischer Anzeiger* 1989/4: 473-494.

Kouka, O.

2002   *Siedlunsorganisation in der Nord- und Ostägäis während der Frühbronzezeit (3 Jt. v. Chr.)*. Internationale Archäologie 58. Rahden/Westfallen: Verlag Marie Leidorf GmbH.

2009a   Cross-cultural links and elite-identities: the eastern Aegean/western Anatolia and Cyprus from the early third through the early second millennium BC. In V. Karageorghis and O. Kouka (eds), *Cypus and the East Aegean: Intercultural Contacts from 3000 to 500 BC*, 31-47. Nicosia: Leventis Foundation.

2009b   Third millennium BC Aegean chronology: old and new data from the perspective of the third millennium AD. In S.W. Manning and M.J. Bruce (eds), *Tree-Rings, Kings, and Old World Archaeology and Environment: Papers Presented in Honor of Peter Ian Kuniholm*, 133-161. Oxford: Oxbow Books.

2016   The built environment and cultural connectivity in the Aegean Early Bronze Age. In B.P.C. Molloy (ed.), *Of Odysseys and Oddities: Scales and Modes of Interaction between Prehistoric Aegean Societies and Their Neighbours*. Sheffield Studies in Aegean Archaeology 10: 203-224. Oxford: Oxbow.

Kozal, E.

2016   Cypro-Anatolian connections in the 2nd millennium BC. In L. Summerer and H. Kaba (eds), *The Northern Face of Cyprus: New Studies in Cypriot Archaeology and Art History*, 51-64. Istanbul: Zero Prodüksiyon.

Kraft, J.D., G. Rapp, I. Kayan and J.V. Luce

2003   Harbor areas at ancient Troy: sedimentology and geomorphology complement Homer's Iliad. *Geology* 31: 163-166.

Kraft, J.D., I. Kayan and O. Erol

1982   Geology and paleogeographic reconstructions of the vicinity of Troy. In G. Rapp, Jr. and J.A. Gifford (eds), *Troy: The Archaeological Geology*. Troy, Supplementary Monograph 4: 11-41. Princeton: Princeton University Press.

Kristiansen, K.

2004   Sea faring voyages and rock art ships. In P. Clark (ed.), *The Dover Bronze Age Boat in Context. Society and Water Transport in Prehistoric Europe*, 111-121. Oxford: Oxbow.

2016   Interpreting Bronze Age trade and migration. In E. Kiriatizi and C. Knappett (eds), *Human Mobility and Technological Transfer in the Prehistoric Mediterranean*, 154-180. Cambridge: Cambridge University Press.

Kuhrt, A.

2002   Greek contact with the Levant and Mesopotamia in the first half of the first millennium BC: a view from the east. In G.R. Tstetskhladze and A.M. Snodgrass (eds), *Greek Settlement in the Eastern Mediterranean and Black Sea*. British Archaeological Reports, International Series 1062: 17-25. Oxford: Archaeopress.

Lackenbacher, S., and F. Malbran-Labat

2005   Ugarit et les Hittites dans les archives de la 'Maison d'Urtenu'. *Studi Micenei ed Egeo-Anatolici* 47: 227-240.

2016   *Lettres en akkadien de la 'Maison d'Urtenu'. Fouilles de 1994*. Ras Shamra-Ougarit 23. Louvain: Peeters.

Lacovara, P.

1982   British Museum 35324 again. *Göttinger Miszellen* 59: 41-50.

Lagarce, J., E. Lagarce, E. Bounni and N. Saliby

1983   Les fouilles à Ras Ibn Hani en Syrie. *Académie des Inscriptions et Belles-Lettres: Comptes Rendus des Séances*: 249-290.

Lambdin, T.O.

1953   The Miši-people of the Byblian Amarna letters. *Journal of Cuneiform Studies* 7: 75-77.

Lambeck, K., and D. Chappell

2001   Sea-level change through the last glacial cycle. *Science* 292/5517: 679-686.

Lambeck, K., and A. Purcell

2005   Sea-level change in the Mediterranean Sea since the LGM: model predictions for tectonically stable areas. *Quaternary Science Reviews* 24: 1969–1988.

Lambrou-Phillipson, C.

1993   Ugarit: a Late Bronze Age thalassocracy? The evidence of the textual sources. *Orientalia* 62: 163-170.

Landström, B.

1970   *Ships of the Pharaohs*. Garden City, New Jersey: Doubleday and Co.

Langgut, D., M.J. Adams and I. Finkelstein

2016   Climate, settlement patterns and olive horticulture in the southern Levant during the Early Bronze and Intermediate Bronze Ages (c. 3600-1950 BC). *Levant* 48: 117-134.

Larsen, M.T.

2015   *Ancient Kanesh: A Merchant Colony in Bronze Age Anatolia*. Cambridge: Cambridge University Press.

Lawall, M.L.

2011   Greek amphorae in the archaeological record. In M.L. Lawall and J. Lund (eds), *Pottery in the Archaeological Record: Greece and Beyond*. Gösta Enbom Monograph 1: 37-50. Aarhus: Aarhus University Press.

Le Bon, L.

1995   Ancient ship graffiti: symbol and context. In O. Crumlin-Pedersen and B. Munch Thye (eds), *The Ship as Symbol in Prehistoric and Medieval Scandinavia*, 172-179. Copenhagen: Nationalmuseet.

Leeson, P.T.

2009   *The Invisible Hook. The Hidden Economics of Pirates*. Princeton: Princeton University Press.

Leidwanger, J.

2013   Opportunistic ports and spaces of exchange in Late Roman Cyprus. *Journal of Maritime Archaeology* 8: 221-243.

2017   From time capsules to networks: new light on Roman shipwrecks in the maritime economy. *American Journal of Archaeology* 121: 595-619.

Leidwanger, J., C. Knappett, P. Arnaud, P. Arthur, E. Blake, C. Broodbank, T. Brughmans, T. Evans, S. Graham, E.S. Greene, B. Kowalzig, B. Mills, R. Rivers, T.F. Tartaron and R. Van de Noort

2014   A manifesto for the study of ancient Mediterranean maritime networks. *Antiquity* 342. Online: http://journal.antiquity.ac.uk/projgall/leidwanger342

Leppard, T.P.

2014a   Modeling the impacts of Mediterranean island colonisation by archaic hominins: the likelihood of an insular Lower Palaeolithic. *Journal of Mediterranean Archaeology* 27: 231-254.

2014b   Mobility and migration in the Early Neolithic of the Mediterranean: questions of motivation and mechanism. *World Archaeology* 46: 484-501.

Lesko, L.H.

1980   The wars of Ramesses III. *Serapis* 6: 83-86.

1996   Egyptian wine production during the New Kingdom. In P.E McGovern, S.J. Fleming and S.H. Katz (eds), *The Origins and Ancient History of Wine*. Food and Nutrition in History and Anthropology 11: 215-230. Philadelphia: Gordon and Breach.

Lev-Yadun, S., M. Artzy, E. Marcus and R. Stidsing

1996   Wood remains from Tel Nami, a Middle Bronze IIa and Late Bronze IIb port, local exploitation and Levantine cedar trade. *Economic Botany* 50: 310-317.

Lichtheim, M.

1973   *Ancient Egyptian Literature*, Volume 1: *The Old and Middle Kingdoms*. Berkeley: University of California Press.

1976   *Ancient Egyptian Literature*, Volume 2: *The New Kingdom*. Berkeley: University of California Press.

Linder, E.

1970   The Maritime Texts of Ugarit: A Study in Late Bronze Age Shipping. Unpublished PhD dissertation: Brandeis University.

1972   A seafaring merchant-smith from Ugarit and the Cape Gelidonya shipwreck. *International Journal of Nautical Archaeology and Underwater Exploration* 1: 163-164.

1973   Naval warfare in the El-Amarna age. In D.J. Blackman (ed.), *Marine Archaeology*. Colston Papers 23: 317-324. Butterworths: London.

1981   Ugarit: a Canaanite thalassocracy. In G.D. Young (ed.), *Ugarit in Retrospect*, 31-42. Winona Lake, Indiana: Eisenbrauns.

Lindqvist, A.

2016   A study of fishing methods used at Hala Sultan Tekke during the Late Bronze Age. In G. Bourogiannis and C. Mühlenbock (eds), *Ancient Cyprus Today: Museum Collections and New Research*. Studies in Mediterranean Archaeology and Literature PB 184: 239-248. Uppsala: Åström Editions.

Liphschitz, N.

2012   The use of *Cedrus libani* (Cedar of Lebanon) as a construction timber for ships as evident from timber identification of shipwrecks in the East Mediterranean. *Skyllis* 12: 94–98.

Liphschitz, N., and C. Pulak

2008   Wood species used in ancient shipbuilding in Turkey: evidence from dendroarchaeological studies. *Skyllis* 8: 74–83.

Lipke, P.

1984   *The Royal Ship of Cheops*. British Archaeological Reports, International Series 225. Oxford: British Archaeological Reports.

Liverani, M.

1962   *Storia du Ugarit*. Studi Semitici 6. Rome: Università di Roma.

1979a   La dotazione dei mercanti di Ugarit. *Ugarit-Forschungen* 11: 495-503.

1979b   Ras Shamra: histoire. In H. Cazelles and A. Feuillet (eds), *Supplément au Dictionnaire de la Bible*, 1295-1348. Paris: Ane.

1990   *Prestige and Interest: International Relations in the Near East ca. 1600-1100 BC.* Padova: Sargon Press.

1998   How to kill Abdi-Ashirta. EA 101, once again. In S. Isre'el, I. Singer and R. Zadok (eds), *Past Links. Studies in the Languages and Cultures of the Ancient Near East*, 387-394. Winona Lake, Indiana: Eisenbrauns.

2001   *International Relations in the Ancient Near East ca. 1600-1100 BC.* New York: Palgrave.

2004   *Myth and Politics in Ancient Near Eastern Historiography.* London: Equinox.

2014   *The Ancient Near East: History, Society and Economy.* London and New York: Routledge.

Lolos, Y.G.

1999   The cargo of pottery from the Point Iria wreck: character and implications. In W. Phelps, Y. Lolos and Y. Vichos (eds), *The Point Iria Wreck: Interconnections in the Mediterranean ca. 1200 BC*, 43-58. Athens: Hellenic Institute of Marine Archaeology.

López-Bertran, M., A. Garcia-Ventura and M. Krueger

2008   Could you take a picture of my boat, please? The use and significance of Mediterranean ship representations. *Oxford Journal of Archaeology* 27: 341-357.

Luraghi, N.

2006   Traders, pirates, warriors: the proto-history of Greek mercenary soldiers in the eastern Mediterranean. *Phoenix* 60: 21-47.

McCaslin, D.

1978   The 1977 underwater report. *Hala Sultan Tekke* 4. Studies in Mediterranean Archaeology 45(4): 97-157. Göteborg: P. Åström's Förlag.

1980   *Stone Anchors in Antiquity: Coastal Settlements and Maritime Trade-Routes in the Eastern Mediterranean ca.1600-1050 B.C.* Studies in Mediterranean Archaeology 61. Göteborg P. Åström's Förlag.

McGeough, K. M.

2007   *Exchange Relationships at Ugarit.* Ancient Near Eastern Studies, Supplement 26. Leuven: Peeters.

2015   'What is not in my house you must give me': agents of exchange according to the textual evidence from Ugarit. In B. Eder and R. Pruzsinszky (eds), *Policies of Exchange: Political Systems and Modes of Interaction in the Aegean and the Near East in the 2nd Millennium B.C.E.* Oriental and European Archaeology 2: 85-96. Vienna: Österreichische Akademie der Wissenschaften.

MacGillivray, J.A.

1998   *Knossos: Pottery Groups of the Old Palace Period.* British School at Athens, Studies 5. London: British School at Athens.

McGovern, P.E.

1997   Wine of Egypt's golden age: an archaeochemical perspective. *Journal of Egyptian Archaeology* 83: 69-108.

1998   Wine for eternity. *Archaeology* 51(4): 28-34.

2000   *The Foreign Relations of the 'Hyksos': A Neutron Activation Study of Middle Bronze Age Pottery from the Eastern Mediterranean.* British Archaeological Reports, International Series 888. Oxford: Archaeopress.

2001   The origins of the tomb U-j Syro-Palestinian type jars as determined by neutron activation analysis. In U. Hartung (ed.), *Umm el-Qaab* II: *Importkeramik aus dem Friedhof U in Abydos (Umm el-Qaab) und die Beziehungen Ägyptens zu Vorderasien im 4. Jahrtausend v. Chr*, 407-416. Mainz: P. von Zabern.

2009   *Uncorking the Past: The Quest for Wine, Beer, and Other Alcoholic Beverages.* Berkeley: University of California Press.

McGovern, P.E., and G. Harbottle

1997   'Hyksos' trade connections beween Tell el-Dabʿa (Avaris) and the Levant: a Neutron Activation study of the Canaanite jar. In Eliezer D. Oren (ed.), *The Hyksos: New Historical and Archaeological Perspectives.* University Museum Monograph 96. University Museum Symposium Series 8: 141-157. Philadelphia: University Museum, University of Pennsylvania.

McGovern, P.E., A. Mirzoian and G.R. Hall

2009   Ancient Egyptian herbal wines. *Proceedings of the National Academy of Sciences of the United States of America* 106(18): 7361–7366.

McGovern, P. E., and G. R. Hall

2016   Charting a future course for organic residues analysis in archaeology. *Journal of Archaeological Method and Theory* 23: 592-622.

McNiven, I.J.

2003   Saltwater People: spiritscapes, maritime rituals and the archaeology of Australian indigenous seascapes. *World Archaeology* 35: 329-349.

Mączyńska, A.

2013   *Lower Egyptian Communities and Their Interactions with Southern Levant in the 4th Millennium BC.* Poznań, Poland: Poznań Archaeological Museum.

Maguire, L. C.

2009   *The Cypriot Pottery and its Circulation in the Levant.* Tell el-Dabʿa 21. Österreichische Akademie der Wissenschaften, Denkschriften der Gesamtakademie 51. Vienna: Österreichische Akademie der Wissenschaften.

Maier, F.-G., and V. Karageorghis

1984   *Paphos: History and Archaeology.* Nicosia: Leventis Foundation.

Manning, S. W.

1993   Prestige, distinction and competition: the anatomy of socio-economic complexity in 4th-2nd millennium B.C.E. Cyprus. *Bulletin of American Schools of Oriental Research* 292: 35-58.

1998   Tsaroukkas, Mycenaeans and Trade Project: preliminary report on the 1996-97 seasons. *Report of the Department of Antiquities, Cyprus*: 39-54.

2014a   A radiocarbon-based chronology for the Chalcolithic through Middle Bronze Age of Cyprus (as of AD 2012). In F. Höflmayer and R. Eichmann (eds), *Egypt and the Southern Levant in the Early Bronze Age.* Orient-Archäologie 31: 207-240. Rahden, Germany: Verlag Marie Leidorf.

2014b   Timings and gaps in the early history of Cyprus and its copper trade—what these might tell us. In J.M. Webb (ed.), *Structure, Measurement and Meaning: Insights into the Prehistory of Cyprus. Studies on Prehistoric Cyprus in Honour of David Frankel.* Studies in Mediterranean Archaeology 143: 23-41. Uppsala: Åström Editions.

Manning, S.W., and F.A. DeMita, Jr

1997   Cyprus, the Aegean and Maroni *Tsaroukkas*. In D. Christou (ed.), *Cyprus and the Aegean in Antiquity*, 103-142. Nicosia: Department of Antiquities, Cyprus.

Manning, S.W., D. Sewell and E. Herscher

2002   Late Cypriot IA maritime trade in action: underwater survey at Maroni *Tsarroukkas* and the contemporary east Mediterranean trading system. *Annual of the British School at Athens* 97: 97-162.

Manning, S.W., L. Crewe and D.A. Sewell

2006   Further light on early LC I connections at Maroni. In E. Czerny, I. Hein, H. Hunger, D. Melman and A. Schwab (eds), *Timelines. Studies in Honour of Manfred Bietak*, Volume 2. *Orientalia Lovaniensia Analecta* 149(2): 471-488. Leuven: Uitgeverij Peeters en Departement Oosterse Studies.

Manzo, A.

2012   Nubians and the others on the Red Sea: an update on the exotic ceramic materials from the Middle Kingdom harbour of Mersa/Wadi Gawasis, Red Sea, Egypt. In D.A. Agius, J.P. Cooper, A. Trakadas and C. Zazzaro (eds), *Navigated Spaces, Connected Places*. British Archaeological Reports, International Series 2346. British Foundation for the Study of Arabia Monographs 12: 47–58. Oxford: Archaeopress.

Maran, J.

2004   The spreading of objects and ideas in the Late Bronze Age eastern Mediterranean: two case examples from the Argolid of the 13th and 12th centuries B.C. *Bulletin of the American Schools of Oriental Research* 336: 11-30.

Marangou, A.

2002   *The Harbours and Ports of Cyprus*. Nicosia: Laiki Group Cultural Centre.

Marcus, E.

1995   A petrographic analysis of storage jars from Tel Nami, Israel: ceramic production and trade networks of the Middle Bronze Age II period (ca. 2000-1750 BC). In P. Vandiver, J. Druzik, J.L.G. Madrid, I. Freestone and G.S. Wheeler (eds), *Materials Issues in Art and Archaeology* 4. Materials Research Society Symposium, Proceedings 352: 597-604. Pittsburgh: Materials Research Society.

2002   Early seafaring and maritime activity in the southern Levant from prehistory through the third millennium BCE. In E.C.M. van den Brink and T. E. Levy (eds), *Egypt and the Levant: Interrelations from the 4th through the Early 3rd Millennium BC*, 403-417. London: Leicester University Press.

2006   Venice on the Nile? On the maritime character of Tell el Dabʿa/Avaris. In E. Czerny, I. Hein, H. Hunger, D. Melman and A. Schwab (eds), *Timelines. Studies in Honour of Manfred Bietak*. Volume 2. Orientalia Lovaniensia Analecta 149(2): 187-190. Leuven: Uitgeverij Peeters en Departement Oosterse Studies.

2007   Amenemhet II and the sea: maritime aspects of the Mit Rahina (Memphis) inscription. *Ägypten und Levante* 17: 137-190.

Marfoe, L.

1987   Cedar forest to silver mountain: social change and the development of long-distance trade in early Near Eastern societies. In M. Rowlands, M. Larsen and K. Kristiansen (eds), *Centre and Periphery in the Ancient World*, 25-35. Cambridge: Cambridge University Press.

Margariti, R. E.

1998   The Seytan Deresi Wreck and the Minoan Connection in the Eastern Aegean. Unpublished MA thesis, Department of Anthropology, Texas A&M University, College Station, Texas.

Márquez-Rowe, I.

1992   Summaries of Ugaritic texts and some new reading suggestions. *Ugarit-Forschungen* 24: 259-262.

Marriner, N.

2009   *Geoarchaeology of Lebanon's Ancient Harbours*. British Archaeological Reports, International Series 1953. Oxford: Archaeopress.

Marriner, N., C. Morhange, M. Boudagher-Fadel, M. Bourcier and P. Carbonel

2005   Geoarchaeology of Tyre's ancient harbour, Phoenicia. *Journal of Archaeological Science* 32: 1302-1327.

Marriner, N., C. Morhange, C. Doumet-Sehal and P. Carbonel

2006a   Geoscience rediscovers Phoenicia's buried harbors. *Geology* 34: 1-4.

Marriner, N., C. Morhange and C. Doumet-Sehal

2006b   Geoarchaeology of Sidon's ancient harbours, Phoenicia. *Journal of Archaeological Science* 33: 1514-1535.

Marriner, N., and C. Morhange

2007   Geoscience of ancient Mediterranean harbours. *Earth-Science Reviews* 80: 137-194.

Marriner, N., C. Morhange and N. Carayon

2008   Ancient Tyre and its harbours: 5,000 years of human-environment relations. *Journal of Archaeological Science* 35: 1281-1310.

Martin, M.A.S.

2008   Egyptians at Ashkelon? An assemblage of Egyptian and Egyptian-style pottery. *Ägypten und Levante* 18: 245-274.

2011   *Egyptian-Type Pottery in the Late Bronze Age Southern Levant*. Contributions to the Chronology of the Eastern Mediterranean 29. Denkschriften der Gesamtakademie 69. Vienna: Austrian Academy of Sciences.

Martin, R.

2016   The development of Canaanite and Phoenician Maritime Transport Containers and their role in reconstructing maritime exchange networks. In S. Demesticha and A.B. Knapp (eds), *Maritime Transport Containers in the Bronze–Iron Age Aegean and Eastern Mediterranean*. Studies in Mediterranean Archaeology and Literature, PB 183: 111-128. Uppsala, Sweden: Åströms Förlag.

Massa, M., and V. Şahoğlu

2015   The 4.2 ka BP climatic event in west and central Anatolia: combining palaeo-climatic proxies and archaeological data. In H. Meller, H.W. Arz, R. Jung und R. Risch (eds), *2200 BC—ein Klimasturz al Ursache für den Zerfall der Alten Welt?* Tagungen des Landesmuseum für Vorgeschichte Halle 12(1): 61-78. Halle, Germany: Landesmuseum für Vorgeschichte.

Matthäus, H.

2014   Ugarit, Zypern und die Ägäis: spätbronzezeitliche Kulturkontakte, Grundlagen und Wirkungen. *Ugarit-Forschungen* 45: 413-472.

Mazar, A.

1988   A note on Canaanite jars from Enkomi. *Israel Exploration Journal* 38: 224-226.

Mee, C.

2008   Mycenaean Greece, the Aegean and beyond. In C. Shelmerdine (ed.), *The Cambridge Companion to the Aegean Bronze Age*, 362-386. Cambridge: Cambridge University Press.

Meller, H., H.W. Arz, R. Jung und R. Risch (eds)

2015   *2200 BC — ein Klimasturz al Ursache für den Zerfall der Alten Welt?* Tagungen des Landesmuseum für Vorgeschichte Halle 12. Halle, Germany: Landesmuseum für Vorgeschichte.

Mellink, M.J.

1986   The Early Bronze Age in west Anatolia: Aegean and Asiatic correlations. In G. Cadogan (ed.), *The End of the Early Bronze Age in the Aegean*. Cincinnati Classical Studies n.s. 6: 139-152. Leiden: Brill.

1991   Anatolian contacts with Chalcolithic Cyprus. *Bulletin of the American Schools of Oriental Research* 282-283: 167-175.

1993   The Anatolian south coast in the Early Bronze Age: the Cilician perspective. In M. Frangipane, H. Hauptmann, M. Liverani, P. Matthiae and M. Mellink (eds), *Between the Rivers and Over the Mountains. Archaeologica Anatolica et Mesopotamica, Alba Palmieri Dedicata*, 495-508. Rome: Università di Roma 'La Sapienza'.

Meriç, R., and P. A. Mountjoy

2002   Mycenaean pottery from Bademgediği Tepe (Puranda) in Ionia: a preliminary report. *Istanbuler Mitteilungen* 52: 79–98.

Merrillees, R.S.

1974   *Trade and Transcendance in the Bronze Age Levant*. Studies in Mediterranean Archaeology 39. Göteborg, Sweden: P. Åström's Förlag.

1984   Ambelikou-*Aletri*: a preliminary report. *Report of the Department of Antiquities, Cyprus*: 1-13.

1992   The government of Cyprus in the Late Bronze Age. In P. Åström (ed.), *Acta Cypria* 3. Studies in Mediterranean Archaeology and Literature, Pocketbook 120: 310-329. Jonsered: P. Åström's Förlag.

2009   The stone vases of the Philia culture from Vasilia: Cypriot, Egyptian or other? In D. Michaelides, V. Kassianidou and R. Merrillees (eds), *Egypt and Cyprus in Antiquity*, 23-28. Oxford: Oxbow.

Michail, M.

2015   Ship graffiti in context: a preliminary study of Cypriot patterns. In I. Hadjikyriakos and M. Gaia Trentin (eds), *Cypriot Cultural Details: Proceedings of the 10th Post Graduate Cypriot Archaeology Conference*, 41-64. Oxford: Oxbow.

Middleton, G.D.

2015   Telling stories: the Mycenaean origin of the Philistines. *Oxford Journal of Archaeology* 34: 45–65.

Millet, N.B.

1987   The first appearance of the loose-footed square-sail rig in the Mediterranean. *Journal of the Society for the Study of Egyptian Antiquities* 17: 89-91.

Mills, J.S., and R. White

1989   The identity of the resins from the Late Bronze Age shipwreck at Ulu Burun (Kaş). *Archaeometry* 31: 37-44.

Molloy, B.P.C.

2016   Nought may endure but mutability: eclectic encounters and material change in the 13th to 11th centuries BC Aegean. In B.P.C. Molloy (ed.), *Of Odysseys and Oddities: Scales and Modes of Interaction between Prehistoric Aegean Societies and Their Neighbours*. Sheffield Studies in Aegean Archaeology 10: 343-383. Oxford: Oxbow.

Mommsen, H., T. Beier and A. Hein

2002   A complete chemical grouping of the Berkeley Neutron Activation Analysis data on Mycenaean pottery. *Journal of Archaeological Science* 29(6): 613-637.

Monroe, C.

2007   Vessel volumetrics and the myth of the Cyclopean Bronze Age ship. *Journal of the Economic and Social History of the Orient* 50: 1-18.

2009   *Scales of Fate: Trade, Tradition, and Transformation in the Eastern Mediterranean*. Alter Orient und Altes Testament 357. Münster: Ugarit-Verlag.

2011   'From luxuries to anxieties': a liminal view of the Late Bronze Age world-system. In T.C. Wilkinson, S. Sherratt and J. Bennett (eds), *Interweaving Worlds: Systemic Interactions in Eurasia, 7th to the 1st Millennia BC*, 87-99. Oxford: Oxbow.

2015   Tangled up in blue: material and other relations of exchange in the Late Bronze Age world. In T. Howe (ed.), *Traders in the Ancient Mediterranean*. Publications of the Association of Ancient Historians 11: 7-46. Chicago: Ares Publishers.

2016   Measure for 'measure': connecting text to material culture through Late Bronze Age shipping jars. In S. Demesticha and A.B. Knapp (eds), *Maritime Transport Containers in the Bronze–Iron Age Aegean and Eastern Mediterranean*. Studies in Mediterranean Archaeology and Literature, PB 183: 79-96. Uppsala: Åströms Förlag.

Moorey, P.R.S.

1990   From Gulf to Delta in the fourth millennium: the Syrian connection. In A. Eitan, R. Gophna and M. Kochavi (eds), *Ruth Amiran Volume*. Eretz Israel 21: 62*-69*. Jerusalem: Israel Exploration Society.

Moran, W.L.

1992   *The Amarna Letters*. Baltimore: Johns Hopkins University Press.

Moreno García, J.C.

2017   Trade and power in ancient Egypt: Middle Egypt in the late third/early second millennium BC. *Journal of Archaeological Research* 25: 87-132.

Morgan, L.

1988   *The Miniature Wall Paintings of Thera. A Study in Aegean Culture and Iconography*. Cambridge Classical Studies 19. Cambridge: Cambridge University Press.

2007   Paintings, harbors, and intercultural relations. In P.P. Betancourt, M.C. Nelson and E.H. Williams (eds), *Krinoi kai Limenai: Studies in Honor of Joseph and Maria Shaw*, 117-129. Philadelphia: Institute for Aegean Prehistory Academic Press.

Morhange, C.

1988-89 Étude géomorphologique du littoral de Byblos: résultats ed la mission de terrain de 1998. *Bulletin d'archéologie et d'architecure Libanaises* 3: 261-265.

Morhange, C., J.-P. Goiran, M. Bourcier, P. Carbonel, J. Le Campion, M.-M. Rouchy and M. Yon

2000   Recent Holocene palaeo-environment evolution and coastline changes of Kition, Larnaca, Cyprus. *Marine Geology* 170: 205-230.

Morhange, C., M.H. Taha, J.-B. Humbert and N. Marriner

2005   Human settlement and coastal change in Gaza since the Bronze Age. *Méditerranée – Journal of Mediterranean Geography* 104: 75-78.

Morillo, A., C. Fernández Ochoa and J. Salida Domínguez

2016   Hispania and the Atlantic route in Roman times: new approaches to ports and trade. *Oxford Journal of Archaeology* 35: 267-284.

Morris, E.F.

2005   *The Architecture of Imperialism: Military Bases and the Evolution of Foreign Policy in Egypt's New Kingdom*. Leiden: Brill.

Morris, I.

2003   Mediterraneanization. *Mediterranean Historical Review* 18(2): 30-55.

Morrison, J.S., and R.T. Williams

1968   *Greek Oared Ships 900-322 B.C.* Cambridge: Cambridge University Press.

Morton J.

2001   *The Role of the Physical Environment in Ancient Greek Seafaring*. Mnemosyne Supplements. History and Archaeology of Classical Antiquity 213. Leiden: Brill.

Mountjoy, P.A.

2005   Mycenaean connections with the Near East in LH IIIC: ships and sea peoples. In R. Laffineur and E. Greco (eds), *Emporia: Aegeans in the Central and Eastern Mediterranean*. Aegaeum 25 (1): 423-427. Liège, Austin: Université de Liège, University of Texas at Austin.

2006   Mycenaean pictorial pottery from Anatolia in the transitional LH IIIB2-LH
        IIIC early and the LH IIIC phases. In E. Rystedt and B. Wells (eds), *Pictorial
        Pursuits: Figurative Painting on Mycenaean and Geometric Pottery*. Skrifter
        Utgivna av Svenska Insitutet i Athen 53: 107-121. Stockholm: Svenska
        Insitutet i Athen.

2011   A Bronze Age ship from Ashkelon with particular reference to the Bronze Age
        ship from Bademgediği Tepe. *American Journal of Archaeology* 115: 483-488.

Mountjoy, P.A., and H. Mommsen

2015   Neutron Activation Analysis of Aegean-style IIIC pottery from 11 Cypriot
        and various Near Eastern sites. *Ägypten und Levante* 25: 421-508.

Muhly, J.D.

1982   The nature of trade in the Late Bronze Age eastern Mediterranean: the
        organization of the metals' trade and the role of Cyprus. In J.D. Muhly, R.
        Maddin and V. Karageorghis (eds), *Early Metallurgy in Cyprus, 4000-500 BC*,
        251-266. Nicosia: Pierides Foundation.

2011   Archaeometry and shipwrecks: a review article. *Expedition* 53(1): 36-44.

Muhly, J.D., T.S. Wheeler and R. Maddin

1977   The Cape Gelidonya shipwreck and the Bronze Age metals trade in the
        eastern Mediterranean. *Journal of Field Archaeology* 4: 353-362.

Murray, M.A. (with N. Boulton and C. Heron)

2000   Viticulture and wine production. In P.T. Nicholson and I. Shaw (eds),
        Ancient Egyptian Materials and Technology, 577-608. Cambridge: Cambridge
        University Press.

Mylona, D.

2003   Archaeological fish remains in Greece: general trends of the research and a
        gazetteer of sites. In E. Kotzabopoulou, Y. Hamilakis, P. Halstead, C. Gamble
        and P. Elefanti (eds), *Zooarchaeology in Greece: Recent Advances*. British School
        at Athens, Studies 9: 193–200. London: British School at Athens.

2014   Aquatic animal resources in prehistoric Aegean, Greece. *Journal of Biological
        Research–Thessaloniki* 21: 2-11. [https://doi.org/10.1186/2241-5793-21-2]

2016   On fish bones, seashells, fishermen and seaside living at Late Minoan IB
        Mochlos. *Kentro* 19: 1-5.

Nakassis, D., M.L. Galaty and W.A. Parkinson

2016   Reciprocity in Aegean palatial societies: gifts, debt, and the foundations of
        economic exchange. *Journal of Mediterranean Archaeology* 29: 61-132.

Nelson, H.H.

1929   The epigraphic survey of the Great Temple of Medinet Habu (seasons 1924-25
        to 1927-28). In *Medinet Habu 1924–28*. Oriental Institute Communications
        5: 1-36. Chicago: University of Chicago Press.

Nelson, H.H., W.F. Edgerton, C. Ransom Wiliams and J.A. Wilson

1930   *Medinet Habu* I. *Earlier Historical Records of Ramses III*. Oriental Institute
        Publicatons 8. Chicago: University of Chicago Press.

Newberry, P.E.

1893   *Beni Hassan*. Part 2. London: Kegan Paul, Trench and Trübner.

Nibbi, A.

1994   A group of stone anchors from Mirgissa on the Upper Nile. *International Journal of Nautical Archaeology* 21: 259-267.

Niemeier, W.-D.

2005   Minoans, Mycenaeans, Hittites and Ionians in western Asia Minor: new excavations in Bronze Age Miletus-Millawanda. In A. Villings (ed.), *The Greeks in the East*. British Museum Research Publication 157: 1-36. London: The British Museum.

Nikolaou, K., and H.W. Catling

1968   Composite anchors in Late Bronze Age Cyprus. *Antiquity* 42: 225-229.

Nougayrol, J.

1955   *Le Palais Royal d'Ugarit* 3. Mission de Ras Shamra 6. Paris: Klincksieck.

1956   *Le Palais Royal d'Ugarit* 4. Mission de Ras Shamra 9. Paris: Klincksieck.

1970   *Le Palais Royal d'Ugarit* 6. Mission de Ras Shamra 12. Paris: Klincksieck.

Nougayrol, J., E. Laroche, C. Virolleaud and C.F.A. Schaeffer

1968   *Ugaritica* 5. Mission de Ras Shamra 16. Paris: P. Geuthner.

Nowicki, K.

2000   *Defensible Sites in Crete c.1200-800 BC (LM IIIB/IIIC through Early Geometric)*. Aegaeum 21. Liège: Université de Liège.

Öbrink, U.

1979   *Excavations in Area 22, 1971-1973 and 1975-1978*. Hala Sultan Tekke 5. Studies in Mediterranean Archaeology 45.5. Göteborg: P. Åström's Förlag.

O'Connor, D.

1995   The earliest royal boat graves. *Egyptian Archaeology* 6: 3-7.

2000   The Sea Peoples and the Egyptian sources. In E.D. Oren (ed.), *The Sea Peoples and Their World: A Reassessment*. University Museum Monograph 108. University Museum Symposium Series 11: 85-102. Philadelphia: University Museum, University of Pennsylvania.

Oleson, J.P.

2014   The evolution of harbor engineering in the ancient Mediterranean world. In S. Ladstätter, F. Pirson and T. Schmidts (eds), *Harbors and Harbor Cities in the Eastern Mediterranean from Antiquity to the Byzantine Period: Recent Discoveries and Current Approaches*. Byzas 19: 509-522. Istanbul: Ege Yayinlari.

Oller, G.H.

1989   The inscription of Idrimi: a pseudo-autobiography? In H. Behrens, D.M. Loding and M.T. Roth (eds), *Studies Presented to A. Sjoberg on the Occasion of His 65th Birthday*. Occasional Publications of the Samuel Noah Kramer Fund 11: 411-417. Philadelphia: University of Pennsylvania Press.

Olsen, B., M. Shanks, T. Webmoor and C. Witmore

2012   *Archaeology: The Discipline of Things*. Berkeley: University of California Press.

Oren, E.D.

1997   The 'Kingdom of Sharuhen' and the Hyksos kingdom. In E.D. Oren (ed.), *The Hyksos: New Historical and Archaeological Perspectives*. University Museum Monograph 96. University Museum Symposium Series 8: 253-283. Philadelphia: University Museum, University of Pennsylvania.

Oren, E.D., and Y. Yekutieli

1992   Taur Ikhbeineh: earliest evidence for Egyptian interconnections. In E.C.M. van den Brink (ed.), *The Nile Delta in Transition: 4th-3rd Millennium BC*, 361-384. Tel Aviv: Edwin van den Brink.

Ormerod, H.A.

1924   *Piracy in the Ancient World: An Essay in Mediterranean History*. Liverpool: Liverpool University Press.

Orton C., P. Tyers and A. Vince

1993   *Pottery in Archaeology*. Cambridge: Cambridge University Press.

Otten, H.

1963   Neue Quellung zum Ausklang des hethitischen Reiches. *Mitteilungen der Deutschen Orient-Gesellschaft* 94: 1-23.

1969   *Sprachliche Stellung und Datierung des Madduwatta-Textes*. Studien zu den Boğazköy-Texten 11. Wiesbaden: Harrassowitz.

Ownby, M.

2010   Canaanite Jars from Memphis as Evidence for Trade and Political Relationships in the Middle Bronze Age. Unpublished PhD thesis, Department of Archaeology, Cambridge University, UK.

2012   The importance of imports: petrographic analysis of Levantine pottery jars in Egypt. *Journal of Ancient Egyptian Interconnections* 3(4): 23-29.

Ownby, M., and J. Bourriau

2009   The movement of Middle Bronze Age transport jars: a provenance study based on petrographic and chemical analysis of Canaanite jars from Memphis, Egypt. In P.S. Quinn (ed.), *Interpreting Silent Artefacts: Petrographic Approaches to Archaeological Ceramics*, 173-188. Oxford: Archaeopress.

Ownby, M., and M.V. Smith

2011   The impact of changing political situations on trade between Egypt and the Near East: a provenance study of Canaanite jars from Memphis, Egypt. In K. Duistermaat and I. Regulski (eds), *Intercultural Contacts in the Ancient Mediterranean*. Orientalia Lovaniensia Analecta 202: 267-284. Louvain: Peeters.

Ownby, M., H. Franzmeier, S. Laemmel and E. Pusch

2014   Late Bronze Age imports at Qantir: petrographic and contextual analysis of fabric groups. *Journal of Ancient Egyptian Interconnections* 6(3): 11-21.

Palaima, T.G., P.P. Betancourt and G.H. Meyer

1984   An inscribed stirrup jar of Cretan origin from Bamboula, Cyprus. *Kadmos* 23: 65-73.

Panagiotopoulos, D.

2011   The stirring sea: conceptualising transculturality in the Late Bronze Age eastern Mediterranean. In K. Duistermaat and I. Regulski (eds), *Intercultural Contacts in the Ancient Mediterranean*. Orientalia Lovaniensia Analecta 202: 31-51. Louvain: Peeters.

2012   Encountering the foreign. (De-)constructing alterity in the archaeologies of the Bronze Age Mediterranean. In J. Maran and P. Stockhammer (eds), *Materiality and Social Practice: Transformative Capacities of Intercultural Encounters*, 51-60. Oxford: Oxbow.

Papageorgiou, D.

2009   The marine environment and its influence on seafaring and maritime routes in the prehistoric Aegean. *European Journal of Archaeology* 11: 199-222.

Pardee, D.

1975   The Ugaritic text 2106:10-18 — a bottomry loan? *Journal of the American Oriental Society* 95: 612-619.

2003   Ugaritic letters. In W. W. Hallo (ed.), *The Context of Scripture* III. *Archival Documents from the Biblical World*, 87-116. Leiden, Boston: Brill.

Parker, A.J.

1981   Stratification and contamination in ancient Mediterranean shipwrecks. *International Journal of Nautical Archaeology and Underwater Exploration* 10: 309-335.

1990   The pattern of commerce as evidence by shipwrecks. In T. Hackens and M. Miró (eds), *Le commerce maritime romain en Méditerranée occidentale*. PACT 27: 147-168. Strasbourg, Rixensart: Conseil de l'Europe, PACT Belgium.

1992   *Ancient Shipwrecks of the Mediterranean and the Roman Provinces*. British Archaeological Reports, International Series 580. Oxford: British Archaeological Reports.

2001   Maritime landscapes. *Landscapes* 1: 22-41.

Parker, B.J.

2000   The earliest known reference to the Ionians in the cuneiform sources. *Ancient History Bulletin* 14(3): 69-77.

Parr, P.J.

1973   The origin of the Canaanite jar. In D.E. Strong (ed.), *Archaeologial Theory and Practice: Festschrift W.F. Grimes*, 173-181. London, New York: Seminar Press.

Patch, D.C., and C.W. Haldane

1990   *The Pharaoh's Boat at the Carnegie*. Pittsburgh: Carnegie Museum of Natural History.

Peachey, C.

1997   Cape Gelidonya wreck. In J.P. Delgado (ed.), *Encyclopaedia of Underwater and Maritime Archaeology*, 84-86. London: British Museum Press.

Pearlman, D.

1985   Kalavassos village, tomb 51: tomb of an unknown soldier. *Report of the Department of Antiquities, Cyprus*: 164-179.

Pedersen, R.

2011   The maritime archaeological survey at Tell el-Burak and nearby environs. *Bulletin d'archéologie et d'architecure Libanaises* 15: 281-290.

Pedrazzi, T.

2007   *Le giare da conservazione e trasporto del Levante: Uno studio archeologico dell'economia fra Bronzo Tardo II e Ferro I (ca.1400–900 A.C.)*. Pisa: Edizione ETS.

2010   Globalization versus regionalism: LB II/Iron I transition in coastal Syria from the storage jars point of view. In F. Venturi (ed.), *Societies in Transition. Evolutionary Processes in the Northern Levant between Late Bronze Age II and Early Iron Age*, 53-64. Bologna: IBS.

2016   Canaanite jars and the maritime trade network in the northern Levant during the transition from the Late Bronze to the early Iron Age. In S. Demesticha and A.B. Knapp (eds), *Maritime Transport Containers in the Bronze–Iron Age Aegean and Eastern Mediterranean*. Studies in Mediterranean Archaeology and Literature, PB 183: 57-77. Uppsala, Sweden: Åströms Förlag.

Peltenburg, E.J.

1986   Ramesside Egypt and Cyprus. In V. Karageorghis (ed.), *Cyprus between the Orient and the Occident*, 149-179. Nicosia: Department of Antiquities, Cyprus.

1991   Kissonerga-*Mosphilia*: a major Chalcolithic site in Cyprus. *Bulletin of the American Schools of Oriental Research* 282-83: 17-35.

1995   Kissonerga in Cyprus and the appearance of faience in the east Mediterranean. In S. Bourke and J.-P. Descoeudres (eds), *Trade, Contact, and the Movement of People in the Eastern Mediterranean*. Mediterranean Archaeology, Supplement 3: 31-41. Sydney: Department of Archaeology, University of Sydney.

2007   East Mediterranean interactions in the 3rd millennium BC. In S. Antoniadou and A. Pace (eds), *Mediterranean Crossroads*, 141-161. Athens, Oxford: Pierides Foundation, Oxbow Books.

2008   Nitovikla and Tell el-Burak: Cypriot mid-second millennium B.C. forts in a Levantine context. *Report of the Department of Antiquities, Cyprus*: 145-157.

2012a   Text meets material culture in Late Bronze Age Cyprus. In A. Georgiou (ed.), *Cyprus: An Island Culture. Society and Social Relations from the Bronze Age to the Venetian Period*, 1-23. Oxford: Oxbow.

2012b   King Kushmeshusha and the decentralised political structure of Late Bronze Age Cyprus. In G. Cadogan, M. Iacovou, K. Kopaka and J. Whitley (eds), *Parallel Lives: Ancient Island Societies in Crete and Cyprus*. British School at Athens, Studies 20: 345-351. London: British School at Athens.

Peltier, W.R., and R.G. Fairbanks

2006   Global glacial ice volume and Last Glacial Maximum duration from an extended Barbados sea level record. *Quaternary Science Reviews* 25: 3322-3327.

Peña, J.T.

2007   *Roman Pottery in the Archaeological Record*. Cambridge: Cambridge University Press.

Peters, E., C. Roberts and P.P. Creasman

2017   Recent research on the "Carnegie Boat" from Dahshur, Egypt. *Journal of Ancient Egyptian Interconnections* 16: 99-103.

Phelps, W., Y. Lolos and Y. Vichos (eds)

1999   *The Point Iria Wreck: Interconnections in the Mediterranean ca. 1200 BC*. Athens: Hellenic Institute of Marine Archaeology.

Philip, G., P.W. Clogg, D. Dungworth and S. Stos

2003   Copper metallurgy in the Jordan Valley from the third to the first millennia BC: chemical, metallographic and lead isotope analysis of artefacts from Pella. *Levant* 35: 71-100.

Phillips, J.

2008   *Aegyptiaca on the Island of Crete in their Chronological Context: A Critical Review*. Contributions to the Chronology of the Eastern Mediterranean 18. 2 Volumes. Vienna: Österreichisches Akademie der Wissenschaften.

Phillips, T.

2003   Seascapes and landscapes in Orkney and northern Scotland. *World Archaeology* 35: 371-384.

Pilides, D.

2000   *Pithoi of the Late Bronze Age in Cyprus*. Nicosia: Department of Antiquities, Cyprus.

Pirazzoli, P.A.

2005   A review of possible eustatic, isostatic and tectonic contributions in eight late-Holocene relative sea-level histories from the Mediterranean area. *Quaternary Science Reviews* 24: 1989–2001.

Pomey, P.

2011   Defining a ship: architecture, function and human space. In A. Catsambis, B. Ford and D. L. Hamilton (eds), *The Oxford Handbook of Maritime Archaeology*, 25-46. Oxford: Oxford University Press.

Porada, E.

1948   The cylinder seal from Tell el-Dab'a. *American Journal of Archaeology* 88: 485-488.

Porat, N., and Y. Goren

2002   Petrography of the Naqada IIIa Canaanite pottery from tomb U-j in Abydos. In E.C.M. van den Brink and T. E. Levy (eds), *Egypt and the Levant: Interrelations from the 4th through the Early 3rd Millennium BC*, 252-270. London: Leicester University Press.

Portugali, Y., and A. B. Knapp

1985   Cyprus and the Aegean: a spatial analysis of interaction in the 17th-14th centuries B.C. In A.B. Knapp and T. Stech (eds), *Prehistoric Production and Exchange: The Aegean and the Eastern Mediterranean*. UCLA Institute of Archaeology, Monograph 25: 44-78. Los Angeles: UCLA Institute of Archaeology.

Poursat, J.-C, and C. Knappett

2006   Minoan amphoras and inter-regional exchange: evidence from Malia. In T. Detorakis and A. Kalokerinos (eds), *Proceedings of the Ninth International Cretological Congress (Elounda, 2001)*, 153-163. Heraklion, Crete: Society of Cretan Historical Studies.

Poursat, J.-C, and M. Loubet

2005   Métallurgie et contacts extérieurs à Malia (Crète) au Minoen Moyen II: remarques sur une série d'analyses isotopiques du plomb. In R. Laffineur and E. Greco (eds), *Emporia. Aegeans in the Central and Eastern Mediterranean*. Aegaeum 25: 117-121. Liège, Austin: Université de Liège, University of Texas at Austin.

Powell, J.

1996   *Fishing in the Prehistoric Aegean*. Studies in Mediterranean Archaeology and Literature, Pocket-book 137. Jonsered: P. Åström's Förlag.

Prag, K.

1986   Byblos and Egypt in the fourth millennium BC. *Levant* 18: 59-74.

Pratt, C.E.

2016   The rise and fall of the transport stirrup jar in the Late Bronze Age Aegean. *American Journal of Archaeology* 120: 27-66.

Pritchard, J.B.

1969   *Ancient Near Eastern Texts Relating to the Old Testament.* (3rd ed.) Princeton, New Jersey: Princeton University Press.

Pryor, J.H.

1988   *Geography, Technology, and War: Studies in the Maritime History of the Mediterranean, 649-1571.* Cambridge: Cambridge University Press.

Pulak, C.

1988   The Bronze Age shipwreck at Ulu Burun, Turkey: 1985 campaign. *American Journal of Archaeology* 92: 1-37.

1998   The Uluburun shipwreck: an overview. *International Journal of Nautical Archaeology* 27: 188-224.

2000   The balance weights from the Late Bronze Age shipwreck at Uluburn. In C.F. Pare (ed.), *Metals Make the World Go Round: The Supply and Circulation of Metals in Bronze Age Europe*, 247-266. Oxford: Oxbow Books.

2000   The copper and tin ingots from the Late Bronze Age shipwreck at Uluburn. In Ü. Yalçin (ed.), *Anatolian Metal* I. Der Anschnitt, Beiheft 13: 137-157. Bochum: Deutsches Bergbau-Museum.

2001   The cargo of the Uluburun shipwreck and evidence for trade with the Aegean and beyond. In L. Bonfante and V. Karageorghis (eds), *Italy and Cyprus in Antiquity, 1500-450 BC*, 13-60. Nicosia: Leventis Foundation.

2005   Who were the Mycenaeans aboard the Uluburun ship? In R. Laffineur and E. Greco (eds), *Emporia: Aegeans in the Central and Eastern Mediterranean.* Aegaeum 25 (1): 295-310. Liège, Austin: Université de Liège, University of Texas at Austin.

2008   The Uluburun shipwreck and Late Bronze Age trade. In J. Aruz, K. Benzel and J.M. Evans (eds), *Beyond Babylon: Art, Trade, and Diplomacy in the Second Millennium BC*, 289-310. New York, New Haven and London: Metropolitan Museum of Art, Yale University Press.

2009   The Uluburun tin ingots and the shipment of tin by sea in the Late Bronze Age Mediterranean. *Tübaar* 12: 189-207.

2010   Uluburun shipwreck. In E.H. Cline (ed.), *The Oxford Handbook of the Bronze Age Aegean*, 862-876. Oxford: Oxford University Press.

Pulak, C., and E. Rogers

1994   The 1993-1994 Turkish shipwreck surveys. *Institute of Nautical Archaeology Quarterly* 21(4): 17-21.

Pungetti, G.

2012   Islands, culture, landscape and seascape. *Journal of Marine and Island Cultures* 1(2): 51-54.

Purcell, N.

2014   The ancient Mediterranean. In P. Horden and S. Kinoshita (eds), *A Companion to Mediterranean History*, 60-76. Chichester: John Wiley and Sons.

Quack, J.F.

1996   Kft3w and 'l3ssy. *Ägypten und Levante* 6: 75–81.

Raban, A.

1980   The Commercial Jar in the Ancient Near East: Its Evidence for Interconnections amongst the Biblical Lands. Unpublished PhD dissertation, Hebrew University, Jerusalem. (in Hebrew, with English summary)

1985   The ancient harbours of Israel in Biblical times (from the Neolithic period to the end of the Iron Age). In A. Raban (ed.), *Harbour Archaeology*. British Archaeological Reports, International Series S257: 11-44. Oxford: British Archaeological Reports.

1987   The harbor of the Sea Peoples at Dor. *Biblical Archaeologist* 50: 118-126.

1991   The port city of Akko in the MBII. *Michmanim* 5: 17*-34*.

1993   The Sea Peoples port at Dor. In A. Biran and J. Aviram (eds), *Biblical Archaeology Today* 1990, 641-643. Jerusalem: Israel Exploration Society, Israel Academy of Sciences and Humanities.

1995   The heritage of ancient harbour engineering in Cyprus and the Levant. In V. Karageorghis and D. Michaelides (eds), *Cyprus and the Sea*, 139-190. Nicosia: University of Cyprus, Cyprus Ports Authority.

1998   Near Eastern harbors: thirteenth-seventh centuries BCE. In S. Gitin, A. Mazar and E. Stern (eds), *Mediterranean Peoples in Transition: Thirteenth to Early Tenth Centuries BCE*, 428-438. Jerusalem: Israel Exploration Society.

Raban, A., and Y. Tur-Caspa

2008   Underwater survey, 1985-1987. In L.E. Stager, J.D Schloen and D.M. Master (eds), *Ashkelon* I. *Introduction and Overview (1985-2006)*, 67-96. Winona Lake, Indiana: Eisenbrauns.

Rahmstorf, L.

2016   Emerging economic complexity in the Aegean and western Anatolia during earlier third millennium BC. In B.P.C. Molloy (ed.), *Of Odysseys and Oddities: Scales and Modes of Interaction between Prehistoric Aegean Societies and Their Neighbours*. Sheffield Studies in Aegean Archaeology 10: 225-276. Oxford: Oxbow.

Rainey, A.F.

1963   Business agents at Ugarit. *Israel Exploration Journal* 13: 313-321.

Rauh, N.

1997   Who were the Cilician pirates? In S. Swiny, R. Hohlfelder and H.W. Swiny (eds), *Res Maritimae: Cyprus and the Eastern Mediterranean from Prehistory through the Roman Period*. Cyprus American Archaeological Research Institute, Monograph 1: 263-283. Atlanta, Georgia: ASOR/Scholars Press.

Rauh, N., M. Dillon and R. Rothaus

2013   Anchors, amphoras, and ashlar masonry: new evidence for the Cilician pirates. In M. C. Hoff and R. F. Townshend (eds), *Rough Cilicia: New Historical and Archaeological Approaches*, 59-86. Oxford: Oxbow Books.

Raymond, A.

2005   Importing culture at Miletus: Minoans and Anatolians at Middle Bronze Age Miletus. In R. Laffineur and E. Greco (eds), *Emporia: Aegeans in the Central and Eastern Mediterranean*. Aegaeum 25 (1): 185-191. Liège, Austin: Université de Liège, University of Texas at Austin.

Redford, D.B.

1997   Textual sources for the Hyksos period. In E.D. Oren (ed.), *The Hyksos: New Historical and Archaeological Perspectives*. University Museum Monograph 96. University Museum Symposium Series 8: 1-44. Philadelphia: University Museum, University of Pennsylvania.

2000   Egypt and western Asia in the late New Kingdom: an overview. In E.D. Oren (ed.), *The Sea Peoples and Their World: A Reassessment*. University Museum Monograph 108. University Museum Symposium Series 11: 1-20. Philadelphia: University Museum, University of Pennsylvania.

Rediker, M.

1987   *Between the Devil and the Deep Blue Sea: Merchants, Seamen, Pirates, and the Anglo-American Maritime World 1700-1750*. Cambridge: Cambridge University Press.

Reese, D.S., H.K. Mienis and F.R. Woodward

1986   On the trade of shells and fish from the Nile River. *Bulletin of the American Schools of Oriental Research* 264: 79-84.

Reese, D., and M.J. Rose

2002   Organic remains from the island and adjacent areas. In D. White, *Marsa Matruh* II: *The Objects*. Institute for Aegean Prehistory, Monograph 2: 73-108. Philadelphia: Institute for Aegean Prehistory Academic Press.

Reisner, G. A.

1913   *Models of Ships and Boats*. Cairo: Institut français d'archéologie orientale.

Renfrew, A.C.

2003   *Figuring it Out: The Parallel Visions of Artists and Archaeologists*. London: Thames and Hudson.

Renson, V., D. Ben-Shlomo, J. Coenaerts, K. Charbit-Nataf, M. Samaes, N. Mattielli, K. Nys and Ph. Claeys

2014   Coupling lead isotope analysis and petrography to characterize fabrics of storage and trade containers from Hala Sultan Tekke (Cyprus). *Archaeometry* 56: 261–278.

Rice, P.M.

2015   *Pottery Analysis: A Sourcebook*. Second edition. Chicago: University of Chicago Press.

Rich, S., S.W. Manning, P. Degryse, F. Vanhaecke, K. Latruwe and K. Van Lerberghe

2016   To put a cedar ship in a bottle: dendroprovenancing three ancient East Mediterranean watercraft with the 87Sr/86Sr isotope ratio. *Journal of Archaeological Science: Reports* 9: 514-521.

Riis, P.J.,

1948   *Les cimetières à crémation*. Hama, fouilles et recherches 1931-1938, vol. 2:3. Copenhagen: Nordisk Verlag.

Riis, P.J., J. Jensen, M.L. Buhl and B. Otzen

1995   *Sukas* X: *The Bronze and Early Iron Age Remains at the Southern Harbour.* Publications of the Carlsberg Expedition to Phoenicia 12. Copenhagen: Det Kongelige Danske Videnskarbernes Selskab.

Rizkana, I., and J. Seeher

1987   *Maadi* I: *The Pottery of the Predynastic Settlement.* Deutsches Archaeologisches Institut, Abteilung Kairo, Archaeologische Veroffentlichungen 64. Mainz: Philipp von Zabern.

1989   *Maadi* III: *The Non-Lithic Small Finds and the Structural Remains of the Predynastic Settlement.* Deutsches Archaeologisches Institut, Abteilung Kairo, Archaeologische Veroffentlichungen 80. Mainz: Philipp von Zabern.

Robb, J.E., and R.H. Farr

2005   Substances in motion: Neolithic Mediterranean 'trade'. In E. Blake and A.B. Knapp (eds), *The Archaeology of Mediterranean Prehistory*, 24-45. Oxford: Blackwell.

Roberts, N., W.J. Eastwood, C. Kuzucuoğlu, G. Fiorentino and V. Caracuta

2011   Climatic, vegetation and cultural change in the eastern Mediterranean during the mid-Holocene environmental transition. *The Holocene* 21: 147-162.

Roberts, R.G.

2009   Identity, choice, and the Year 8 reliefs of Ramesses III at Medinet Habu. In C. Bachhuber and R. G. Roberts (eds), *Forces of Transformation: The End of the Bronze Age in the Mediterranean.* BANEA Publication Series 1: 60-68. Oxford: Oxbow.

2014   Changes in perceptions of the 'other' and expressions of Egyptian self-identity in the Late Bronze Age. In A.B. Knapp and P. van Dommelen (eds), *The Cambridge Prehistory of the Bronze and Iron Age Mediterranean*, 352-366. New York: Cambridge University Press.

Robertson, B.M.

1999   The Chronology of the Middle Bronze Age Tombs at Tell el Ajjul. Unpublished PhD dissertation, Department of Anthropology, University of Utah, Salt Lake City.

Rogers, A.

2013   Social archaeological approaches in port and harbour studies. *Journal of Maritime Archaeology* 8: 181-196.

Routledge, B., and K. McGeough

2009   Just what collapsed? A network perspective on 'palatial' and 'private' trade at Ugarit. In C. Bachhuber and R. G. Roberts (eds), *Forces of Transformation: The End of the Bronze Age in the Mediterranean.* BANEA Publication Series 1: 22-29. Oxford: Oxbow.

Runnels, C.

2014   Early Palaeolithic on the Greek Islands? *Journal of Mediterranean Archaeology* 27: 211-230.

Runnels, C., C. DiGregorio, K.W. Wegmann, S.F. Gallen, T.F. Strasser and E. Panagopoulou

2014   Lower Palaeolithic artifacts from Plakias, Crete: implications for hominin dispersals. *Eurasian Prehistory* 11: 129-152.

Russell, A.

2017   Sicily without Mycenae: a cross-cultural consumption analysis of connectivity in the Bronze Age central Mediterranean. *Journal of Mediterranean Archaeology* 30: 59-83.

Russell, A., and A. B. Knapp

2017   Sardinia and Cyprus: an alternative view on Cypriotes in the central Mediterranean. *Papers of the British School at Rome* 85: 1-35.

Rutter, J.

2006   Southwestern Anatolian pottery from Late Minoan Crete: evidence for direct contacts between Arzawa and Keftiu? In M.H. Wiener, J.L. Warner, J. Polonsky and E.E. Hayes (eds), *Pottery and Society: The Impact of Recent Studies in Minoan Pottery*, 138-153. Boston: Archaeological Institute of America.

2008   The Anatolian roots of Early Helladic III drinking behavior. In H. Erkanal, H. Hauptmann, V. Şahoğlu and R. Tuncel (eds), *The Aegean in the Neolithic, Chalcolithic and Early Bronze Age*. Ankara University Research Center for Maritime Archaeology, Publication 1: 461-481. Ankara: Ankara University.

2014   The Canaanite transport amphora within the Late Bronze Age Aegean: a 2013 perspective on a frequently changing picture. In D. Nakassis, J. Gulizio and S.A. James (eds), *KE-RA-ME-JA: Studies Presented to Cynthia W. Shelmerdine*. Prehistory Monographs 46: 53-69. Philadelphia: Institute for Aegean Prehistory Academic Press.

Sader, H., and J. Kamlah

2010   Tell el-Burak: a new Middle Bronze Age site from Lebanon. *Near Eastern Archaeology* 73: 130-141.

Safadi, C.

2016   Wind and wave modelling for the evaluation of the maritime accessibility and protection afforded by ancient harbours. *Journal of Archaeological Science, Reports* 5: 348–360.

Saghieh, M.

1983   *Byblos in the Third Millennium BC: A Reconstruction of the Stratigraphy and a Study of the Cultural Connections*. Warminster: Aris and Phillips.

Sagona, A.G.

1982   Levantine storage jars of the 13th to 4th century BC. *Opuscula Atheniensia* 14: 73-110.

Şahoğlu, V.

2005   The Anatolian Trade Network and the Izmir region during the Early Bronze Age. *Oxford Journal of Archaeology* 24: 339-361.

2007   Çeşme-Bağlararası: a new excavation in western Anatolia. In F. Felten, W. Gauss and R. Smetana (eds), *Middle Helladic Pottery and Synchronisms*. Denkschriften der Gesamtakademie 42. Contributions to the Chronology of the Eastern Mediterranean 14: 309-322. Wien: Verlag der Österreichischen Akademie der Wissenschaften.

2008a   Crossing borders: the Izmir region as a bridge between the east and the west during the Early Bronze Age. In C. Gillis and B. Sjöberg (eds), *Crossing Borders: Trade and Production in Premonetary Greece 7-9*. Studies in Mediterranean Archaeology and Literature, Pocket-book 173: 153-173. Sävedalen, Sweden: P. Åström's Förlag.

2008b   New evidence for the relations between the Izmir region, the Cyclades and the Greek mainland during the third millennium BC. In H. Erkanal, H. Hauptmann, V. Şahoğlu and R. Tuncel (eds), *The Aegean in the Neolithic, Chalcolithic and Early Bronze Age*. Ankara University Research Center for Maritime Archaeology, Publication 1: 483-501. Ankara: Ankara University.

2010   Ankara Research Center for Maritime Archaeology (ANKÜSAM) and its role in the protection of Turkey's underwater cultural heritage. In *Proceedings* II: *2010 World Universities Congress*, 1571-1580. Çanakkale: Çanakkale Onsekiz Mart University.

2011   Trade and interconnections between Anatolia and the Cyclades during the 3rd millennium BC. In V. Şahoğlu and P. Sotirakopoulou (eds), *Across: The Cyclades and Western Anatolia during the Third Millennium BC*, 172-177. Istanbul: Sabanci University, Sakip Sabanci Muzesi.

2015   Çeşme–Bağlararası: a western Anatolian harbour settlement at the beginning of the Late Bronze Age. In N.C. Stampolidis, Ç. Maner and K. Kopanias (eds), *Nostoi. Indigenous Culture, Migration and Integration in the Aegean Islands and Western Anatolia during the Late Bronze and Early Iron Age*, 593-608. Istanbul: Koç University Press.

2016   Early Bronze Age cemeteries at Bakla Tepe: changing patterns. In E. Pernicka, S. Ünlüsoy and S.W.E. Blum (eds), *Early Bronze Age Troy: Chronology, Cultural Development and Interregional Contacts*. Studia Troica Monographien 8: 167-182. Bonn: Verlag Dr Rudolf Habelt GmbH.

Salles, J.-F.

1980   *La Nécropole 'K' de Byblos*. Recherche sur les grandes civilisations, mémoire 2. Paris: Maison de l'Orient.

Samaras, V.

2015   Piracy in the Aegean during the Postpalatial Period and the Early Iron Age. In A. Babbi, F. Bubenheimer-Erhart, B. Marín-Aguilera and S. Mühl (eds), *The Mediterranean Mirror. Cultural Contacts in the Mediterranean Sea between 1200 and 750 B.C.* Tagungen 20: 189-204. Mainz: Römisch-Germanisches Zentralmuseum.

Sapir-Hen, L., and E. Ben-Yosef

2014   The socioeconomic status of Iron Age metalworkers: animal economy in the 'Slave's Hill', Timna, Israel. *Antiquity* 88/341: 775-790.

Sasson, J.M.

1966   Canaanite maritime involvement in the second millennium BC. *Journal of the American Oriental Society* 86: 126-138.

Sauvage, C.

2005   Quelques figures de commerçants d'après les textes égyptiens et ougaritiques, au Bronze Récent. In Ph. Clancier, F. Joannès, P. Rouillard and A. Tenu (eds), *Polanyi: vocabulaires, théories et modalités des échanges*, 155-170. Paris: de Boccard.

2011   Evidence from old texts: aspects of Late Bronze Age international maritime travel and trade regulations in the eastern Mediterranean? In K. Duistermaat and I. Regulski (eds), *Intercultural Contacts in the Ancient Mediterranean*. Orientalia Lovaniensia Analecta 202: 427-437. Louvain: Peeters.

2012   *Routes maritimes et systèmes d'échanges internationaux au Bronze récent en Méditerranée orientale*. Travaux de la Maison de l'Orient et de la Méditerranée 61. Lyon: Maison de l'Orient et de la Méditerranée–Jean Pouilloux.

Sauvage, C., and D. Pardee

2015   L'itinéraire maritime d'une reine d'Ougarit: note sur le texte RS 94.2406. *Syria* 92: 239-254.

Säve-Söderbergh, T.

1946   *The Navy of the Eighteenth Egyptian Dynasty*. Uppsala Universitets Arsskrift 1946:6. Uppsala: Universitets Uppsala.

1957   *Four Eighteenth Dynasty Tombs*. Oxford: Griffiths Institute, University of Oxford.

Sawicky, B. A.

2007   Enkomi and Kition: Cypriot Case Studies of the Late Bronze Age Eastern Mediterranean Maritime Landscape. Unpublished MA dissertation. London: University College London.

Sayed, A.M.A.

1977   Discovery of the site of the 12th Dynasty port at Wadi Gawasis on the Red Sea shore. *Revue d'Egyptologie* 29: 140-178.

Sazcı, G.

2013   Maydos Kilisetepe Höyüğü–eine Bronzezeitliche Hafensidelun an den Dardanellen. *Archäologisches Korrespondenzblatt* 43: 29-40.

Schäfer, J.

1991   Amnisos: harbour-town of Knossos? In R. Laffineur and L. Basch (eds), *Thalassa: L'Égée Préhistorique et la Mer*. Aegaeum 7: 111-116. Liège: Université de Liège.

Schaeffer, C.F.A.

1929   Les fouilles de Minet el-Beidha et de Ras Shamra (campagne du printemps 1929). *Syria* 10: 285-297.

1931   Les fouilles de Minet el-Beidha et de Ras Shamra, deuxième campagne (printemps 1930). *Syria* 12: 1-14.

1932   Les fouilles de Minet el-Beidha et de Ras Shamra, troisième campagne (printemps 1931). *Syria* 13: 1-27.

1933   Les fouilles de Minet el-Beidha et de Ras Shamra. *Syria* 14: 93-127.

1936   *Missions en Chypre, 1932-1935*. Paris: P. Geuthner.

1937   Fouilles de Ras Shamra-Ugarit: huitième campagne (printemps 1936). *Syria* 18: 125-154.

1952   *Enkomi-Alasia* I. *Nouvelles Missions en Chypre 1946-1950*. Paris: Klincksieck.

1962   (ed.) *Ugaritica 4. Découvertes des XVIIIe et XIXe campagnes, 1954-1955.* Bibliothéque Archéologique et Historique 74. Paris: P. Geuthner.

1978   Remarques sur les ancres en pierre d'Ugarit. In C.F.A. Schaeffer (ed.), *Ugaritica* 7. Mission de Ras Shamra 18. Bibliothéque Archéologique et Historique 99: 371-381. Paris: P. Geuthner.

Schloen, J. D.

2001   *The House of the Father as Fact and Symbol: Patrimonalism in Ugarit and the Ancient Near East.* Studies in the Archaeology and History of the Levant 2. Winona Lake, Indiana: Eisenbrauns.

Schneider, H.D., G.T. Martin, J. Van Dijk, B. Greene Aston, R. Perizonius and E. Strouhal

1993   The Tomb of Iniuia: preliminary report on the Saqqâra excavations, 1993. *Journal of Egyptian Archaeology* 79: 1-9.

Schofield, L., and R.B. Parkinson

1994   Of helmets and heretics: a possible Egyptian representation of Mycenaean warriors on a papyrus from el-Amarna. *Annual of the British School at Athens* 89: 157-170.

Serpico, M.

2005   The Canaanite amphora project. http://www.amarnaproject.com/pages/ recent_projects/material_culture/canaanite.shtml

Serpico, M., and R. White

1996   A report on the analysis of the contents of a cache of jars from the tomb of Djer. In A.J. Spencer (ed.), *Aspects of Early Egypt*, 128-139. London: British Museum Press.

2000   The botanical identity and transport of incense during the Egyptian New Kingdom. *Antiquity* 74/286: 884-897.

Serpico, M., J. Bourriau, L. Smith, Y. Goren, B. Stern and C. Heron

2003   Commodities and containers: a project to study Canaanite amphorae imported into Egypt during the New Kingdom. In M. Bietak (ed.), *The Synchronisation of Civilisations in the Eastern Mediterranean in the Second Millennium BC* II. Denkschrften der Gesamtakademie 29. Contributions to the Chronology of the Eastern Mediterranean 4: 365-375. Wien: Verlag der Österreichischen Akademie der Wissenschaften.

Sethe, K.

1906   *Urkunden der 18. Dynastie.* Urkunden des Aegyptischen Altertum 4, Band 3. Leipzig: Akademie Verlag.

Sewell, D.A.

2015   The seafarers of Maroni. In C.F. Macdonald, E. Hatzaki and S. Andreou (eds), *The Great Islands: Studies of Crete and Cyprus presented to Gerald Cadogan*, 186-191. Athens: Kapon Editions.

Shackleton, J.C., T.H. van Andel and C.N. Runnels

1984   Coastal paleogeography of the central and western Mediterranean during the last 125,000 years and its archaeological implications. *Journal of Field Archaeology* 11: 307-314.

Sharvit, J., E. Galili, E., B. Rosen and E.C.M. van den Brink

2002   Predynastic maritime traffic along the Carmel coast of Israel: a submerged find from north Athlit Bay. In E.C.M. van den Brink (ed.), *In Quest of Ancient Settlements and Landscapes*, 159-166. Tel Aviv: Ramot Publishing.

Shaw, I.

2000   Egypt and the outside world. In I. Shaw (ed.), *The Oxford History of Ancient Egypt*, 314-329. Oxford: Oxford University Press.

Shaw, J.W.

1990   Bronze Age Aegean harboursides. In D. Hardy, C.G. Doumas, J.A. Sakellarakis and P.M. Warren (eds), *Thera and the Aegean World* 3(1): 420-436. London: Thera Foundation.

1999   A proposal for Bronze Age Aegean ship-sheds in Crete. In H. Tzalas (ed.), *Tropis* V: 368-382. Athens: Hellenic Institute for the Preservation of Nautical Tradition.

Shaw, J.W., and M.C. Shaw (eds)

2006   *Kommos: An Excavation on the South Coast of Crete by the University of Toronto under the Auspices of the American School of Classical Studies in Athens.* Kommos V: The Monumental Minoan Buildings at Kommos. Princeton and Oxford: Princeton University Press.

Shaw, M.C.

1985   Late Minoan I buildings J/T, and Late Minoan III buildings N and P at Kommos: their nature and possible uses as residences, palaces, or emporia. *Scripta Mediterranea* 6: 19-25.

Sherratt, A.G., and E.S. Sherratt

1991   From luxuries to commodities: the nature of Mediterranean Bronze Age trading systems. In N.H. Gale (ed.), *Bronze Age Trade in the Mediterranean*. Studies in Mediterranean Archaeology 90: 351-386. Göteborg: P. Åström's Förlag.

1993   The growth of the Mediterranean economy in the early first millennium BC. *World Archaeology* 24: 361-378.

1998   Small worlds: interaction and identity in the ancient Mediterranean. In E.H. Cline and D. Harris-Cline (eds), *The Aegean and the Orient in the Second Millennium*. Aegaeum 18: 329-343. Liège: Université de Liège.

2001   Technological change in the east Mediterranean Bronze Age: capital, resources and marketing. In A. Shortland (ed.), *The Social Context of Technological Change in Egypt and the Near East, 1650-1550 BC*, 15-38. Oxbow: Oxford.

Sherratt, S.

1998   'Sea Peoples' and the economic structure of the late second millennium in the eastern Mediterranean. In S. Gitin, A. Mazar and E. Stern (eds), *Mediterranean Peoples in Transition: Thirteenth to Tenth Centuries BCE*, 292-313. Jerusalem: Israel Exploration Society.

2016   From "institutional" to "private": traders, routes and commerce from the Late Bronze Age to the Iron Age. In J.C. Moreno García (ed.), *Dynamics of Production in the Ancient Near East*, 289-302. Oxford: Oxbow Books.

Sievertsen, U.

1992   Das Messer vom Gebel el-Arak. *Baghdader Mitteilungen* 23: 1-75.

Simmons, A.H. (with K. DiBenedetto)

2014   *Stone Age Sailors: Paleolithic Seafaring in the Mediterranean.* Walnut Creek, California: Left Coast Press.

Simpson, W.K.

1960   Papyrus Lythgoe: a fragment of a literary text of the Middle Kingdom from El-Lisht. *Journal of Egyptian Archaeology* 46: 65-70.

2003   The Shipwrecked Sailor. In W.K. Simpson (ed.), *The Literature of Ancient Egypt: An Anthology of Stories, Instructions, Stelae, Autobiographies, and Poetry*, 45-53. Third ed. New Haven: Yale University Press.

Singer, I.

1999   A political history of Ugarit. In W.G.E. Watson and N. Wyatt (eds), *Handbook of Ugaritic Studies*. Handbuch der Orientalistik, Abteilung 1, Der Nahe und Mittlere Osten, Band 39: 603-733. Leiden: Brill.

2000   New evidence on the end of the Hittite empire. In E. D. Oren (ed.), *The Sea Peoples and Their World: A Reassessment*. University Museum Monograph 108. University Museum Symposium Series 11: 21-33. Philadelphia: University Museum, University of Pennsylvania.

2006   Ships bound for Lukka: a new interpretation of the companion letters RS 94.2530 and RS 94.2523. *Altorientalische Forschungen* 33: 242-262.

2008   Purple-dyers in Lazpa. In B.J. Collins, M. R. Bachvarova and I. Rutherford (eds), *Anatolian Interfaces: Hittites, Greeks and Their Neighbours*, 21-43. Oxford: Oxbow Books.

2011   *The Calm before the Storm: Selected Writings of Itamar Singer on the Late Bronze Age in Anatolia and the Levant*. Society of Biblical Literature: Writings from the Ancient World, Supplement 1. Atlanta, Georgia: Society of Biblical Literature.

2012   The Philistines in the north and the kingdom of Taita. In G. Galil, A. Gilboa, A. M. Maeir and D. Kahn (eds), *The Ancient Near East in the 12th–10th Centuries BCE: Culture and History*. Alter Orient und Altes Testament 392: 451-472. Münster: Ugarit-Verlag.

2013   'Old country' ethnonyms in 'new countries' of the 'Sea Peoples' diaspora. In R. B. Koehl (ed.), *Amilla. The Quest for Excellence. Studies Presented to Guenter Kopcke in Celebration of His 75th Birthday*. Prehistory Monographs 43: 321-333. Philadelphia: Institute for Aegean Prehistory Academic Press.

Sivan, D., S. Wdowinski, K. Lambeck, E. Galili and A. Raban

2001   Holocene sea-level changes along the Mediterranean coast of Israel, based on archaeological observations and numerical model. *Palaeogeography, Palaeoclimatology, Palaeoecology* 167: 101-117.

Sjöqvist, E.

1940   *Problems of the Late Cypriote Bronze Age*. Stockholm: Swedish Cyprus Expedition.

Skeates, R.

2007   Abstract and figurative representation and the politics of display in Neolithic southeast Italy. In C. Renfrew and I. Morley (eds), *Image and Imagination: A Global Prehistory of Figurative Representation*, 199-210. Cambridge: McDonald Institute.

Smith, A.F.

1998   From *garum* to ketchup: a spicy tale of two fish sauces. In H. Walker (ed.), *Fish: Food from the Waters*, 299-306. Blackawton (Devon), England: Prospect Books.

Smith, J.S.

2007   Theme and style in Cypriot wooden roller impressions. *Cahier du Centre d'Études Cyphriotes* 37: 347-374.

2012   Seals, scripts, and politics at Late Bronze Age Kourion. *American Journal of Archaeology* 116: 39-103.

Smith, L.M.V., J. Bourriau, Y. Goren, M. J. Hughes and M. Serpico

2004   The provenance of Canaanite amphorae found at Memphis and Amarna in the New Kingdom: results 2000–2002. In J. Bourriau and J. Phillips (eds), *Invention and Innovation: The Social Context of Technological Change* 2: *Egypt, the Aegean, and the Near East, 1650–1150 BC*, 55-77. Oxford: Oxbow.

Snape, S.R.

2003   Zawiyet Umm el-Rakham and Egyptian foreign trade in the 13th century BC. In N.C. Stampolidis and V. Karageorghis (eds), *Ploes.. Sea Routes...: Interconnections in the Mediterranean, 16th-6th c. BC*, 63-70. Athens: University of Crete, Leventis Foundation.

Snape, S.R., and P. Wilson

2007   *Zawiyet Umm el-Rakham* 1: *Temples and Chapels*. Liverpool: Rutherford Press Ltd.

Soar, K.

2014   Sects and the city: factional ideologies in representations of performance from Bronze Age Crete. *World Archaeology* 46: 224-241.

Sotirakopoulou, P.

2008   The Cyclades, the east Aegean islands and western Asia Minor: their relations in the Aegean Neolithic and Early Bronze Age. In H. Erkanal, H. Hauptmann, V. Şahoğlu and R. Tuncel (eds), *The Aegean in the Neolithic, Chalcolithic and Early Bronze Age*. Ankara University Research Center for Maritime Archaeology, Publication 1: 533-557. Ankara: Ankara University.

South, A.K.

1983   Kalavasos-*Ayios Dhimitrios* 1982. *Report of the Department of Antiquities, Cyprus*: 92-116.

1991   Kalavasos-*Ayios Dhimitrios* 1990. *Report of the Department of Antiquities, Cyprus*: 131-139.

1995   Urbanism and trade in the Vasilikos Valley in the Late Bronze Age. In S. Bourke and J.-P. Descoeudres (eds), *Trade, Contact, and the Movement of People in the Eastern Mediterranean*. Mediterranean Archaeology, Supplement 3: 187-197. Sydney: Department of Archaeology, University of Sydney.

1997   Kalavasos-*Ayios Dhimitrios* 1992-1996. *Report of the Department of Antiquities, Cyprus*: 151-175.

2008   Feasting in Cyprus: a view from Kalavasos. In L.A. Hitchcock, R. Laffineur and J. Crowley (eds), *DAIS. The Aegean Feast*. Aegaeum 29: 309-316. Liège, Austin: Université de Liège, University of Texas at Austin.

South, A.K., P. Russell and P.S. Keswani

1989   *Vasilikos Valley Project 3: Kalavasos-Ayios Dhimitrios* II *(Ceramics, Objects, Tombs, Specialist Studies)*. Studies in Mediterranean Archaeology 71.3 Göteborg: P. Åström's Förlag.

Sowada, K.N.

2009   *Egypt in the Eastern Mediterranean during the Old Kingdom: An Archaeological Perspective*. Oriens Biblicus et Orientalis 237. Fribourg, Göttingen: Academic Press, Vandenhoeck and Ruprecht.

Sparks, R.T.

2003   Egyptian stone vessels and the politics of exchange (2617-1070 BC). In R. Matthews and C. Roemer (eds), *Ancient Perspectives on Egypt*, 39-56. London: UCL Press.

Spondylis, E.

2012   A Minoan shipwreck off Laconia. *Enalia* 11: 6-7.

Stager, L.E.

1985   The first fruits of civilization. In J. Tubb (ed.), *Palestine in the Bronze and Iron Ages: Papers in Honour of Olga Tufnell*. University of London, Institute of Archaeology, Occasional Paper 11: 172-187. London: Institute of Archaeology.

2001   Port power in the Early and Middle Bronze Ages: the organization of maritime trade and hinterland production. In S.R. Wolff (ed.), *Studies in the Archaeology in Israel and Neighboring Lands in Memory of Douglas L. Esse*. Studies in Ancient Oriental Civilization 59: 625-638. Boston: American Schools of Oriental Research.

Stanley Price, N.P.

1979   *Early Prehistoric Settlement in Cyprus: A Review and Gazetteer of Sites, c.6500-3000 BC*. British Archaeological Reports, International Series 65. Oxford: British Archaeological Reports.

Staubwasser, M., and H. Weiss

2006   Holocene climate and cultural evolution in late prehistoric–early historic West Asia. *Quaternary Research* 66: 372–387.

Steel, L.

1999   Wine, kraters and chariots: the Mycenaean pictorial style reconsidered. In P. Betancourt, V. Karageorghis, R. Laffineur and W. D. Niemeier (eds), *Meletemata: Studies in Aegean Archaeology Presented to Malcolm H. Wiener as He Enters His 65th Year*. Aegaeum 20: 803-811. Liège, Austin: Université de Liège, University of Texas.

2002   Consuming passions: a contextual study of the local consumption of Mycenaean pottery at Tell el-'Ajjul. *Journal of Mediterranean Archaeology* 15: 25-51.

2004   *Cyprus before History: From the Earliest Settlers to the End of the Bronze Age*. London: Duckworth.

Steel, L., and C. McCartney

2008   Survey at Arediou *Vouppes* (Lithosouros), a Late Bronze Age agricultural settlement on Cyprus: a preliminary analysis of the material culture assemblages. *Bulletin of the American Schools of Oriental Research* 351: 9-37.

Steel, L., and S. Thomas

2008   Excavations at Aredhiou *Vouppes* (Lithosouros): an interim report on excavations 2005-2006. *Report of the Department of Antiquities, Cyprus*: 227-249.

Steffy, R.J.

1985   The Kyrenia ship: an interim report on its hull construction. *American Journal of Archaeology* 38: 71-101.

1994   *Wooden Ship Building and the Interpretation of Shipwrecks*. Texas: Texas A & M University Press: College Station.

Steiner, G.

1989   Schiffe von Ahhijawa oder Kriegschiffe von Amurru im Sauskamuwa-Vertrag? *Ugarit-Forschungen* 21: 393-411.

Stern, B., C. Heron, M. Serpico and J. Bourriau

2000   A comparison of methods for establishing fatty acid concentration gradients through potsherds: a case study using Late Bronze Age Canaanite amphorae. *Archaeometry* 42: 399-414.

Stern, B., C. Heron, T. Tellefsen and M. Serpico

2008   New investigations into the Uluburun resin cargo. *Journal of Archaeological Science* 35: 2188-2203.

Stern, E.

1977   A Late Bronze temple at Tel Mevorakh. *Biblical Archaeologist* 40: 89-91.

1984   *Excavations at Tel Mevorakh 1973-1976*. Volume 2: *The Bronze Age*. Qedem 18. Jerusalem: Israel Exploration Society.

Stevenson, A.

2016   The Egyptian predynastic and state formation. *Journal of Archaeological Research* 24: 421-468.

Stewart, I., and C. Morhange

2009   Coastal geomorphology and sea-level change. In J.Woodward (ed.), *The Physical Geography of the Mediterranean*, 385-413. Oxford: Oxford University Press.

Stewart, J.R.

1962   The Early Cypriote Bronze Age. In P. Dikaios and J.R. Stewart, *Swedish Cyprus Expedition* IV.1A: 205-401. Lund: Swedish Cyprus Expedition.

Stewart, J. R. (with Hanna Kassis)

1974   *Tell el-'Ajjul: The Middle Bronze Age Remains*. Studies in Mediterranean Archaeology 38. Göteborg: P. Åström's Förlag.

Stieglitz, R.R.

1972a   Inscribed Egyptian stone anchors. *Sefunim* 4: 42-43.

1972b   An ancient terra-cotta ship from Cyprus. *Sefunim* 4: 44-46.

1991   The city of Amurru. *Journal of Near Eastern Studies* 50: 45-48.

Stos, Z. A.

2009   Across the wine dark seas... sailor tinkers and royal cargoes in the Late Bronze Age eastern Mediterranean. In A.J. Shortland, I.C. Freestone and T. Rehren (eds), *From Mine to Microscope: Advances in the Study of Ancient Technology*, 163-180. Oxford: Oxbow.

Stos-Gale, Z.

2001   Minoan foreign relations and copper metallurgy in Protopalatial and Neopalatial Crete. In A. Shortland (ed.), *The Social Context of Technological Change in Egypt and the Near East, 1650-1550 BC*, 195-210. Oxford: Oxbow.

2015   Patterns of trade in Cypriot copper in the Bronze Age eastern Mediterranean revealed using data from Oxford Archaeological Lead Isotope Database (OXALID). In K. Rosińska-Balik, A. Ochal-Czarnowicz, M. Czarnowicz and J. Debowska-Ludwin (eds), *Copper and Trade in the South-Eastern Mediterranean: Trade Routes of the Near East in Antiquity*. British Archaeological Reports, International Series 2573: 111-122. Oxford: Archaeopress.

Stos-Gale, Z.A., and N.H. Gale

2003   Lead isotopic and other isotopic research in the Aegean. In K.P. Foster and R. Laffineur (eds), *Metron: Measuring the Aegean Bronze Age*. Aegaeum 24: 83-101. Liège, Austin: Université de Liège, University of Texas at Austin.

Strange, J.

1980   *Caphtor/Keftiu: A New Investigation*. Acta Theologica Danica 14. Leiden: Brill.

Strasser, T.G.

2010   Location and perspective in the Theran flotilla fresco. *Journal of Mediterranean Archaeology* 23: 3-26.

Strasser, T.F., and A. Chapin

2014   Geological formations in the flotilla fresco from Akrotiri. In G. Touchais, R. Laffineur and F. Rougemont (eds), *Physis: l'environnement naturel et la relation homme-milieu dans le monde égéen protohistorique*. Aegaeum 37: 57-64. Leuven, Liège, Belgium: Peeters.

Strasser, T.G., E. Panagopoulou, C.N. Runnels, P.M. Murray, N. Thomspon, P. Karkanas, F.T. McCoy and K.W. Wegmann

2010   Stone Age seafaring in the Mediterranean: evidence from the Plakias region for Lower Palaeolithic and Mesolithic habitation of Crete. *Hesperia* 79: 145-190.

Strasser, T.G., C.N. Runnels, K.W. Wegmann, E. Panagopoulou, F.T. McCoy, C. DeGregorio, P. Karkanas and N. Thomspon

2011   Dating Palaeolithic sites in southwestern Crete, Greece. *Journal of Quaternary Science* 26: 553-560.

Strudwick, N.

2005   *Texts from the Pyramid Age*. Atlanta, Georgia: Society of Biblical Literature.

Sugerman, M.

2000   Webs of Commerce: The Archaeology of Ordinary Things in Late Bronze Age Israel and Palestine. Unpublished PhD dissertation, Department of Anthropology, Harvard University: Cambridge, Massachusetts.

2009   Trade and power in Late Bronze Age Canaan. In J.D. Schloen (ed.), *Exploring the Longue Durée: Essays in Honor of Lawrence E. Stager*, 439-448. Winona Lake, Indiana: Eisenbrauns.

Swiny, S., G. Rapp and E. Herscher (eds)

2003   *Sotira Kamminoudhia: An Early Bronze Age Site in Cyprus*. American Schools of Oriental Research, Archaeological Reports 8. Cyprus American Archaeological Research Institute, Monograph 4. Boston: American Schools of Oriental Research.

Tallet, P.

1998   Quelques aspects de l'économie du vin en Égypte ancienne, au Nouvel Empire. In N. Grimal and B. Menu (eds), *Le commerce en Égypte ancienne*, 240-267. Paris: Institute Français d'Archéologie Orientale.

2012   Ayn Sukhna and Wadi el-Jarf: two newly discovered pharaonic harbours on the Suez Gulf. *British Museum Studies in Ancient Egypt and Sudan 18: 147–168*. Open access online journal: http://www.britishmuseum.org/research/publications/online_journals/bmsaes/issue_18/tallet.aspx

Tallet, P., and D. Laisney

2012   Iry-Hor et Narmer au sud-Sinaï (Ouadi 'Ameyra): un complément à la chronologie des expéditions minières égyptiennes. *Bulletin de l'Institut Français d'Archéologie Orientale* 112: 381-398.

Tallet, P., and G. Marouard

2014   The harbor of Khufu on the Red Sea coast at Wadi al-Jarf, Egypt. *Near Eastern Archaeology* 77: 4-14.

Tallet, P., G. Marouard and D. Laisney

2012   Un port de la IVe dynastie au Ouadi al-Jarf (mer Rouge). *Bulletin de l'Institut Français d'Archéologie Orientale* 112: 399-446.

Tartaron, T.F.

2013   *Maritime Networks in the Mycenaean World*. Cambridge: Cambridge University Press.

Thalmann, J.-P.

2007   A seldom used parameter in pottery studies: the capacity of pottery vessels. In M. Bietak and E. Czerny (eds), *The Synchronisation of Civilisations in the Eastern Mediterranean in the Second Millennium BC* III. Denkschriften der Gesamtakademie 37. Contributions to the Chronology of the Eastern Mediterranean 9: 431-438. Wien: Verlag der Österreichischen Akademie der Wissenschaften.

Thalmann, J. P., and K. Sowada

2014   Levantine 'combed ware'. In M. Lebeau (ed.), *ARCANE Interregional: Ceramics*, 323–345. Turnhout, Belgium: Brepols.

Todd, I.A.

2016   *Vasilikos Valley Project 10: The Field Survey of the Vasilikos Valley*. Volume 2. *Artefacts Recovered by the Field Survey*. Studies in Mediterranean Archaeology 71.10. Stockholm: Åström Editions.

Tomlinson, J.E., J. B. Rutter and S.M.A. Hoffman

2010   Mycenaean and Cypriot Late Bronze Age ceramic imports to Kommos: an investigation by Neutron Activation Analysis. *Hesperia* 79: 191-231.

Toth, J.A.

2002   Composite stone anchors in the ancient Mediterranean. *Acta Archaeologica Hungarica* 53: 85-118.

Tufnell, O.

1962   The courtyard cemetery at Tell el-'Ajjul. *Bulletin of the Institute of Archaeology, University of London* 3: 1-37.

Uerpmann, M., and W. Van Neer

2000   Fischreste aus den neuen Grabungen in Troia (1989-1999). *Studia Troica* 10: 145-179.

Ünlü, E.

2016   The handle wagging the cup. Formal aspects of alcohol consumption in the transfer of ideology: Anatolia and the Aegean towards the end of the third millennium BC. *Oxford Journal of Archaeology* 35: 345-358.

van Andel, T.H.

1989   Late Quaternary sea-level changes and archaeology. *Antiquity* 63/241: 733-745.

Van De Mieroop, M.

2007   *The Eastern Mediterranean in the Age of Ramesses II*. Oxford: Blackwell.

van den Brink, E.C.M., and T.E. Levy (eds)

2002   *Egypt and the Levant: Interrelations from the 4th through the Early 3rd Millennium BC*. London: Leicester University Press.

Van der Post, J.

1991   Cypriots in Tell Abu Hawam? Unpublished MA thesis, Groningen University, Groningen, The Netherlands.

van Dommelen, P.

2014   Moving on: archaeological perspectives on mobility and migration. *World Archaeology* 46: 477-483.

van Dommelen, P., and A.B. Knapp (eds)

2010   *Material Connections in the Ancient Mediterranean: Mobility, Materiality and Mediterranean Identities*. London: Routledge.

Van Neer, W., and M. Waelkens

2007   Fish remains from Bronze Age to Byzantine levels. In N. Postgate and D. Thomas (eds), *Excavations at Kilise Tepe 1994–98: From Bronze Age to Byzantine in Western Cilicia*. British Institute at Ankara, Monograph 30: 607-612. Cambridge, London: McDonald Institute for Archaeological Research, British Institute at Ankara.

Van Neer, W., E. Paulissen and P.M. Vermeersch

2000   Chronology, subsistence and environment of the Late Palaeolithic fishing sites of Makhadma-2 and 4. In P.M. Vermeersch (ed.), *Palaeolithic Living Sites in Upper and Middle Egypt*, 271-287. Leuven: Leuven University Press.

Van Neer, W., O. Lernau, R. Friedman, G. Mumford, J. Poblome and M. Waelkens

2004   Fish remains from archaeological sites as indicators of former trade in the eastern Mediterranean. *Paléorient* 30(1): 101-148.

van Soldt, W.H.

1990   Fabrics and dyes at Ugarit. *Ugarit-Forschungen* 22: 321-358.

van Wijngaarden, G.J.

2002   *Use and Appreciation of Mycenaean Pottery in the Levant, Cyprus and Italy*. Amsterdam: Amsterdam University Press.

Vella, N.C.

2004   A maritime perspective: looking for Hermes in an ancient seascape. In J. Chrysostomides, C. Dendrinos and J. Harris (eds), *The Greek Islands and the Sea*, 33-57. Camberley (Surrey), UK: Porphyrogenitus and Hellenic Institute, Royal Holloway, University of London.

Vidal, J.

2005   Beirut and Ugarit in the 13th century BCE. *Studi Micenei ed Egeo-Anatolici* 47: 291-298.

2008   The men of Arwad, mercenaries of the sea. *Bibliotheca Orientalis* 65: 5-15.

Vinson, S.

1993   The earliest representations of brailed sails. *Journal of the American Research Center in Egypt* 30: 133-150.

Virolleaud, C.

1957   *Le Palais Royal d'Ugarit* 2. *Textes en cuneiformes alphabetiques des Archivs Est, Ouest et Centrales*. Mission de Ras Shamra 7. Paris: P. Geuthner.

1965   *Le Palais Royal d'Ugarit* 5. Mission de Ras Shamra 11. Paris: Klincksieck.

Vita, J.-P.

1995   *El ejército de Ugarit*. Madrid: Consejo Superior de Investigaciones Cientficas.

1997   Remarques épigraphiques à propos de quatre textes ougaritiques. *Ugarit-Forschungen* 29: 705-707.

2017   Ships and diplomacy. The historical connection between the Letters RS 18.031 (from Tyre) and RS 94.2483 (from Ugarit). *Ash-sharq* 1(1): 69–71.

von Kroll, H.

1989   Die Pflanzenfunde von Maadi. In I. Rizkana and J. Seeher, *Maadi* III: *The Non-Lithic Small Finds and the Structural Remains of the Predynastic Settlement*. Deutsches Archaeologisches Institut, Abteilung Kairo, Archaeologische Veroffentlichungen 80: 129-136. Mainz: Philipp von Zabern.

von Rüden, C.

2015   Making the way through the sea: experiencing Mediterranean seascapes in the second millennium BCE. In A. Lichtenberger and C. von Rüden (eds), *Multiple Mediterranean Realities: Current Approaches to Spaces, Resources, and Connectivities*. Mittelmeerstudien 6: 31-65. Paderborn, Munich: Ferdinand Schöningh Verlag, Fink-Verlag.

Voskos, I., and A. B. Knapp

2008   Cyprus at the end of the Late Bronze Age: crisis and colonization, or continuity and hybridization? *American Journal of Archaeology* 112: 659-684.

Voss, B.L.

2007   Image, text, object: interpreting documents and artifacts as 'labors of representation'. *Historical Archaeology* 41: 147-171.

Votruba, G.F., and H. Erkanal

2016   Anchor finds from the harbour basin of ancient Klazomenai and Chyton, Turkey. *Archaeologia Maritima Mediterranea* 13: 105-116.

Votruba, G.F., M. Artzy and H. Erkanal

2016   A set Archaic anchor arm exposed within *P. oceanica* matte at Klazomenai/Liman Tepe, Turkey: a contribution for understanding marine stratigraphy. *Journal of Field Archaeology* 41: 671-683.

Wachsmann, S.

1981   The ships of the Sea Peoples. *International Journal of Nautical Archaeology and Underwater Exploration* 10: 187-220.

1987   *Aegeans in the Theban Tombs.* Orientalia Lovaniensia Analecta 20. Leuven: Peeters.

1997   Were the Sea Peoples Mycenaeans? The evidence of ship iconography. In S. Swiny, R. Hohlfelder and H.W. Swiny (eds), *Res Maritimae: Cyprus and the Eastern Mediterranean from Prehistory through Late Antiquity.* Cyprus American Archaeological Research Institute, Monograph 1: 339-356. Atlanta, Georgia: ASOR/Scholars Press.

1998   *Seagoing Ships and Seamanship in the Bronze Age Levant.* Texas A&M University Press: College Station, Texas.

2000a To the sea of the Philistines. In E.D. Oren (ed.), *The Sea Peoples and Their World: A Reassessment.* University Museum Monograph 108. University Museum Symposium Series 11: 103-143. Philadelphia: University Museum, University of Pennsylvania.

2000b Some notes on Mediterranean seafaring during the second millennium BC. In S. Sherratt (ed.), *The Wall Paintings of Thera* 2: 803-824. Athens: Thera Foundation.

2008   Underwater survey, 1996-1997. In L.E. Stager, J.D Schloen and D.M. Master (eds), *Ashkelon* I. *Introduction and Overview (1985-2006)*, 97-100. Winona Lake, Indiana: Eisenbrauns.

2013   *The Gurob Ship-cart Model and its Mediterranean Context.* College Station, Texas: Texas A&M University Press.

Wachsmann, S., and K. Raveh

1984   A concise nautical history of Dor/Tantura. *International Journal of Nautical Archaeology and Underwater Exploration* 13: 223-241.

Walsh, K.

2014   *The Archaeology of Mediterranean Landscapes: Human-Environment Interaction from the Neolithic to the Roman Period.* Cambridge: Cambridge University Press.

Ward, C.A.

2006   Boat-building and its social context in early Egypt: interpretations from the First Dynasty boat-grave cemetery at Abydos. *Antiquity* 80/307: 118-129.

2010a Seafaring in the Bronze Age Aegean: evidence and speculation. In D.J. Pullen (ed.), *Political Economies of the Aegean Bronze Age*, 149-160. Oxford: Oxbow.

2010b From river to sea: evidence for Egyptian seafaring ships. *Journal of Ancient Egyptian Interconnections* 2(3): 42-49.

Ward, C.A., and C. Zazzaro

2010   Evidence for pharaonic seagoing ships at Mersa/Wadi Gawasis, Egypt. *International Journal of Nautical Archaeology* 39: 27-43.

Ward, C., P. Couser, D. Vann, T. Vosmer and M.M. Abd el-Maguid

2012   Reconstruction and sailing performance of an ancient Egyptian ship. In N. Gunsenin (ed.), *Between Continents. Proceedings of the Twelfth Symposium on Boat and Ship Archaeology, Istanbul 2009*, 287-292. Istanbul: Ege Yayinlari.

Ward, W.A.

1961   Egypt and the east Mediterranean in the early second millennium BC. *Orientalia* n.s. 30: 22-45, 129-155.

1963   Egypt and the east Mediterranean from Predynastic times to the end of the Old Kingdom. *Journal of the Economic and Social History of the Orient* 6: 1-57.

Watrin, L.

2002   Tributes and the rise of a predatory power: unraveling the intrigue of EB I Palestinian jars found by E. Amélinou at Abydos. In E.C.M. van den Brink and T. E. Levy (eds), *Egypt and the Levant: Interrelations from the 4th through the Early 3rd Millennium BC*, 435-463. London: Leicester University Press.

Weaver, A. J., O.A. Saenko, P.U. Clark and J.X. Mitrovica

2003   Meltwater Pulse 1A from Antarctica as a trigger of the Bølling-Allerød warm interval. *Science* 299: 1709–1713.

Webb, J. M.

2013   'The mantle of Vasilia': have Stewart's views on the centrality of the copper trade in prehistoric Bronze Age Cyprus stood the test of time? In A.B. Knapp, J.M. Webb and A. McCarthy (eds), *J.R.B. Stewart: An Archaeological Legacy*. Studies in Mediterranean Archaeology 139: 59-71. Uppsala: Åström's Förlag.

2014   Cyprus in the Early Bronze Age. In M.L. Steiner and A.E. Killegbrew (eds), *The Oxford Handbook of the Archaeology of the Levant (c.8000-332 BCE)*, 347-360. Oxford: Oxford University Press.

2015   The production and distribution of plank-shaped figurines in Middle Bronze Age Cyprus: the role of Lapithos. *Cahiers du Centre d'Études Chypriotes* 45: 241-254.

2016   Lapithos revisited: a fresh look at a key Middle Bronze Age site in Cyprus. In G. Bourogiannis and C. Mühlenbock (eds), *Ancient Cyprus Today: Museum Collections and New Research*. Studies in Mediterranean Archaeology and Literature PB 184: 57-67. Uppsala: Åström Editions.

2017   *Vounoi* (*Vounous*) and Lapithos in the Early and Middle Bronze Age: a reappraisal of the central north coast of Cyprus in the light of fieldwork and research undertaken since 1974. In D. Pilides and M. Mina (eds), *Four Decades of Hiatus in Archaeological Research in Cyprus: Towards Restoring the Balance*. Studies on Ancient Cyprus 2: 128-139. Vienna: Holzhausen der Verlag.

Webb, J., and D. Frankel

2013   *Ambelikou Aletri: Metallurgy and Pottery Production in Middle Bronze Age Cyprus*. Studies in Mediterraenan Archaeology 138. Uppsala: Åström's Förlag.

Webb, J., D. Frankel, Z.A. Stos and N. Gale

2006   Early Bronze Age metals trade in the eastern Mediterranean. New compositional and lead isotope evidence from Cyprus. *Oxford Journal of Archaeology* 25: 261-288.

Webb, J.M., D. Frankel, K. Eriksson and J.B. Hennessy

2009   *The Bronze Age Cemeteries at Karmi Paleolana and Lapatsa in Cyprus. Excavations by J.R.B. Stewart*. Studies in Mediterranean Archaeology 136. Göteborg: P. Åström's Förlag.

Wedde, M.

1991 Aegean Bronze Age ship imagery: regionalisms, a Minoan bias, and a 'thalassocracy'. In R. Laffineur and L. Basch (eds), *Thalassa. L'Égée préhistorique et la mer*. Aegaeum 7: 73-94. Liège: Universite de Liège.

1999 War at sea: the Mycenaean and early Iron Age oared galley. In R. Laffineur (ed.), *Polemos: Le Contexte Guerrier en Égée à l'âge du Bronze*. Aegaeum 19: 465-476. Liège: Université de Liège.

2000 *Towards a Hermeneutics of Aegean Bronze Age Ship Imagery*. Peleus: Studien zur Archäologie und Geschichte Griechenlands und Zyprerns 6. Mannheim und Möhnesee: Bibliopolis.

Weeden, M.

2013 After the Hittites: the kingdoms of Karkamish and Palistin in northern Syria. *Bulletin of the Institute of Classical Studies* 56(2): 1–20.

Wegner, J.

2017 A royal boat burial and watercraft tableau of Egypt's 12th Dynasty (c.1850 BCE) at south Abydos. *International Journal of Nautical Archaeology* 46: 5-30.

Weinstein, J.M.

2008 Nefertiti scarab. In J. Aruz, K. Benzel and J.M. Evans (eds), *Beyond Babylon: Art, Trade, and Diplomacy in the Second Millennium BC*, 358. New York, New Haven and London: Metropolitan Museum of Art, Yale University Press.

Weinstein Balthazar, J.

1990 *Copper and Bronze Working in Early through Middle Bronze Age Cyprus*. Studies in Mediterranean Archaeology and Literature, Pocket-book 84. Göteborg: P. Åström's Förlag.

Wengrow, D.

2006 *The Archaeology of Early Egypt: Social Transformations in North-East Africa, 10,000 to 2650 BC*. Cambridge: Cambridge University Press.

Westerberg, K.

1983 *Cypriote Ships from the Bronze Age to c. 500 BC*. Studies in Mediterranean Archaeology and Literature, Pocket-book 22. Göteborg: P. Åström's Förlag.

Westerdahl, C.

1992 The maritime cultural landscape. *International Journal of Nautical Archaeology* 21: 5-14.

1994 Maritime cultures and ship types: brief comments on the significance of maritime archaeology. *International Journal of Nautical Archaeology* 23: 265-270.

2005 Seal on land, elk at sea: notes on and applications of the ritual landscape at the seaboard. *International Journal of Nautical Archaeology* 34: 2-23.

2010 'Horses are strong at sea': the liminal aspect of the maritime cultural landscape. In A. Anderson, J. Barrett and K. Boyle (eds), *The Global Origins and Development of Seafaring*, 275-287. Cambridge: McDonald Institute for Archaeological Research.

2013 Medieval carved ship images found in Nordic churches: the poor man's votive ships? *International Journal of Nautical Archaeology* 42: 337-347.

Westley, K., and J. Dix

2006 Coastal environments and their role in prehistoric migrations. *Journal of Maritime Archaeology* 1: 9-28.

White, D.

1986   1985 excavations on Bates's Island, Marsa Matruh. *Journal of the American Research Center in Egypt* 23: 51-84.

1999   Water, wood, dung and eggs: reciprocity in trade along the LBA Mamarican coast. In P.P. Betancourt, V. Karageorghis, R. Laffineur and W.-D. Niemeier eds), *Meletemata: Studies in Aegean Archaeology Presented to Malcolm H. Weiner as He Enters his 65th Year.* Aegaeum 20(3): 931-935. Liège, Austin: Université de Liège, University of Texas.

2002a   *Marsa Matruh* I: *The Excavation. The University of Pennsylvania Museum of Archaeology and Anthropology's Excavations on Bates's Island, Marsa Matruh, Egypt 1985-1989.* Institute for Aegean Prehistory, Prehistory Monographs 1. Philadelphia: Institute for Aegean Prehistory Academic Press.

2002b   *Marsa Matruh* II: *The Objects. The University of Pennsylvania Museum of Archaeology and Anthropology's Excavations on Bates's Island, Marsa Matruh, Egypt 1985-1989.* Institute for Aegean Prehistory, Prehistory Monographs 2. Philadelphia: Institute for Aegean Prehistory Academic Press.

2003   *Multum in parvo*: Bates's island on the NW coast of Egypt. In N.C. Stampolidis and V. Karageorghis (eds), *Ploes.. Sea Routes...: Interconnections in the Mediterranean, 16th-6th c. BC,* 71-82. Athens: University of Crete, Leventis Foundation.

Whitewright, J.

2011   The potential performance of ancient Mediterranean sailing rigs. *International Journal of Nautical Archaeology* 40: 2-17.

Wiener, M.

2013   Realities of power: the Minoan thalassocracy in historical perspective. In R. B. Koehl (ed.), *Amilla. The Quest for Excellence. Studies Presented to Guenter Kopcke in Celebration of His 75th Birthday.* Prehistory Monographs 43: 149-173. Philadelphia: Institute for Aegean Prehistory Academic Press.

Wilkinson, T.

2010   *The Rise and Fall of Ancient Egypt.* London: Bloomsbury.

Williams, B.B.

1986   *Excavations between Abu Simbel and the Sudan Frontier. Part 1. The A-Group Royal Cemetery at Qustul: Cemetery L.* Chicago: Oriental Institute, University of Chicago.

Wilson, D.E.

1999   *Ayia Irini: Period I-III. The Neolithic and Early Bronze Age Settlements. Part 1: The Pottery and Small Finds.* Keos 9. Mainz: Phillip von Zabern.

Winther-Jacobsen, K.

2002   Cypriot transport amphorae in the Archaic and Classical periods. In A. Rathje, M. Mielsen and B. Bundgaard-Rasmussen (eds), *Pots for the Living, Pots for the Dead.* Acta Hyperborea 9: 169-184. Copenhagen: Museum Tusculanum Press.

Witmore, C.

2014   Archaeology and the new materialisms. *Journal of Contemporary Archaeology* 1: 203-246.

Wodzińska, A., and M. Ownby

2011   Tentative remarks on Levantine combed ware from Heit el-Ghurab, Giza. In J. Mynárová (ed.), *Egypt and the Near East-The Crossroads*, 285-295. Prague: Charles University, Czech Institute of Egyptology.

Wood, B.G.

1987   Egyptian amphorae of the New Kingdom and Ramesside periods. *Biblical Archaeologist* 50: 75-83.

Wreschner, E.

1971   Prehistoric rock engravings in Nahal ha-Me'arot, Mount Carmel. *Israel Exploration Journal* 21: 217-218.

Xella, P.

1982   Die Ausrüstung eines kanaanäischen Schiffes (KTU 4.689). *Welt des Orient* 13: 31-35.

Yalçin, Ü., C. Pulak and R. Slotta (eds)

2005   *Das Schiff von Uluburun: Welthandel vor 3000 Jahren*. Bochum: Deutsches Bergbau-Museum.

Yanklevitz, S.

2007   Provenience of Imported Pottery and Pebbles from Tell Abu Hawam 2001: Excavations as Evidence of Maritime Trade in the Late Bronze Age IIB. Unpublished MA thesis, University of Haifa, Israel.

Yardeni, A.

1994   Maritime trade and royal accountancy in an erased customs account from 475 B.C.E. on the Aḥiqar Scroll from Elephantine. *Bulletin of the American Schools of Oriental Research* 293: 67-78.

Yasur-Landau, A.

2010   *The Philistines and Aegean Migration at the End of the Late Bronze Age*. Cambridge: Cambridge University Press.

Yener, K. A.

2000   *The Domestication of Metals: The Rise of Complex Metal Industries in Anatolia*. Culture and History of the Ancient Near East 4. Leiden: Brill.

Yon, M.

1997   Ougarit et le port du Mahadou/Minet el-Beida. In S. Swiny, R. Hohlfelder and H.W. Swiny (eds), *Res Maritimae: Cyprus and the Eastern Mediterranean from Prehistory through the Roman Period*. Cyprus American Archaeological Research Institute, Monograph 1: 357-369. Atlanta: ASOR/Scholars Press.

2000   A trading city: Ugarit and the west. *Near Eastern Archaeology* 63: 192-193.

2006   *The City of Ugarit at Tell Ras Shamra*. Winona Lake, Indiana: Eisenbrauns.

2016   Aux échelles du Levant. Échanges commerciaux au Bronze Récent. *Cahier du Centre d'Études Chypriotes* 46: 33-50.

Yon, M., and C. Sauvage

2015   La navigation en Méditerranée orientale à l'Âge du Bronze Récent. In B. Argémi and P. Tallet (eds), *Entre Nil et mers. La navigation en Égypte ancienne*. Nehet 3: 73-103. Paris, Brussels: Centre de Recherches égyptologiques de la Sorbonne; Centre de Recherches en Archéologie et Patrimoine de la Université libre de Bruxelles.

Zangani, F.

2016   Amarna and Uluburun: reconsidering patterns of exchange in the Late Bronze Age. *Palestine Exploration Quarterly* 148: 230-244.

Zangger, E.

1992   *The Flood from Heaven: Deciphering the Atlantis Legend.* London: Sidgwick and Jackson.

2008   The port of Nestor. In J.L. Davis (ed.), *Sandy Pylos: An Archaeological History from Nestor to Navarino* (2nd edn.), 69–74. Princeton: American School of Classical Studies at Athens.

Zazzaro, C.

2007   Stone anchors and pierced stones. In K.A. Bard and R. Fattovich (eds), *Harbor of the Pharaohs to the Land of Punt: Archaeological Investigations at Mersa/Wadi Gawasis, Egypt, 2001-2005*, 153-163. Naples: Università degli Studie di Napoli 'l'Orientale'.

Ziegler, C.

1993   *Le Mastaba d'Akhethétep. Une chapelle funéraire de l'Ancien Empire.* Paris: Editions de la Réunion des musées nationaux.

Zimmerman, T.

2005   Perfumes and policies–a 'Syrian bottle' from Kinet Höyük and Anatolian trade patterns in the advanced third millennium BC. *Anatolica* 31: 161-169.

Zingarelli, A.P.

2010   *Trade and Market in New Kingdom Egypt: Internal Socio-economic Processes and Transformations.* British Archaeological Reports, International Series 2063. Oxford: Archaeopress.

Zomeni, Z.

2014   Appendix VIII: The Quaternary environment of the Pyla-*Kokkinokremos* Area. In V. Karageorghis and A. Kanta, *Pyla-Kokkinokremos: A Late 13th Century BC Fortified Settlement in Cyprus. Excavations 2010-2011.* Studies in Mediterranean Archaeology 141: 215-216. Uppsala: Åström Editions.

INDEX

Number in *italics* denotes figure; number in **bold** denotes table

57, 92, *93*, 170, 186; 'piriform' 101; Proto-White Painted 144; Red Polished III 98; southeast Aegean 52; transport 52; wine 50. See also Canaanite Jars (CJs)

Amun Temple (Karnak) 151

Amuq Plain 45, *157*

Amurru 42, 46–48, 111, 117, 189

Anatolian Trade Network (ATN) 66, 67, 72, 75–78, *76,* 168, 186, 192

anchor: Anatolia 78, *100*, 101, 164–165, 177; Byblian- (or Syrian) type 68–69, 96, 137, 151; Byblos 68–69, 95, 137, 164, 168, 178; Cape Gelidonya shipwreck 162, 164, 178; composite 61, 101, 136–137, 148–151, *150*, 164, 177; Cypro-Minoan marks 148–149, 151; Egypt 68, 95, 137, 151, 168, 176; Hala Sultan Tekke *Vyzakia* 148–149, *150*, 177; Kition 137, 148, 151, 164, 177, 193; Kition *Bamboula* 151; Kouklia *Achni* 139, 148–151; Levantine 24, 51, 61, 68–69, 159, 194; limestone 64, 96, 164; Maroni *Tsaroukkas* 140, 148, 149, *150*, 177; miniature 95, 138, 151, 176, 177; mineral and petrographic analysis 159, 164, 177–178; pictorial representation 168; sand(stone) 61, 136, 164; *shfifonim* 68–69, 96; single-holed 61, 95, 162, 164, 177, 178; Syro-Canaanite 137; Ugarit 69, 95, 116, 137–138, 164, 178, 193; Uluburun shipwreck 51, 137, 159, 164, *165*, 176–178, 194; weight 61, 95, 101, 136–138, 149–151, 164, 176–177; wooden 78

Aphrodisias 76

Apliki **145**, 152

Appian 35

Arameans 26

archaeology, maritime 21, 32, 51, 196

archives **106–107**, 110, 113, 124, 172, 187–188

Argolid 120, 147

Arnuwanda I 42

Aromatics 82, 89

Arpera *Mosphilos* 57, 94, 97, **145**

Arwad (*Arwada*): Amarna letters 44, 46, 47–48, 111, 173, 189, 190; (proto-) harbour 47–48, 55, 84, 118, 172

Arzawa 44

Asherah 89

Ashkelon: Egyptian jars 135; (proto-) harbour 66, 87, 169, 186–187, 191, 195; Nilotic fish 138; part of a small world 182

Assyria 26, 42, 47, 111, 188

Aswan stele 44

Atalligu 109

Athena Temple (Miletos) 156, 163

Atlit 55, 87, 96, 121

Atlit bay 70

Avaris. *See* Tell ed-Dab'a

Ayia Irini (Keos) 77

Ayn Sukhna 64, 91

Aziru 48

B

b'l any (ship's captain) 110, 113, 114

Ba'al Ṣapon 89, 95, 116

Babylon 98, 187

Babylonia 26

Badari 65

Bademgediği Tepesi 40, 162–163, *162*, 177, 192, 193

Bakla Tepe 75, 76

ballast stones 120

barracuda 152

Base-ring ware, Cypriot pottery 117, 120, 157, 161

Batroun 88

Bay of Haifa 86, 118–119, *119*, 120, 121, 134–135, 175

Bay of Iskenderun 101, 157, *157*, 171

Bay of Izmir 55, 75–76, 78, 101, 102, 155, 168

bdlm (merchant representative) 114, 188. See also *bidāluma*

beads 74, 98, 99, 153, 158, 168

beer 112, 136, 188

SEAFARING AND SEAFARERS IN THE BRONZE AGE EASTERN MEDITERRANEAN

151; ships' representations 40, 59, 140, 144, *144*, 176; Transport Stirrup Jars (TSJs) 146

Enkomi, *Ayios Iakovos* 142

Ephesos 54

Episkopi *Bamboula* 72, 139, 146, *146*

Erimi *Laonin tou Porakou* 153

Euboea 76

Exotica 124, 158, 172, 185, 192

'Ezbet Rushdi. *See* Tell ed-Dab'a

F

faience: beads 74, 98, 158, 168; cylinder seal 118; pin inlay 98; miniature vessel 118; necklace 99; scarab 124, 174

Famagusta (Bay) 72, 139, 182

fat 105, 135, 136, 175

Fayyum 131, 136

feasting and drinking 39

figs 148

fish: bones 59–60, 76, 138, 151–152, 165, 176–177; depiction 126, 138, 143, 144, 153, 163, 195; Egyptian jar 136, 175–176; freshwater 101; Mediterranean 138, 176; Nilotic 89, 129, 138, 152, 176; preserving, 60, 110; sauce 52, 60; shoals 30; trading 60

fisher-foragers 32–33

fishermen, seafaring 29, 30, 32, 33, 58, 84, 177

fishhook 32, 59–61, 118, 151, 152, 164, 177

fishing equipment: fishhooks 32, 59–61, 118, 151, 152, 164, 177; fleets 29, 179; floaters 59, 60; forks 59; harpoon 32, 59; installations 29; net weights 60, 140, 151–152, 164, 165, 177; pierced pebbles 138, 176; sinkers 59, 138, 151, 165, 176, 177; spear 151; trident 59, 60, *60*, 151

fleet: *Alašiya* (Cyprus) 43, **107**, 108, 189; Arwad 111; Beirut 111; Byblos 110, 111; commercial 110, 111, 189, 190; fishing 29, 179; Hittite

43, 44, **107**, 108; military 44, 111; Ramesses III 131, 175; Roman 37; royal 35, 43, 110, 131; Sidon 111; Tyre 111; Ugarit 44, 108, 110, 116, 172, 188

floaters 59, 60

fresco: marine and nautical depictions 60; 'miniature' (Thera) 38, 53, 55, 58; 'Flotilla' 163

funerary barge 68, 82, 89, 90, 193

G

Galilee, Sea of 65, 68, 69

Galinoporni **145**

galley: Aegean 131, 175, 193; depicted at Medinet Habu 38, 128, 131, 175; Helladic 126, 128; Levantine 193; Mycenaean 39, 131–132, 143–144; oared 125, 128. See also long boat; *pentekonter*; warship

Gaza 50, 51, 52, 67, 122, 182. See also Wadi Gaza

Gaza River 63, 66

Gebel el-Araq 67

Gerzeh 67

gift exchange 179, 188

Giza 70

glass: 24, 51, 109, 155, 158, *158*, 162

Golan plateau 70

gold: cargo 105, 109, 162, 194–195; circulation of 77; extraction and distribution 75; decorated daggers 82; jewellery 76, 98–99, 158; -leaf 60

Gözlükale (Tarsus) 67, 74, 76, *157*

graffito of ships: Dakleh Oasis 132; Dor 126; Enkomi 140, 176, 193; Hala Sultan Tekke *Vyzakia* 140, *141*, 176, 193; Kition 59, 126, 140, *141*, 176, 193; on built structures or shrines 30, 57; Tell Abu Hawam 126, 174; Wadi 'Ameyra 68; Wadi Rôd el-'Air 90

grain: Akkadian text 43, **107**, 108, 109, 113; Armana letters 47, 109, 111; bulk transport 33; hieratic

Makhadma 60

malaḫḫu (mariners) 113

Malia 93, 98

Manapa-Tarhunta 42

Manika 77

Mari 98, 187

maritime archaeology 32, 51, 196

maritime transport containers (MTCs),
    definition 55–56

Marmaris 41

Maroni *Tsaroukkas*: anchors 140, 148,
    149, *150*, 177; boat models 142–
    143, *142*, 176; harbour 139, 140,
    176, 195; imported pottery 140; key
    node in exchange networks 189–
    190, 192

Maroni *Vournes* 145, **145**

Marsa Matruh: Aegean transport stirrup
    jars 124, 174; Cannaanite jars (CJs)
    124, 134, 174; Cypriot *pithoi* 124,
    148, 174; destruction by end of
    Bronze Age 186; harbour 39, 55,
    115, 124, *124*, 173, 174; key node
    in exchange networks 180, 189–190,
    195; Mediterranean (shell)fish 138;
    piracy 39

Maydos Kilisetepe 101

Medinet Habu 38, 40, 44–45, 58,
    128–130, *130*, 175

Megadim 69, 87, 96, 137

Megiddo: Amarna letter 111; Egyptian
    jars 135; Mediterranean (shell)
    fish 138, 176; Nilotic fish 89, 138;
    production of imitation Cypriot
    juglets 121; ships' representations
    68, 168

Memphis: Canaanite jars (CJs) 117,
    135; Egyptian jar production 136,
    175–176; Helwan tombs 70; Kom
    Rabia 94, 117; Mit Rahina 81, 170,
    186; Saqqara necropolis 129, *129*;
    ships' representation 129, *129*

Menderes plain 76

Menelaus 37, 49

mercenaries 36, 42, 47, 49, 160

merchant ships ('round boats'): Amarna
    letters 111, 189; Cypriot 143;
    Hittite document 43; Kenamun
    Tomb 53, *53*, 184, 185; Levantine
    design 175, 184; Medinet Habu
    131, 175; tomb reliefs at Memphite
    cemetery, Saqqara 175, 185. See also
    br

merchantman 160, 161, 177

Merneptah 44, 46

Mersa/Wadi Gawasis 83, *83*, 91, 95,
    134, 169

meru wood 63

Mesopotamia 23, 48, 77, 115, 169, 188

metal: -based value equivalencies 23;
    cargo 33, 45, 81, 105, 109, 161–
    162; demand 23, 185; deposition
    in hoards or tombs 72–73, 74, 76,
    99; fishing equipment 59–60, *60*;
    imports 23, 75, 98, 139, 171; ores
    72–73, 98, 115, 161, 167, 168;
    Philia-phase artefacts 73; production
    74, 99, 168; scrap 158, 161, 162;
    ship models 59, 90; -smith 73, 75,
    162; tools 73, 89, 109, 161, 168;
    (maritime) trade 66, 77, 115, 167,
    169, 187, 191–192; vessels 158;
    weapons 38, 73, 74, 77, 89, 168

'metallic' or 'combed' ware jars 56, 66,
    70–71, *71*, 186

metallurgy: bronze 38; Cyprus 71–72,
    139, 168; Kastri 77; transmission of
    technology 77; Troy 75

middlemen 148, 176, 177, 180, 192

migration 25, 38, 39

Miletos 40, 54, 155–156, *156*, 163,
    177, 181

minerals 81

Minet al-Beidha: Aegean pottery 173;
    anchors 137–138, 164, 176, 177–
    178; Canaanite jars (CJs) 116, *116*,
    134, 173, 175; Cypriot *pithoi* 117,
    173; harbour 24, *24*, 88, 115, 159,
    185, 195; murex shells 138; Ugaritic
    texts 108–109, 111, 113, 116, 187

mining 64, 73, 171

Minoanising 101, 155

Minoans 23, 24, 57, 155, 181

Mirabello Bay 93

Mirgissa 95

miši 41, 44, 46–47, 48, 189

Mit Rahina (Memphis) 81, 89, 93, 170, 182, 186–187

mnš (type of Egyptian ship) 130–131, 135, 140

mobility: contribution of seafaring practices to 185; degree of 34; hubs of 195; intensification of 31; maritime 23–24, 32, 36, 49, 98, 190, 196; seasonal 32; 'technologies of' 179

Modi island shipwreck 41, 51

mole 78, 155, 168–169

molluscs 70, 76, 120, 165, 177

Monochrome ware, Cypriot pottery 117, 120, 157

moringa oil 105, 135

mortuary rituals 57, 59

Mount Hermon 70

Mukish 43, 104, *105*, **107**, 108, 113, 192

murex shells 42, 138, 152

Muwatalli II 42

Mycenaeans 38–39, 47, 128, 132, 153, 160, 181

N

NAA. *See* Neutron Activation Analysis

Na'aman River 118

Nahal Alexander 87

Nahal Ayalon 87, 123

Nahal Besor 123

Nahal Ga'aton 87

Nahal Keziv 87

Nahal Lachish 87

Nahal Me'arot 121, 127, 132, 140

Nahal Oren 87, 121, 127

Nahal Qishon 87, 119

Nahal Soreq 87

Nahal Tanninim 122

Nahal Yarqon 63, 66, 87

Nahariya 87

Naveh Yam 137

Naxos 76

Nebamun Tomb 129, 131, 133, 140, 175, 193

'necked liquid storage or transport jars' ('beer jars') 91, 92

necropolis: Abydos, royal 68, 69–70, 82, 90–92, *91*, 126, 170; Bakla Tepe 76; Bellapais *Vounous* 96, 99; Beşik-Yassıtepe 153; Deir el-Balah 135; Hagia Photia 72; Hama 125, 174; Karmi *Palealona* 99; Lapithos *Vrysi tou Barba* 72, 73, 74, 98–100, 143, 171; Nami East 121; Memphis, Saqqara 129, *129*, 133, 175, 185; Panaztepe 155; Thebes 130, *130*; Vasilia *Kafkalla* 72, 73, 74, 99

net weights 60, 140, 151–152, 164, 165, 177

network: Anatolian Trade (ATN) 66, 67, 72, 75–78, *76* , 168, 186, 192; commercial 172, 190, 196; dendritic 56; diplomatic 25; exchange 22, 25, 49, 55–56, 120, 189, 192; interaction 24; long-distance exchange 122, 185; maritime/ seaborne 33, 35, 86, 89, 160, 178–183; Mediterranean trade 174; palace-centred trading 25; Red Sea centred exchange 83, 92; 'super-' 66, 75, *76*; terrestial 86

Neutron Activation Analysis (NAA) 93, 101, 119, 134, 136, 145

Neve Yam 96

Nile (River): clay 70; Delta 23, 24, 57, 64, 69, 82; 'Delta wine' 69; eastern Delta 174, 186; fish 89, 129, 138, 152, 176; molluscs 70; mouth 67; naval battle(s) 40, 45; northeastern Delta 69, 182; port 105, 129, 160, 186–187; ships 82, 91, 92; trade 83, 92; travel 63, 65, 68; upper Delta 136; 'Venice on the' 82, 170, 174

Niqmaddu III 109

Nubia 68, 83, 94

64–65; documents from Ugarit 109;
ebony 24, 51, 109, 158; imported
63; juniper 65; *meru* 63; pine 65;
plunder from ships 45, 105; ship
remains 51, 64, 161, 178; Turkish
Oak (*Quercus cerris*) 66, 159;
Uluburun shipwreck cargo 158, 159,
159, 162
wool 42, 109, 110

Y

Yabninu 112, 187, 188
Yapah-Adda of Beirut 44
Yapah-Hadda 44
Yapu (Jaffa) 123. See also Jaffa
Yarqon river 63, 66, 87
Yavne-Yam 86, 87
Yemen 83

Z

Zawiyet Umm el-Rakham 115, 124,
134, 173, 174
Zire 85, 118
Zizaḫallima 112